AMERICAN THOUGHT AND CULTURE
IN THE 21ST CENTURY

AMERICAN THOUGHT
AND CULTURE
IN THE 21ST CENTURY

Edited by

Martin Halliwell and Catherine Morley

EDINBURGH UNIVERSITY PRESS

© editorial matter and organisation Martin Halliwell and Catherine Morley, 2008
© the chapters their several authors, 2008

Edinburgh University Press Ltd
22 George Square, Edinburgh

Typeset in Monotype Garamond by
Norman Tilley Graphics Ltd, Northampton, and
printed and bound in Great Britain by
CPI Antony Rowe, Chippenham, Wilts

A CIP record for this book is available from the British Library

ISBN 978 0 7486 2601 4 (hardback)
ISBN 978 0 7486 2602 1 (paperback)

CONTENTS

ACKNOWLEDGEMENTS

This volume has provided us with the chance to work with some amazingly talented scholars and we are very grateful to all the contributors for their incisive commentary on the 'time of our time', to evoke the words of the late Norman Mailer. When we were working on the early stages of this project we were very aware that time always catches up on books dealing with the present. Many readers will come to this volume when the 44th President of the United States of America is in the White House: either the first black president or the oldest man ever to take office. This book does not discuss in detail the 2008 presidential campaign, as we were keen for it to appear in print before the 2008 election to bookend the dramatic years that have formed the first phase of the 21st century.

I am very grateful to Nicola Ramsey, Senior Commissioning Editor at Edinburgh University Press, for her early encouragement when I emailed excitedly from the Library of Congress in 2003, and for helping us to develop these embryonic ideas into this published volume. I am also indebted to the Rothermere American Institute at the University of Oxford for granting me the status of Senior Academic Fellow in 2007. That year was a very profitable one for this volume, as it enabled me to work very closely in Oxford with my co-editor Catherine Morley. This has been a very happy project, largely because Catherine has been such a delightful colleague to work alongside – and extremely tolerant of my nocturnal e-habits. Catherine and I would like to warmly thank the Saatchi Gallery for enabling us to use a reproduction of Jules de Balincourt's painting *US World Studies II* (2005) as our cover image.

I would like to extend my sincere thanks to colleagues in the Centre for American Studies and the Department of English at the University of Leicester; to my co-editor on another Edinburgh project, Andy Mousley; and to colleagues and friends in the British Association for American Studies. Finally, my greatest debts go to my families in Derby and Leicester, and especially to Laraine Porter.

Martin Halliwell

While I was working on this collection, I was also carrying out my duties as a lecturer at Oxford Brookes University. I would like to thank everyone at Brookes for their help and advice, especially Alex Goody, Daniel Lea and Steve Matthews. I have also benefited enormously from a fellowship at the Rothermere American Institute, where I have tapped the experiences and expertise of many of my co-fellows. Colleagues in the British Association for American Studies have offered sage advice on a range of issues, for which I am most grateful. One of the greatest gifts to the editor of a collection such as *American Thought and Culture in the 21st Century* is to have a co-editor such as Martin Halliwell, who has made this job both immensely enjoyable and much less burdensome. I am deeply appreciative to have worked with such a consummate professional.

As well as colleagues, I thank my parents and family, Deirdre, Elaine and Rachel for their faith, love and encouragement. Above all, my heartfelt gratitude goes to Dominic Sandbrook, for great stoicism and patience in the face of innumerable evenings and weekends lost to the rigours of the editing process.

Catherine Morley

NOTES ON THE CONTRIBUTORS

Howard Brick is Professor of History at Washington University in St Louis. He specialises in 20th-century intellectual and cultural history and is the author of several books, including *Age of Contradiction: American Thought and Culture in the 1960s* (2000) and *Transcending Capitalism: Visions of a New Society in Modern American Thought* (2006).

Max Dawson is Assistant Professor in the Department of Communication and Culture at Indiana University, Bloomington. His work explores the idea that new technologies ranging from the remote control to the mobile telephone will reform or rehabilitate television. He has published articles on both television and new media.

John Dumbrell is Professor of Government at the University of Durham and a specialist on the US presidency and international relations. He is the author of numerous publications, most recently *President Lyndon Johnson and Soviet Communism* (2004) and *A Special Relationship: Anglo-American Relations from the Cold War to Iraq* (2006), and co-editor of two volumes, *Vietnam in Iraq* (2007) and *America's War on Terrorism* (2008).

Martin Halliwell is Professor of American Studies and Director of the Centre for American Studies at the University of Leicester. He has published six monographs on American and transatlantic intellectual, cultural and literary history, most recently *The Constant Dialogue: Reinhold Niebuhr and American Intellectual Culture* (2005), *Transatlantic Modernism* (2006) and *American Culture in the 1950s* (2007).

Liam Kennedy is Professor of American Studies and Director of the Clinton Institute at University College Dublin. He specialises in American urban studies, visual culture, globalisation and transatlantic relations. He is the author of *Susan Sontag: Mind as Passion* (1995) and *Race and Urban Space in American Culture* (2000), and is currently working on a book on photography and international conflict.

Peter Kuryla teaches history at Belmont University, Nashville and in the Department of English at Vanderbilt University. He specialises in 20th-century intellectual and cultural history and is currently working on a book project entitled 'The integration of the American mind: intellectuals and the creation of the Civil Rights Movement'.

Elisabeth Lasch-Quinn is Professor of History at Syracuse University, New York. She specialises in 20th-century American social, cultural and intellectual history and has written extensively on race and the family. Amongst her publications, she is the author of *Black Neighbours* (1993) and *Race Experts* (2002) and co-editor of *Reconstructing History* (1999).

Wilfred M. McClay is SunTrust Chair of Excellence in Humanities, University of Tennessee at Chattanooga. He specialises in intellectual, religious and cultural history. He has authored and edited many works including *The Masterless: Self and Society in Modern America* (1994), *Religion Returns to the Public Square* (2003) and *Figures in the Carpet* (2007).

Kevin Mattson is Connor Study Professor of Contemporary American History at the University of Ohio, specialising in 20th-century American politics and culture. Among many other works, he is author of *When America was Great: The Fighting Faith of Postwar Liberalism* (2004) and *Upton Sinclair and the Other American Century* (2006), and co-editor of *Liberalism for a New Century* (2007).

Catherine Morley is Lecturer in American Literature at the University of Leicester, formerly RCUK Academic Fellow in the Cultures of Modernism at Oxford Brookes University and Fellow of the Rothermere American Institute, Oxford. She has recently published *The Quest for Epic in Contemporary American Fiction* (2008) and her work has appeared in numerous academic journals and edited collections.

Carroll Pursell is Adjunct Professor of Modern History at Macquarie University, Sydney with specialist interests in the history of technology and the environment. He is the author of *The Machine in America,* 2nd edn (2007) and *Technology in Postwar America* (2007) and editor of *A Hammer in Their Hands* (2004) and *A Companion to American Technology* (2004).

David Ryan is Senior Lecturer in US Diplomatic History and Foreign Policy at University College Cork. He specialises in US intervention and regional conflict in the post-Vietnam context. Recent books include *US Foreign Policy in World History* (2000), *Frustrated Empire: US Foreign Policy from 9/11 to Iraq* (2007) and (with John Dumbrell) co-editor of *Vietnam in Iraq* (2007).

Dominic Sandbrook is a member of the Oxford University history faculty and a columnist for the London *Evening Standard*. His books include a biography of Eugene McCarthy (2004), two bestselling histories of Britain in the 1950s and 1960s, *Never Had It So Good* (2005) and *White Heat* (2006), and a forthcoming history of the United States in the 1970s, *Spirit of '76* (2009).

Christopher Thomas Scott is Senior Research Scholar in the Center for Biomedical Ethics at Stanford University. He is director of three pro- grammes on stem cell technology, including the founding Director of the Stanford Program on Stem Cells in Society. He has published widely on the political, legal, ethical, technological and economic impacts of stem cell research.

Nancy Snow is Associate Professor in the S. I. Newhouse School of Public Communications at Syracuse University. She is a frequent media com- mentator on American foreign policy, propaganda and the causes of anti- Americanism, and amongst her publications are *Propaganda, Inc.* (2002), *Information War* (2004) and the *Routledge Handbook of Public Diplomacy* (2008).

Lynn Spigel is the Frances E. Willard Professor of Screen Cultures in the School of Communication at Northwestern University. She has written extensively on broadcasting, consumption and media in post-war and contemporary America. She is author of *Make Room for TV* (1992), *Welcome to the Dreamhouse* (2001) and *TV by Design* (2008) and, amongst other volumes, editor of *Television after TV* (2004).

Rebecca Tillett is Lecturer in American Literature and Culture at the University of East Anglia. She specialises in 20th- and 21st-century multi- ethnic American literature and film, race, environmental history and postcolonial theory. As well as numerous articles, she is the author of *Contemporary Native American Literature* (2007).

Paul Wells is Professor of Animation Studies in the Animation Academy at Loughborough University. He is a broadcaster, writer and filmmaker, and has published widely on animation, performance and digital culture, including *Understanding Animation* (1998), *Animation and America* (2002) and *Funda- mentals of Animation* (2006).

John Wills is Lecturer in American History at the University of Kent. His research is in US environmental, cultural and visual history, with special interest in nuclear protest, popular tourism and cyberculture. Among his book-length publications are *Invention of the Park* (2005), *Conservation Fallout* (2006) and *The American West* (2009).

INTRODUCTION
THE NEXT AMERICAN CENTURY?

Martin Halliwell and Catherine Morley

One of the most symbolic political speeches of the early 21st century was given by the British Prime Minister Tony Blair. Speaking at the Labour Party Conference a month after the terrorist attacks on the World Trade Center and the Pentagon, Blair gave a lasting image of the political and moral chaos created by events of 11 September 2001. After discussing the need to extend freedom around the globe, Blair proclaimed 'This is a moment to seize. The kaleidoscope has been shaken. The pieces are in flux. Soon they will settle again. Before they do, let us reorder this world around us.'[1] Although Blair did speak of 'the starving, the wretched, the dispossessed, the ignorant' and 'those living in want and squalor', behind these now famous words was the implication that, at least as long ago as the symbolic end of the Cold War in 1989, relative harmony and stability had characterised world affairs. Perhaps bolstered by the robust economies of the United States and United Kingdom in the late 1990s, Blair's speech did not reference the Gulf War of 1990–1, the recent ethnic wars in East Europe or ongoing political turbulence on the Asian subcontinent, which might have detracted from the vision of a world of certainty shaken to the core by the atrocities of 9/11.[2] Within this mythic structure – and with the ashes still falling in Manhattan – Blair detected a moment of rupture, of irrevocable change, which would take time to assess and even longer to settle down into a meaningful pattern. It was a speech primed for a moment of adversity, but also one born out of fear – 'let us reorder this world around us' – that global power was, perhaps, being wrenched away from North America and West Europe and new blocs were forming elsewhere.[3]

The fact that in the years following this speech there grew a close but, for some, uncomfortable relationship between the British leader and the US President, George W. Bush, revealed that Blair's fears of national decline within a new world order were real ones. This was at least part of the reason that Blair attempted to revive a North Atlantic alliance which would help both countries to renew their 'special relationship' and, more imperiously, to 'reorder' the world. Blair was accused by many during the Iraq War (which began in March 2003) of ignoring domestic politics and pandering to Bush, particularly as the US President sidestepped United Nations protocol and entered into what would prove to be a long and bloody conflict in Iraq. In his speech, Blair resurrected the Enlightenment idea of America as a beacon of liberty, which had not been extinguished by the trauma of 9/11, and a political 'model for the world' enshrined in the US Constitution 'with its inalienable rights granted to every citizen'.

Part of the problem with the United States in the early years of the 21st century has been one of perception, particularly for those on the outside looking in. Sympathies around the world were focused on New York City in the immediate aftermath of 9/11 and even during the invasion of Afghanistan in search of Osama Bin Laden and the al-Qaeda terrorists. However, pre-emptive war in Iraq jeopardised the liberal values that Blair upheld for what many saw as myopic 'moral clarity' (a term wedded to neoconservative philosophy), which masked the newly aggressive foreign policy of the Bush administration and also hid economic and, very possibly, personal motives that looped back to the earlier Gulf War when Bush's father George H. W. Bush was in the White House. Many critics have argued that 9/11 rescued George W. Bush's presidency, giving it a sense of mission that it lacked in his first eight months. Such views were reinforced because Bush repeatedly seemed to use the national trauma of 9/11 for his own political advantage – most notably in the wake of Hurricane Katrina in September 2005, which conveniently, for the President, coincided with the four-year anniversary of the terrorist attacks.

Most critical accounts of Bush have a liberal slant though, blaming the Republican Party (particularly the think-tank of neoconservatives with its figurehead of Dick Cheney, Bush's running partner and later his Vice-President) for stealing the premiership away from Clinton's natural successor, Al Gore, in the 2000 presidential election. The culture wars of the 1990s fuelled full-scale political warfare in the early 21st century, even leading to blue states in the North East threatening to secede from the union in the immediate aftermath of Bush's second victory over the Democrat candidate John Kerry in the 2004 election.[4] However, what many such criticisms of Bush's executive decisions overlook is that 9/11 had been a long time coming, rooted in a history of antagonism between the US and Middle Eastern countries and with intelligence about potential attacks available during the Clinton presidency.

HISTORICAL RUPTURE OR CONTINUITY?

One of the purposes of *American Thought and Culture in the 21st Century* is to broaden the debate about whether 9/11 did represent a rupture – ushering in a new kaleidoscopic pattern and the symbolic beginning of the new millennium – or whether the lines of political, social and cultural continuity with the recent and more distant past are much stronger than many early 21st-century accounts credit.

The 'turning point' theory of history is one that is seductively neat. Blair began his October 2001 speech by claiming that 9/11 'marked a turning point in history' and a journalistic account of 9/11 begins with the words: 'significant days in world history are like turning points of fate'.[5] We are still drawn toward taking (from a US perspective) 1776, 1861, 1917, 1941 and 2001 as moments in which the continuous threads of history are broken and rewoven through national or international conflict. Millennial thought in the months leading up to the turn of the 21st century became obsessed with numbers and dates, fuelling widespread panic that the Y2K computer bug (in which all digital clocks would be reset) would crash business and economies around the world. More specifically, a number of accounts of the terrorist attacks have drawn parallels between 11 September 2001 and 7 December 1941 when the Japanese attack on Pearl Harbor marked US entry into World War II – a parallel that gives some weight to this idea of a turning point in which American sovereignty is threatened by foreign forces. Theories proposing that 9/11 was a repeat of Pearl Harbor were shared by the general public, professional critics and conspiracy theorists alike.[6] That 9/11 was an attack on mainland America, rather than on a trading and military outpost in the Pacific, gives greater weight to this theory. And amongst the devastating loss to families bereft of loved ones in the collapse of the twin towers, was a larger transnational story, in which the World Trade Center represented a triumphant symbol of global capitalism – perhaps, even, to use Francis Fukuyama's potent image from 1989, a supreme symbol of the 'end of history'. But, as a number of essays in this volume explore, Fukuyama's account of the end of history in *The End of History and the Last Man* (1992), in which he argued that all nations were converging on a model of Western democratic capitalism, was premature and overlooked strong currents elsewhere across the globe.

The 'turning point' theory of history has a number of problems. It tends to reduce complex historical forces to a mechanistic theory of cause and effect, or privileges catastrophic events at the expense of more subterranean political, social and cultural currents that might turn out to have more profound effects on shaping the future. The exhaustive media coverage of 9/11 was without precedent, but much of it overlooked the broader historical patterns that inform and help to explain the contours of the early 21st century. It is tempting to seize on momentous and dramatic occasions –

the fall of the Berlin Wall, the fall of the Twin Towers – to mark new values and belief systems but, as the historian Robert McElvaine noted in 2005, 'political turning points are often hard to recognize. Sometimes events that seem certain to have a redefining impact on political allegiances turn out not to do so'.[7] Without diminishing the significance or horror of 9/11, or ignoring the subsequent internationalist turn in US foreign policy, McElvaine argues that 'in terms of political realignment' 9/11 appears 'to have been such a non-turning point' in that the 2004 presidential elections were close to a rerun of those four years earlier. McElvaine does not want to dismiss the turning point theory out of hand, but he points to other less dramatic moments – specifically a scientist in Seoul National University in South Korea who, in spring 2005, produced stems cells that provided a 'genetic match' for diseased patients. One of the purposes of this book is to reconsider the events and consequences of 9/11, but also to explore other spheres of activity (such as McElvaine's example, drawn from medicine and biotechnology) which have contributed to the shifts in thought and culture in the early years of this millennium.

The political thinker David Marquand has criticised Blair's use of the 'turning point' theory as an example of national leaders not knowing enough about history and indulging in presentism – a criticism that could also be made of Bush in not heeding the warnings of the Vietnam War when he chose to invade Iraq.[8] Two more recent potent metaphors have challenged the turning point model of history, suggesting that history is in continuous motion, accreting change rather than exploding through violent rupture. In 1993, conservative thinker Samuel Huntington first outlined what he saw as a long-standing clash between the ideologies of East and West, a 'clash of civilizations', which discourses of multiculturalism in the 1990s did little to disguise or ameliorate. This is a story that goes back at least as far as the Korean War (1950–3) in which President Truman's engagement in military conflict in Southeast Asia was a key phase in the foreign policy of containment (a philosophy devised by statesman George F. Kennan in 1947), which attempted to keep at bay communist forces that threatened American democratic values. Huntington's thesis evokes much longer antagonisms, which bring into focus religious belief systems that position Christianity in conflict with Muslim and Confucian traditions and pits the growing moral relativism in the West against a version of moral absolutism in the East. Huntington's thesis, expanded in his 1996 book *The Clash of Civilizations and the Remaking of World Order*, is arguably as limited as Fukuyama's 'end of history', but it does indicate that the apocryphal calls in the 1990s that globally we could 'relax' into a new postmodern epoch (to evoke the French theorist Jean-François Lyotard) were short-sighted.[9]

Another metaphor that has come to the fore since 9/11 has been the journalist Thomas Friedman's theory of a 'flat earth'. The fall of the Berlin Wall, for Friedman, did not just liberate 'all the captive peoples of the Soviet

Empire', but 'it tipped the balance of power across the world to those advocating democratic, consensual, free-market-oriented governance'.[10] This description can be read as another inflection of Fukuyama's 'end of history' thesis. But Friedman is critical of the Bush administration for 'exporting fear' rather than 'hope', and his vision is more nuanced than Fukuyama in suggesting that other important factors (including the dotcom boom, the development of sophisticated computer and digital technologies, and the outsourcing of jobs to other countries) have contributed to a flatter globe, in which the borders between nations have become more permeable and economic and technology flows are swifter.[11] There are dangers of living in such a world – Friedman worries that the opportunities for terrorism are much greater – but also cause for optimism as the most creative and imaginative individuals (one would hope regardless of class, race, creed or gender) will prosper in this brave flat world. Rather than focusing on the catastrophe of 9/11, with its emphasis on death, destruction and trauma, Friedman encourages his readers to use the stimulus of 11/9 (when the Berlin Wall fell) to become part of a generation of 'strategic optimists', a generation 'that wakes up each morning and not only imagines that things can be better but also acts on that imagination every day'.[12] Friedman not only encourages his American readers to look beyond the spectre of 9/11 and the borders of national identity, but he wishes to offset the critical tradition of the jeremiad (into which Huntington's thesis fits) with the more optimistic American currents of resourcefulness and renewal.

REMAPPING AMERICA

One aspect of Thomas Friedman's work is that it shifts attention away from temporal processes of change and rupture towards thinking about global relationships in spatial terms where location and dislocation become key tropes. This turn towards spatialisation can be seen as a growing discourse in the academy (at least in North America and West Europe) since the 1990s, highlighting geographical and geopolitical issues which broaden the understanding of global markets, climate change, immigration and technological forces. If we want to resist the argument that 9/11 represented a moment of historical rupture, then we might be convinced by the theory of a tipping point in which 9/11 intensified certain emergent patterns through a process of reterritorialisation. While this theory is tempting, as the French-born artist Jules de Balincourt emphasises in his artwork *US World Studies II* (reproduced on the cover of this volume) the topographical shifts that have occurred – both in the real world and in the international imaginary – over the last few years have remapped what appeared to be fixed coordinates.

Balincourt's image was the centrepiece of the 'USA Today' exhibition held at the Royal Academy of Arts in London in autumn 2006, showcasing a generation of artists born in the 1960s and 1970s grappling with the problems of a 'post-9/11' world. Balincourt's *faux-naif* style draws critical attention to the geopolitics of the contemporary landscape and exemplifies one of the aims of the 'USA Today' exhibition: to 'situate art made in any given place between the global and the local, art that is both multivalent and grounded in locational matters'.[13] As one of Balincourt's series of cartographical paintings of the United States, *US World Studies II* turns the familiar national map upside down, rearranges the states and depicts the Mississippi River dividing the country in two, roughly into blue and red states. This painterly remapping forces viewers to rethink their geographical assumptions, national perspectives and regional allegiances within this strangely familiar and yet uncanny landscape. As a young French critic of economic hegemony, the fact that Balincourt has crammed the rest of the world into a small pencil sketch in the bottom of the painting reveals that territorialisation and geopolitics are in urgent need of reassessment in the early 21st century.

Balincourt's *US World Studies II* is indeed critical of a US-centred perspective of the globe, and the artist's sense that transnational identities and institutions are those most in need of critical attention is reflected in the surge of scholarship on transnationalism since the 1990s. On the one hand, it might be argued that the proliferation of partial and often highly specialised mechanisms for cross-border governance since the 1980s has contributed to this rapidly growing intellectual field of inquiry, which spans disciplines from economic policy to literature and the humanities. As Saskia Sassen observes, the most prominent of such mechanisms are those that cover global trade (the International Standards Organization, for instance), the global art market and 'the cross-border circulation of professional workers contained in all the major trade agreements (notably NAFTA and the GATTs)'.[14] An alternative view, though not entirely unrelated in terms of trade networks and communications, is that international migration has forced political and economic scientists to consider new means of discussing the channels between nation states.[15]

Though rooted in the real phenomena of transcultural governance and migration, the term 'transnationalism' is not without considerable complexity, especially since the terrorist attacks of 9/11 and the events in its aftermath when the very notion of global networks has taken on a more sinister hue. The sociologist Steven Vertovec, for example, identifies six different variations, arguing that it is at once a term to describe social morphology that spans borders, including ethnic diasporas and technological networks, and a mode of cultural reproduction emphasising the fluidity of constructed styles and social institutions. Drawing on Arjun Appadurai's notion of 'new maps of desire and attachment' in the diasporic subject, transnationalism also denotes a kind of consciousness. This consciousness is one of decentred attachments, with the idea of an identity being fastened to more than one nation and even partaking of a shared imagination.[16] Finally, according to Vertovec, the term describes sites of political engagement (especially in terms of International Non-Governmental Organisations – INGOs), the (re)construction of place or locality, and avenues of capital: the supply, transfer, marketing, investment of information transfer strategies of corporations.[17]

While at the beginning of the new century the term transnationalism has, according to Vertovec, become something of a catch-all phrase amongst academics, it is worth bearing in mind that it originated in the United States with the essayist and critic Randolph Bourne. His essay 'Transnational America' (1916) referred to the nation as 'a federation of cultures', 'a cosmopolitan federation of national colonies, of foreign cultures' with 'an intellectual internationalism … [interested in] different cultural expressions.' Of course Bourne's essay must be read in the context of his rejection of the war fever that was beginning to overtake many American ethnic groups in 1915, when the cry for 'preparedness' was often a code for heightening the will to fight on an international scale. But the essay is also a challenging rethinking of the 'melting pot' metaphor, rejecting it on the basis that it would inevitably produce a homogenous culture based on the dominant Anglo-Saxon model, 'washed out into a tasteless, colorless fluid of uniformity'. Responding to an intellectual climate which was beginning to question the success of assimilation and to look unfavourably on those who became known as 'hyphenated Americans', Bourne claimed that 'if freedom means a democratic cooperation in determining the ideals and purposes and industrial and social institutions of a country, then the immigrant has not been free'. In discussing the rhetoric of war advocates, he remarked:

> We have had to listen to publicists who express themselves as stunned by the evidence of vigorous traditionalistic and cultural movements in this country among Germans, Scandinavians, Bohemians and Poles, while in the same breath they insist that the alien shall be forcibly assimilated to that Anglo-Saxon tradition which they unquestionably label 'American'.[18]

Furthermore, Bourne clearly advocated an interrogation of the nature of 'American-ness', envisaging the United States as a nation of immigrants who could 'retain that distinctiveness of their native cultures' and hence be 'more valuable and interesting to each other for being different', a nation of 'cosmopolitan interchange … in spite of the war and all its national exclusiveness'.

The spirit of Bourne's thinking informs current work in studies in transnationalism, much of which is resistant to the notion of an unquestioned American nationalism. For American Studies scholars, this has engendered something of a paradigm shift in terms of the conception of the discipline. However, this is not necessarily a new trend for the field; indeed, much of the intellectual vigour of American Studies comes from its ongoing tendency towards self-examination. As Karen Haltunnen points out, since the 1960s, American Studies has undergone three successive challenges: the assault on the myth-and-symbol school of the 1950s and its sense of the homogenous American 'mind' or 'character'; the response to Benedict Anderson's 'imagined community' by way of exposing the fictive qualities of American bourgeois nationalism; and finally the disruption caused by globalisation to the isomorphism of culture and place.[19] Haltunnen regards these challenges, which are all clearly interlinked, as especially problematic, and she laments the loss of 'the national' in current American Studies, largely because it erodes the sense of place which is the bedrock of the discipline. This absence of the national, or at least the desire to erase it, was evident in Janice Radway's 1998 address to the American Studies Association. Her address, entitled 'What's in a name' – later reprinted in Donald Pease and Robyn Weigman's *The Futures of American Studies* (2003) – examined three alternative titles for the discipline, including United States studies, intercultural studies and inter-American studies, before concluding that while it might be possible to keep the name, the discipline ought to pursue a more comparative agenda. What she advocated, therefore, was a 'bifocal vision, a capacity to attend simultaneously to the local and the global, as they are intricately inter-twined.'[20]

The idea of the American nation state, or the need to be attentive to the nation, is not considered by Radway. But, as Vertovec, Haltunnen and others such as Edward Said, Paul Jay and Thomas Friedman observe, the nation is a crucial component of any transnational identity. John Carlos Rowe detects that the nation 'in the twenty-first century ... will undergo dramatic changes and other social, economic, and political organizations will challenge the nation's hegemony.'[21] Similarly, Appadurai suggests that the rise of the global landscape, rather than obliterating the nation state, presents a weakening of its structure and composition:

> The waves of debate about multiculturalism that have spread through-out the United States and Europe is surely testimony to the incapacity of states to prevent their minority populations from linking themselves to wider constituencies of religious or ethnic affiliation. These examples, and others, suggest that the era in which we could assume that viable public spheres were typically, exclusively, or necessarily national could be at an end.[22]

This destabilising of the nation state has profound repercussions for any study of the United States based on nativist and nationalist paradigms: it heralds the disruption of traditional connections in national culture, which for Rowe and Appadurai is both positive and empowering. Clearly resistant to the notion that globalised cultures themselves become homogenous,

Appadurai insists upon the process as 'the conscious mobilization of cultural differences in the service of a national or transnational politics'.[23]

The theorist Julia Kristeva, like Rowe, perceives the 21st century as 'a transitional period between the nation and international or polynational confederations' and calls for a reconfiguration of the national in terms of a 'universal, transnational principle of Humanity that is distinct from the historical realities of nation and citizenship.'[24] For Kristeva this universal principle of Humanity, which she derives from the 1789 *Declaration of the Rights of Man and of the Citizen*, must include the negative and violent aspects of its history. Thus, the old model of national ideology is not to be discarded completely. It is to be recovered and utilised for all its expansive and inclusive possibilities, taking something of the shape of Montesquieu's *esprit général* that goes beyond national and political ideologies into higher entities set forth by a spirit of concord and economic development.[25]

Regardless of whether one believes, like Rowe, Kristeva, Appadurai and others, that the demise of the nation state is upon us or, indeed, whether one shares their universalist humanism, the fact remains that in the post-millennial global environment of economic, cultural and ideological exchange, the self-sufficiency and definition of the nation state has been radically altered. Thus, as American Studies scholars, we are impelled to question preconceived ideas of an ingrained national identity. Kristeva's notion of a 'universal, transnational principle of Humanity' is problematic for a number of reasons, the most obvious being its erasure of cultural difference and assimilation of 'minority' cultural practices, literatures and groups. Furthermore, the idea of a universal principle can only exist in opposition to an exclusionary principle, thus strengthening the binaries Kristeva strives to eradicate. Ultimately, then, the appropriate stance is perhaps less one of a blanket humanist universality than of a model that acknowledges the continued existence and relevance of the nation state, and the means whereby it infects and inflects cultural thought. In the defamiliarised topography of Jules de Balincourt's painting, America may no longer be what it once seemed, and the rest of the world may no longer have the same relationship it once had with the United States, but the nation state remains.

In part stimulated by worries about these changing power relationships, a number of critics have recently focused on founder of *Time* and *Life* magazines Henry Luce's famous phase, 'the American Century'. Luce used the phrase in February 1941 as a call to the nation 'to assume leadership of the world' – a call which he reiterated later in 1941 in the wake of Pearl Harbor to 'create the first American Century'.[26] The phrase has been revived recently to contrast the rise of the US as an economic and political superpower in the 20th century with the realisation that this new historical phase is unlikely to be the 'next American century'.[27] President Clinton optimistically ended his 1999 State of the Union address with such an image: 'Let us lift our eyes as one nation, and from the mountaintop of this

American century, look ahead to the next one'.[28] However, a number of commentators have already predicted that the 21st century may well be a 'Chinese century' or even an 'Indian century', where the hegemony of North America and Europe is challenged or completely reshaped. Many have responded with unease to China's disturbing human rights record,[29] but *The Economist* highlighted the 2008 Beijing Olympics as an opportunity to 'show off China's rapid modernisation to the outside world' and a chance 'to prove just how much China's Communist rulers have achieved in restoring the country's prestige'.[30] Thomas Friedman and other thinkers answer the rise of other global players with the call for the US to become more resourceful; a renewal of hope, but also the sense that in a competitive world American industry and enterprise can prosper.

FRAMING 21ST-CENTURY THOUGHT AND CULTURE

Another aspect of this shuttling between the hope of renewal and the potency of critique is to widen the field of inquiry to look beyond national politics and the Bush administration, which has dominated the way in which the world has viewed America in the first eight years of the 21st century. It is the attempt of this volume to assess the character and legacy of the Bush presidency, but also to broaden the focus far beyond this. Another collection of essays published 50 years ago, entitled *The Search for America* (1959), embarked on an exploration of 'American values' by subjecting them to 'double scrutiny with social science and humanistic perspectives interlacing one another in tension and complement'.[31] The editor of this volume, Walter Huston, assembled a very distinguished cast of mid-20th-century thinkers, including Eleanor Roosevelt, Benjamin Mays, J. K. Galbraith, Margaret Mead, Erich Fromm, Reinhold Niebuhr and Paul Tillich, and provided an early example of what the then-emerging field of 'American Studies' could do. But Huston realised that such 'interlacing' of critical perspectives is an extremely difficult task. The danger in searching for a holistic picture is that the detail often gets left out; it is easy for snapshots to speak to a set of historical truths, rather than simply capturing a particular moment of time within a single photographic frame.

American Thought and Culture in the 21st Century takes its inspiration from the goals of *The Search for America*, particularly Walter Huston's aim to provide 'a thoughtful and suggestive discussion of the chief problems that confront us, individually and as a nation'. Huston did not seek to provide a panacea (there were enough social panaceas in the 1950s) nor an uncritical celebration of American life. Indeed, he notes that the net effect of such widespread examination

> is not soothing: those who talk about the United State these days as if it
> were a completed society, one which has achieved its purposes and has

no further great business to transact will, I fear, draw little comfort from these chapters.[32]

The protean nature of American identity is one that thinkers such as William James, Erik Erikson, Robert Jay Lifton and Christopher Lasch have identified as deeply rooted in the history of the United States. But the counterforce to this proteanism is an exceptional sense of national coherence that has persisted since the early Republic, even despite 'all its contradictions and silences', as Michael Kazin and Joseph McCartin have recently described.[33] Rather than searching for unified theories or grand narratives, though, this volume tries to strike a balance between interrogative and critical approaches, while also acknowledging that the diversity of American thought and culture is one of its most enduring qualities. *American Thought and Culture in the 21st Century* tries to broaden the frame further than Huston by looking at the United States both from the inside and from without. To facilitate this, the volume draws contributors based in North America, Europe and Australia to examine the ways in which the flux and diversity of American identity and thought can be given shape and definition in the early years of the new millennium.

Divided into three discrete sections dealing with Politics, Society and Culture, *American Thought and Culture in the 21st Century* offers a range of challenging and unique perspectives on contemporary issues such as leadership, diplomacy, health, the environment, the mass media and digital culture. The opening essays of the three sections sketch some of the broader coordinates in recent and current political, social and cultural life, providing routes into the following five essays in each section, which deal in turn with more specific topics.

In the book's opening essay, for instance, Dominic Sandbrook reminds us that in many important ways American politics remains in the shadow of Ronald Reagan, the 'Great Communicator'. Reagan's passing in 2004 was lamented on both sides of the political spectrum: his career proved an inspiration for the supposedly new conservatism of George W. Bush; and he even re-emerged in a heated discussion during the Democratic primaries in January 2008 when Hillary Clinton accused Barack Obama of praising Reagan's leadership style. Amidst the more hysterical commentary on the Bush era, Sandbrook sounds a note of caution: beneath the surface of American politics, he argues, there is a remarkable continuity between the late 20th and early 21st centuries.

John Dumbrell's essay develops this point, tracing the continuities between the Clinton and the Bush presidencies in the context of their increasingly militarised global leadership. Moving from American diplomatic policy to the arena of domestic security, Dumbrell makes the case that 9/11 had profound repercussions, propelling Bush towards increased executive power and authority at home. Tracing assertions of presidential authority in foreign policy, especially concerning the invasion of Iraq, Dumbrell explores Bush's war with the Democratic Congress and the development of the administration's absolutist stance, concluding that at the end of the first decade of the 21st century the agenda would seem to be one of restraining presidential authority at home and adjusting to a deeply uncertain situation abroad.

On the subject of US relations with the international community, David Ryan argues that even at the dawn of the 21st century, memories of defeat in Vietnam hang heavily over foreign relations. He contends that the Bush administration's reaction to 9/11, rather than offering a departure from established policy, built on trends that have been evident since the 1960s. Furthermore, Ryan argues that the fallout from Iraq will be the toppling of the normative authority that the US has enjoyed unchecked since the end of the Cold War. Meanwhile, Nancy Snow's piece on propaganda takes a fresh look at official rhetoric, noting the influence of marketing and public relations techniques on government operations. Like the other authors in this section, Snow traces supposedly current phenomena back to the later decades of the 20th century. Returning to the Cold War, she examines the language of Reagan's Evil Empire speeches to demonstrate how the President made full use of the media, information, propaganda and cultural diplomacy to overthrow the Soviet Union. Similarly, she argues, in the immediate post-9/11 environment global public relations and advertising techniques were applied in an effort to win hearts and minds in the global War on Terror.

These complex cultural patterns are explored in terms of political theory in the essays by Peter Kuryla and Kevin Mattson on liberal and conservative thought. Both authors argue that in the transformed political landscape there are still currents of old-fashioned heartland conservatism and reform liberalism jostling alongside the extreme partisanship of culture-war adversaries like Ann Coulter and Michael Moore and other more nuanced ideological expressions. What unites all the essays in the Politics section is the legacy of the later decades of the outgoing century, from Vietnam to the Cold War to the Great Communicator to postmodern relativism. In this respect, 9/11 emerges as much less of a turning point than is commonly imagined.

Elizabeth Lasch-Quinn laments the lost art of the public intellectual in her essay on contemporary social criticism, which leads the second section on Society. Citing thinkers such as Russell Jacoby, George Cotkin and Sven Birkerts on the rise of celebrity culture, the demise (or reduced readership and relevance) of the intellectual journal, and the proliferation of the gratuitous insult, Lasch-Quinn argues that a revived and more widespread social criticism is a necessity to inject new life into democratic politics, and to measure the nation at the turn of the new century against its founding ideals and incipient promise. Indeed, Howard Brick's essay on globalisation takes up this very issue. Contrary to common assumptions regarding the relative newness of the concept of globalisation, Brick argues that the tension between insularity and a cosmopolitan appeal to the world has marked American culture since the early Republic. According to Brick, the growth of US power, particularly after 1898, was registered conceptually by more explicit attention to world contexts and a willingness to understand the American experience in terms strikingly similar to those adopted by other peoples across the globe.

Foundational issues of this kind are also addressed by Wilfred McClay's penetrating examination of the resurgence of religious debate in what he describes as a 'post-secular' nation. McClay makes the point that the apparent resurrection of religion at the beginning of the 21st century has less to do with 9/11 than with the inability of secularism to fill the shoes of religion in providing a moral framework by which individuals might live their lives. Emphasising the same kind of historical continuities that are fore-grounded in the Politics section, McClay observes that the resurgence of religion in public life is not a recent phenomenon. Since the presidency of Jimmy Carter, the taboo on the public expression of religious belief has been steadily eroding. George W. Bush's intensely Christian rhetoric, especially since his address at the National Cathedral on 14 September 2001, is not without presidential precedents or successors, as evidenced in the 2008 presidential party candidate campaigns of Mike Huckabee and Barack Obama. Finally, McClay suggests that the ubiquity of religion in public life is undoubtedly linked to the idea of an American civil religion, the same kind of national creed that was enthusiastically celebrated after the 9/11 attacks. What Americans face as they move deeper into the 21st century, therefore, is not a split between religious denominations, but a political division between religious conservatives and religious liberals.

Christopher Thomas Scott's compelling essay on medicine makes much of George W. Bush's religiously motivated antipathy toward embryonic stem cell research by imagining a fictional future scenario in which President Bush suffers from Guillain-Barré Syndrome (GBS), an immune system disorder that mercilessly attacks the body's nervous system. Scott's essay examines the Bush administration's record on stem cell research, and takes the long view by returning to the first embryo war in the 1973 *Roe* v. *Wade* case, since when no government funds have been allocated to embryonic research. Comparing the US to the UK, in which the fictional future Bush is to be treated, Scott observes that Britain's Human Fertilisation and Embryology Authority oversees IVF clinics and laboratories making embryonic stem cells. He notes that the President's greatest ally is home to the British Stem Cell Bank, a facility that catalogues, stores, characterises and distributes to researchers around the world. Appealing to his compatriots to emulate the British record of biomedical research, Scott concludes with a passionate call to arms – foreshadowing Carroll Pursell's and John Wills's illuminating essays on technology and the environment – in defence of science which is so often the bugbear of public debates.

Martin Halliwell's piece, which opens the third section on Culture, examines cultural eclecticism and diversity at the turn of the century. Halliwell develops Kuryla's and Mattson's earlier explorations of conservative and liberal crosscurrents in contemporary American life by assessing the interpenetration of politics and culture. Moving from a discussion of American intellectuals and the culture wars he focuses on musical protests against the Iraq War and the ways in which filmmakers, both within and outside Hollywood, have reengaged with pressing political issues. This emphasis on diversity is given historical and social context in Rebecca Tillett's essay on pluralism and national identity, which traces the long history of multicultural relations in the United States in order to cast new light on the emerging discourse of nationalism in the wake of 9/11.

Catherine Morley's essay on literature after 9/11 examines the widespread sense among American writers that words were impotent, even redundant, in the aftermath of the terrorist attacks on the World Trade Center. Looking at a range of novels from Claire Messud's *The Emperor's Children* (2006) to Don DeLillo's *Falling Man* (2007), Morley explains how the visual has come to haunt the literary writer, much as the visual technologies that sent images of the burning towers across the globe on 11 September permeated the global cultural consciousness. This idea is developed in Paul Wells's essay on digital culture and animation in the form of technologically mediated 'virtual histories', and in Lynn Spigel and Max Dawson's essay on television. Spigel and Dawson explore how television's future and its possible influences on social and political life are dependent upon a new set of developments related to its convergence with digital technologies, the rise of multichannel systems and the growth of multinational media conglomerates. They examine how all of these developments have already changed an 'old' television culture; and yet, as they point out, television still functions to define the nation in often exceedingly nationalist ways.

This point is elaborated in Liam Kennedy's essay on photojournalism, which argues that the medium has had a long and complex relationship with the production of national identity and its international extensions. For Kennedy, photojournalism provides a very useful medium for analysing the close yet shifting relationship between visual media, the mythos of the nation, and the geopolitical visions of the state. Kennedy examines the role of photojournalism in the framing of US foreign policy and explores how the photojournalistic image has mutated in the 21st century both to support and to challenge the state's geopolitical ambitions.

Persistent themes recur through these eighteen essays, from the importance of religion in American life, to the interfusion of politics and culture, to the prevalence of technology and the image, to the continuities between the new and old centuries. But what strikes us most about these eighteen provocative pieces is the sheer diversity, energy and force of their ideas, which is testament to the vitality and promise of American public discourse. Certainly, the nation faces unprecedented global challenges, from the growing economic power of China and India to the constant threat of political and religious extremism. But, if the 21st century encourages us to remap the United States and reassess its place in world affairs, it does not mean that the experience and energies (as well as the social problems) of 20th-century America have vanished. As the shaken kaleidoscope – which Tony Blair spoke of in autumn 2001 – starts to settle on the first decade of the new millennium, these essays remind us that the spirit of the American Century remains a reality.

NOTES

1. For Tony Blair's Labour Party Conference Speech 1 October 2001 see http://politics.guardian.co.uk/speeches/story/0,,590775,00.html.
2. Nor did Blair in his 2001 speech refer to the dotcom crash of March 2000, which, together with 9/11, was to destabilise the US economy until September 2002.
3. The then British Ambassador to the United States, Christopher Meyer, often quoted Blair's words from this speech: 'we were with you at the first. We will stay with you to the last'. For discussion see Kathleen Burk, *Old World New World: The Story of Britain and America* (New York, NY: Little, Brown, 2007), pp. 648–9.
4. This notion of a 'divided America' has appeared in numerous accounts since the millennium, Simon Schama going as far as using the acronym 'DSA' ('Divided States of America') in his article 'Onward Christian soldiers', *The Guardian*, G2, 5 November 2004.
5. *Inside 9-11: What Really Happened*, by the reporters, writers and editors of *Der Spiegel* magazine (New York, NY: St. Martin's, 2001), p. ix.
6. For an extended discussion of conspiracy theories around 9/11 (including the frequent parallels with Pearl Harbor), see Peter Knight, 'Outrageous Conspiracy Theories: popular and official responses to 9/11 in Germany and the United States', *New German Critique*, 103(35), Spring 2008, 165–93.
7. Robert S. McElvaine, 'Are we at a turning point in history', *History News Network*, 27 June 2005, http://hnn.us/articles/12405.html.
8. David Marquand, 'A man without history', *New Statesman*, 7 May 2007, http://www.newstatesman.com/200705070031.
9. For a reading of Huntington's 'clash of civilizations' thesis see Richard Crockatt, *After 9/11: Cultural Dimensions of American Global Power* (London: Routledge, 2007), pp. 10–35.
10. Thomas Friedman, *The World is Flat: A Brief History of the Globalized World in the 21st Century* (London: Allen Lane, 2005), p. 49.
11. Ibid., p. 450.
12. Ibid., p. 469.
13. Meghan Dailey, 'Made in America', in *USA Today: New American Art from the Saatchi Gallery* (London: Royal Academy of Arts, 2006), p. 13.

14. Saskia Sassen, 'The multiplication of cross-border governance mechanisms: implications for democracy and social order', *The Transnationalism Project*, http://transnationalism.uchicago.edu/gov.html.
15. Roger Waldinger and David Fitzgerald, 'Transnationalism in question', *American Journal of Sociology*, 109(5), March 2004, 1177.
16. See Benedict Anderson's *Imagined Communities: Reflections on the Origin and Spread of Nationalism* (London and New York, NY: Verso, 1983).
17. Steven Vertovec, 'Conceiving and researching transnationalism', *Ethnic and Racial Studies*, 22(2), 447–62.
18. Randolph Bourne, 'Transnational America' [1916], in Paul Lauter (ed.), *The Heath Anthology of American Literature* (Boston, MA: Houghton Mifflin, 2006), pp. 139–48.
19. Karen Haltunnen, 'Transnationalism and American Studies in Place', *The Japanese Journal of American Studies*, 18, 2007, 5–6.
20. Janice Radway, 'What's in a Name?', in Donald E. Pease and Robyn Weigman (eds), *The Futures of American Studies* (Durham, NC: Duke University Press, 2002), p. 65.
21. John Carlos Rowe, *The New American Studies* (Minneapolis, MN: University of Minnesota Press, 2002), pp. xxi–xxii.
22. Arjun Appadurai, *Modernity at Large: Cultural Dimensions of Globalization* (Minneapolis, MN: University of Minnesota Press, 1996), p. 22.
23. Ibid., p. 13.
24. Julia Kristeva, *Nations without Nationalism*, trans. Leon S. Roudiez (New York, NY: Columbia University Press, 1993), pp. 7, 26.
25. Ibid., pp. 44–55.
26. See John Morton Blume, *V was for Victory: Politics and American Culture during World War II* (New York, NY: Harcourt, Brace, Jovanavich, 1976) and James L. Baughman, *Henry Luce and the Rise of the American News Media* (Boston, MA: Twayne, 1987).
27. For recent uses of the phrase 'American century' see Nicholas Guyatt, *Another American Century?: The United States and the World Since 9/11* (New York, NY: Zed Books, [2000] 2003), Kent H. Hughes, *Building the Next American Century: The Past and Present of American Economic Competitiveness* (Baltimore, MD: Johns Hopkins University Press, 2005) and Richard Crockatt, 'America at the Millennium', in Howard Temperley and Christopher Bigsby (eds), *A New Introduction to American Studies* (London: Longman, 2007), pp. 376–96.
28. For Clinton's State of the Union address of 19 January 1999 see http://www.cnn.com/ALLPOLITICS/stories/1999/01/19/sotu.transcript/.
29. In early 2008 film director Steven Spielberg resigned as artistic advisor to the Beijing Olympics in protest against China's history of violence in Tibet and Darfur; the lighting of the Olympic torch in Athens in March 2008 was met with televised protests by the activist group Reporters Without Borders; and the journey of the torch was met by numerous protests and disruptions.
30. Simon Long, 'China's Great Game', *The Economist*, Special Issue: *The World in 2008* (2007), 16. In February 2008, *Time* magazine ran a feature on the mass suburbanisation of China, comparing it to suburban growth in the US

after World War II: Bill Powell, 'The Short March', *Time*, 25 February 2008, 26–32.

31. Walter Huston (ed.), *The Search for America* (Englewood Cliffs, NJ: Prentice-Hall, 1959), p. vii.
32. Ibid., p. viii.
33. Michael Kazin and Joseph A. McCartin (eds), *Americanism: New Perspectives on the History of an Ideal* (Chapel Hill, NC: University of North Carolina Press, 2006), p. 12.

PART I
POLITICS

1. AMERICAN POLITICS IN THE 1990s AND 2000s

Dominic Sandbrook

On 11 June 2004, the American people bade farewell to President Ronald Reagan with a day of mourning on a scale not seen for 30 years. For Reagan's funeral, the first such state occasion since the death of Lyndon Johnson in 1973, the nation appeared united in grief. A few days earlier, more than 100,000 people had filed past the former governor's coffin at his presidential library in California. In Washington, a similar number queued to pay their respects as Reagan lay in state at the Capitol Rotunda. And on the day of the funeral itself, every American military base in the world fired a 21-gun salute in Reagan's honour, while church bells across the nation tolled 40 times and several states held a minute's silence. Breaking off from an agonisingly close re-election campaign, President George W. Bush told the nation that 'when the sun sets … a great American story will close.'[1]

That Reagan would be deeply mourned on the right, among the conservatives who had propelled him into office and by the Republican Party whose success he had done so much to assure, was no surprise. Some called for him to replace Alexander Hamilton on the ten-dollar note or John Kennedy on the half-dollar coin, while the Senate Republican leader Bill Frist even suggested that the Pentagon be renamed in his honour. Foreign observers wryly noted the efforts of the Ronald Reagan Legacy Project, which campaigned for every county in the nation to name something, whether a street, highway, school or plaza, after the late President.[2] The remarkable thing, however, was how far this spirit of affection, even reverence, transcended partisan boundaries. During the dog days of the Iran-Contra scandal and the virtual collapse of Reagan's administration after 1986, few would have predicted that he would be remembered as a great president. Yet almost

20 years later, equally few doubted it. Democrats joined Republicans in paying tribute to Reagan's legacy; black joined white in the crowds and the queues. Three years later Gallup found that only Abraham Lincoln matched Reagan's standing as 'the greatest United States president', while millions of viewers of the Discovery Channel voted Reagan 'the greatest American' ahead of Lincoln, Martin Luther King and George Washington.[3]

A Conservative Consensus

If nothing else, the extraordinary outpouring of grief and nostalgia for Reagan's life and achievements suggested that the centre of American life had shifted well to the right by the first years of the new century, an impression cemented by George W. Bush's re-election in November 2004. And although the debacle of the occupation of Iraq, as well as such perceived fiascos as the slow reaction to the Katrina disaster, badly wounded the Republicans during the 2006 mid-term elections, it is hard to deny a general impression of conservative momentum. Indeed, Reagan's high posthumous standing was only one indication of the widespread respectability of conservative ideas and values among large swathes of the American public, something that would have been difficult to imagine during the 1960s and 1970s, when the California governor was often written off as an extremist or a crank. Even if conservatives bemoaned the erosion of Bush's popularity under the pressure of the Iraq imbroglio, they could console themselves that in three successive national contests (2000, 2002 and 2004) the Republican Party had shown itself a remarkably resilient and effective vote-winning force. They could also reassure themselves that for all the failings of the Bush administration, the ideas that underpinned political and economic conservatism remained alive and well. Across the political spectrum, in fact, Reagan's prescription of free markets, low taxes and patriotic populism was widely accepted.

In this context, the Democrats' gains in the 2006 mid-terms actually made oddly depressing news for old-fashioned liberals. In almost every major initiative or referendum, voters opted for the most conservative option on the ballot, the exceptions being in Missouri, where they approved stem cell research, and minimum-wage initiatives. And in Congress, as Bush's disaffected former speechwriter David Frum reminded readers of Britain's conservative *Daily Telegraph*, the Class of 2006 was very different from previous Democratic intakes of 1958, 1974 or 1986, being in general much more conservative than the caucus they joined. In Virginia, for example, Democrats celebrated James Webb's Senate victory over George Allen; yet, astonishingly, Webb was an unashamed conservative and Confederate enthusiast who had served as Reagan's Secretary of the Navy. In neighbouring Tennessee, meanwhile, the defeated Democratic candidate Harold Ford identified God as his campaign manager and printed the Ten Commandments on the back of his business cards. This was no great liberal revival, for exit polls, too, showed strong and continuing support for the military campaign against Islamic extremism, anti-terrorist surveillance measures, the prison at Guantánamo Bay and an aggressive stance against Iran. 'America', wrote Frum, 'remains a very, very conservative country'.[4]

As in recent periods of Republican dominance, notably the administrations of Richard Nixon (1969–74) and Reagan (1981–9), conservative success was accompanied by liberal howls of pain about the alleged collapse of civil liberties, the rise of a new moneyed elite, the undeclared war on the working poor, and other dire predictions of a right-wing apocalypse. The likes of Michael Moore, in other words, were nothing new, but merely heirs to the liberal Cassandras who had warned in the early 1970s that Richard Nixon was about to launch a military coup, or that the United States teetered on the brink of fascism. A more sensible and level-headed verdict on American politics in the early 21st century, however, would be that despite the surface froth and bubble of invective and denunciation, the country actually remained surprisingly calm, peaceful and united. For all the exaggerated, even hysterical commentary about 'culture wars' and 'red and blue states', American society continued to display a remarkable degree of consensus. While almost all Americans remained wedded to the values of free-market capitalism, polls consistently showed their disapproval of racism, sexism and general intolerance. The hard-line evangelicals on whom foreign journalists often relied for entertaining copy remained little more than an eccentric minority; indeed, church attendance continued its long decline since the high point of the Eisenhower years.

Indeed, George W. Bush himself, rather like Reagan before him, typified this unacknowledged consensus. Like Reagan, he often subordinated hard-right dogma to practical politics; like Reagan, he failed to dismantle popular social programmes like Medicare, and he abandoned attempts to reform Social Security after encountering severe Congressional resistance. The first Republican President to appoint an openly homosexual man to his administration, he belied charges of callous racism by appointing the first black Secretary of State (Colin Powell), the first black National Security Advisor (Condoleezza Rice) and the first Hispanic Attorney General (Alberto Gonzalez). It was a reflection of how much attitudes had changed that Bush also appointed more women and members of minority groups to his administration than any of his predecessors, Republican or Democratic; while liberals charged that this was mere window-dressing, it nevertheless sent a powerful signal that the old prejudices were, in theory at least, no longer acceptable. And even Bush's deeply controversial immigration proposals, which promised to grant 'temporary guest-worker' status to some 12 million illegal immigrants, suggested an underlying pragmatism that belied the frequent charges that he was no more than a fanatical conservative ideologue.

Despite all the breathless, often ill-informed commentary surrounding them, the terrorist attacks of 11 September 2001 played little part in shaping the broad consensus of the early 21st century, the contours of which were already visible during the Clinton years. Perhaps the most remarkable thing about this consensus, and certainly the one that would immediately strike an observer from, say, the 1950s and 1960s, was the virtual collapse of economic and political liberalism. In his essay for this volume, Peter Kuryla notes that most definitions of liberalism are vague and unsatisfactory, and one reason is that scholars show curiously little interest in what liberal politicians themselves claim to espouse. In fact, post-war liberalism can be defined quite precisely. What united liberal champions like Harry Truman, Adlai Stevenson, John Kennedy, Lyndon Johnson, Hubert Humphrey and Edward Kennedy was their shared commitment to protecting and extending the New Deal state, usually along the lines promised by Truman in his Fair Deal platform of 1948. Liberals also believed, often in a rather vague way, in the efficacy of Keynesian demand management to sponsor economic growth and with it, they hoped, domestic prosperity and equality without the need for punitive redistribution of wealth. As time went on, they became increasingly identified with the cause of civil rights, too, although by the mid-1970s racial segregation had become unacceptable on both sides of the partisan divide. Finally, they were united in their commitment to defeating international Communism; indeed, muscular liberals of the Kennedy stripe were often more gung-ho than their Republican counterparts, as the experience of Vietnam was to prove.

The collapse of liberalism was one of the two big political stories of the 1970s and 1980s. Although older historians often blame the searing experiences of the Vietnam War, black urban unrest and the meteoric rise and fall of the counterculture, the real causes were rather more mundane. The passage of Lyndon Johnson's Great Society meant that the promise of the Fair Deal, nursed and nurtured for almost two decades, had largely been fulfilled. Having put most of their proposals into effect, therefore, older liberals had simply run out of ideas. More seriously, however, the premise of painless growth on which their programme had been based was utterly shattered by the economic downturn of the 1970s. A combination of runaway inflation, rising world commodity prices, tumbling productivity growth, the decline of heavy industry and, especially, vast increases in the cost of Middle Eastern oil meant that liberals could no longer fall back on the innocent optimism that had underpinned their appeal in the preceding decades. To make matters worse, they had few answers to the crime wave that blighted so many American cities during the Nixon years, and with stagflation and cultural change driving a wedge between working-class trade unionists and their well-educated white-collar allies, liberals found it hard to repudiate the famous caricature of 'pointy-headed intellectuals'. By 1976, the Democratic Party had clearly shifted to the right, nominating the fiscally conservative Jimmy Carter; four years later, even after Carter had adopted a tough anti-inflation programme in defiance of the party's traditional supporters, Edward Kennedy's liberal challenge failed to unseat him. Perhaps the last genuine liberal of the old school nominated for the presidency was the luckless Walter Mondale in 1984; afterwards, the Democratic Party belonged to a succession of technocratic centrists, from Michael Dukakis to John Kerry.

The other big story of the late 20th century, of course, was the rise of conservatism. Liberals often liked to argue that conservatism was nothing more than rampant greed or thinly disguised racism, or that its advance was really a question of big-business sponsorship.[5] But this missed the point. Conservatism was unarguably the most exciting and dynamic political creed of the 1970s and 1980s, and it also, equally unarguably, held genuine appeal for millions of Americans. Like liberalism before it, the conservative movement was an often uneasy coalition, shot through with tensions and contradictions, but its basic thrust was clear. Drawing on old Republican traditions of small government and self-reliance, New Right champions like Ronald Reagan and Jack Kemp promised to slash taxes, roll back the reach of the federal state and unleash a new era of entrepreneurship and prosperity. With American corporations suffering in an age of rising wage costs and foreign competition, business leaders handed over millions of dollars in sponsorship and funding, and a flood of policy proposals poured forth from the new foundations and think-tanks of the age. And while liberals struggled to make sense of the economic malaise of the 1970s, conservatives offered an appealingly simple agenda, insisting that tax cuts, deregulation and steadfast austerity to squeeze inflation out of the system would relieve the miseries of millions of their fellow citizens.

Of course there was more to conservatism than economics: indeed, the Republican presidential victories of 1988, 2000 and 2004 were won largely on social and cultural issues, from urban crime to homosexual marriage. But although liberals often insisted that their adversaries wanted to turn back the clock to some forgotten age of reactionary prejudice, what is really striking is the extent to which conservatives accepted, or at least struck a compromise with, the changing social and cultural values of the modern world. Both Ronald Reagan and George H. W. Bush drew considerable flack from evangelical leaders like Jerry Falwell for their refusal to turn back the clock in matters of abortion, gender and sexuality. Indeed, it is remarkable that despite having been born again and reaching out to Christian fundamentalists during his presidential campaigns, George W. Bush, too, made sure that his administration contained a high proportion of black and female faces. Conservatism's appeal, in other words, was all the stronger because it was not merely reactionary. While its champions might appeal to old-fashioned prejudices in their election campaigns – the so-called 'dog whistle' effect, as exemplified by George Bush's famous Willie Horton ad in 1988, or his son's visit to Bob Jones University in 2000 – they took care to strike a more accommodating pose in office.

During the early 1970s, Richard Nixon, the first major Republican figure to grasp the appeal of the new conservatism, had often been accused of campaigning to the right but governing from the centre. To some extent, his successors did the same. Much of Ronald Reagan's success can be attributed to his keen sense of pragmatism: not only did he effectively ditch radical supply-side economics within his first few months, he preserved much of the welfare state and, thanks to his defence spending, ran up a huge federal deficit, a far cry from the balanced-budget conservatism of old. George Bush, who memorably promised not to raise taxes but then did precisely that to try and address his predecessor's deficit, was frequently accused of being nothing more than a woolly East Coast centrist. At first glance his son, who stuck much more closely to a narrow partisan base under the tutelage of Karl Rove, did the opposite: after initially presenting himself as a 'compassionate conservative', playing down ideological differences during his contest with Al Gore in 2000, the second Bush then infuriated liberals with his unilateral foreign policy and enthusiasm for faith-based projects at home. Again, though, this can be overstated: he made little effort to roll back the state, abandoned controversial welfare reforms, and disappointed many conservative zealots with his Supreme Court selections. And historians may well judge George W. Bush not as some extremist anomaly, but as merely one in a succession of conservative presidents stretching back to the mid-1970s, albeit one governing at a time when the opportunity to flex presidential muscles – as John Dumbrell's essay explains – was probably greater than at any point since the Johnson era.

If American politics in the early 21st century was governed by an underlying, undeclared consensus, then how do we explain the extraordinarily frenzied and vituperative tone of public debate during this period? Any reader of Michael Moore's enormously successful broadside *Stupid White Men … And Other Sorry Excuses for the State of the Nation* (2003), for example, or of Ann Coulter's wildly hysterical tracts *Treason: Liberal Treachery from the Cold War to the War on Terrorism* (2003) or *Godless: the Church of Liberalism* (2006), would certainly be hard pressed to recognise much bipartisanship. However, a little caution and common sense are in order. As with most bestsellers, many Americans had the good sense neither to buy nor to read such effusions (despite the vast publicity surrounding them), while polls since the 1970s consistently found that just under a third identified with neither party, but considered themselves independents.[6] In fact, harsh rhetoric and negative campaigning were products not of vast ideological divergence but of an electoral system that relied heavily on television and, above all, on highly personalised, character-based campaigns. What is more, although the strident tone of American political debate since the 1980s shocked many foreign observers, it did not really represent anything new. During the 1930s, for example, Franklin D. Roosevelt had been attacked in just as fierce terms as those used to describe George W. Bush, while the ferocity of political campaigning in the nineteenth century would make even many modern consultants blanch. In fact, a glance at the platforms of both parties since the 1990s suggests remarkably little difference, and journalists reporting on the presidential debates of 2000 and even 2004, when passions were said to be higher than ever, often complained that there was little to choose between the two adversaries. 'Predictable', 'plodding' and downright 'dull', wrote one columnist on the website Mediavillage.com; he was referring to the first Bush–Kerry contest, but in truth he could have been writing about any debate since 1992.[7]

BILL CLINTON AND THE END OF IDEOLOGY

If there was one moment when the contours of this new post-Cold War consensus became clear, it was not the aftermath of the World Trade Center bombing, but the aftermath of Bill Clinton's election victory in November 1992. Initially hailed as a moment of liberal resurgence, Clinton's triumph was actually nothing of the kind. True, he had worked for George McGovern in 1972, but the Arkansas governor was a very different kind of Democrat: cautious, fiscally prudent, always keen to blur the ideological boundaries between himself and his opponents. Even before he took office, in fact, Clinton had taken the key decision to reject major public investment in favour of paying off the Reagan deficit, a choice that went down extremely well with the bond market and with the conservative Federal Reserve chief Alan Greenspan, but which deeply disappointed his liberal advisor, friend and fellow Rhodes scholar Robert Reich, who now found himself pushed to the sidelines of the administration. Although some accounts have Clinton moving to the right only after the Republican landslide of 1994, his centrist instincts had in fact been in evidence from the very beginning.[8]

As a consensual, centrist politician who relied on distinctly non-liberal advisors like Dick Morris and David Gergen, Clinton was the ideal politician for the times. With the Cold War over at last, ideological conflict now seemed distinctly old-hat; indeed, Clinton took office just months after Francis Fukuyama published his controversial book *The End of History and the Last Man* (1992), which argued that the end of Soviet socialism meant the 'unabashed victory of economic and political liberalism'. What Fukuyama meant by this was the victory of free-market capitalism, parliamentary democracy and consumerist individualism, forces against which politicians and nation states were increasingly powerless.[9] Clinton himself spent much of his few weeks in office bitterly bemoaning his impotence against the great forces of global capital: in an early meeting with his economic team, he complained incredulously that 'the success of the program and my re-election hinges on the Federal Reserve and a bunch of fucking bond traders?'[10] Yet if Clinton privately chafed against the constraints of presidential leadership in the age of bond markets, outsourcing and globalisation, he proved distinctly willing to ditch long-cherished liberal programmes in the name of the new order. When Clinton signed the Personal Responsibility and Work Opportunity Reconciliation Act in August 1996, for example, he horrified traditional liberal Democrats opposed to the idea of welfare reform. Yet the issue did him no harm in the November election; indeed, some commentators believed that it cemented his victory over the Republican senatorial warhorse Robert Dole, whose aggressive rhetoric went down less well with suburban floating voters than did Clinton's emollient centrism. By the time he left office four years later, Clinton could plausibly argue that despite the miserable sexual scandal that overshadowed his second term, he presided over a nation more at ease with itself than at any time since the 1950s.[11]

Had it not been for its unprecedented conclusion in the Supreme Court, the presidential election of 2000 would have gone down in history as one of the least inspiring of modern times, and arguably the least interesting since Dwight Eisenhower's re-election in 1956. The exhaustion of liberal ideas in the Democratic Party was well illustrated by the contest between Al Gore and Bill Bradley for the presidential nomination. Although perceived as the more liberal candidate, Bradley had in fact been a leading 'Atari Democrat' of the early 1980s, part of a group of so-called 'neoliberals' (the label never stuck and soon came to mean something quite different) who urged their comrades to abandon old welfare-state ideas and to embrace the technological, managerial possibilities of the Reagan era. His campaign hamstrung by the assistance of the present author, Bradley attempted to campaign against Gore from the left, but promptly lost every primary he entered. Within months of the New Hampshire primary, in fact, he had bowed out of political life. As for Gore, he effectively promised a continuation of Clinton's technocratic centrism, which left him open to attack from the self-selected gadfly Ralph Nader, with, as it turned out, disastrous consequences for Gore's electoral prospects. Meanwhile, the Republican primaries were expected to present easy pickings for the wealthy, well-funded Texas governor George W. Bush, but complacency dragged him into a bruising, dirty battle with the unpredictable John McCain. Bush beat McCain only by swinging sharply to the right, especially in the brutal South Carolina primary. Once McCain was out of the race, however, Bush swung just as sharply back towards the centre, suggesting that American politics in the new century would not be dominated by the clash of ideological opposites, but by the time-honoured battle for the centre ground.

Looking back at the results of the 2000 election, the unexpected denouement aside, the two really striking things are how little had changed since 1996 and how little would change by 2004. In all three elections, the Democrats drew most of their strength from the urban Northeast,

California, and the industrial states of the Midwest, while the Republicans, as in previous elections, could rely on winning much of the South, the Mountain states and the rural Midwest. No election was a landslide: even in 1996, when the Republicans were judged to have fought a lacklustre campaign, they picked up 40.7 per cent of the total ballots cast and 159 electoral votes. The similarities between 2000 and 2004 were particularly remarkable. Both elections were extremely close, with John Kerry finishing just 2.5 per cent short of the President in the latter. Even though turnout increased by some 12 million votes, thanks largely to high voter interest in the aftermath of the war in Iraq and frantic get-out-the-vote efforts by both parties, the electoral maps also looked astonishingly similar. On both occasions, the Democrats piled up big leads on the West Coast and in the North East, while the Republicans swept the entire South, the Great Plains and Mountains, and the industrial states of Ohio and Indiana. Only three states changed hands, with Iowa and New Mexico moving into the Republican camp and New Hampshire falling to the Democrats, almost certainly because Kerry was a local candidate. In most states, the margin of victory shifted by only a few per cent over four years, indeed, despite the manifold foreign policy controversies of Bush's first term, a casual observer might easily think that nothing had changed – or indeed happened – at all.

What this suggests, of course, is that in the context of the broad sweep of American political and social history, the terrorist attacks of September 2001 were much less significant than is often alleged. Despite the immediate devastation and enormous shock, the outpourings of flag-waving rage or tortured introspection, there is no evidence that the attacks radically altered the course of American political life. In 2004, a comprehensive *Los Angeles Times* exit poll found that despite all the attention paid to the issue, just 29 per cent of voters named terrorism amongst their two primary concerns in choosing their candidate, while even fewer, 16 per cent, cited the war in Iraq. As in 2000, and as in almost every other election since World War II, in fact, domestic issues predominated: 40 per cent cited 'moral/ethical values', 33 per cent chose 'jobs/economy', and smaller percentages opted for such issues as education, health and homosexual marriage.[12] Insofar as the issues of terrorism and Iraq had an impact, therefore, they probably acted to strengthen existing ideological instincts and patterns of allegiance, driving up levels of partisan enthusiasm (and hence turnout) without actually producing any great electoral shifts. The obvious conclusion is that, as in the period between the late 1940s and the early 1960s, or most famously in the Gilded Age, politics in the early 21st century had settled into a pattern, with the two parties confirmed in their regional strongholds and enjoying a roughly equivalent share of the national vote. For all the politicians' rhetoric about an age of change, therefore, American politics was notable above all for its predictable stability.

With the two parties locked in a virtual dead heat at the presidential level, and given the lack of movement since 2000 as well as the intemperate, even violent tone of public debate, many commentators drew the conclusion that the nation was divided into two implacably opposed camps, or 'red' (Republican) and 'blue' (Democratic) states.[13] In fact this formula, much beloved of those for whom it reinforced old regional prejudices, made little sense. Once again, a look at the results of the 2004 election proves instructive. Of course, as in any other period of American history, an obvious regional pattern revealed itself, but within each state there could be enormous variations. Even in the most partisan regions, the losing candidate could generally be assured of a third or more of the vote, so while Kerry picked up 37 per cent of the vote in Alabama, 40 per cent in Mississippi and 41 per cent in Georgia, Bush won 37 per cent in Massachusetts, 39 per cent in Vermont and 44 per cent in Connecticut. Indeed, although caricatures often painted the South or New England as ideologically homogenous, one-party regions, the reality, especially when Congressional and gubernatorial elections were taken into account, was of intense, passionate competition at almost every level. Only one group of electors, in fact, came close to deserving the one-party 'blue' label: the people of the District of Columbia, who gave John Kerry almost 90 per cent of the vote in 2004, after voting in similar numbers for Al Gore four years earlier. In the so-called 'red states', meanwhile, the picture was always more variegated than much commentary suggested. Even at the height of the Bush presidency, a visitor to Austin, Texas or Chapel Hill, North Carolina or New Orleans, Louisiana, would have a hard time recognising the red-raw blood-and-Bibles stereotypes beloved by many Democratic writers. Similarly, even states like Massachusetts and Minnesota, famously the heartlands of Democratic liberalism in the 1950s and 1960s, sent Republicans like Mitt Romney, Norm Coleman and Tim Pawlenty to the governor's mansion or the Senate.

THE MYTH OF THE CULTURE WARS

The other stereotype beloved of press commentators during the Clinton and Bush years, of course, was that of 'culture wars'. Although the phrase was occasionally used during the 1980s, it owed its popularity to a thoughtful and influential bestseller by the sociologist James Davison Hunter, *Culture Wars: the Struggle to Define America* (1992). As so often, the timing was no accident. Hunter's analysis appeared at a point when traditional liberal-conservative debates about the role of the state and the proper management of the economy had run out of steam; indeed, only months after Hunter's book came out the Democrats elected a president who turned out to be more Reagan's heir than his repudiator. Hunter's thesis – that politics was increasingly dominated and defined by cultural issues such as abortion, censorship, gun control, gender and sexuality and the relationship between church and state – therefore seemed eminently sensible. He argued that whereas in earlier periods American society had been splintered along denominational lines, pitting Protestants against Catholics during the Gilded Age or the 1920s, for example, the true divide in the 1990s was that between 'Progressivism' and 'Orthodoxy'. Progressives, he thought, tended to be relativists, tolerant of competing moral viewpoints; their orthodox neighbours, however, claimed to derive their morality from some external authority (usually God), which meant that they were much less flexible on issues like abortion.[14]

Hunter's argument clearly made a lot of sense, not least since it explained such recent developments as the alliance between traditionalist Catholics and evangelical Protestants, two groups that had loathed one another for years but had now come together to fight abortion, feminism, homosexuality and the march of godless secularism. His terminology soon found its way into public discourse, most famously when the maverick conservative Patrick Buchanan told the 1992 Republican National Convention that 'there is a religious war going on in our country for the soul of America. It is a cultural war, as critical to the kind of nation we will one day be as was the Cold War itself'. Pausing to denounce 'environmental extremists' and 'radical feminism', Buchanan warned that the agenda 'Clinton and Clinton would impose on America – abortion on demand, a litmus test for the Supreme Court, homosexual rights, discrimination against religious schools, women in combat … is not the kind of change we can tolerate in a nation that we still call God's country.' Needless to say, the Republican faithful loved it.[15]

Although Buchanan's rhetoric soon passed into political legend, it is worth remembering that at the time his speech was regarded as something of a gaffe, striking a tone of strident negativity that went down less well with the nation at large than did the relentless baby-boomer optimism of the Democratic convention the same year. This is not to deny that cultural issues clearly played a crucial role in electoral politics under Clinton and Bush: in 2004, for example, it was the issue of homosexual marriage that brought out many Republican and independent voters in swing states like Ohio, where Bush benefited from heavy support from church-goers and, especially, Catholics. But whether all this really deserves the label of a 'culture war' is another matter entirely. Nobody died. And despite much commentary to the contrary, polls suggested that even the most ostensibly divisive social issues elicited a surprising degree of consensus. In the case of abortion, for example, polls since at least 1980 consistently indicated that no more than one in five Americans thought that the practice should be made illegal. As for gun control, at least two-thirds of the electorate consistently supported it, while three out of four Americans consistently opposed the concept of homosexual marriage.[16] The picture that emerges, therefore, is that of an electorate not split down the middle into two rigid, monolithic blocs, nor that of a conservative electorate obsessed by social and cultural deviance, but a much messier, more variegated one: an electorate that was increasingly tolerant but nevertheless slow to change; an electorate that flickered inconsistently between moral traditionalism and individualist libertarianism; an electorate, in fact, that looked not unlike the American people of 20, 50 or 100 years before.

*　　*　　*

This sense of complexity is well captured by the five essays in this section of the book. Peter Kuryla's thoughtful essay on contemporary American liberalism traces the different intellectual origins of an ideology that often appears vague or inchoate, placing 21st-century liberal debates in a long continuum that encompasses the likes of John Dewey, Reinhold Niebuhr, John Rawls and Richard Rorty. For Kuryla, the future of liberalism lies in a compromise between what he identifies as its divergent components: the philosophical heirs of John Rawls, often concerned more with principles than practice; the pragmatic 'muscular liberals', fixated on the everyday imperatives of practical politics; and the 'polemicists', for whom politics is above all a matter of tearing down the ideological edifice of the Bush administration. Kevin Mattson, meanwhile, concentrates on what he sees as the parallels between conservatism and postmodernism, arguing that insofar as they are both concerned with challenging the 'grand narratives' of post-war politics and culture, they can be seen as strange bedfellows in the 21st-century world of 'cultural fragmentation and dissonance'. Yet paradoxically, as Mattson notes, the triumph of conservatism was also based on 'the populist and anti-intellectual tendencies deeply rooted in American history', forces to which Kuryla's liberals stand opposed, but which remain as marked today as they did when Richard Hofstadter identified them in the early 1950s.

The three other essays that complete this section are all concerned not with political creeds but with particular aspects of modern American political life. David Ryan's essay on American diplomacy argues that even at the dawn of the 21st century, memories of defeat in Vietnam hung heavily over foreign relations. The Bush administration's reaction to the attacks of September 2001, he argues, did not represent a departure from established policy, but its culmination, building on trends that had long been evident. Meanwhile, Nancy Snow's piece on propaganda takes a fresh look at official rhetoric during the period, noting the influence of marketing and public-relations techniques on government operations, as well as the apparent contradictions between principles and practice. Finally, John Dumbrell's essay on leadership suggests that conceptions of the nation's global role were influenced by a curious mixture of arrogance and anxiety, pointing out a number of divergent influences on American foreign policy from Wilsonian idealism to the kind of hard-headed realism that would do Henry Kissinger proud. At home, meanwhile, leadership was above all a question of the shifting balance between the White House and Congress, which after September 2001 tipped decisively in the President's favour, only to tip back again when the occupation of Iraq ran into serious trouble in 2005 and 2006. As Dumbrell rightly notes, much of the commentary on Bush's administration 'tends towards the hysterical'; the challenge for the next few years, both for politicians and for commentators, is to restore a sense of balance.

If there is one theme that unites the five writers in this section, it is the sheer influence and longevity of the Reagan revolution. All five contributors agree that the contours of American political life had already been traced, if only thinly, during the 1980s, when the so-called Great Communicator demonstrated the enormous electoral appeal of his mixture of economic conservatism, moral traditionalism and patriotic populism. During the years of Reagan's ascendancy, critics often wrote him off as a stooge, a front man, an ignorant actor parroting the views of his sponsors and advisors. But, as his most acclaimed biographer, Lou Cannon, points out, Reagan's success was a tribute not so much to the messenger but to the message, which clearly resonated with millions of Americans.[17] They voted for Reagan, and later for George W. Bush, not because they were idiots or were duped or were brainwashed by the nation's major corporations, but because they were attracted by a message that emphasised hard work, low taxes, traditional morality and old-fashioned optimistic patriotism – values that in an age of dizzying economic and technological change appealed more than ever. And it was Reagan's funeral in 2004, far more than the presidential election that followed it, that really brought home the degree of his post-presidential ideological victory. Fifteen years before, his old Democratic opponents had congratulated themselves that they had seen the last of their most dangerous adversary. Little did they know that he would cast such a long shadow.

NOTES

1. *New York Times*, 11 June 2004, 12 June 2004.
2. *The Times*, 12 June 2004.
3. *USA Today*/Gallup poll, 9–11 February 2007, http://www.pollingreport.com/wh-hstry.htm. On *The Greatest American*, see *New York Times*, 7 July 2005.
4. *Daily Telegraph*, 9 November 2006.
5. See, for example, Thomas Byrne Edsall and Mary Edsall, *Chain Reaction: The Impact of Race, Rights, and Taxes on American Politics* (New York, NY: Norton, 1991); Thomas Frank, *What's the Matter with Kansas: How Conservatives Won the Heart of America* (New York, NY: Metropolitan, 2004).
6. See the database of Harris polls since 1969 at http://www.pollingreport.com/institut2.htm.
7. Ed Martin, writing at http://www.mediavillage.com/jmentr/2004/10/04/jmer-10-04-04/, 10 October 2004.
8. See Robert B. Reich, *Locked in the Cabinet* (New York, NY: Knopf, 1997); George Stephanopoulos, *All Too Human: A Political Education* (New York, NY: Little, Brown, 1999).
9. Francis Fukuyama, 'The End of History?', *The National Interest*, 16, Summer

1989; Francis Fukuyama, *The End of History and the Last Man* (New York, NY: Free Press, 1992).

10. Bob Woodward, *The Agenda: Inside the Clinton White House* (New York, NY: Simon and Schuster, 1994), p. 84.

11. See Ron Haskins, *Work Over Welfare: The Inside Story of the 1996 Welfare Reform Law* (Washington, DC: Brookings, 2006).

12. *Los Angeles Times* poll, 2 November 2004, http://www.pollingreport.com/2004.htm#Exit.

13. See, for example, Thomas Byrne Edsall, *Building Red America: The New Conservative Coalition and the Drive for Permanent Power* (New York, NY: Basic Books, 2006).

14. See James Davison Hunter, *Culture Wars: the Struggle to Define America* (New York, NY: Basic Books, 1992).

15. Patrick Buchanan, Republican National Convention speech, 17 August 1992, http://www.buchanan.org/pa-92-0817-rnc.html.

16. See the historical databases at http://www.pollingreport.com/abortion.htm, http://www.pollingreport.com/guns.htm and http://www.pollingreport.com/civil.htm.

17. Lou Cannon, *Governor Reagan: His Rise to Power* (New York, NY: Public Affairs, 2003), pp. 116–17.

2. AMERICAN LEADERSHIP INTO THE NEW CENTURY

John Dumbrell

In 1987, George Shultz, Secretary of State under President Reagan, declared that 'the great ideological struggle that has marked this century ever since the Bolshevik revolution of 1917 has essentially been decided'.[1] Speaking two years before the fall of the Berlin Wall, George Shultz was a little premature in proclaiming the termination of the Cold War. However, the significance, not least for American thought and culture, of the late 20th-century ideological and material 'victory' over Soviet communism can scarcely be overstated. The international business of the 20th century – admittedly diverted by the rise of fascism in the 1930s – was the contest between communism (or at least bureaucratised state socialism) on the one hand and democratic capitalism on the other. The geopolitical cataclysm symbolised by the crashing wall in Berlin appeared not only a vindication of national mission and American exceptionalism. It also seemed to signify, as Francis Fukuyama famously put it, that 'all the really big questions had been settled' – in favour of America and the liberal idea.[2]

The present chapter concerns itself with ideas of American global leadership as they developed between 1989 and the first decade of the new century. The discussion will then turn to consider leadership in a domestic context. Just as Fukuyama's 'end of history' had huge implications for American leadership in the world, so did the end of the Cold War and the onset of the War on Terror profoundly affect concepts of leadership at the national level. By 2002, contrary to the expectations of the early 1990s, the power of the US President was following an aggrandising trajectory. Not only did the conditions of the post-9/11 era stimulate an enormous growth of executive power and authority in the realms of foreign policy and domestic security, the early 21st-century White House also advanced a species of 'big government' presidentialist conservatism, which had severe implications for traditional Madisonian notions of fragmented national leadership. We turn first to the international debate over leadership.

POST-COLD WAR AMERICAN GLOBAL LEADERSHIP

The global transformations that accompanied the collapse of Soviet communism brought with them an almost inevitable burst of American triumphalism. Neoconservative commentator Charles Krauthammer hailed in 1991 'the unipolar moment' and called on American elites to make the most of the unique opportunities presented by the Soviet implosion.[3] The national mood, however, in this immediate post-Cold War period was far from universally confident. Perceptions of American decline overshadowed the electoral politics of the early 1990s and even had an impact on the first presidential effort to set out a framework for American leadership in the new global context: President George H. W. Bush's New World Order speech of September 1990. Though attacked from the left as revamped imperialism, the New World Order rather reflected a conception of American leadership that was rooted in multilateralism, limited liability and the upholding of international law.[4] In a speech at West Point military academy in January 1993, the outgoing President Bush declared that the US would use force in the future only 'where its application can be limited in space and time, and where the potential benefits justify the potential costs and sacrifice'.[5] If this was a new imperialism, it was an imperialism tailored to an awareness of the limits to US globalism.

The 1992 presidential election was concerned more with the trade and budget deficits than with any post-Cold War celebration. President Bill Clinton's conception of America's world leadership was circumspect and geared primarily to the economic sphere. Clinton followed the route of 'selective engagement', prioritising international issues that had either a significant domestic overspill or which had direct relevance to core US economic or security interests. Presidential Decision Directive 25, issued in May 1994, declared that the US would participate in United Nations peacekeeping only if risks were 'acceptable' and objectives clear. In Stephen Walt's marvellous phrase, Clinton sought 'hegemony on the cheap'.[6]

Lurking behind this cautious approach to international leadership were memories of over-extension in Vietnam, along with the post-Cold War visibility of the kind of 'new populism' that surfaced in Ross Perot's 1992 electoral challenge to both Bush and Clinton. 'New populism' disavowed seamless international engagement, especially when (on the right) it was associated with the United Nations and 'foreign policy as social work', and (on the left) when it appeared to embrace capitulation to the forces of economic globalisation. Elements of the 'new populism' of the right – notably a revived nationalism and a willingness to favour unilateralism in foreign relations – found their way into the Republican Party programme which triumphed in the 1994 Congressional elections, and continued to affect attitudes towards international leadership into the new century.

During the 1990s, those politicians and intellectuals who favoured strong US global leadership battled consciously against what they perceived as the forces of isolationism. Within the Republican Party, this contest took the form of neoconservative assaults on the narrow nationalism that distinguished the programme of the post-1994 majority in Congress. Joshua Muravchik rebuked 'neo-isolationism' in 1996, noting 'History will long marvel at the denouement of the cold war'. Not only had Soviet leaders 'just upped and threw in the towel', their American counterparts responded to victory 'not with triumphalism but with a similar collapse of confidence'.[7] On the Democratic side, Bill Clinton attacked protectionists and 'neo-isolationists' on the left and labour wing of his party. In his second inaugural address (January 1997) Clinton used a phrase that came to signify his administration's commitment to international leadership: 'America stands alone as the world's indispensable nation'.[8]

By the time Clinton made this inaugural address, the US debate over post-Cold War global leadership had shifted significantly. The recessionary economic climate of the early 1990s had disappeared. The huge Reagan budget deficit was now under control. The American consumer boom, the computer revolution and US-sponsored globalising free trade had transformed outlooks and expectations. The promise of 1989 at last seemed to have been made real. Clinton announced that 'for the very first time in all of history, more people on this planet live under democracy than dictatorship'.[9] US leadership was now geared to the 'family of nations': market democracies embracing free trade and acknowledging the indispensability of American leadership. The new confidence of the late 1990s, underpinned by the nationalism of the Republican Congress, also contributed to a new willingness to conceive international leadership in unilateralist terms: certainly, as in Kosovo in 1999, to act militarily without any United Nations remit. This new assertion of leadership also required a degree of remilitarisation, reversing the secular decline in defence spending which had begun in the very last years of the Cold War. By 2000, the US was spending $280 billion annually on defence – a sum completely beyond the aspiration of any rival.

As American political and intellectual elites looked forward to the new century, concerns ranged from the emergence of 'new threats' to the problems and possibilities of undisputed global supremacy. By 2000, America's international eminence was indeed extraordinary. The most cited threats of this period were the 'borderless threats' identified by the Clinton administration: refugee flows, HIV-AIDS, environmental pollution and international terrorism. Two major reports produced in 1999 by the US Commission on National Security, chaired by former Senators Gary Hart and Warren Rudman, concluded that 'borderless threats' embraced new vulnerabilities, notably over-reliance on attackable information systems and the unpredictable nature of globalised economic shifts.[10] Clinton's 'bridge' to the new century involved a cornucopia of programmatic 'pathways', emphasising cultural diversity as well as the 'indispensability' of American international leadership. More ominously, Samuel Huntington's notion of the 'clash of civilizations', the putative replacement of global economic and ideological cleavages by cultural ones, gained huge currency, even before the terror attacks of 9/11.[11]

In general, however, the American turn-of-the-century mood was as much preoccupied with the undisputed nature of US global leadership per se, as with any threats to that leadership. By the turn of the century, the combination of 'hard' military power, economic strength and 'soft' cultural assets – the international attractiveness of the United States – seemed to have carried all before it.[12] National Security Advisor Sandy Berger announced in January 2001, 'Today, as President Clinton leaves office, America is by any measure the world's unchallenged military, economic and political power. The world counts on us to be a catalyst of coalitions, a broker of peace, and a guarantor of financial stability'.[13]

In the early post-Cold War years, Robert Tucker and David Hendrickson warned America of 'the imperial temptation'.[14] As the new century dawned, shelves of books appeared, all criticising, condemning or celebrating a new imperial age. Andrew Bacevich wrote that empire was un-American. Its characteristics – 'pomp and privilege, corruption and excess' – were 'quite alien to America's Puritan heritage'.[15] Yet Rome had travelled a not dissimilar path. Could the US not learn from Rome's mistakes? What about Britain's more recent experiences with empire? Perhaps the US could pick up tips from its imperial predecessors. At least on the neoconservative right, the whiff of 'empire' was in the air even before 9/11. What 9/11 did, of course, at least in the short term, was to weaken those inhibitions on the projection of power that had so affected the presidencies of the elder Bush and Clinton.[16]

As the younger Bush entered the White House in January 2001, the US was poised between 'unilateralist' and 'cooperativist' conceptions of international leadership. In some ways, the US was now so unlike other countries – its economic and military power was now so unchallenged – that cooperative leadership, at least in so far as that concept implied some kind of partnership among equals, was scarcely feasible. Under the new President, however, American global leadership was to become increasingly militarised and its global instincts more unilateralist.

The presidency of George W. Bush saw a prolonged debate between 'new nationalist' and 'neoconservative' understandings of how America should exercise global leadership. 'New nationalism' seemed to be the President's own default position on leadership. It derived from a tradition that weaves its way back to the Frontier and the nationalism of President Andrew Jackson.[17] More immediately, it derived from the rather narrowly defined nationalism that had been such a prominent feature of Republican Party thinking in the 1990s. Bush, particularly early on, presented himself as a 'new nationalist': prepared to exercise international leadership, but only in a manner congruent with strictly and narrowly understood American interests. Remove those interests and the world would have to resolve its own problems.[18] In 1999, Bush declared that, unless the leader of America 'sets his own priorities, his priorities will be set by others'.[19]

Against the new nationalist version of international leadership, the version embraced by the top echelon of Bush's foreign policy team, stood neo-conservatism and militarised democracy-promotion. The tradition of democracy-promoting global leadership associated with President Woodrow Wilson stood opposed to that deriving from Jackson and President Theodore Roosevelt. Sometimes understood as a form of interests-based realism, neoconservatism is more sensibly construed as a coming together of democratising idealism with a commitment to military primacy, all strongly rooted in the soil of American exceptionalism.[20] Neoconservatives, like Paul Wolfowitz, deputy to Defence Secretary Donald Rumsfeld in the first George W. Bush administration, tend to see 'interests' and 'ideals' as interpenetrative.[21] In America's case, at least, the one reinforces the other. Neoconservatism frequently, as with the 1992 Defence Guidance (the framework for post-Cold War US leadership written under Wolfowitz's sponsorship by Lewis Libby and Zalmay Khalilzad), does express itself in 'interests' terms.[22] Yet America's exceptionalist, democratising vision never lags far behind. For Charles Krauthammer, the realist/idealist circle is squared by the concept of 'democratic realism', wherein pro-democracy interventionists accept a commitment to more traditionally conceived national interests, such as access to Middle Eastern oil and strong national defence.[23]

The shock of 9/11 immeasurably strengthened the hand of those within the administration, and particularly within the Pentagon, who favoured a neoconservative construction of American global leadership. Charles Krauthammer wrote on 21 September 2001 that this was no time for 'agonized relativism'.[24] As originally conceived, the War on Terror reflected new nationalist rather than neoconservative conceptions of global leadership: more forward defence than democracy-promotion, more Theodore Roosevelt than Woodrow Wilson. The neoconservative position was that 9/11 had opened the way for transformative action, conceived in moral as much as in narrow strategic terms. At least in relation to the Middle East, the neoconservative agenda rapidly gained ground. 'Forward defence' in Afghanistan gave way to an approach that embodied more strongly the theme of democracy-promotion/imposition. The shift to a democracy-promoting rhetoric, seen at its most spectacular in Bush's second inaugural address of January 2005, was also unquestionably connected to the failure to unearth weapons of mass destruction in Iraq. However, the notion of leadership defended by the administration after 9/11 always combined the new nationalist (with 'American interests' defined more expansively than before 9/11) and the neoconservative versions of global leadership. Speaking at West Point in June 2002, Bush not only claimed a virtually absolute right to 'pre-empt' threats from other countries by taking military action against them, he also promised to 'extend the peace by encouraging free and open societies on every continent'.[25] By November 2003, speaking in London, Bush was defending a Wilsonian form of world leadership: a concept of leadership rooted in the interdependence of ideals and interests, drawing also from the post-Cold War doctrine, very dear to the Clinton administration, that international democracy guarantees international peace.[26] The administration's mind-set was still shaped by the Cold War victory. The events of 1989 had, it felt, been a vindication of American ideals; market democracy was *bound* to prevail, provided always that Washington did not lose its nerve. The 2002 National Security Strategy opened thus: 'The great struggles of the 20th century between liberty and totalitarianism ended with a decisive victory for the forces of freedom – and a single sustainable model for national success: freedom, democracy and free enterprise'.[27]

Failure and chaos in Iraq called into question the entire expansive conception of global leadership that underpinned Washington's response to 9/11. The terror attacks themselves revealed starkly that the global hyper-power was vulnerable to the asymmetric threat mounted by international terrorism. The widespread opposition to American action in Iraq – not least in the ranks of traditional allies – threatened also to erode US 'soft power'.[28] By this time, American commentators were examining problems of over-extension and international 'blowback'.[29] John Ikenberry called on America to rediscover its cooperativist version of global leadership, 'based on the view that America's security partnerships are not simply instrumental tools but critical components of an American-led world political order that should be preserved'.[30] Global domination, argued Stephen Walt in 2005, was simply too demanding and was ultimately destructive of sustainable leadership.[31]

By the second half of the first decade of the new century, it was clear that America would face significant challenges to its global leadership. A specialist literature emerged on yet more 'new threats': not just 'borderless' ones like terrorism, but also the more traditional 'threat' posed by a rising (and in political terms at least, still communist) China. Such threat-mongering tended to underplay the difficulties in China's path and to overplay the likelihood of conflict between what are almost bound to be the world's two most powerful countries in the medium-term future.[32] What was evident, however, some years after the Iraq invasion, was that American conceptions of global leadership were likely – as in the era following the Vietnam War – to develop against the background of a keen awareness of limits. Hillary

Clinton, running for the Democratic nomination in 2007, gave her support to US democracy promotion, but only in 'digestible packages'.[33]

LEADERSHIP AT HOME

The end of the Cold War affected conceptions of leadership at home almost as much as views on America's world role. The domestic and international politics of the pre-1989 era combined to create a 'heroic' model, in particular, of presidential leadership. The 'imperial presidency' of Richard Nixon (1969–74) and the defeat in Vietnam had, it is true, produced a reaction to various excesses and abuses of presidential authority. The presidency of Jimmy Carter (1977–81) was, at some level, an antidote to the heroic presidential model. Yet the conditions of the Cold War – high levels of defence mobilisation, ever-present nuclear threat, prolonged invocation of crisis – invited enhanced executive power. The heroic model of presidential leadership was not simply the product of international conditions. It related also to the rise of television and to expectations of mobilisation for domestic change, whether in a liberal (as in the cases of John Kennedy and Lyndon Johnson) or (as in the case of President Reagan) a conservative direction. Heroic presidential leadership also reflected the relative strengths of state and federal levels of political authority; although, of course, the Cold War era also witnessed the spectacle of heroic presidents, notably Nixon and Reagan, actually espousing the cause of rolling power back to the states. What was undeniable about the strong post-New Deal presidency was the sustaining context of the Cold War.[34]

In a sense, the Cold War victory was a victory for presidential power, a victory made possible (according to preference) by John Kennedy's handling of the Cuban missile crisis, or by Ronald Reagan's strategy of negotiation from strength. Despite all this, the ending of the Cold War was accompanied by expectations that the ability of the presidency to survive as the prime focus for national leadership would be compromised. A 1993 report by the American Assembly on 'Public Engagement in US Foreign Policy after the Cold War' noted: 'We have inherited a conception of the "man in the Oval Office" hearing all the evidence, making lonely decisions, and then persuading the nation.' With the ending of the Cold War, however, 'foreign policy making increasingly resembles the process by which domestic policies are made, and the president must be prepared to build mutually supportive coalitions at home and abroad that will give authority and legitimacy to his/her decisions'.[35]

Bill Clinton's leadership style was certainly presidentialist and activist. He had no intention of emulating the semi-detached style of President Reagan, nor of surrendering to a constrained model of post-Cold War leadership. Yet Clinton's own orientation to the job of being leader involved more than mere super-activity. To some extent Clinton's thinking on national leadership reflected at least a hint of the suspicion of power that was characteristic of the generation that came to political maturity during the era of the Vietnam War. More importantly, Clinton's leadership was consciously fashioned for a post-liberal, 'post-heroic' America. As a founder of the Democratic Leadership Council in 1985, Clinton had been part of a movement within the Democratic Party to prepare for executive office in times that demanded fiscal caution and the exaltation of compromise ('triangulation') over ideology. In this line of thought, successful leadership meant not repeating the McGovern mistakes of 1972 by racing too far ahead of public opinion. Clinton's style was emotional; it involved a good deal of 'listening' and searching out consensual 'pathways' to the new century. According to Margaret Hermann, his style was one of 'search and check': 'search for information that will bring about good policy and check where relevant constituencies stand to see if consensus is possible'.[36]

Clinton's contribution to the development of presidential leadership – his legacy to the new century – differed significantly between domestic and foreign policy. In foreign policy, in defiance of the expectations of the early 1990s, Clinton generally kept the process under presidential control. Congress and other non-executive actors gained important new leverage in some areas; such an area was policy towards Cuba, now relegated from the high importance accorded to it during the Cold War. However, the reins of 'high' foreign and security policy-making were kept in the White House. The means of doing so involved, as during the Cold War, the frequent invocation of external 'threat' and the plausible assertion that, if the US were to have a clear international direction, only the President could provide it. Like his Republican predecessor and his Republican successor in office, Clinton paid only minimal and largely symbolic heed to legislative war powers.[37]

On the domestic side, especially after the 1995 Republican takeover of Congress, Clinton was more obviously committed to 'listening', 'triangulation' and compromise. A key example here was the welfare policy reform of 1996. Even in domestic policy, however, Clinton achieved some remarkable victories for traditional, liberal notions of strongly activist presidential leadership. The 1994 Republican Contract with America was, in effect, a blueprint for a system of national Congressional government. The Contract was complex and included provisions, notably the item veto (allowing the President to cancel specific items in appropriations bills), which actually augmented presidential authority. The main thrust of the Contract, however, was to put forward a national manifesto for Congressional leadership, with a detailed schedule for '100 days' legislative action. In the event, this new era of post-Cold War Congressional government never appeared. It was destroyed by Clinton's grasping of the initiative in foreign policy; by overreaching and misjudgement by the would-be 'prime minister', House Speaker Newt Gingrich; by the lack of a veto- or filibuster-proof Republican majority in the Senate; and by a skilled combination of compromise and confrontation (especially in the annual budget battles) by the White House. In 2001, Clinton handed on to George W. Bush a presidential office whose wings remained surprisingly unclipped, despite the impeachment and the vicious partisan political warfare of the 1990s.

The new, post-2000 presidential style was assuredly not one of 'search and check'. The Republicans who entered the White House in 2001 were strong proponents, not of Gingrich-style Congressional government, but of firm executive leadership. The White House developed doctrines of the strong presidency, rooted in notions of 'inherent power', which echoed those advanced by President Richard Nixon's Justice Department in the early 1970s, and in ideas of the 'unitary executive', which had been developed during the 1990s.[38] In a truly Nixonian touch (though also one which echoed Clinton's response to the Lewinsky scandal), the new administration relied heavily on notions of 'executive privilege' in order to protect sensitive information.[39] The argument advanced by Vice-President Richard Cheney and other leading administration conservatives was that America needed to rediscover the tradition of assertive presidential leadership which had been lost during the national overreaction to Watergate and the Vietnam War. Cheney himself emerged as possibly the most powerful Vice-President in US history. According to White House Chief of Staff Andrew Card, President George W. Bush (even before 9/11) 'wanted to restore the executive authority the president had traditionally been able to exercise'.[40] Management in this new order was perfunctory in style and, despite Bush's famous status as the first President with an MBA, strangely disordered.[41] Bush tended to equate explanation with weakness. Bob Woodward quoted him thus: 'I'm the commander – see, I don't need to explain – I do not need to explain why I say things'.[42] According to James Pfiffner, Bush 'eschewed deliberation, and his White House does not adhere to any regularized policy development process'.[43]

At the level of legal argument, the White House put its faith in a controversially presidentialist reading of constitutional history.[44] Such assertions of authority naturally found fertile ground in the political conditions which followed the 9/11 attacks. The US Congress lacked the political will seriously to raise issues of constitutional propriety when, for example, it delegated huge powers relating to national security surveillance to the executive in the Patriot Act of 2001. Such legislation raised major questions relating to civil liberties and to legislative authority. Democrat Senator Robert Byrd of West Virginia emerged as the most conspicuous defender of Congressional prerogatives after 9/11; in the atmosphere that prevailed, at least in the period 2001–5, his case for Congress asserting *its* right to lead assumed the same practical irrelevance as that of the legislative opponents of the 1964 Gulf of Tonkin resolution.[45] In domestic policy, the administration was, of course, anxious to obtain legislation. This was 'big government', rather than 'do nothing', conservatism. Legislation such as the

No Child Left Behind education reform, signed into law by President Bush in January 2002, sprang from a familiar process of compromise and adjustment in Congress, though it certainly marked a new high point for federal involvement in (usually state government-led) educational practice. Unsurprisingly, it was for policy areas related to the War on Terror that the fiercest assertions of executive power were reserved.

The most swingeing assertion of presidential authority in foreign policy was the doctrine of pre-emption. At West Point in June 2002 and in the National Security Strategy published later in the year, President Bush averred a limitless personal authority to order military action against any nation that posed – in the President's judgement, and in the President's judgement alone – either an immediate or even a longer-term threat to US security.[46] The doctrine thus effectively conflated 'pre-emption' (the heading-off of an immediate threat) with 'prevention' (cancelling remote threats). The Iraq invasion of 2003 was, in this terminology, actually 'preventive' rather than 'pre-emptive'.[47] Presidentially adjudicated pre-emption is not entirely novel, but never before had this aspect of effective executive authority been expressed quite so starkly. Anthony Lewis wrote that the doctrine overthrew 'the commitment that the United States and all other members' of the United Nations 'have made … to eschew attacks across international frontiers except in response to armed aggression'.[48] As an 'inherent' presidential power, pre-emption also left no apparent room for checks by the US Congress, much less by any international body. Assertion of executive authority was remorseless, with particularly striking examples involving the treatment of 'enemy combatants'. In 2002, following the invasion of Afghanistan, Bush's Justice Department argued that Congress could 'no more regulate the President's ability to detain and interrogate enemy combatants than it may regulate his ability to direct troop movements in the battlefield'. The President, according to the Office of Legal Counsel, 'has the inherent authority to convene military commissions to try and punish enemy combatants even in the absence of statutory authority'.[49] Such claims amount to an assertion of presidential supremacy. Intense controversy extended not only to the detention of 'combatants' – notably at Guantánamo in Cuba, but also in a range of clandestine sites – but also to their interrogation. Republican Senator John McCain of Arizona led a major effort in 2005 to outlaw torture of terror suspects. The resulting legislation was accepted by President Bush, but only with the attachment of a 'signing statement', declaring the executive's intention to enforce the law only 'in a manner consistent with the constitutional authority of the President to supervise the unitary executive branch and as Commander in Chief'.[50]

Sweeping and controversial claims of executive authority are bound to be challenged, at least in the medium to long term. In the case of the Bush presidency, formal and effective challenge emerged firstly at the judicial level. The key Supreme Court cases involved the *habeas corpus* rights of detainees.

In *Hamdi* v. *Rumsfeld* (2004), Justice Sandra O'Connor, writing for the Court, held that the administration position on denying legal appeals from detainees could not be supported by 'any reasonable view' of the constitutional doctrine of separation of powers, since it 'serves only to condense power within a single branch of government'. The Court reaffirms 'today the fundamental nature of a citizen's right to be free from involuntary confinement by his own government without due process of law'.[51]

The *Hamden* v. *Rumsfeld* decision of 2006 further damaged the administration's absolutist stance. The military commissions established to deal with War on Terror detainee cases were deemed improper, since they lacked statutory backing and contravened the Geneva Conventions. Justice Stevens, writing for the Court, opposed the administration's assertion of a 'sweeping mandate for the President to invoke military commissions whenever he deems them necessary'.[52] As with the McCain torture legislation, the administration found an escape: this time by achieving statutory backing for the tribunals. The Military Commissions Act of 2006 explicitly denied admissibility to evidence extracted under torture; yet it also provided a framework for trial by military commission, with no clear right for a non-US citizen to appeal detention before American courts. Towards the end of 2007, the stage appeared set for further Supreme Court determinations regarding *habeas corpus* and due process rights.[53]

Legislative reassertion was part of the agenda for the Democratic Congress, which convened in January 2007 and proceeded to investigate executive conduct of foreign policy and to challenge administration claims to exclusive leadership rights over the conflict in Iraq. For House Speaker Nancy Pelosi, the priority was to achieve legislation that 'ends the blank check for the President's war without end'.[54] The ability of the new Congress radically to affect the conduct of the Iraq conflict was reduced by its inability to muster enough votes to override presidential vetoes. The administration view was clearly put by Vice-President Cheney: 'military operations are to be directed by the President of the United States, period.'[55]

As America waved goodbye to the Cold War, it seemed that leadership by and in the United States might be transformed. When George Washington returned to his farm at the end of his presidency in 1797, he invoked the memory of the Roman leader Cincinnatus, who had swapped dictatorship and the ways of war for modesty and peace. As we have seen, any expectation that post-1989 America would emulate Cincinnatus, destroy its sword and revert to modest leadership was quickly disappointed. The Cold War victory produced a long, albeit initially hesitant, period of extreme confidence in the universal currency of American democratic, capitalist values. By the early years of the new century, White House assertion of presidential authority also matched, in truth exceeded, those made by Cold War presidents. The political conditions of the immediate post-9/11 years encouraged sweeping assertions of American global power, just as they underpinned presidential aggrandisement at home.

Much commentary on Bush's presidential leadership – certainly much European commentary – tends towards the hysterical. In the final few sentences of this chapter, let us try to restore a sense of proportion. Bush's globalist presidentialism was driven by ideology: a mixture, as we have seen, of new nationalism, neoconservatism and the assumption that Congress is incapable of acting responsibly, especially in any area connected to foreign policy. Such doctrines and assumptions are highly contentious at best; at worst, they transgress fundamentally constitutional provisions concerning checks on executive power and separation of powers. Yet the American system of shared and limited leadership will work only if all elements within it act to protect their interests and jurisdictions. In the period between 2001 and early 2007, the US Congress – at the federal level, *the* representative branch – singularly failed to do this. From 2008 onwards, the agenda would seem to be one of 'rebalancing': at home, the move to restrain presidential authority; and abroad, adjustment (yet again) to a newly constrained internationalism.

NOTES

1. *American Foreign Policy: Current Documents 1987* (Washington, DC: Department of State, 1988), p. 29.
2. Francis Fukuyama, 'The End of History', *The National Interest*, 16, 1989, 3–18, 4.
3. Charles Krauthammer, 'The Unipolar Moment', *Foreign Affairs*, 70, 1991, 23–33.
4. See John Dumbrell, *American Foreign Policy: Carter to Clinton* (Basingstoke: Macmillan, 1997), pp. 162–4. Also, Noam Chomsky, *World Orders: Old and New* (London: Pluto Press, 1994).
5. *Public Papers of the Presidents of the United States: George Bush: 1992–3*: Book 2 (Washington, DC: US Government Printing Office, 1993), pp. 2228–9.
6. Stephen Walt, 'Two cheers for Clinton's foreign policy', *Foreign Affairs*, 79, 2000, 63–76.
7. Joshua Muravchik, *The Imperative of American Leadership: A Challenge to Neo-Isolationism* (Washington, DC: American Enterprise Institute, 1996), p. 9.
8. Available on Clinton Presidential Library website: http://www.clintonlibrary. gov/.
9. Ibid.
10. See Ian Roxborough, *The Hart-Rudman Commission and Homeland Defense* (Carlisle, PA: Strategic Studies Institute, 2001).
11. See Samuel P. Huntington, *The Clash of Civilizations and the Remaking of World Order* (New York, NY: Simon and Schuster, 1996).
12. See Joseph S. Nye, *Bound to Lead: The Changing Nature of American Power* (New York, NY: Basic Books, 1991).
13. 'A Foreign Policy for the Global Age', 17 January 2001, available on Clinton Presidential Library website.
14. Robert W. Tucker and David C. Hendrickson, *The Imperial Temptation* (New York,

NY: Council on Foreign Relations, 1992).

15. Andrew J. Bacevich, *The Imperial Tense: Prospects and Problems of American Empire* (Chicago, IL: Dee, 2003), p. ix.

16. See Robert Kaplan, *Warrior Politics: Why Leadership Demands a Pagan Ethos* (New York, NY: Random House, 2002); Michael Cox, 'Still the American Empire', *Political Studies Review*, 5, 2007, 1–10.

17. Anatol Lieven, *America Right or Wrong: The Anatomy of American Nationalism* (London: HarperCollins, 2004), p. 96.

18. Condoleezza Rice, 'Promoting the National Interest', *Foreign Affairs*, 79, 2001, 45–62.

19. Cited in Stanley Renshon, 'The Bush Doctrine Considered', in Stanley Renshon and Peter Suedfeld (eds), *Understanding the Bush Doctrine: Psychology and Strategy in an Age of Terrorism* (New York, NY: Routledge, 2007), p. 13.

20. See Gerard Alexander, 'International Relations Theory meets World Politics', in Renshon and Suedfeld (eds), *Understanding the Bush Doctrine*, p. 42.

21. See Mark Bowden, 'Wolfowitz: The Exit Interviews', *The Atlantic Monthly*, July–August 2005, 110–22.

22. See James Petras and Morris Morley, *Empire or Republic? American Global Power and Domestic Decay* (New York, NY: Routledge, 1995).

23. Charles Krauthammer, 'In Defense of Democratic Realism', *The National Interest*, 77, 2004, 15–27.

24. Charles Krauthammer, 'Visions of Moral Obtuseness', in Micah L. Sifry and Christopher Cerf (eds), *The Iraq War Reader: History, Documents, Opinions* (New York, NY: Touchstone, 2003), pp. 217–18.

25. See John Dumbrell, 'The Bush Doctrine', in George C. Edwards and Philip J. Davies (eds), *New Challenges for the American Presidency* (New York, NY: Pearson Longman, 2004), p. 231.

26. Cited in David H. Dunn, 'Bush, 11 September and conflicting strategies of the "War on Terrorism"', *Irish Studies in International Affairs*, 16, 2005, 11–33, 23.

27. *The National Security Strategy of the United States* (Washington, DC: The White House, 2002), p. 1.

28. See Josef Joffe, *Überpower: The Imperial Temptation of America* (New York, NY: Norton, 2006), p. 131.

29. See Chalmers Johnson, *Blowback: The Costs and Consequences of American Empire*, 2nd edn (New York, NY: Henry Holt, 2004).

30. G. John Ikenberry, *Liberal Order and Imperial Ambition* (Cambridge: Polity, 2006), p. 228.

31. Stephen Walt, *Taming American Power: The Global Response to US Primacy* (New York, NY: Norton, 2005).

32. See Robert Ash, David Shambaugh and Seiichiro Takagi (eds), *China Watching: Perspectives from Europe, Japan, and the United States* (New York, NY: Routledge, 2006).

33. Jeffrey Goldberg, 'The Starting Gate', *The New Yorker*, 15 January 2007, 26–36, 28.

34. See Jon Roper, *The American Presidents: Heroic Leadership from Kennedy to Clinton* (Edinburgh: Edinburgh University Press, 2000).

35. Daniel Yankelovich and I. M. Destler (eds), *Beyond the Beltway: Engaging the Public*

   in US Foreign Policy (New York, NY: Norton, 1994), p. 283.

36. Margaret Hermann, 'Advice and advisers in the Clinton presidency: the impact of leadership style', in Stanley Renshon (ed.), *The Clinton Presidency: Campaigning, Governing, and the Psychology of Leadership* (Boulder, CO: Westview Press, 1995), p. 161.

37. See Ryan C. Hendrickson, *The Clinton Wars: The Constitution, Congress, and War Powers* (Nashville, TN: Vanderbilt University Press, 2002).

38. See Steven G. Calabresi and Kevin H. Rhodes, 'The structural constitution: unitary executive, plural judiciary', *Harvard Law Review*, 105, 1992, 1153–216.

39. See Robert M. Pallitto and William G. Weaver, *Presidential Secrecy and the Law* (Baltimore, MD: Johns Hopkins University Press, 2007).

40. Cited in John E. Owens, 'Presidential power and congressional acquiescence in America's "war" on terrorism: a new constitutional equilibrium?', *Politics and Policy*, 34, 2006, 258–303, 265.

41. See James P. Pfiffner, 'The First MBA President', *Public Administration Review*, 67, 2007, 6–20.

42. Bob Woodward, *Bush at War* (New York, NY: Simon and Schuster, 2002), pp. 146–7.

43. Pfiffner, 'The first MBA President', p. 8.

44. See John Yoo, *The Powers of War and Peace: The Constitution and Foreign Affairs after 9/11* (Chicago, IL: University of Chicago Press, 2005); Richard Posner, *Not a Suicide Pact: The Constitution in a Time of National Emergency* (New York, NY: Oxford University Press, 2006); Anita Miller (ed.), *George W. Bush versus the US Constitution* (Chicago, IL: Academy Chicago, 2006).

45. See Robert C. Byrd, *Losing America: Confronting a Reckless and Arrogant Presidency* (New York, NY: Norton, 2004).

46. See Dumbrell, 'The Bush Doctrine', in Edwards and Davies (eds), *New Challenges for the American Presidency*.

47. See, for example, remarks of Senator Edward Kennedy: www.truthout. org/docs_02/10.9A.kennedy.html.

48. Anthony Lewis, 'Bush and Iraq', *New York Review of Books*, 7 November 2002, 7–13, 8.

49. Cited in Jules Lobel, 'The Commander in Chief and the Courts', *Presidential Studies Quarterly*, 37, 2007, 49–65, 49.

50. Ibid. See also Phillip J. Cooper, 'George W. Bush, Edgar Allen Poe, and the use and abuse of presidential signing statements', *Presidential Studies Quarterly*, 35, 2005, 512–32.

51. *Hamdi* v. *Rumsfeld* (542 US 507, 2004). *Rasul* v. *Bush* (542 US 466, 2004) established that a non-US citizen could petition against detention.

52. *Hamden* v. *Rumsfeld* (126 S.Ct. 2749, 2006). See David Cole, 'Why the Court said no', *New York Review of Books*, 10 August 2006, 41–3.

53. Various cases, notably *Boumedienne* v. *Bush,* are pending.

54. See www.house.gov/pelosi/press/release/May07/newiraq.html.

55. Cheney, remarks to the Heritage Foundation, 13 April 2007 (available on Heritage Foundation website).

3. 9/11 AND US FOREIGN POLICY

David Ryan

For all the horror of that Tuesday and the fathomless pain and grief visited on countless families, 9/11 was an event that thus far does not represent a significant turning point in US diplomatic history or foreign policy.[1] It was quickly superseded by other events unrelated to the causes of 9/11. Influential strategists within the Bush administration seized on the horror to gain assent from liberal Americans to move the country towards a war in Iraq that neoconservative strategists desired, but that many within the US, albeit with considerable liberal acquiescence, shunned because of the memories of Vietnam.

This chapter contends that the dominant reaction led by the Bush administration instantaneously broadened the context by falling back on old ideas associated with notions of victory and confrontation, with ideologies resulting from defeat in Vietnam, and with the Cold War inclination to think in dualistic terms. While the event was and is of immense importance in order to understand US foreign policy, one must also understand the 'ideological system of the epoch in question'.[2] As the French historian Fernand Braudel famously wrote:

> I remember the night near Bahia when I was enveloped in a firework display of phosphorescent fireflies; their pale lights glowed, went out, shone again, all without piercing the night with any true illumination. So it is with events; beyond their glow, darkness prevails.[3]

The Bush administration's decision to take war to Iraq has meant that in many ways 9/11 has been overshadowed; its specific implications for US foreign policy will still need to be addressed after settlement of the Iraq War.

9/11 has been widely interpreted as an act of ill-defined opposition to Western modernism and US power. The symbolic termini were important: the Twin Towers of the World Trade Center, architectural expressions of power and mastery, control and lordship, were constructed in 1973 just as concepts and cultures of postmodernism were identified as resulting from 'cultural logic of late capitalism' and the 'crisis of endless accumulation'.[4] Postmodernism simultaneously undermined and augmented the architectural narratives associated with the Twin Towers. The Pentagon, the other target of 9/11, represented the strategic node of US military power and hegemony. These buildings also embodied the two dominant theses on US foreign policy: the 'end of history' and the 'clash of civilizations'. The Twin Towers of the World Trade Center represented the material manifestation of US leadership in the world economy and economic integration since the end of World War II, whereas the Pentagon stood as a potent symbol of US 'hard power'. As this chapter will explore, these discourses, associated in the 1990s with conservative thinkers Francis Fukuyama and Samuel Huntington respectively, were both revived after 9/11.

The 'end of history' thesis suggested that the story of progress had culminated in the Western dream of liberal democracy, with all peoples and cultures moving towards that inexorable end. The 'clash of civilizations' thesis proposed that with the end of the Cold War the struggle over ideas of freedom, democracy and justice had ended. Henceforth international relations would be characterised as a clash of civilisations, centred particularly on the conflict between the West versus Islam and the so-called Confucian world, but ultimately reduced to a clash between the 'West and the rest'.[5] Flawed though the thesis was, its cultural resonance was widespread at the time that Huntington published his essay in 1993, and then again after 9/11. The two theses represented a strong urge towards a restoration of US ideological and cultural power. Fukuyama and Huntington both had a deep appreciation of the importance of the constructed notion of 'the West' and the values that it ostensibly represented. Reacting to the intellectual and cultural developments of the 1960s and building on both the triumphalism of the 1980s and the simultaneous 'rise of Islamism', these narratives envisaged new horizons that harkened back to the Cold War of the 1950s, a period of relative consensus, material wealth, of Rockwellesque certainty and confidence, a period in which Daniel Bell had proclaimed the 'end of ideology'. Nevertheless, it was a period that was simultaneously tempered by an anxiety attuned to external Soviet threats and internal cultural narratives of subversion.[6]

The intellectual and cultural ramifications of the 1973 US defeat in Vietnam were far-reaching. Understanding these ramifications is pivotal to understanding US foreign policy after 9/11. The strategic implications of the US loss in Vietnam were profound. That experience induced widespread US inhibition on the use of hard power associated with the Vietnam syndrome, precipitating a significant readjustment in US relative power that undermined their preponderance to which they had become accustomed. Policy-makers had to adjust to a post-heroic age, in which there was widespread reticence on sending US troops into protracted ground warfare. Henceforth intervention would be circumscribed by a set of criteria, articulated by Secretary of Defense Caspar Weinberger and later by Colin Powell, which had to be addressed before the intervention or application of hard power. These limitations were anathema to other strategists who seized on the opportunity of 9/11 to extract the nation from these constraints.

If hegemony rested on the acceptance of US ideas and legitimating discourses, these too were increasingly threatened by a multipolar world order and the multiplicity of postcolonial voices after Vietnam. Even if the neoconservative columnist Charles Krauthammer extolled the 'unipolar moment' in the early 1990s, the construction was premised on the end of Cold War bipolarity, which privileged a view of the world that masked many other forces and ideas.[7] As early as 1969 the US National Security Advisor Henry Kissinger recognised that

> many of the salient characteristics of the present period of international politics spring from the diffusion of independent political activity among and within states following the decline of the cold war, the loosening of cold-war alliances, and the assertion of national and subnational loyalties in the wake of colonial dissolution.[8]

The centrifugal forces in world politics were obvious and US strategists immediately crafted instrumental lessons of the Vietnam War that would facilitate further US intervention.

Beneath this, the meta-narrative of US diplomacy and foreign policy lay in tatters. The elite cultural affinity with certain ideas linked to US identity – democracy, liberty, self-determination – were fundamentally challenged in Vietnam, but also crucially within the US as the civil rights and feminist movements challenged ingrained conceptions. The 1960s, precursor to the advent of postmodernism, exercised an enormous social and psychological displacement that dislodged traditional attitudes.[9] Yet, there were limits. Perry Anderson credits Alex Callinicos and Terry Eagleton for emphasising that the immediate origin of postmodernity was in the experience of defeat: 'within another few years, all the signs were reversed as, one by one, the political dreams of the sixties were snuffed out.'[10]

The process of decentring took many forms. There was the rise of alternative centres of global power in Europe, China and Japan, the OPEC challenge that limited cheap oil (a basis for so much Western wealth and cultural confidence), whilst Third World revolutionary politics and post-colonial thought threatened the stability and meaning of Western ideologies. Cumulatively, these changes ushered in a period of doubt, fragmentation, pluralism and a decentring of power and influence away from Washington and Wall Street. Postmodernity and postcolonial interpretations of power undermined US meta-narratives and social constructions of US identity from within and beyond its borders.[11] The phenomenon was a fundamentally disorienting experience for elite decision-makers engaged in US foreign policy.[12]

US leaders turned to realism to guide their foreign policies. Open-ended commitments and universal ideals were shunned while national interests were narrowly defined to foster the longevity of US power. Kissinger warned that 'we must be wary both of the zealous ideologues who would over-commit us and of those who would withdraw us from meeting our legitimate responsibilities and interests'.[13] The observation was prompted by reaction to a piece in the *Wall Street Journal* by Robert Nisbet, which reflected on John Kenneth Galbraith's article 'Who needs the Democrats?' (1970). Galbraith argued that wars came with a certain and devastating reliability every time the Democrats were in power, while Nisbet adopted the pragmatist philosopher William James's dichotomy between the 'tender-minded' and 'tough-minded' to contrast the foreign policies of the idealist Democrats and the realist Republicans. Nisbet recounted:

> Among modern intellectuals ... there is a frequently observed fondness for the uses of power, especially centralized, bureaucratized power in service to large-scale moral objectives. In a modern nation state, war is the supreme crisis, the highest expression of a complex of elements including love of large-scale undertakings involving masses of people, power, centralization, bureaucracy and chronic political moralism.[14]

Kissinger's antidote centred on an 'intelligent tough-mindedness' that balanced foreign policy capabilities and aspirations. The tender-minded who took the US into Vietnam, according to Kissinger, put too much emphasis on the structures of their thought rather than examining actualities of the enemy or Southeast Asian culture. Kissinger credited the Republicans for stripping away 'the moralisms that still suffocate our thinking' and facilitating a more effective pursuit of US national interests and security. The Republican Party was divided on the attractions of realism. When the Iraq Study Group reported in late 2006 and recommended similar tough-minded ways in which to conclude the US occupation of Iraq, divisions within the GOP were exposed.[15] While President Nixon and Kissinger advocated such amoral realism, the traditional reading of American history and diplomacy was far more appealing to a range of intellectual strategists – some of them later neoconservatives – who distanced themselves from this realism and eventually found a home in both the Reagan and George W. Bush administrations. The sense of limits imposed after the Vietnam War and at the conclusion of the Gulf War of 1991 chaffed against the tender-minded sentiments and ambitions of these figures. Whether it was the reassertion of US power and a restoration of its hegemony, the ostensible promotion of democracy, or the desire to overthrow and deliver a crushing defeat on Iraq, it was this tide of intellectual engagement (often pulling against the current of US culture) that assumed one Vietnam was enough. This is pivotal for understanding the turn in foreign policy that separates the 20th century from the 21st century.[16] The events of 9/11 provided the opportunity, and briefly allowed these intellectuals to row with the emotional tide built on grief and outrage, which swept along previously war-weary and reticent liberals.

THE RESTORATION

After Vietnam, few Americans advocated a return to isolationism. There was a move away from internationalism, but more particularly a majority of Americans briefly favoured demilitarising US power.[17] Most pertinently for this essay, the emergence of the Vietnam syndrome – that reluctance to commit US troops to ground combat abroad unless interests were defined, objectives articulated and success assured – became more pronounced over subsequent decades.

The post-Vietnam attitude to ground warfare represented a strand of democratic constraint on executive power. Intellectuals closely related to power and policy formation in Washington and the think tanks were keen to limit such constraints. With the 1968 Tet Offensive it became acutely apparent that the Vietnamese opposition had found the point of vulnerability in the American mind – 9/11 provided the opportunity to overcome this reticence on ground warfare. But 9/11 did not fundamentally change the culture of US foreign policy; it gave certain intellectual strategists the chance to redress old mentalities. Albert Wohlstetter (the Cold War intellectual and University of Chicago academic, who was also an influence on then Deputy Secretary of Defense, Paul Wolfowitz) pointed out that 'of all the disasters of Vietnam the worst may be the "lessons" that we'll draw from it'. The popular lessons might indeed inhibit White House agendas.[18] State Department analysis reaffirmed the fear. In 1975, a high level study observed that

> having been badly burned in Viet-Nam, the American people now appear to have quite different, and more limited, visions of our proper role in the world and our ability to influence events. In a sense a control mechanism has evolved within our society which is likely to prevent for the foreseeable future any repetition of a Viet-Nam style involvement.[19]

Such constraints, domestic or foreign, were anathema to a growing number of intellectual strategists, and particularly those involved in the neoconservative movement. Initially Kissinger tried to limit the impact of the lessons of Vietnam on US strategy.[20] But certain lessons were worth learning.

And, while Kissinger and Nixon placed interests above values, many subsequent administrations tried to reverse that formula with the re-injection of values into their policies. It took on different forms in the Carter, Reagan, Clinton and George W. Bush administrations, but ultimately the return of the tender-minded proclivity would again force the US to face the results of the 'quagmire of the vanities'.[21]

Kissinger recognised that Americans would not long support a foreign policy that jarred with their traditional attitudes.[22] Jimmy Carter's electoral victory over Gerald Ford in 1976 represented, in part, a repudiation of the particular interest-focused approach to foreign policy, the sense of cultural moral confusion and identity crisis associated with the Vietnam War, and the turmoil of the early 1970s.[23] Carter's National Security Advisor Zbigniew Brzezinski described a 'sharp contrast' with the past, especially, as he wrote to Carter, because

> you have re-identified the United States with an ideal. Traditionally, the United States has been seen abroad as a society that is associated with certain basic values. During the last several years, however, the impression became widespread that domestically we are concerned with consumption and abroad only with the balance of power. Your stress on human rights has corrected this.[24]

Brzezinski went on to outline the world the Carter administration had inherited:

> The international position of the United States at the end of 1976 was not good. Our Allies were uneasy about our constancy, our will, and our ability to lead. Our adversaries were openly speculating about the political consequences of 'the general crisis of capitalism'. The third world was generally hostile or disappointed. The American public distrusted our policies and deplored the apparent lack of moral content in our actions and goal.

He suggested that there was a sense amongst overseas nations that Americans were fearful of change and indifferent to emerging global aspirations. Collectively, the Carter administration intended to 'restore our spirit', inject a moral content into US foreign policy, to cooperate and work multilaterally with allies, seek reconciliation in regional conflict, and finally to seek strategic accommodation.[25]

Here was the re-injection of values, but William James's tender-minded description could not be applied because, if anything, Carter did not over commit the nation. Despite the constraints on the use of force during the Reagan era, there was a considerable cultural shift to the right.

The meaning of US power and the fundamental purpose of its foreign policy were central to neoconservative thinking.[26] Fukuyama's thesis on the 'end of history' had widespread appeal, particularly his view that the terminus of progress through liberal democratic capitalism had been reached.[27] The confidence with which the argument was advanced belied the narratives of US decline that were simultaneously put forward. During the 1960s, the 'American Idea, of unlimited possibility and the transformation of humanity, no longer convinced some Americans themselves'. The neo-conservatives reacted to this cultural doubt and pushed the beliefs in 'American worth and American primacy' up the agenda. William Pfaff suggests that it was inconceivable that the US cultural acceptance of its international role, its engagement and the sacrifices of the various wars could produce much less than anticipated.[28]

The 'end of history' thesis provided an antidote. Fukuyama stipulated that, despite the necessary adjustments in philosophical developments, the present condition represented the culmination of the orthodox or traditional meta-narrative of US foreign policy, of the march of freedom and the progress of democracy. Triumphal histories of the Cold War abounded during the 1990s. Indeed, one of the reasons why Vietnam is relatively neglected in school and college curricula is that that war raised fundamental questions about US identity and history.[29]

The gist of the argument found its way into President Bush's 2002 National Security Strategy. It asserted that 'the great struggles of the 20th century between liberty and totalitarianism ended with a decisive victory for the forces of freedom – and a single sustainable model for national success: freedom, democracy, and free enterprise'.[30] Yet, the philosophical confidence was still tempered by doubts about US power and the collective memory of its earlier defeat. The combination of these cultural and intellectual uncertainties, coupled with the inhibitions on US power, produced a bitter and dangerous sentiment that would measure US primacy through its ability to employ unilateral military action. It was an imperative for the Reagan administration to reconstruct a strong American identity through military power. Yet despite the obvious but unsatisfactory 'victory' in the Cold War and the more traditional but limited victory in Iraq in 1991 the idea of America had been tarnished. The 'culture of defeat' had to be reversed: a sense of defeat that could not be fully satiated by the fall of the Berlin Wall in 1989.[31]

The 2003 'victory' in Iraq briefly fulfilled the yearning for triumph. But this was soon confounded by various forms of resistance from Falluja, Najaf and elsewhere. Initially, Bush exuded confidence following the short-term success in Afghanistan over the autumn of 2001. The neoconservatives celebrated. Charles Krauthammer pointed out that 'power is its own reward. Victory changes everything, psychology above all. The psychology in the region is now one of fear and deep respect for American power.'[32] Next, they took up the old project. Stung by the decision of George H. W. Bush to halt the Gulf War in 1991, where the lessons of Vietnam suggested it ought to stop, they decided to return. US victory in that country would become an example and produce a demonstration effect across the region. The confidence of American opponents would be shattered, their actions inhibited. That sense of victory was reflected in the visions that emerged in 2002, primarily contained in Bush's National Security Strategy and in the idea to 'democratise' the Middle East over the next generation.

The explicit and implicit narratives of a desire to recreate preponderance can be traced backward from the National Security Strategy of 2002, which indicated that 'our forces will be strong enough to dissuade potential adversaries from pursuing a military build-up in hopes of surpassing, or equalling, the power of the United States.' The military priorities included the need to 'dissuade future military competition; deter threats against U.S. interests, allies, and friends; and decisively defeat any adversary if deterrence fails'.[33] The desire for the restoration of primacy of US power was also clear in the leaked 1992 *Defense Planning Guidance* document that sought to 'discourage' advanced industrial nations 'from challenging our leadership or seeking to overturn the established political and economic order'. Moreover competitors must be deterred 'from even aspiring to a larger regional or global role'.[34] Earlier still, Reagan's National Security Council worried about the 'loss of U.S. strategic superiority', not just because of perceived Soviet advances, but also because of 'the increased political and economic strength of the industrial democracies' in Europe.[35] A world characterised by a greater distribution of power disturbed these strategic thinkers who were nostalgic for the earlier US preponderance and 'disparity of power'.[36] After the Iran-Contra affair of 1986, Robert McFarlane, a former National Security Advisor, reflected predominant Reagan administration beliefs in hearings before Congress:

> We had just witnessed a five year period where the Soviet Union tried out a stratagem of sponsoring guerrilla movements that would topple moderate regimes, and install their own totalitarian successor, and they had phenomenal success ... If we could not muster an effective counter to Cuban-Sandinista strategy in our own backyard, it was far less likely that we could do so in the years ahead in more distant locations ... We had to win this one.[37]

There was probably no need for such a victory in Nicaragua except that the Sandinista government had been constructed as a Soviet puppet regime in a Manichaean view of the global order.

As such events demonstrate, much of US identity and one basis of its nationalism is formed in opposition and opprobrium directed at an 'Other'. Despite the early injunctions in US foreign policy not to go in search of monsters to destroy, they have usually animated its foreign policy and provided it with an overarching purpose. Broad conceptual dichotomies have provided a momentum and a point of contrast to bring US identity into sharp relief. These dualities – the product of intellectual conception but with some basis in historical fact – have defined US policy and ideology from inception, but particularly through the Monroe Doctrine, which advanced the conceptual divide between the old and the new world, updated in the discourses of civilization and barbarism at the turn into the 20th century. Woodrow Wilson's foreign policy ostensibly updated the Monroe Doctrine, but with universal application. And as the Cold War ended, a range of work reflected the vindication of Wilsonian liberal internationalism, from Tony Smith's *America's Mission* (1994) to Frank Ninkovich's *The Wilsonian Century* (2001) and Akira Iriye's *Cultural Internationalism and World Order* (1997).[38]

These dichotomies returned in the early Cold War, at the outset of which President Truman enjoined audiences to make a choice at that juncture in world history between two – and only two – ways of life. His doctrine of 1947 represented the popular articulation of containment, which according to the dominant narratives of US diplomatic history took the US into Vietnam.[39] Head of Policy Plannng, George Kennan, understood that the effects of the Soviet challenge would make US culture and society more cohesive.[40] Similarly, Bush's early response after 9/11 presented another dualistic choice of either standing with the US or against it. The administration's rhetorical conflation of all sorts of disparate opponents belied reality and set Washington on course for Iraq, thus evading the implications of 9/11.

Fukuyama's book *The End of History and the Last Man* might have provided the philosophical aspiration long associated with US liberalism, prefacing a decade of heightened consumerism and the rise of globalisation. The project complete, there was no further need for the 'strenuous life' or the 'barbarian sentiment' articulated by President Theodore Roosevelt a century earlier. But, as a source of motivation, Fukuyama's thesis failed to grasp other models of political and cultural life. The triumph of the market was unsatisfactory; the 'last man', in Fukuyama's reading of Nietzsche, was 'a comfortable slave, with physical security and material plenty, a person who believes in nothing (or everything) …'[41] Clinton's vision of the 'globalization of the free market had undermined the efficacy of military power', which chaffed against neoconservative agendas. On this subject, Irving Kristol once lamented that 'what's the point of being the greatest most powerful nation in the world and not having an imperial role?'[42]

QUAGMIRE OF THE VANITIES

'It is possible', Wolfgang Schivelbusch suggests, that 'the destruction of September 11 uncovered the suppressed remains of Vietnam'.[43] After Vietnam the malaise of the late 1970s was quickly reversed through Reagan's rhetorical constructions and re-imagining of America. Such reversal is not unique, but part of the 'recognizable set of patterns or archetypes that recur across time and national boundaries'. Schivelbusch remarks how surprising it is that the depression is so short lived 'before turning into a unique type of euphoria'.[44] The dreamscape of that United States (again in part a construction) contrasted explicitly with the identification of the Other as the 'evil empire' in 1982 and coincided with the demise of the Soviet bloc and the Soviet Union itself by 1991. Interpretations of that collapse are diverse and at times unrelated to US foreign policy. Yet in the United States the analyst, historian and cultural commentator 'who stands on the side of the victorious is easily tempted to interpret triumphs of the moment as the lasting outcomes of an ex-post facto teleology'.[45] That is, they take the demise of the Soviet Union as necessarily a result of the application of US policies of containment rather than a series of alternatives relating to the Soviet economy and managerial system, the rise of religion and nationalism within the USSR, or other internal issues. The intellectual and cultural echoes of the triumphal outcomes of both the Cold War and the Gulf War masked a deeper lingering cultural doubt, expressed specifically in the US indecision and ambivalence on conditions and potential interventions in Bosnia, Somalia, Rwanda and Haiti.

'Paradigms do not have to be true to become accepted wisdom', yet without paradigms, as Ernest Gellner has appropriated Hobbes, 'the life of ideas would be nasty, brutish and short'.[46] After the Cold War, and again after 9/11, Huntington's 'clash of civilizations' thesis was far more appealing than Fukuyama's soporific 'end of history'. Huntington's thesis created an abstract and reductive understanding of the new dynamics in international relations. Although criticised in many regards, it was widely referred to after 9/11 as the nation searched for an overarching understanding of what the atrocities meant.[47] The thesis was predicated on a sense of 'fear and loathing'. For Huntington, 'it is human to hate. For self-definition and motivation people need enemies.'[48] Bruce Cumings has declared that 9/11 'appeared to bring this theory to life'. The US realism of earlier thinking or the idealism associated with the Fukuyama thesis found no cultural resonance immediately after 9/11.[49] Yet in Huntington's thesis, as Edward Said suggests, 'the basic paradigm of West versus the rest (the Cold War opposition reformulated) remained untouched, and this is what has persisted, often insidiously and implicitly, in discussion since the events of 9/11.'[50] The thesis was certainly echoed in cultural discourse. Intellectual analyses of the US response to 9/11 played on the title of two books published in 2002: Tariq Ali's *The Clash of Fundamentalisms* and of Gilbert Achcar's *The Clash of Barbarisms*.

Despite the official denial that the wars taken to Afghanistan or Iraq – or that more amorphous war on global terrorism – represented such a clash, this is not the way that much cultural discourse projected it. Moreover, the

Manichaean strain that pervaded Bush's rhetoric both before and after 9/11 is telling. The complexity of the heterogeneous world and the origins of the conflict in US policy in the Middle East and elsewhere were elided with simplistic formulae. The mindset was palpable *before* and *after* 9/11. In 2000, Bush admitted that he did not know who the enemy was, but soon explained: 'when I was coming up, with what was a dangerous world, we knew exactly who they were. It was us versus them, and it was clear who the them were. Today we're not so sure who the they are, but we know they're there.'[51] After 9/11, such identities settled into cultural caricatures as the President conflated the attacks with the benign meta-narratives and ideologies of US history and diplomacy. He told his audience that these attacks were on American freedom and its way of life. He warned citizens all over the world that they were either with the United States or against it. That dualism, intended to bring Americans together, papered over ongoing cultural fragmentation. It obscured conditions and understandings of US policy, past, present and future: Washington had ongoing ties to many authoritarian regimes that reflected the realities of power but jarred with the ideologies Bush identified as under attack on and after 9/11.

Moreover, the dualism found multiple echoes throughout US culture.[52] The conflation of figures and forces into 'the enemy' reinforced the dualistic predisposition. First, al-Qaeda was conflated with the Taliban, and then they were conceived as the 'terrorists', before quickly merging with the 'tyrants'.[53] Not content to remain 'philosophical realists' willing to leave opponents alone so long as they leave the US alone, tender-minded moralism returned to the fore in foreign policy, particularly when it came to Saddam Hussein. The Iraqi leader found himself the immediate subject of discussion and the target of retribution in the wake of 9/11, even despite the incongruity of the association between *that* tyrant and *those* terrorists.[54]

Nevertheless, despite widespread condemnation, opposition and wariness of the US inclination to change the regime in Iraq (unilaterally if necessary), the emphasis was now on the structure of the strategists' thought rather than the actuality of the particular enemy, the Iraqi terrain, or the 'people over which they fought'. While direct comparisons to Vietnam are difficult, frequently misguided and sometimes motivated by ideological or political agendas, at least one here is worth noting. Both Presidents Johnson and Bush enjoyed the support of public opinion at the times of the decision to escalate (1965) or invade (2003) and even though a particular sense of idealism informed their decisions, 'inside this idealism', Robert Brigham writes, 'lay the belief that the United States knew no limits to its power'.[55] It was precisely this lack of significant public debate and the absence of effective checks and balances on the imperious executive that facilitated US entry into both Vietnam and Iraq. Writing in the aftermath of 9/11 and Afghanistan, Walter LaFeber identified a nation 'so strong that others could not check it, and so self-righteous that it could not check itself'.[56] And so the familiar pattern of acquiescence and exceptionalism, of deference and difference, prefaced the path to the interventions in Afghanistan and Iraq that will have a profound and inhibiting impact on US foreign policy.

The commitment in Iraq produced another interest that closely resembled previous administrations' concerns with US credibility. The need to 'stay the course', to demonstrate resolve and the tenacity of the American people in the face of a war – the end of which became even more elusive beyond the narrative of Iraqification and US withdrawal – was dogged by the structures of thought evident since the end of the Vietnam War.

The Iraq War represented another of those occasions not seen since the earlier decades of the Cold War in which the tender-minded values took precedence over the US national interests. The costs in terms of human lives, both Iraqi and American, in terms of dollars, in terms of strategic positioning and, fundamentally, in terms of attitudes towards US foreign policy and power were considerable. It was manifest in the extensive diplomatic opposition, in the widespread anti-Americanism across the globe since 2002, the internal doubt and scepticism of the Executive and in the loss of US normative authority.[57]

There are obvious dangers associated with such overarching intellectual adventures related to the paradigms advanced by intellectuals closely associated with power.[58] This is particularly the case if such ideas are implemented through military power; indeed Fukuyama defected from the neoconservative cause because of the overemphasis on militarism.[59] It took the Vietnam War and the global changes that characterised the 1970s to deconstruct the Cold War paradigm (particularly that formulated by tender-minded strategists) and to turn the US off grand designs and universal projects. But the fallout from Iraq promises not only to erode the appeal of the tender 'end of history' and the tough 'clash of civilizations' theses, but also to reinforce the Vietnam (and now Iraq) syndrome and its lessons, and usher in a period of relativism, particularism and further erosion of the meta-narratives of US diplomatic history and foreign policy. The very yearning to re-inject a purpose and moralism into US foreign policy, in many ways against the current, squandered a fleeting opportunity engendered by the widespread sympathy and outrage of 9/11.

NOTES

1. See David L. Anderson, 'One Vietnam War should be enough and other reflections on diplomatic history and the making of foreign policy', *Diplomatic History*, 30(1), January 2006, 18.
2. Roger Chartier, *Cultural History: Between Practices and Representations*, trans. Lydia G. Cochrane (Cambridge: Polity, 1988), p. 34.
3. Fernand Braudel, *On History*, trans. Sarah Matthews (London: Weidenfeld and Nicolson, 1980), pp. 10–11.

4. Wolfgang Schivelbusch, *The Culture of Defeat: On National Trauma, Mourning, and Recovery* (New York, NY: Henry Holt, 2003), p. 292.
5. See Francis Fukuyama, *The End of History and the Last Man* (London: Penguin, 1992) and Samuel P. Huntington, 'The Clash of Civilizations', *Foreign Affairs*, 72(3), Summer 1993, 22–49.
6. Perry Anderson, *The Origins of Postmodernity* (London: Verso, 1998), p. 89; Alan Ryan, 'Introduction', *After the End of History* (London: Collins and Brown, 1992), p. 3.
7. Charles Krauthammer, 'The Unipolar Moment', *Foreign Affairs*, 70(1), Winter 1990–1, 23–33.
8. Henry Kissinger, memorandum from the President's Assistant for National Security Affairs to President Nixon, 20 October 1969, document 41, Foundations of Foreign Policy 1969–1972, vol. 1, *Foreign Relations of the United States 1969–1976*, p. 131.
9. Fredric Jameson, *Postmodernism, or, the Cultural Logic of Late Capitalism* (London: Verso, 1991), p. xx.
10. Perry Anderson, *The Origins of Postmodernity*, p. 91.
11. See Part 2 of Joyce Appleby *et al.*, *Telling the Truth about History* (New York, NY: Norton, 1994).
12. Alfred E. Eckes and Thomas W. Zeiler, *Globalization and the American Century* (Cambridge: Cambridge University Press, 2003), pp. 181–90; Immanual Wallerstein, *Historical Capitalism with Capitalist Civilization* (London: Verso, 1983), pp. 75–93.
13. Henry A. Kissinger, memorandum for the Staff Secretary, The White House, n.d., NSC files, Subject files, box 378, press, TV, news 1970–1, vol. 1, Nixon Presidential Materials.
14. Robert Nisbet, 'War, Crisis and Intellectuals', *Wall Street Journal*, 25 January 1971.
15. Kissinger, memorandum for the Staff Secretary, 1970–1; James A. Baker and Lee H. Hamilton, *The Iraq Study Group Report* (New York, NY: Vintage, 2006).
16. David Anderson, 'One Vietnam should be enough', 1–21.
17. Richard Sobel, *The Impact of Public Opinion on U.S. Foreign Policy Since Vietnam* (New York, NY: Oxford University Press, 2001), p. 37. Sobel demonstrates through a review of public opinion that there was considerable wariness on the use of military solutions in regional conflicts.
18. Andrew J. Bacevich, *The New American Militarism: How Americans are Seduced by War* (New York, NY: Oxford University Press, 2005), pp. 157–8; David Ryan, '"Vietnam", victory culture and Iraq: struggling with lessons, constraints and credibility from Saigon to Falluja', in John Dumbrell and David Ryan (eds), *Vietnam in Iraq* (London: Routledge, 2006), p. 113.
19. W. R. Smyser, memorandum to Secretary Kissinger, 'Lessons of Vietnam', 12 May 1975, NSA, Presidential Country Files for East Asia and the Pacific. Country file: Vietnam (23), box 20, Gerald R. Ford Library (GRF).
20. Henry A. Kissinger, memorandum for the President, 'Lessons of Vietnam', 12 May 1978.
21. The term is that of Slavoj Žižek. See also his *Iraq: The Borrowed Kettle* (London: Verso, 2004).
22. Kissinger, 'Lessons of Vietnam', 12 May 1975.

23. See, for example, Carter's statement: 'our country has been through difficult times in the last few years – with an unpopular war in Vietnam and Cambodia, with the Watergate revelations bringing disgrace on the White House itself, with doubt being cast on the legality of operations within our intelligence community and within the FBI itself', Jimmy Carter, Remarks of the President at the Department of Defense, The Pentagon, 1 March 1977, Defense Department Visit, Jimmy Carter Library (JCL).

24. Zbigniew Brzezinski, memorandum for the President, 22 April 1977, Presidential Interviews, JCL.

25. Brzezinski, memorandum for Rick Hertzberg and Rick Inderfurth, The White House, 11 January 1978, State of the Union 1978, 'Beloved Community', JCL.

26. Francis Fukuyama, *After the Neocons: America at the Crossroads* (London: Profile, 2006), pp. 48–50.

27. Fukuyama, *The End of History and the Last Man*, p. xi.

28. William Pfaff, *Barbarian Sentiments: How the American Century Ends* (New York, NY: Hill and Wang, 1989), pp. 182–3, 188.

29. Rick Berg and John Carlos Rowe (eds), *The Vietnam War and American Culture* (New York, NY: Columbia University Press, 1991), p. 13.

30. The White House, *The National Security Strategy of the United States of America* (Washington, DC: September 2002).

31. See Schivelbusch, *Culture of Defeat* and Tom Engelhardt, *The End of Victory Culture: Cold War America and the Disillusioning of a Generation* (Amherst, MA: University of Massachusetts Press, 1995).

32. Cited in Michael Cox, 'American power before and after 11 September: dizzy with success?', *International Affairs*, 78(2), 2002, 275.

33. Ibid.

34. Patrick Tyler, 'U.S. strategy plan calls for insuring no rivals develop', *The New York Times*, 8 March 1992; David Ryan, *US Foreign Policy in World History* (London: Routledge, 2000), p. 190.

35. US National Security Strategy and accompanying papers, April 1982, document 8290283 (NSDD 32) System II, NSC Records, Reagan Presidential Library.

36. See David Ryan, *Frustrated Empire: US Foreign Policy, 9/11 to Iraq* (London: Pluto, 2007), pp. 97–114.

37. Peter Kornbluh, 'The US role in the Counterrevolution', in Thomas W. Walter (ed.), *Revolution & Counterrevolution in Nicaragua* (Boulder, CO: Westview Press, 1991), p. 325.

38. Anderson, 'One Vietnam War should be enough', p. 16.

39. Ibid., p. 4.

40. See George Kennan, 'The Sources of Soviet Conduct', *Foreign Affairs*, 25, July 1947.

41. Bruce Cumings, 'Time of Illusion: Post-Cold War Visions of the World', in Ellen Schrecker (ed.), *Cold War Triumphalism* (New York, NY: The New Press, 2004), p. 80.

42. Corey Robin, 'Remembrance of Empires Past: 9/11 and the End of the Cold War', in Schrecker (ed.), *Cold War Triumphalism*, pp. 275–81.

43. Schivelbusch, *The Culture of Defeat*, p. 293. See also Marilyn B. Young, 'Still stuck in the big muddy', in Schrecker (ed.), *Cold War Triumphalism*, pp. 262–73.

44. Schivelbusch, *The Culture of Defeat*, p. 10.
45. Reinhart Koselleck cited in Schivelbusch, *The Culture of Defeat*, pp. 3–4.
46. Ervand Abrahamian, 'The US Media, Samuel Huntington and September 11', *Middle East Report*, 223, Summer 2002, 62; Ernest Gellner, *Reason and Culture: The Historical Role of Rationality and Rationalism* (Oxford: Blackwell, 1992), p. 113.
47. Richard E. Rubenstein and Jarle Crocker, 'Challenging Huntington', *Foreign Policy*, 96, Fall 1994, 113–28; Edward Said, *The Politics of Dispossession: The Struggle for Palestinian Self-Determination 1969–1994* (London: Chatto and Windus, 1994), pp. 384–92.
48. Huntington cited by Nicholas Guyatt, *Another American Century? The United States and the World after 2000* (Sydney: Pluto, 2000), p. 193.
49. Cumings, 'Time of illusion: post-Cold War visions of the world', in Schrecker (ed.), *Cold War Triumphalism*, p. 92. Samuel Huntington actually opposed the US war in Iraq but his ideas nevertheless informed broad cultural comment.
50. Edward Said, 'The clash of ignorance', in Don Hazen *et al.* (eds), *After 9/11: Solutions for a Saner World* (San Francisco, CA: AlterNet, 2001), p. 84.
51. Cited in Frances Fitzgerald, 'George Bush and the world', *New York Review of Books*, 26 September 2002, 84.
52. President George Bush, address to a Joint Session of Congress and the American People, The White House, www.whitehouse.gov/news/releases 2001/09/20010920-8.html, 20 September 2001.
53. President George Bush, Graduation Speech at West Point, The White House, www.whitehouse.gov/news/releases/2002/06/print/20020601-3.html, 1 June 2002.
54. Pfaff, *Barbarian Sentiments*, p. 188.
55. Robert K. Brigham, *Is Iraq Another Vietnam?* (New York, NY: Public Affairs, 2006), p. xiii.
56. Cited in Fredrik Logevall, *Choosing War: The Lost Chance for Peace and the Escalation of War in Vietnam* (Berkeley, CA: University of California Press, 1999), pp. 412–13; Walter LaFeber, 'The Bush Doctrine', *Diplomatic History*, 26(4), Fall 2002, 558.
57. See Jürgen Habermas, *The Divided West* (Cambridge: Polity, 2006).
58. See Bruce Kuklick, *Blind Oracles: Intellectuals and War from Kennan to Kissinger* (Princeton, NJ: Princeton University Press, 2006).
59. See Fukuyama, *After the Neocons*.

4. THREE VARIATIONS ON AMERICAN LIBERALISM

Peter Kuryla

Liberalism in the United States refers to a politico-cultural persuasion that has advocates almost exclusively in the American Democratic Party. The word also describes a group of political theorists who 'do' philosophy, and who tend to complicate and defy mainstream American party identifications and labels because their concerns largely transcend them: a debate that pits theorists called 'liberal' against those called 'communitarian'. Most books and articles written about liberalism in the United States in recent years consider political culture and strategy, which can appeal to most every liberal, especially those of the more partisan variety. Less frequent, knottier treatments take on philosophical or historical issues and tend to attract a much smaller, primarily academic readership. Sometimes the different approaches reach across audiences, but not very often. Nonetheless, for purposes of convenience, we might describe American liberalism at the start of the 21st century as a set of variations on a theme, the variations being (1) pragmatic/pluralist, (2) Rawlsian/rights-based and (3) polemical/radical.

A first, tradition-seeking liberal mode might be described as meliorist or pragmatic – or, to borrow a more expressive phrase from the philosopher William James, an 'ever not quite'.[1] A second, philosophical variation travels best under the terms of a Rawlsian debate, often concerned with what the political theorist John Rawls referred to as 'public reason', an idea that has inspired a vigorous transatlantic exchange ever since the appearance of Rawls's *Theory of Justice* in 1971. A final, more popular trend merits the description of anti-authoritarian or polemical, sometimes concerned with exposing the perfidy of that plutocratic cabal whom the filmmaker and provocateur Michael Moore has called, with characteristic subtlety, 'Stupid

White Men'.[2] Obviously, these variations require explanations. Playing in these modes means offering some context for each of them, which helps to account for the domestic, international and stylistic contours of contemporary liberalism in light of recent developments: the terrorist attacks of 11 September 2001 and especially the George W. Bush presidency.

AMERICAN LIBERALISM, CONTESTED AND ELUSIVE

First, though, it is important to provide a framework. American liberalism has long invited wonderfully vague and aphoristic descriptions of its essential nature because its applications have been so various, making it impossible to define adequately. 'Protean', as one historian has chosen to put it, but the underlying logic of liberalism remains elusive.[3] To understand what liberalism means and speculate about its prospects requires something that many liberals will find unsatisfying and even dead wrong no matter how one approaches the topic: an extended attempt at a reasonably encompassing definition. American liberalism has been defined as much by its champions as by its critics, each having absorbed something of the other's perspective. Not surprisingly, the literature of liberalism and its critics is remarkably vast, and liberals can disagree amongst themselves over the finer points of their persuasion (this is especially true for Rawlsians and their critics). Such rutted and muddy terrain inevitably transforms definitions into arguments, and, provided one doesn't get too mired along the way, arguments into both proscriptions and prescriptions. Gaps are inevitable in any brief treatment, personnel and ideas overlap, popular understandings are at best vague and amorphous, and conceptual slippage occurs between the modes of liberalism.

In any event, nearly every variation on liberalism in the US draws lines of descent from the historic creation of the limited American welfare state, starting with the New Deal of the 1930s and proceeding through the Great Society of the 1960s. While liberals disagree about their precise history and about the wisdom of one or another state-sponsored effort to achieve a greater measure of social and political equality for American citizens, in nearly every case they throw in their lot with the general history of government action on this score.[4] Yet, even this identification can be illusory.[5]

Liberals in the United States also claim affiliation of one kind or another with the Civil Rights Movement of the 1960s and with the rights revolution it spawned, which came to include women, Latino Americans, Native Americans, Asian Americans, Americans with disabilities, and, uneasily for some, gay Americans. Liberals in the 21st century prize diversity and debate as a general proposition, though some confusion exists over the proper tenor and method for rights-talk and acquisition. Against the potential chaos of a multicultural America, the Civil Rights Movement and its heroes exist as unassailable examples of liberal values, especially figures like Martin Luther

King Jr and Rosa Parks. Such monumental historic figures lend moral clarity to the liberal respect for individual rights and freedoms. Still, the relationship between liberal and minority politics in the US has long been complex and even fractious, and it remains problematic. Minority groups alternately resist and affirm their alliance with liberals. Forthright expressions of bigotry routinely merit liberal condemnation, but for the most part painful and difficult discussions of race and ethnicity among liberals and minority spokespersons have faded since the culture wars of the 1990s. Especially after 2001, arguably liberals have dedicated much more attention to conservative opponents and to shoring up consensus than to stirring up troubling divisions.

Liberals tend to be suspicious of political realism and lean toward idealism in international relations. In this field more than any other, liberals show an acute sense of history. The precise lessons of this history remain unclear. The tough, anticommunist internationalism of Harry S. Truman and later John F. Kennedy still inspire, but American liberals in the 21st century feel the residual aches and pains of the war in Vietnam, a debacle undertaken by a liberal administration under Lyndon Baines Johnson. The common narrative of American left liberal politics witnessed the short-lived liberal consensus or triumph of the early 1960s rent apart by Vietnam.[6] As President Johnson put it, playing characteristically blue: 'If I left the woman I really loved – the Great Society – in order to get involved with that bitch of a war on the other side of the world, then I would lose everything at home'.[7] He was spot on. What followed was a period of confusion and ambivalence in which liberals evinced little faith in unilateralism and felt some reluctance to use military power, some even questioning the importance of foreign policy altogether. As a result, liberals have not established a consistent regime for deciding when and if international events warrant the use of force. By 2006, all were opposing the Iraq War, but some are hawkish and more are dovish. Nonetheless, liberals do tend to espouse internationalist solutions to the problems posed by the status of the US as world superpower. They have some faith in diplomacy, multilateralism and in transnational organisations like the United Nations, against the current Bush administration.

THREE VARIATIONS

Thinking about liberalism as variations on a theme requires some respect for disconnections between theory and praxis and between popular and scholarly applications. Politicians and journalists, who influence up to the minute popular understandings in the greatest measure, rarely consider publicly the theory or method that underpins their beliefs and as a result resist philosophical labels. Rawlsian or pragmatic modes of liberal thought have adherents who work out the theoretical and philosophical implications of their beliefs, but this is rare in American politics. Suffice it to say that a small minority of American liberals actively theorise their political beliefs, creating and cultivating liberalism with some fidelity to its specific variations, while the vast number play much more freely in whatever mode suits them at a given time. Thus in more precise terms, variations should not be confused with immediately discernible groups or with followers of a given creed or way of thinking. While each variation does have more sophisticated and doctrinaire adherents who hail primarily from the academy, for the most part liberal commentators, journalists, politicians, policy makers, wonks and hacks choose the forms that fit their eye best when the situation warrants. Like Americans of almost any political persuasion, liberals can espouse a commonsensical, vulgarised pragmatism.

PRAGMATIC LIBERALISM

The pragmatic mode of American liberalism is different from simple common sense. It has become increasingly relevant and conscious of itself in recent years for at least three reasons. First, amidst a debate following the philosopher Richard Rorty's revival of the thought of John Dewey, which took shape during the 1980s and reached something like maturity in the 1990s, pragmatism emerged as an alternative to academic postmodernism and to the culture wars of the mid-1990s. Second, pragmatic liberals attempted to define and locate their ideas within a usable tradition of conscientious statecraft in the wake of the Democratic Party's move to the centre under the second term of President Clinton, from 1997 to 2001. Finally, some liberals have begun the search for coherent and hard-minded alternatives to the apparent dominance of conservatism – or neoconservatism – during the current Bush administration, particularly after the terrorist attacks of 9/11.

Pragmatic liberals when aware of a tradition, draw insights from *fin-de-siècle* pragmatic thinkers like William James and, two decades later, John Dewey. Thus, they are not pragmatists in the vernacular conception of that term, which denotes a type of moral relativism or tractability. Rather, like James and Dewey, they value tolerance, for ideas and for people's experiences, cherish free but rigorous experiment, and view society as always unfinished but consistently made and remade with human hands, which demands a high degree of moral responsibility and humane consideration for the results. No doubt, many liberals would probably eschew the term pragmatic as a description of themselves. Most would harbour suspicion for pragmatist theories of truth, which posit contingency rather than foundations or absolutes. But given their hopes for the world and for American society, they understand politics and policy-making as 'the art of the possible', to use a phrase that the Democratic Senator (and liberal warhorse) Edward Kennedy offered recently when working in the pragmatic liberal mode.[8]

Whether explicitly cognizant of it or not, pragmatic liberals draw even more from the Cold War anticommunist successors of the earlier pragmatists, especially from thinkers like the theologian Reinhold Niebuhr and the historian Arthur M. Schlesinger Jr, along with literary and cultural critics like Alfred Kazin and Lionel Trilling. This group of mid-century public intellectuals wrote continuously about complexity and tragedy, from which they begat something of a tradition. As such, they tended to think historically, looking to the past for individual examples of their mood with heroism as their common theme. The mistaken optimism of the years immediately following World War II gave way to a dark, threatening and uncertain world where even prosperity invited banality and conformity and where contingencies reigned – all of which demanded moral intelligence, or in some cases, as Kevin Mattson has recently explored, a 'fighting faith'.[9]

At the close of the 20th century and into the 21st century, the historical circumstances are certainly different, but the mood is quite similar. Post-modern excesses, regarded as 'relativistic', demand the academic pragmatist's sober and complex sense of social hope and meliorism in the face of irony, cynicism, and whimsy. The dilution of programmatic efforts meant to address problems of inequality and poverty, best encapsulated by the Clinton administration's cooperation with conservatives in the dismantling of government welfare programmes in the late 1990s, require the pragmatist policymaker's relentless capacity for social and political experiment. Such things require a certain measure of optimism, but must always be tempered by the realisation that such experiments will inevitably lead to further testing. The increased presence of religious intolerance at home and abroad should lead away from crushing binaries like those of the Cold War – the forces of freedom versus the 'Axis of Evil' to use George W. Bush's language – and toward realistic, openly debated, tolerant solutions unsullied by the hubristic stain of rank Americanism.

In the wake of the attacks of 9/11 and the Bush administration's handling of the war in Iraq, pragmatic liberalism has enjoyed something of a renais-sance. Before his death in 2007 at the age of 89, Arthur Schlesinger called for renewed attention to the thought of Niebuhr, who, in his estimation 'was tireless … in cautioning Americans not to succumb to self-righteous delusions of innocence and infallibility'. He wondered, moreover, amidst the recent revival of popular religiosity in the US, and a 'faith based administration' under George W. Bush, whether or not 9/11 had 'revived the myth of our national innocence'.[10]

Such a weary sense of tragedy and fallibilism has yet to find widespread purchase among less seasoned liberals. More hawkish sorts have used Cold War pragmatic liberalism to strike out against dovish elements to their left in the Democratic Party. Peter Beinart, for example, a columnist for *The New Republic*, has called for a 'tough liberalism' of the muscular type advocated by anticommunist liberals like Schlesinger, particularly in the latter's idiosyn-cratic but essential 1949 Cold War work, *The Vital Center*.[11] In this case, worldwide terrorism equals totalitarianism as the object of combat.[12]

But foreign policy realism is far from the only contemporary application of the pragmatic liberal variation. More generally, many liberals in the pragmatic mode often espouse some version of a benign, tolerant nationalism that respects cultural pluralism and particularism – yet, with a sense of complexity that refuses to let it overwhelm sources of solidarity.[13] This perspective has found some traction, but is certainly not without its critics. The cultural historian Eric Lott, for one, derisively labels this tendency 'The New Cosmopolitanism' of the 'Color Blind Club'.[14] Nonetheless, for supporters of this view America can be a great nation, but only with a sense of responsibility, rigor, or, as one of its most able defenders James Kloppenberg has argued, the proper 'virtues'.[15] This also speaks, with some significant disagreements over the details, to the philosopher Richard Rorty's recent emphasis on 'national hope' as a route toward 'achieving our country'.[16] In a more popular application, the pragmatic renaissance deals in what former Secretary of Labor for the Clinton administration, Robert Reich, has dubbed 'positive patriotism':

> a patriotism that's based on love of America, but not on contempt for what's not American; that cherishes our civil liberties and our democratic right to dissent; that understands that our national security depends as much on America's leadership and moral authority in the world as it does on our military might; and that emphasizes what we owe to one another as members of the same society.[17]

Thus pragmatic liberalism, whatever its proponents' claims to the contrary, has somewhere deep in its essential makeup a sort of residual Puritanism. This is surely what Lionel Trilling, perhaps the most perceptive Cold War critic, was writing about in 1950 when he famously championed liberalism's 'first essential imagination of variousness and possibility' while criticising its 'impulse to organization.'[18] At their best, pragmatic liberals would tell others how the world should be yet are often reluctant for having done so. Unnervingly, the moralistic, elitist side of this brand of liberalism has always been tempered by a characteristic lack of confidence, a refusal to levy that final judgment – an 'ever not quite', to borrow again from William James. Pragmatic liberals style themselves the own quintessentially jittery elect of modern America.[19] This includes a hopeful and whiggish sense of national history used to defend their discomfiting but necessary position at the centre of affairs.

This is why the American pragmatic liberal's capacity for criticism – of self and others – is so compelling. As often as not, in pragmatic mode liberals express with consummate skill the belief that their faith can be stronger or better than its current uses allow. Thus, today as in the past, pragmatic liberals in the US make frequent use of declension narratives of one kind or another, even when things seem to be going their way. At its best, this tendency is sharp-minded, radically empirical and breathlessly experimental; at its worst it is frustrating in its predilection for collective hand wringing and gradualism.[20] In its pragmatic mode American liberalism can never be revolutionary; its impatience for abstractions and for utopias doesn't allow such things. In the future, however, it promises to remain a prominent liberal variation. Its tradition is weighty and inclusive, carefully maintained by expert practitioners. Yet its greatest advocates are baby boomer intellectuals, now a generation of senior citizens. Nearly four decades after the tumult and failed utopianism of their late 1960s youth, they find some solace in the realisation that Dad was probably on to something, although Mom and lots of others now deserve a fair hearing. However careful and intelligent, calls for complexity, rigor, moral responsibility or fallibility by cultural aristocrats have rarely set younger generations afire. In the early 21st century, amidst a very unpopular war, the irony is keenly felt.

THE RAWLSIAN DEBATE: RIGHTS VERSUS THE GOOD

Rawlsians are similarly unpersuaded by radicalism, but for somewhat different, rather subtle reasons. The pragmatist's search for a usable tradition flitters around but rarely seeks and even defies any concrete resolution of the practical dialectic of American liberalism, whether pragmatic, polemic, or Rawlsian: the protection of individual liberty from forms of authority on the one hand and the use of the state to ensure the free exercise of that liberty on the other. Of course, this involves the difficult problem of equality, and of what conditions in the form of rights and/or entitlements are necessary for citizens to pursue the ends they wish, which supposes some definition of citizenship more generally. Along that sliding scale, political philosophers tend to drop in all over the place, but at least with a high degree of analytical clarity.

If pragmatic philosophers like Dewey or James, mid-century pragmatists like Trilling, Niebuhr and Schlesinger and more recently Rorty have played a major role in shaping modern pragmatic liberalism, then John Rawls deserves the credit for developing liberalism as a comprehensive type of political philosophy. Countless political thinkers in the US identified themselves as liberals long before John Rawls, but generally speaking they understood it normatively, as with Louis Hartz's *The Liberal Tradition in America* (1955), or even presupposed its (often vague) meaning. Starting in 1971 with the appearance of *A Theory of Justice*, a remarkable synthesis of Immanuel Kant and the classic social contract theorists, and continuing with *Political Liberalism* (1993), Rawls's ideas have dominated formal political thought in the US for nearly 40 years. A caveat is necessary: the Rawlsian variation here refers not to Rawls's thought specifically, but to the massive debate that continues over his work, which by now has taken on a life of its own even after Rawls's death in 2002.

In the Rawlsian mode then, the task becomes less one of intellectual history than the history of ideas, less one of national institutional history than a questioning of basic, universal principles. Liberalism moves beyond considerations of utilitarian, majoritarian democracy or of the practical give and take of politics, concerning itself with staking out the inviolable rights that each person possesses because of their status as human beings. In Kantian terms, liberalism means the basic framework through which people are treated not as means to some end but as ends in themselves. In Rawlsian terms, politics can only be just when human beings, through self-interested, purely rational means, establish the basic principles that govern political activity, which, being reasonable, are based on fair and equal conditions free from contingencies like political affiliation, race, ethnicity, and gender.[21]

Liberals who take part in this debate disagree over whether liberalism can be an all-encompassing moral worldview or doctrine, or if it refers only to those shared values that are explicitly political: in other words, 'society's main political, constitutional, social and economic institutions and how they fit together to form a unified scheme of social cooperation over time'.[22] There is concern that liberalism in this mode, when considered in universal terms, indulges in a familiar Enlightenment conception of values that *a priori* supersede or undergird all others for their basic 'rationality'. As a solution to this problem, many Rawlsians instantiate some form of political space or blank proceduralism that both protects and respects a plurality of more fundamental or comprehensive value systems.

For John Rawls, at least, a politically liberal society exists when people subject problems and issues to a tribunal of 'public reason', where the standard for judging the merits of a certain argument or policy is reciprocity, so that people use political power for some end only when it is clear that those affected can reasonably accept the justifications offered for such ends. Appeals to absolutist or all-encompassing doctrine and authority are unacceptable in the space of public reason because such creeds inevitably exclude others, discarding mutual respect and ignoring the things that people – in their political role as citizens – share. Rawls and those like him hope that despite basic differences among citizens in a democracy over what creeds and doctrines they hold most dear, some 'overlapping consensus' can exist over time about political matters. When it doesn't, the only recourse is political philosophy.[23]

Arguably, the Kantian or Rawlsian variation of liberalism best explains common and very prevalent liberal claims to the Civil Rights Movement and its major figures, especially Martin Luther King Jr. Despite significant differences of opinion about the wisdom of the tactics employed by civil rights activists and those who learned from such tactics, then and now, the Rawlsian liberal's dismissal of utilitarian and majoritarian ideas (the greatest good for the greatest number) mark an appeal to fundamental individual human rights and to the necessity of public reason – values shared by the movement. Dr King and the movement, it follows, merely desired that national authorities enforce the social contract.

Yet, the healthiest disagreements among liberals in the Rawlsian mode are about whether life in a body politic necessitates an idea of the good or of virtue, which recalls the ancients, especially Aristotle. Here, more orthodox Rawlsian 'liberals' do battle with 'communitarians'. With the exception of some neo-Marxist and Catholic communitarian thinkers and some 'minimal state' libertarian thinkers, both groups would merit the label 'liberal' in the commonplace American sense of the word. Generally speaking, Rawlsian liberals make clear, against classical Republican traditions, that a commonly sought after conception of a virtuous or good society violates the individual's conception of the good, which demands respect.[24] Regarding the Civil Rights Movement, Rawlsian communitarians might argue, against their liberal opponents, that Martin Luther King Jr valued tradition and dreamt of a 'beloved community', whose members shared some idea of the good. The movement dealt with much more than individual rights; its members demanded national recognition that certain people had for too long been excluded from the American community.[25]

With the exception of the pragmatic liberal thinker Richard Rorty, liberals working in the Rawlsian mode tend not to engage too much with their pragmatic counterparts. This could be an academic disciplinary boundary, in that many tradition-minded pragmatists are historians or philosophers in the Continental tradition, while most liberals of the Rawlsian variation are political theorists or philosophers in the analytic tradition. The Rawlsian variation is thus not confined to the US but is very much an Anglophone debate. One suspects that theorists working in this mode find pragmatists provincial or lacking when it comes to analytical rigor for their 'evasion of philosophy'. In this sense, Rorty garners their attention primarily because he has recognisable international and analytical *bona fides*.[26]

This is too bad. Some liberals and communitarians voice concern that more orthodox Rawlsian liberals and their libertarian cousins offer a thin, rather arid conception of political life. While potentially chaotic, the pragmatist brings in much of the day-to-day warp and woof of human experience. The pragmatic stress upon experience might present a way for liberals and communitarians to talk to one another more effectively. Recently, for example, some effort has been made to bridge the distinction between community and autonomy, often with John Dewey as the thinker of choice.[27] In any case, the differences are perhaps too profoundly rooted in disagreements over basic philosophical perspectives and traditions.

In popular terms, the theoretical divide between liberal and communitarians is lost on most American liberals, who can alternately embrace one or the other position, or more often, some combination of the two at the same time. Liberals carry the Rawlsian debate without much sense of contradiction. Almost all seek stronger constitutional protections for their individual rights against incursions by the state: they roundly condemn the Patriot Act, for example, or vigorously support the American Civil Liberties Union. At the same time, they fear the loss of older, intermediate forms of association apart from the state, particularly in the latter's alliance with national and multinational business interests on whatever level of federalism: national, state or municipal. They worry, with Robert Putnam, about the dissolution of American civic culture and its 'declining social capital'.[28] Liberals often lament the collapse of small independent businesses in the face of big-box retailers such as Wal-mart; they excoriate the swallowing up of unaffiliated forms of media by massive conglomerates like Clear Channel Communications; some believe that 'it takes a village to raise a child', all the while proclaiming the inviolability of the Bill of Rights and civil rights protections against local prejudices.[29] In sum, the Rawlsian debate translates into a largely uncritical embrace of both liberal and communitarian elements by liberals in 21st-century America.

Whatever its peculiarities, for the time being at least this variation on liberalism in America shows little sign of abating, having become something of an academic industry on both sides of the Atlantic. It remains to be seen whether many of its adherents will take on a more expansive role as politically involved public intellectuals. Nonetheless, some of the most interesting work in this area involves conceptions of global universal human rights, of whether certain procedures or political spaces can transcend traditional national boundaries. The Rawlsian idea of overlapping consensus negotiated within a space of political reason suggests that multilateral solutions to international problems can be arrived at periodically whatever the differences in comprehensive belief systems, especially religious ones like Christianity or Islam. The cosmopolitanism of the debate, partly the result of its abstraction, immediately separates it from many other US liberal variations, which can be provincial and partial to domestic issues.[30]

POLEMICAL LIBERALISM

Liberals have often found themselves under attack in recent US history, whether from different kinds of American conservatives, from this or that minority group whose cause they purport to defend, or from traditionally very small but often very vocal groups of American leftists – as a general rule liberals tend to have a soft spot for American leftists, who in turn love to spurn them. If the effective practice of politics is necessarily an adversarial art, then real or imagined persecution is its most effective rallying cry. American liberals follow this logic along with American conservatives, the truth of the matter being that in the past two decades conservatives have used such tactics far better than the liberals.[31]

Simply put, in the context of mainstream US politics, liberalism has become a bad word. It is nearly suicidal for any American politician to openly espouse it. While countless Democratic politicians work in any one of its modes, they refuse to embrace the label. More than a few self-described liberals today use the word 'progressive' as a preferred label in order to rid themselves of the opprobrious stink of the term. Yet, because of the conservative success in recent years, liberals now talk a great deal about taking a page from their conservative opponents. Because of a reaction against the Bush administration, progressive liberals now list among their number a group of writers whom the sociologist Alan Wolfe has called 'the New Pamphleteers'.[32] Stridently partisan, a touch angry, at times unreasonable, cynical, and often bitingly funny, liberals in this polemical mode represent perhaps the most vibrant strain of the persuasion in the 21st century. Alongside the pamphleteers, others working in the mode write screed in print media, crack jokes on cable networks, and flood their opinions onto the blogosphere. The humorists Jon Stewart of the *Daily Show* and Stephen Colbert of *The Colbert Report* are heroes-cum-clown princes for this liberal variation. The adversarial, largely unprogrammatic style of the 'DailyKos' liberal weblog represents the position nicely, as does the vaguely populist, anti-authoritarian style of the documentary filmmaker Michael Moore. 'Stupid [read: wealthy, conservative] White Men' are indeed targets. Polemicists call for populist rhetoric and policies designed to cull votes from proletarian and petite (rather than haute) bourgeoisie elements. Many have come to disdain the heightened identity politics climate of the 1990s, discarding 'political correctness'. Thus, in addition to wondering 'What's the Matter with Kansas' (to cite the title of Thomas Frank's 2004 critique), liberals of this cast puzzle over how it is that, in the title of Geoffrey Nunberg's 2006 book, 'Conservatives Turned Liberalism into a Tax-Raising, Latte-Drinking, Sushi-Eating, Volvo-Driving, New York Times-Reading, Body-Piercing, Hollywood-Loving, Left-Wing Freak Show'.[33]

While a very recent phenomenon, it would be hasty to assume that polemical liberals lack any tradition whatsoever; they are merely ignorant or dismissive of such things. While the direct provenance is impossible to trace, polemical liberals have adopted some of the existentialist absurdity prevalent in the humour of civil rights activists, the New Left, and some Cold War liberals. The style is somewhat unique though, in that, to use Stewart's phrase, many liberal outlets for humor offer 'fake news', the forebears of which are certainly skits from ensemble comedy television shows such as *Monty Python's Flying Circus* in the UK (1969–74) and later *Saturday Night Live* in the US (est. 1975). Perhaps to the disappointment of more established liberals, the newest generation gets much of its news from comedy shows and the blogosphere – formats which encourage polemics rather than programmes, running somewhat counter to the traditional liberal emphasis on fair hearing and patient toleration for opposing perspectives.

Yet polemical liberalism owes its vibrancy to its unqualified embrace of multimedia formats: print, of course, but especially the web, movies, and even music. In movie houses and on home video, Michael Moore has found receptive soil, seeding Americans' historic appetite for conspiracies with the wildly suggestive *Fahrenheit 9/11* (2004). In the film documentary *Sicko* (2007), Moore joined an increasingly widespread chorus of calls for some form of national health coverage, offering devastating and characteristically intimate portraits of people horribly mistreated by colossally insensitive insurance companies. And more than a few liberals probably took some pleasure in finding that the venerable rock 'n' roll artist Neil Young has aged with welcome and only slightly unexpected irascibility. As Martin Halliwell discusses in this volume, Young's *Living with War* album (2006) launched a devastating salvo against the current Bush administration and a complacent American public. In these kinds of areas, pragmatists and Rawlsians have yet to fully embrace the 21st century and can seem rather toothless when it comes to the raw, sanguinary delights of a polemic done up just right.

Still, the stubborn unreality and sometimes ham-fisted sloganeering of the current Bush administration (Young critiques the slogans 'Shock & Awe' and 'Mission Accomplished' in *Living with War*) no doubt has much to do with the popularity of 'fake news' and partisanship, so the staying power of this variation is questionable after the end of the Bush presidency. The polemicist move toward populism and 'bread and butter' domestic issues are part of a suite of concerns that include problems such as globalisation ('flattening' to use Thomas Friedman's term) and restrictions on greenhouse gases, the negative implications of which find ultimate coherence in the policies of George W. Bush and his allies in government and in corporate America.

If polemical liberalism is to survive much further into the 21st century, its momentarily fruitful adversarialism must be replaced by a positive programmatic effort. In turn, George W. Bush, its principle organising symbol, must be superseded by a more nuanced understanding of larger local, national and transnational socio-economic forces, particularly those wrought by global capitalism and its glitteringly clean and sophisticated technologies. But the impersonality of 'forces', their multiplicity and complexity, makes pointed appeals and criticisms difficult in a political system that cherishes its binaries: us versus them, Democrat versus Republican, liberal versus conservative. Perhaps the answer lies in more communication and interaction, or somewhere in the thick of middlebrow culture and in multimedia formats à la Thomas Friedman and Al Gore: in other words, between the leading lights of the three variations. Perhaps not. Can Rawlsian debaters abandon philosophy momentarily for more immediate concerns? Can pragmatists eschew a measure of complexity to embrace propaganda? Will polemicists tighten up their arguments, and if they do, will they be nearly as witty? Barring the incredible, liberals in the 21st century will find themselves amidst the familiar push and pull of American party politics. Acknowledging the inevitable, the liberals who stay around, as well as those to come, will bear the familiar burdens of trying to clear some space and time for moral complexity, unencumbered communication and cultural achievement in a democracy that has rarely admitted such things.

NOTES

1. William James, 'A Pluralistic Universe', in *Writings, 1902–1910* (New York, NY: Modern Library, 1987), p. 776.
2. See Michael Moore, *Stupid White Men … and Other Excuses for the Sorry State of the Nation!* (New York, NY: Regan Books, 2001).
3. Gary Gerstle, 'The Protean Character of American Liberalism', *The American Historical Review*, 99, October 1994, 1043.
4. American liberalism is nominally part of global liberalism *writ large*, which has been conflated with democratic institutions and free enterprise economics. Roger M. Smith, 'Liberalism and Racism: The Problem of Analyzing Traditions' in David Ericson and Louisa Bertch Green (eds), *The Liberal Tradition in American Politics: Reassessing the Legacy of American Liberalism* (New York, NY: Routledge, 1999), pp. 9–27, argues that even the common *laissez faire* conception of liberalism is a product of 20th-century thinkers. American liberalism, then, arises *in response* to an older liberal tradition, which had only recently been identified as such, stemming from Protestantism and developing through Hobbes and Locke, the Enlightenment, American revolutionary thinkers, utilitarians and Social Darwininsts.
5. The exception here are Kantian liberals like Robert Nozick, who against more egalitarian-minded Kantians like John Rawls, advocate the 'minimal state', which most American liberals would label 'libertarian'. See Robert Nozick, *Anarchy, State, and Utopia* (New York, NY: Basic Books, 1978).
6. For example Alan Matusow, *The Unraveling of America: A History of Liberalism in the 1960s* (New York, NY: Harper and Row, 1984).
7. Doris Kearns Goodwin, *Lyndon Johnson and the American Dream* (New York, NY: Harper and Row), p. 263.
8. Edward M. Kennedy, 'Kennedy on immigration agreement', http://kennedy.senate.gov/newsroom/press_release.cfm?id=80405880-2B4F-4E23-80D4-A11142E93803.
9. For the origins of 'fighting faith' see Arthur M. Schlesinger Jr (adopting Oliver Wendell Holmes Jr's phrase), *The Vital Center* (Boston, MA: Houghton Mifflin, 1949), p. 256.
10. Arthur M. Schlesinger Jr, 'Forgetting Reinhold Niebuhr', *The New York Times*, 18 September 2005, Section 7.
11. Peter Beinart, 'A fighting faith: an argument for a new liberalism', *The New Republic*, 13 December 2004, 17. See also Kevin Mattson, *When America Was Great: The Fighting Faith of Postwar Liberalism* (New York, NY: Routledge, 2004).
12. Casey Nelson Blake neatly points out a common misuse of Niebuhr: 'Curiously, many of Niebuhr's contemporary admirers miss the irony (as it were) of enlisting their hero in the service of projects to remake the Middle East that are stunning in their naiveté, hubris, and utopianism': Casey Nelson Blake,

'Obama and Niebuhr', *The New Republic*, Open University, 4 May 2007, http://www.tnr.com/blog/openuniversity?pid=104944, p. 2.

13. The intellectual historian David Hollinger calls his specific and nuanced version of this a 'postethnic America'. See Hollinger, *Postethnic America: Beyond Multiculturalism* (New York, NY: Basic Books, 1995).

14. See Eric Lott, *The Disappearing Liberal Intellectual* (New York, NY: Basic Books, 2006), pp. 45–93. Lott rightly points out the pragmatic liberal's increasing appreciation of the novelist Ralph Ellison for the latter's emphasis on possibility and complexity.

15. James T. Kloppenberg, *The Virtues of Liberalism* (Oxford: Oxford University Press, 1998).

16. Richard Rorty, *Achieving Our Country: Leftist Thought in the Twentieth Century* (Cambridge, MA: Harvard University Press, 1997). For the differences, see John Pettegrew (ed.), *A Pragmatist's Progress?: Richard Rorty and American Intellectual History* (Lanham, MD: Rowman and Littlefield, 2000).

17. Robert Reich, *Reason: Why Liberals Will Win the Battle for America* (New York, NY: Knopf, 2004), pp. 146–85. Reich includes a reading list with Dewey, Schlesinger, and Rorty as prominent figures.

18. Lionel Trilling, *The Liberal Imagination* (Garden City, NY: Doubleday, 1954), p. 10.

19. This residual sense of election probably comes from mid-century pronouncements, like Trilling's, that liberalism was America's 'sole intellectual tradition' (*The Liberal Imagination*, p. 5), and certainly Louis Hartz's similar observations in *The Liberal Tradition in America* which first appeared in 1955 and has remained in print since.

20. While unhinged at some moments, Eric Lott details such instances nicely: Lott, *The Disappearing Liberal Intellectual*, pp. 1–23. Declension is played nicely by a sampling of phrases from titles of books about liberalism by liberals: 'The Collapse'; 'The Decline'; 'The Failure; 'The Wrong Turn', and so on.

21. John Rawls, *A Theory of Justice* (Cambridge, MA: Harvard University Press, [1971] 1999), pp. 3–40.

22. Rawls, *Political Liberalism* (New York, NY: Columbia University Press, [1993] 2005), p. xli.

23. Ibid., pp. 3–46.

24. See Michael Sandel (ed.), *Liberalism and Its Critics* (New York, NY: New York University Press, 1984); Ellen Frankel Paul, Fred D, Miller and Jeffrey Paul (eds), *The Communitarian Challenge to Liberalism* (Cambridge: Cambridge University Press, 1996). Ludvig Beckman argues that Rawlsian liberalism can be expanded to include ideas of virtue: see Ludvig Beckman, *The Liberal State and the Politics of Virtue* (London: Transaction, 2001).

25. See Sandel (ed.), *Liberalism and Its Critics*, p. 6.

26. A good example is Mark Evans, 'Pragmatist Liberalism and the Evasion of Politics', in Mark Evans (ed.), *Edinburgh Companion to Contemporary Liberalism* (London: Fitzroy Dearborn, 2001), pp. 148–61. See also Cornel West, *The American Evasion of Philosophy: A Genealogy of Pragmatism* (Madison, WI: University of Wisconsin Press, 1989).

27. See for example Daniel M. Savage, *John Dewey's Liberalism: Individual, Community,*

and Self-Development (Carbondale, IL: Southern Illinois University Press, 2002) and most recently Archon Fung, 'Democratic theory and political science: a pragmatic method of constructive engagement', *American Political Science Review*, 101, August 2007, 443–58. An earlier, significant, Emersonian effort to include sociability as a *sine qua non* of rights-based liberalism is George Kateb, *The Inner Ocean: Individualism and Democratic Culture* (Ithaca, NY: Cornell University Press, 1992).

28. See Robert Putnam, *Bowling Alone: The Collapse and Revival of American Community* (New York, NY: Simon and Schuster, 2000).

29. See Hillary Clinton, *It Takes a Village and Other Lessons Children Teach Us* (New York, NY: Simon and Schuster, 1996).

30. It should come as no surprise here that Thomas Friedman enlists the help of the communitarian Michael Sandel in his increasingly influential recent book *The World is Flat* (New York, NY: Farrar, Strauss and Giroux, 2005).

31. For a review of some recent literature on this subject see Michael Tomasky, 'How Democrats should talk', *The New York Review of Books*, 31 May 2007, 26–8.

32. Alan Wolfe, 'The new pamphleteers: when the establishment disappears, polemics fill the void', *The New York Times Book Review*, 11 July 2004, 12.

33. See Thomas Frank, *What's the Matter with Kansas?: How Conservatives Won the Heart of America* (New York, NY: Metropolitan Books, 2004) and Geoffrey Nunberg, *Talking Right: How Conservatives Turned Liberalism into a Tax-Raising, Latte-Drinking, Sushi-Eating, Volvo-Driving, New York Times-Reading, Body-Piercing, Hollywood-Loving, Left-Wing Freak Show* (New York, NY: Public Affairs, 2006).

5. THE RISE OF POSTMODERN CONSERVATISM

Kevin Mattson

If an American talks about contemporary politics with a citizen of the European Union, the term neoconservatism will likely come up. This is not the neoconservatism of the 1970s, when the term originated, but the neoconservatism that propelled George W. Bush's decision to invade Iraq. It suggests a conservatism that draws from Leo Strauss and emphasises America's role in spreading democracy abroad; a conservatism of grand universals willing to embrace the nasty practice of war; a conservatism that hopes to make democratic omelettes by breaking caseloads of eggs. This type of conservatism is important and has been discussed widely elsewhere, symbolising a new and, for obvious reasons, important constellation of ideas in American life.[1]

It is also likely that our make-believe EU citizen will have heard of the 'culture wars' – the idea that Americans are divided between red and blue, between NASCAR fans and latte drinkers, between traditionalists and modernists. What is not so recognised is just how much these culture wars have transformed the intellectual landscape of America, especially the broad contours of conservative intellectual life today. With the recent critical interest on the neoconservatism of the Bush administration it is easy to overlook what I will call in the essay 'postmodern conservatism', a type of conservatism that relates directly to the rise of the culture wars during the 1980s and 1990s.

THE POSTMODERN TURN IN CONSERVATIVE THOUGHT

Though a slippery term, postmodernism can be defined first and foremost as a long-term exhaustion in modern rationalism. The cultural historian

Morris Dickstein once connected this strain of postmodernity to the 1960s: 'One of the healthier things we learned in the sixties, and are unlikely to forget, was to be more skeptical of the pose of objectivity.' Distrust about the claims of powerful actors who used tones of rationality, disinterestedness and objectivity lasted long after debates surrounding the Vietnam War (they are nicely captured in shots of Defense Secretary Robert McNamara displaying charts and graphs to justify troop escalation in Vietnam, shown evocatively in Errol Morris's documentary, *The Fog of War: Eleven Lessons from the Life of Robert S. McNamara*, 2003). Rationality itself started to look irrational – this was a central feature of so much 1960s protest and political criticism discussed in numerous places, including the *Intercollegiate Review*. Writers like Theodore Roszak believed that the decade's counterculture radicalised the idea as it grew disillusioned with 'the conventional scientific world view' and 'man's infatuation with the machine'. The counterculture's expressive individualism pushed aside McNamara's cold-hearted scientific outlook and conjured a 'non-intellective consciousness' through drugs, rock music, and, of course, the 'new sensibility' of the time.[2]

'Tenured radicals' carried much of the 1960s spirit into the halls of academe during the 1970s and 1980s. Critiques of 'logocentrism' and universal claims to truth became the intellectual tools of the academic left, most prominently visible in literary and aesthetic theory. Consider Susan Sontag's critique of interpretation as an act of violation of art's visual erotics; Richard Rorty's and Jacques Derrida's anti-foundationalism; Jean François Lyotard's dissection of meta-narratives; or Stanley Fish's rejection of objective meaning and an embrace of the individual reception of texts. All these arguments questioned the universal foundations for Western truth-claims. Postmodernism exploded the universalistic pretensions of the West (for instance, the language of 'rights' and 'reason') as too tightly bound up with domination and power, especially when placed in the context of the colonial domination of the non-Western world. Universalism, one philosopher explained in a long work that tried to define the term postmodernism, is 'now seen as an anxious and pretentious and yet ultimately futile effort to enforce rigor and uniformity in an unruly world'. Thus, 'universalism has been replaced by eclecticism and pluralism'. By embracing these ideas, the academic left threw off its own intellectual inheritances. As the historian John Patrick Diggins once quipped: 'The Academic Left was the first Left in American history to distrust the eighteenth-century Enlightenment.'[3]

The postmodern turn generated suspicions about intellectuals' role in public life. This was particularly evident in Europe, where there was once a great deal of respect paid to intellectuals and where post-structuralism made its first splash. As Mark Lilla puts it: 'The days' in Europe 'when intellectuals turned to philosophers to get their political bearings, and the public turned to intellectuals, are all but over'.[4] During the 1960s and 1970s, Michel Foucault criticised Jean-Paul Sartre for speaking in grand and universalistic tones that simply wound up justifying Soviet totalitarianism. The idea of critics standing outside and passing universal and objective judgment on their society's injustices was no longer defensible, especially as truth claims appeared culturally and historically bound. Foucault himself, we now know, showed a frightening sympathy for the Iranian revolutionists who, in 1979, threw off the Western prejudices of the Shah for Islamic fundamentalism. For Foucault, the universal project of the Enlightenment associated with the West had exhausted itself, and 'the 'universal' intellectual' was now dead.[5]

So what do these developments usually associated with post-structuralism and the academic left have to do with the conservative intellectual movement? A great deal. There has always been an anti-intellectual current in post-war conservative thought, starting with William F. Buckley's famous *God and Man at Yale* (1951). By the 1970s, this anti-intellectual strain grew more explicit. The New Right activist Paul Weyrich argued that 'the Old Right was strong on intellectualism', pointing his fingers at the *National Review*. For Weyrich, the 'intellectualization of conservatism' limited the movement's impact.[6] He echoed Kevin Phillips's celebration of George Wallace's attack on 'pointy headed intellectuals'. Though neoconservatives during the 1970s, writers like Norman Podhoretz and Irving Kristol, might have appeared as the right's last gasp of high intellectualism, Kristol's condemnation of an overeducated 'new class' and Podhoretz's personal diminution of intellectuals in his autobiographies such as *Making It* (1967) suggest otherwise. The intellectual, in all of these treatments, appears not only snobbish and self-important but self-interested, certainly not deserving of pronouncing truths that transcend the faiths and beliefs of ordinary citizens. In other words, conservatives had got to Foucault's position much easier and often much earlier.[7]

This feature of postmodern conservatism, strange as it might sound at first, helps explain the rise of one of the more prominent new groupings among right-wing intellectuals: the 'theocons', who rose to prominence during the 1990s and published their writings in the pages of *First Things*.[8] These thinkers spoke directly from their religious faith and rejected the need to translate their ideas into a more universal language or separate them from their Catholic roots. Neoconservatives might have touted the virtues of religious belief, but it was from a rationalistic perspective: that is, the sociological benefit of belief. Writers like Richard John Neuhaus, George Weigel and Michael Novak, in contrast, criticised American public policy from the standpoint of papal declarations and even went so far as to declare the legitimacy of civil disobedience against a corrupt judiciary in the name of Catholic moral principles. Theocons built upon the New Right of the late 1970s, especially Jerry Falwell, the Moral Majority and Christian Voice, that already displaced the more secular language of Barry Goldwater. The terms of the Enlightenment became for theocons simply an impediment to faith, little else. Witnessing 9/11, they called for 'Christian America' to battle 'militant Islam', making their religious particularism more explicit and reaching back to the religious war metaphor used by Whittaker Chambers during the Cold War in his famous book, *Witness* (1952). Theocons might appear a logical extension of Chambers's Cold War thinking, but their prominence also represented a postmodern imperative to find alternatives to Enlightenment rationalism. Religious particularism matched the era better than neoconservative secularism. And so we see a strange amalgamation of absolutist faith and relativistic ramifications.[9]

This is evidenced in the right's own contribution to contemporary cultural fragmentation. Again, this development is traditionally associated with the academic left, especially the rise of multiculturalism and 'identity politics' in the wake of the black power and feminist movements of the 1960s.[10] Faith in a unified culture trumping disparate identities grew tentative after the battles of the 1960s exposed racial oppression and gender disparities; the 1970s emphasis on 'black is beautiful' and ethnic pride only pushed the envelope further. The resulting feel of postmodernity is largely a sense of fracturing and splitting apart, of pluralistic identities breaking up any overarching sense of collective belonging. Though conservatives are traditionally known as critics of identity politics and multiculturalism, they have contributed to cultural fragmentation in increasingly louder tones.

The clearest indication is the vituperative style that marks popular, best-selling conservative writing today, its highly charged rhetoric and shrillness evident to any casual observer. Prominent conservative intellectuals do not conceptualise their role as engaging a wider public through civilised debate. Instead, they act as cheerleaders for their side's belief system, reconfirming pre-held opinions among the already-believing and preaching to the choir. Their writing style mirrors the advice given to politicians by Karl Rove, the Republican Party's political mastermind between 2000 and 2007, who argued that conservatives should play to their 'base', build a politics out of pillorying the enemy, and win through small margins. In a society that fragments political opinions and associates those opinions with 'lifestyles' of red versus blue states (beer swilling NASCAR fans versus wine drinking liberals), conservative intellectuals feel obliged to stoke the anger of their own segmented audience. Thus, the historionic feel of writers like Ann Coulter and Michael Savage, two of the right's bestselling authors. Their books serve as the finest expressions of how postmodern conservative intellectual life contributes to and is informed by cultural fragmentation.[11]

Ann Coulter has accrued the most fame (through what some might label intellectual 'branding') on this front, more than any other conservative writer. She has cultivated a persona of venom and meanness that sells large quantities of books. But nobody reads Coulter's books to learn anything they didn't already know. The tone is of red-faced shouting and screaming, not the sort of style that prompts people to reconsider their opinions. For instance, liberals aren't just wrong for Coulter, they are demonic. 'If Americans knew' what liberals 'really believed', she writes, 'the public would boil them in oil'. For Coulter, 'liberals are like Arabs without the fighting spirit'. It's better to go to war with them. As Coulter put it in her book *How to Talk to a Liberal (If You Must)* (2004) – that parenthetical portion of the title evokes her thesis – the way to argue is this: 'You must outrage the enemy. If the liberal you're arguing with doesn't become speechless with sputtering, impotent rage, you're not doing it right.' Coulter plays well to an audience that wants to secede from a wider public sphere, nurturing a conservative fan club that holds its opinions in airtight vacuums and disengages from the demands of civilised discourse, leaving its enemies 'sputtering' with 'rage'.[12]

Alongside Ann Coulter stands Michael Savage, a man who acquired fame in the world of talk radio, not exactly known as an intellectually sophisticated medium. Savage is especially interesting since his biography highlights another postmodern theme: a sense that the postmodern self lacks co-herence and is simply a series of different poses that rely upon social confirmation. Consider Savage's biography: born Michael Alan Weiner over 65 years ago, he became a hippie who once 'swam naked with Allen Ginsberg' and got 'married in a rain forest and studied ethno-medicine at the University of California at Berkeley'. During the 1970s, he hung out at City Lights Bookstore, the capital of Beatnik culture, and wrote about herbal medicine and health food. He then became a small capitalist, marketing herbal supplements and teas. Then as the country drifted rightward, he decided to become a talk-show host of 'The Savage Nation' where he calls for nuking the Middle East, shooting illegal immigrants, and taking out 'commies, pinkos, and perverts'.[13]

Savage's books read like the rants of a talk-radio-show host whose bellowing is matched by his audience's frantic nodding and cheering. His treatment of liberalism is akin to Coulter's. Liberalism for Savage is a 'mental disorder' that has 'so twisted reality' that 'the terrorists are tolerated when they should be annihilated' and that glorifies 'Arafat, Kinsey, and Clinton … when they should be vilified.' Savage moves with blistering speed from one opinion to another, failing to check if they make sense together. For instance, he condemns liberals for a 'godless worldview' and then quickly leaps into a treatment of the pop singer 'Madonna and the Kabala', as if his own mind's instantaneous connection should be obvious to all. His books become a group of incoherent thoughts that only those already convinced might find convincing. They succeed (at least in terms of sales) due to the postmodern currents into which they play. And they point to a general rise in what some call 'smashmouth' commentary that has defined the right.[14]

APOCALYPSE NOW: THE CULTURE WARS AS DEFINING MOMENT

As Coulter and Savage make clear, the postmodern conservative mind is in a state of permanent apocalypse. This was true already by the Cold War when

Whittaker Chambers and James Burnham saw the conflict between the West in absolutist and religious terms. Throughout the 1990s, a new set of culture wars – fought at home – became all the more important. In three major conservative battles – (1) the legislative push to police America's colleges to cut down on 'liberal bias', (2) the introduction of 'intelligent design' in public schools, and (3) the continuing war against the 'liberal media' – postmodern conservatism crystallised in more perfect form than in Iraq. Crossing the postmodern divide, conservatives came out the other side stronger. The conservative mind drew upon the battle lines drawn earlier by the New Right over public school textbooks and abortion and ingested these battle lines into its own permanent psychic state. David Horowitz would call these 'wars of aggression'; Coulter would speak of 'throttling' liberals. Out of the struggles of war, the postmodern conservative mind emerged more clearly.

POLICING COLLEGES

Gaining political power during the 1990s, conservatives grew annoyed that their reach did not extend to academe. New Leftists (or 'tenured radicals') still seemed to hold all the power there. For conservative writers, academia was now a hotbed of multiculturalism, speech codes, political correctness, identity politics, and an incoherent canon that threw out the 'great books' tradition of yore. And academe for conservative intellectuals throughout the 1990s symbolised liberalism writ large. Conservatives pummelled the postmodern university, blaming liberalism for shoddy education – Alan Bloom's *The Closing of the American Mind* (1987) and Dinesh D'Souza's *Illiberal Education* (1991) key among them – but these books didn't change anything. The problem demanded building upon the electoral successes of conservatives throughout the 2000s and thus bolder activism: something more akin to war.

Enter the gladiator David Horowitz, the leading conservative activist on all things academic and a prolific author. In 2003, he helped form Students for Academic Freedom (SAF). He urged the organisation to mimic the academic left: 'I encourage' students, Horowitz explained, 'to use the language that the left has deployed so effectively on behalf of its own agendas. Radical professors have created a "hostile learning" environment for conservative students … The university should be an "inclusive" and intellectually "diverse" community.'[15] Horowitz clicked off the key words of the academic left to justify right-wing student activism. To embolden the cause of right-wing 'diversity', Horowitz drafted the Academic Bill of Rights (ABOR), a boilerplate piece of legislation that scolded liberal professors for indoctrinating their students and encouraged state legislatures to police higher education classrooms to ensure intellectual diversity. Starting in 2004, Horowitz pushed for its passage in numerous states.[16]

Horowitz took up the tradition of conservative activism against academe but rejected his elders' objective universalism. Consider William F. Buckley's original attack against Yale in his *God and Man at Yale* (1951). Buckley had been an absolutist on questions surrounding academic freedom, while Horowitz had turned postmodern. Buckley wrote: 'It is my view that as long as academic freedom takes the implied position that all ideas are equal, or that all ideas should, in the student's mind, start out equal, it is a dangerous ... concept.'[17] Horowitz reversed this logic, his idea of intellectual 'diversity' growing out of contemporary theories about the indeterminacy of knowledge. Here is the original ABOR statement: 'Human knowledge is a never-ending pursuit of the truth' since 'there is no humanly accessible truth that it not in principle open to challenge, and that no party or intellectual faction has a monopoly on wisdom.'[18] So though Horowitz shared Buckley's vision, he also knew that the terms of activism and intellectual politics had changed.

Horowitz also knew that he could play upon popular strains of anti-intellectualism and populist hatred of academe. But he went one step further by arguing for legislation that would allow state legislatures to police class-rooms because professions wouldn't police their own members. Professional codes of conduct simply shrouded power and domination. The professoriate would never stop imposing its political views on college students unless policed by the state. The ABOR called for the 'protection of students' from 'the imposition of any orthodoxy of a political, religious or ideological nature'.[19] Horowitz combined this paternalistic language with the political language of the 1960s. He pierced claims to objectivity, arguing that professors simply wanted to indoctrinate young minds with liberal ideology.[20] Horowitz echoed New Left students of the 1960s who had questioned scientific neutrality and professional objectivity, but he hardened the critique. He also sounded like Michel Foucault delineating an inherent nexus between knowledge and power, discovering the conservative benefits of postmodern theory.

Horowitz's activism conjures memories of New Left radicalism in other ways. Right-wing students demanding the curriculum reflect their own ideological orientation sound a lot like students who wanted 'relevant' curriculum during the 1960s that would help them understand Vietnam. The language of 'rights' and participatory democracy also live on in Horowitz's activism, conceptualising, as it does, the student as a consumer of academic goods and thus sharing a voice in their delivery. Both right-wing students and their New Left progenitors exerted pressure that challenges claims to institutional stability and professional authority. After all, Horowitz encouraged right-wing students to police classrooms and document bias. And one offshoot from the ABOR is a bill in Arizona that would force professors to provide 'alternative coursework' if students 'find the assigned material "personally offensive"'.[21] The utter absurdity of such a programme seems obvious, loading up institutions with ridiculous demands. Although

Horowitz disagrees with this particular version of legislation, it clearly sprang from his own ABOR activity, and it is hard to see how it diverges from his own thought. It simply pushes the demand that students determine their own education to its logical conclusion. And it is clearly in line with the 1960s ethic of student empowerment.

Horowitz also assumes that winning political power ensures cultural transformation – that political revolution demands cultural transformation. After two years of SAF activism, Horowitz reflected on the 2004 presidential election and when asked stated, 'the election is a big boost for the academic bill of rights, no question.'[22] One of the sponsors he linked up with in late 2004 made the connection between political power and the right to police classrooms explicit, illustrating the dangerous blowback for an intellectual-activist alliance on the right. Larry Mumper, a state senator from Ohio, endorsed the ABOR and asked: 'Why should we as fairly moderate to conservative legislators continue to support universities that turn out students who rail against the very policies that their parents voted us in for?'[23] Buckley's original desire for the executive power of alumni and trustees acting through the university president was now placed in the hands of state legislatures. Horowitz champions populist democracy amassing power in the halls of state legislatures and then transforming the university.

Horowitz's activism on behalf of right-wing students exemplifies the postmodern conservative mindset. He sees knowledge as relative and celebrates diversity and plurality. He believes politics is king and that power always colours any claim to objectivity. And he sees his activism as a legitimate and rightful inheritance of the 1960s' spirit. Tenured radicals with poststructuralist ideas bouncing around in their minds might be the embodiment of the 1960s to some, but so too is Horowitz. Call it the horseshoe effect of cultural politics in the age of postmodernity: the academic left and postmodern right coming full circle. Horowitz's own biographical zigzags suggest that this should not come as a surprise.

INTELLIGENT DESIGN IN SCHOOLS

If conservatives have traditionally questioned academia for its liberal machinations, their dislike of modern science is no less pronounced. Go back to the Cold War and listen to the conservative intellectual Frank Meyer (an editor at *National Review*) complaining about liberalism's 'science-wor-ship'.[24] Conservatives nurtured their own romantic streak, one that perceived limits to materialism and scientific inquiry. Whittaker Chambers – who excommunicated Ayn Rand in part for her attacks on the irrationalities of religion and what today would be called her 'logocentrism' – believed science had displaced marvelling at the 'wonder of life and the wonder of the universe, the wonder of life within the wonder of the universe'. As he sat at the breakfast table and examined his daughter's ear with its beautiful features,

Chambers came to believe that 'design presupposes God', that nature could not be explained by cold-hearted scientific rationalism.[25]

Chambers's critique of science found an odd set of characters taking it up during the 1960s. The critique found resonance in America's counterculture. As the leading theorist of the counterculture, Theodore Roszak, pointed out in 1969, 'the leading mentors of our youthful counter culture have … called into question the validity of the conventional scientific world view'. The young, he believed, were 'dropping out' of a technocratic system built upon the prosperity ensured by science and technology. When hippies 'returned to nature' and kids started drifting away from Christianity towards eastern mysticism (such as Shamanism and Zen), they were embracing a 'magical world view' that renewed the sort of wonder about the world Chambers had experienced with his daughter's ear at the breakfast table. The 'scientific world view' no longer persuaded the young. Science's authority collapsed, much like the authority of parents and government.[26]

The counterculture's impact and shockwaves were felt long after the 1960s, though the more radical and transformative talk of Roszak became quickly dated, blowing away like so much marijuana smoke. Still, academic postmodernists who worked in philosophy and history continued to argue that science's foundations were more historically rooted and less objective than previously believed. The writings of Thomas Kuhn and Paul Feyarbend most explicitly explored these themes, and their criticisms resonated with the academic left and its theories about the indeterminacy of knowledge developed in philosophy and English departments. Generally though, doubts about science drifted back to the right – especially as the New Right pressed an evangelical basis for conservative activism. Conservative intellectuals criticised scientists' amoral outlook about genetic engineering and their tendency to see biological roots to all behaviour, as they questioned the immorality of abortion. But it was the call to teach 'intelligent design' in public schools that became the most important movement critical of science and constitutive of postmodern conservatism. Here, conservative intellectuals did not just criticise science's power, but offered a new vision to explain the world.[27]

'Intelligent design' (ID) is typically understood as an updated version of Biblical creationism, a view that seemed to have disappeared from public sight after the Scopes Trial of 1925. But 'intelligent design' offered something creationism had not. It did not begin with the Biblical story of creation but rather with doubts about Darwin's explanations of evolution, a distinctly postmodern starting point. In 1996, ID's leading exponents formed a think tank called the Discovery Institute based in Seattle, Washington. Led by Phillip Johnson, the author of *Darwin on Trial* (1991), a leading evangelical critic of evolution and a demi-intellectual of sorts, the writers and publicists gathered here came up with the 'teach the controversy' approach to presenting ID, sometimes called the 'wedge' strategy (named after a controversial paper known as the 'Wedge Document' discovered in 1999 that showed how anti-evolution activism could help 'replace materialistic explanations with the theistic understanding that nature and human beings are created by God').[28] The Discovery Institute has offered fellowships to writers and support for grassroots initiatives (that created numerous successes) in states like Ohio, Kansas and Texas. And it has accomplished this by arguing that Darwinian evolution is one theory that should be taught alongside other theories, including Chambers's argument that 'design pre-supposes God'.[29]

ID proponents argue that teachers have the right and responsibility to expose students to diverse viewpoints about evolution. In 2001, Senator Rick Santorum used that rationale to introduce a Senate Amendment promoting ID and tying it to the No Child Left Behind Act (this ultimately failed), and President Bush echoed it a few years later in 2005 when he lent his support to the movement.[30] 'Both sides ought to be properly taught so people can understand what the debate is about', the President explained, implying that liberal teachers were repressing diversity in America's classrooms. The goal in introducing ID into the classroom was to 'expose people to different schools of thought'.[31] Exponents of ID have, in the words of the *New York Times*, successfully 'transformed the debate into an issue of academic freedom rather than a confrontation between biology and religion'.[32] As Horowitz mined the postmodern concept that all knowledge is indeter-minate in order to justify the ABOR, defenders of ID embrace the postmodern view of science as one of many 'paradigms' that help human beings make sense of their world.

The history of this movement is more detailed than my treatment here suggests (indeed, an entire book about the movement was published in 2004). And there are numerous less-well-known intellectuals arguing its case. But most important in this context is the *style* of argument made on ID's behalf. No scientists confirm the nature of the arguments made by proponents of ID, which allows figures like Phillip Johnson to think of themselves as rebels against a steadfast liberal establishment. Because of this, postmodern theories have informed their battle plans. 'Teach the con-troversy' is indebted, after all, to the postmodern doubts about truth being singular. Johnson once explained: 'I'm no postmodernist' but 'I've learned a lot' from reading postmodern theory. This makes his thinking, as he put it, 'dead-bang mainstream' in 'academia these days'.[33] In this, he is certainly right. Like Horowitz, Johnson has taken up the language of radical relativism and postmodern theories of knowledge in order to do battle against the 'liberal establishment' – all for the purpose of conservative aims and giving insight into a mindset framed by the necessity of war.

Those who have studied the success of ID admire its well-orchestrated media and publicity campaign. Most proponents of the theory are not working in laboratories garnering counter-evidence against Darwin's findings. They are, instead, writing for a wider public and mobilising action at the state and local level. The success of the movement is due to the conservative movement's capacity to transform the world of the mass media and to a decline in citizens' view of journalistic ethics over the last few years. And this brings us to the final culture war that informs the contemporary conservative mind.

AT WAR WITH THE LIBERAL MEDIA

The right's war against the 'liberal media' is an old one. Complaints about the media littered the pages of the *National Review* during the 1950s, and Barry Goldwater's run prompted more. In 1964, M. Stanton Evans argued that 'managed news' shut Barry Goldwater out of the mainstream.[34] This view found more prominent voices during the late 1960s. In 1969, Vice-President Spiro Agnew famously berated television news as hostile to President Richard Nixon's oversight of the Vietnam War. He condemned the 'instant analysis and querulous criticism' of television news shows perpetrated by a 'small band of network commentators and self-appointed analysts, the majority of whom' were hostile to Nixon. Television news people were 'urbane' and lived within 'the geographical and intellectual confines of Washington D.C. or New York City.' Agnew took Evans's critique and pushed it in more explicitly populist directions, a touch of Kevin Phillips's Wallace-ism added to the mix.[35]

Two years later, Edith Efron, a right-wing writer at *TV Guide*, would blast liberal 'bias' in her bestselling book *The News Twisters* (1971). The book was chock full of charts showing that, indeed, Spiro Agnew was right: the press *had* treated Nixon harshly. From here, Efron argued that the FCC fairness doctrine and the First Amendment were too broadly interpreted. 'The First Amendment', she wrote, 'gives the press the right to be biased'. For instance, it allowed the mainstream media to treat the 'white middle class' and 'provincial' people with disdain. The media also flattered the New Left, or what she referred to as 'the kids'. She believed that a 'silent majority' would rise up in revolt against the press's bias (her argument won an invitation to Nixon's White House that she declined). And then in passing, Efron pointed out something else: that 'study after study has revealed that people buy publications with whose editorials they agree'. This insight, more than her call for a revolt on the part of the silent majority, transformed the future of the mass media.[36]

Efron's view worked in tandem with the initiatives of 'New Journalists' who were writing around the same time and had questioned the importance of 'objectivity' in reporting. During the late 1960s, the new sensibility joined the world of journalism witnessed in the pioneering work of Tom Wolfe, Joan Didion (who wrote for *National Review* briefly), Norman Mailer, and Hunter S. Thompson. New Journalism's *subjectivity* – its faith that the reporter's consciousness deserved attention and should be included in any and all stories – was easily radicalised into profound doubt about the possibility of *any* objective treatment of events. This was the postmodern kernel in the movement. New Journalism could be understood as a product of the 1960s, but it could also be gleaned in the *National Review*'s early editorial in favour of a 'personal journalism – the manly presentation of deeply felt convictions' and necessarily an accompanying ethic of 'controversy'. That didn't sound all that different from Tom Wolfe's original definition of New Journalism as 'personality, energy, drive, bravura'.[37]

Efron's argument that consumers buy the media they prefer and the rebellion against objectivity found in the work of New Journalists helped clear the way for the 'new' media that defines our own age: cable television with its widespread choice and a plurality of 'political' news shows; the Internet with its 'search driven culture' and opinionated blogs; and talk radio, a medium highly favourable to populist rantings with explicit partisan leanings. All of these outlets have effectively dismantled the ideal of 'objective' journalism. As do the incessant complaints about the mainstream media – now labelled simply MSM – by conservative writers and their search for a more authentic 'personal journalism'.

Just how far these changes have gone and how much the right is responsible for them can be seen in the stodgier world of book publishing. Today, niche marketing has generated an array of conservative book publishers (or divisions within existing houses): Random House's Crown forum, Penguin's imprint Sentinel, Simon and Schuster's Threshold Editions (run by Mary Matalin), Encounter Books in San Francisco, and the oldest conservative publisher, Regnery. Publishers hunt for opinionated and bold arguments that can be marketed to well-defined political audiences. Judith Regan, once an editor at Pocket Books (Simon and Schuster) who signed Sean Hannity (and more memorably O. J. Simpson), explained: 'What people respond to in this culture is loud and brash and pointed and sometimes vulgar – that's what gets people's attention, on TV and radio and in books. Shades-of-gray books are very difficult to sell.'[38] Publishers now promote conservative books that are clearly tagged as such – books by Coulter, Savage, O'Reilly – through a well-defined segment of networks, including conservative websites and magazines, Fox News, right-wing talk radio, and right-wing book clubs.

By the mid-1990s, some conservatives were honest enough to admit that they had transformed the MSM.[39] In essence, the 'counterestablishment' of *National Review* and a few other publications now started to look more like a full-fledged postmodern establishment, if such a term makes sense. In 1996, one writer for the *Weekly Standard* explained that conservatives dominated talk radio and some television outlets, 'from Limbaugh to the Capital Gang'. Talk radio, of course, was a medium that reached large numbers with no pretence of professionalism or objectivity, and it carried with it a more widespread revolution in the media. This same *Weekly Standard* author went on to explain that the liberal media – with its air of 'press-as-clerisy' – would reject the 'new regime of radio gas-bags, TV shoutathons, and Internet yahoos.'[40] But the revolution *would* be televised and could not be held back by the elite trying to suppress the populist rage that an Efron could only dream about. This new conservative counter-regime would soon include Fox News and then Internet blogs.[41] Conservatives created a new media landscape that blurred the line between news and opinion, eliciting a profoundly post-modern cultural victory. As Nicholas Lemann pointed out, 'conservatives are relativists when it comes to the press. In their view, nothing is neutral: there is no disinterested version of the news; everything reflects politics and relationships to power and cultural perspective.'[42] That was the essence of their revolt and its transformational success in making a new world fraught with cultural fragmentation and dissonance – the world of postmodernity.

THE END GAME OF POSTMODERN CONSERVATISM

The postmodernism of MSM critics, ID proponents, and ABOR activists work in tandem. So too does the stridency of Horowitz, Coulter, and Savage. Other critics have noticed a growing postmodern streak in conservative activism and thought today. For instance, the literary critic Stanley Fish believes ID proponents adopt postmodern ideas for the sake of strategy, to win influence and to wedge their ideas into a culture that rejects absolutist claims. But in reality the strategy is much more pervasive than Fish's interpretation suggests. Postmodernity frames numerous culture wars fought by the post-war conservative mind and has helped create something resembling a ragtag establishment – an establishment that glorifies rebellion, loudmouthed rantings, a debunking of professional authority, and a relativist view of truth. Postmodern conservatism has been much more trans-formational than the term 'strategy' suggests.

What critics like Stanley Fish miss (most likely because they want to hold on to their own left-leaning postmodernism) is that the conservative mind was a mind born in a state of war. Its sense of apocalypse and rightfulness lends itself to the use of whatever means necessary – including relativistic tactics. It is not that the conservative mind adopts relativism and post-modernism as tools that are simply strategic in nature, slyly chosen to make headway. It is that the mindset of war propels fervent choices of war-like tactics. These are not just convenient tools being adapted, they are weapons – weapons that reflect the apocalyptic mindset making the choice. The tactics and the mindset are much more closely wedded than critics like Fish imagine. And the tactics and mindset make for the odd combination of fervent absolutism matched with postmodern relativism.

As postmodern conservative intellectuals have waged their wars, they have helped create a culture in which the fine art of discerning truth from falsehood seems unnecessary. A culture in which the line between news and opinion no longer holds, where all truth claims are shields covering up political belief and prejudice; a culture which is disrespectful of professional competence and holds intelligence in contempt, pilloried as elitism and snobbery; a culture that no longer thinks it important to discern high culture from low or good argument from bad so long as entertainment is found.

But there is no reason to believe that any of this will stop conservative activists from hurdling forward. David Horowitz has too much gleam in his eyes – similar to the student radicals who took over Columbia University with great gusto in 1968 – to stop any time soon. Ann Coulter seems too angry and seems to do too well in book sales to wonder if there's something corrosive about yelling and demonising opponents. ID proponents have won too many victories to wonder if perhaps their own relativistic conception of knowledge might do damage to education or respect for scientific inquiry. And the *Weekly Standard* editors are just too hip to wonder if popular culture and suburban sprawl might not be the utopian agents they want them to be. The post-war conservative mind has unleashed new forces that feed into the populist and anti-intellectual tendencies deeply rooted in American history and this has won it popularity. Today, it becomes imperative for critics of the conservative mind to point out how it threatens civil culture, faith in professions and scientific knowledge, the ability to discern facts from political opinion, and the general pursuit of the life of the mind. In the end 'wars of aggression' create blowback and damage. We should not forget that.

NOTES

1. For more on neoconservatism there are many sources. See Jim Mann, *The Rise of the Vulcans: The History of Bush's War Cabinet* (New York, NY: Viking, 2004); George Packer, *The Assassins' Gate: America in Iraq* (New York, NY: Farrar, Straus and Giroux, 2005), Chapter 2; Gary J. Dorrien, *Imperial Designs: Neoconservatism and the New Pax Americana* (New York, NY: Routledge, 2004).
2. Morris Dickstein, *Gates of Eden* (New York, NY: Basic Books, 1977), p. 248. Theodore Roszak, *The Making of a Counterculture* (Berkeley, CA: University of California Press, [1968] 1995), pp. 205, 227, 207.
3. Albert Borgmann, *Crossing the Postmodern Divide* (Chicago, IL: University of Chicago Press, 1992), pp. 55, 57. John Patrick Diggins, *The Rise and Fall of the American Left* (New York, NY: Norton, 1992), p. 347.
4. Mark Lilla, *The Reckless Mind: Intellectuals in Politics* (New York, NY: New York Review Books, 2001), pp. 186–7.
5. Michel Foucault, *Power/Knowledge* (New York, NY: Pantheon, 1980), p. 126. On Foucault's fascination with the Iranian revolution see Janet Afary and Kevin Anderson, *Foucault and the Iranian Revolution* (Chicago, IL: University of Chicago Press, 2005).
6. Paul Weyrich, 'Blue collar or blue blood?: The New Right compared with the

Old Right', in Robert Whitaker (ed.), *The New Right Papers* (New York, NY: St. Martin's Press, 1982), p. 50.

7. For more on this theme see Kevin Mattson, *Rebels All!: A Short History of Postwar Conservative Ideas in America* (New Brunswick, NJ: Rutgers University Press, 2008).

8. See on this point, Mary Brennan, *Turning Right in the Sixties* (Chapel Hill, NC: University of North Carolina Press, 1995), p. 142.

9. Damon Linker, *The Theocons: Secular America Under Siege* (New York, NY: Doubleday, 2006); see also my review, 'Attacking Secular America', *Dissent*, Winter 2007, 139–41.

10. See here especially Todd Gitlin, *The Twilight of Common Dreams* (New York, NY: Metropolitan, 1995).

11. This tendency is mirrored on the left in the work of Al Franken and Michael Moore. For more on this point, see Mattson, 'The Perils of Michael Moore', *Dissent*, Spring 2003, 75–81.

12. Ann Coulter, *Slander* (New York, NY: Crown, 2002), p. 197 and *How To Talk to a Liberal (If You Must)* (New York, NY: Crown, 2004), pp. 37, 10.

13. David Gilson, 'Michael Savage's long, strange trip', www.Salon.com, 5 March 2003.

14. Michael Savage, *Liberalism is a Mental Disorder* (Nashville, TN: Nelson Current, 2005), pp. xx, xxvi.

15. Horowitz quoted in Stanley Fish, 'Intellectual Diversity: The Trojan horse of a dark design', *Chronicle of Higher Education*, 13 February 2004, p. B14.

16. For a fine overview of this history see Chapter 2 of Michael Bérubé, *What's Liberal About the Liberal Arts?* (New York, NY: Norton, 2006).

17. William Buckley, 'The Ivory Tower: here lies the empty mind', *National Review*, 20 April 1957, 382.

18. Academic Bill of Rights, http://www.studentsforacademicfreedom.org/abor. htm.

19. Ibid.

20. For more on this see Mattson, 'A Student Bill of Fights', *The Nation*, 4 April 2005, 16–17.

21. Quoted in 'Avoid whatever offends you', *Inside Higher Education*, 17 February 2006, insidehighered.com

22. Quoted in Jeffrey Brainard *et al.*, 'GOP looks to put its mark on higher education', *Chronicle of Higher Education*, 12 November 2004, A11.

23. Larry Mumper quoted in Joe Hallett, 'Right winger's bill to stifle campus left-leaners is a surefire backfire', *Columbus Dispatch*, 30 January 2005.

24. Frank Meyer, 'Principles and heresies: the bigotry of science', *National Review*, 8 March 1958, 234. See also Albert Hobbs, 'The falseface of science', *Intercollegiate Review*, January 1965, 17–22.

25. Whittaker Chambers, *Witness* (Washington, DC: Regnery, [1952] 2002), pp. 19, 16.

26. Theodore Roszak, *The Making of a Counterculture* (Berkeley, CA: University of California Press, [1969] 1995), pp. 205, 258. Howard Brick, *The Age of Contradiction: American Thought and Culture in the 1960s* (Ithaca, NY: Cornell University Press, 1998), p. 116.

27. Andrew Ferguson, 'How Steven Pinker's mind works', *The Weekly Standard*, 12 January 1998, 16–24.
28. Quotation of Wedge Document in Chris Mooney, *The Republican War on Science* (New York, NY: Basic Books, 2005), p. 173.
29. For more on this history, see Michael Ruse, 'Liberalism, Science, and Evolution', in Neil Jumonville and Kevin Mattson (eds), *Liberalism for a New Century* (Berkeley, CA: University of California, 2007).
30. Barbara Forrest and Paul Gross, *Creationism's Trojan Horse: The Wedge of Intelligent Design* (New York, NY: Oxford University Press, 2004), pp. 240–1.
31. Bush quoted in Linker, *Theocons*, p. 187.
32. Jodi Wilgoven, 'Politicized scholars put evolution on defensive', *New York Times*, 21 August 2005, 1.
33. Quoted in Stanley Fish, 'Academic Cross-dressing: how intelligent design gets its arguments from the left', *Harper's*, December 2005, 71.
34. See for instance, M. Stanton Evans, 'At Home', *National Review*, 21 January 1964, 6.
35. Agnew quoted in Chris Lehmann, 'The Eyes of Spiro are upon You', *The Baffler*, 14, 2001, 27.
36. Edith Efron, *The News Twisters* (Los Angeles, CA: Nash, 1971), pp. 19, 68, 132, 142, 168. The quotation about agreeing with the press can be found on p. 27.
37. *National Review* Editorial, 'Statement of Intentions', in Gregory Schneider (ed.), *Conservatism in America Since 1930* (New York, NY: New York University Press, 2003), p. 198. Tom Wolfe quoted in Howard Brick, *The Age of Contradiction* (Ithaca, NY: Cornell University Press, 1998), p. 38. For more on new journalism see Marc Weingarten, *The Gang That Wouldn't Write Straight* (New York, NY: Crown, 2006).
38. Paula Span, 'Making Books: The Politics of Publishing', *Washington Post*, Book World, 6 November 2005: posted on the net at http://www.washingtonpost.com/wp-dyn/content/article/2005/11/03/AR2005110301847.html.
39. See here Michael Massing, 'The End of News?', *New York Review of Books*, 1 December 2005, 23–7.
40. Andrew Ferguson, 'Media-bashing, Liberal Style', *The Weekly Standard*, 29 January 1996, 39.
41. See for instance Jonathan Last, 'What Blogs have Wrought', *The Weekly Standard*, 27 September 2004, 27–31.
42. Nicholas Lemann, 'Fear and Favor', *New Yorker*, 14–21 February 2005, 172.

6. US PROPAGANDA

Nancy Snow

In September 1992, a relatively obscure international treaty took effect in the United States. Originally signed by Democratic President Jimmy Carter in 1977, the International Covenant on Civil and Political Rights (ICCPR) ultimately oversaw passage by Carter's Republican successor once removed, President George H. W. Bush, after a two-thirds Senate vote. Article 20 of the ICCPR reads: '1. Any propaganda for war shall be prohibited by law. 2. Any advocacy of national, racial or religious hatred that constitutes incitement to discrimination, hostility or violence shall be prohibited by law'.[1]

The covenant makes no attempt to legally define propaganda. It was signed into law in the US within the context of a country that had just one year earlier successfully defeated Iraq using methods of mass persuasion that were then unparalleled since the Cold War. Saddam Hussein was referred to as the Hitler of the Middle East from the President's lips down to the newsrooms of the mainstream media and every manner of commercial product was created with his tyrannical visage: from T-shirts to golf balls to urinal mats making him the object of ire for democracy-loving Americans. Even if average Americans could not locate Iraq on a map, they certainly knew that this Hussein guy was another bad 'H' who mandated ultimate humiliation and defeat. Following the swift and overwhelming US-led coalition victory in pushing Iraq out of Kuwait, General Colin Powell responded to a question about the number of Iraqi dead from ground troops or air sorties: 'It's really not a number I'm terribly interested in'.[2]

Were the communication techniques used to transform a former US ally in the Iran/Iraq war to a desert Hitler exemplary of this prohibited propaganda for war? It is unlikely, since the US was responding forcefully to an aggressive breach of territory by Iraq into Kuwait. The ICCPR, though general in its language, suggests that propaganda in response to a warlike act (exhibited in this case by Saddam Hussein) is not prohibited. Nevertheless, it is likely that the US would not define any advocacy for its persuasive cause as propaganda for war, whether in response to an aggressive act by Iraq in August 1990 or in anticipation of aggression by Iraq with its elective military invasion in 2003. To this day, the US officially and popularly views the contested 'P' word with much derision. It is viewed as inherently deceitful and thus morally repugnant to democracy-loving people who value the truth over the big lie. American propaganda in the late 20th and early 21st centuries is conceived as something that only totalitarian states engage in, notably the 'axis of evil' coalition of nation states like North Korea, Iraq and Iran that President Bush derided in his January 2002 State of the Union address:

> States like these, and their terrorist allies, constitute an axis of evil, arming to threaten the peace of the world. By seeking weapons of mass destruction, these regimes pose a grave and growing danger. They could provide these arms to terrorists, giving them the means to match their hatred. They could attack our allies or attempt to blackmail the United States. In any of these cases, the price of indifference would be catastrophic.[3]

Totalitarian states are known to lie to citizens, censor the media, conceal operations, and generally view the open society with disdain. Propaganda is used to serve the interests of the totalitarian state by manipulating the emotions, attitudes, and behaviours of citizens in service of the state. When democracies go to war, they elect to use propaganda in preparation for war but do so reluctantly and reserve their most manipulative propaganda methods for the enemy or enemy sympathisers. In peacetime, democracies like the US are thought to engage in mass persuasion through consensus, open debate, and dissent, with minimal censorship (for national security purposes only), and promotion of hard news facts over biased views.

It is a well-established myth that democracies are reluctant to use propaganda. The US as the leading democratic republic is also the world's largest producer and consumer of propaganda. Its crowning achievement in propaganda is that it has managed to convince many of its citizens that propaganda is what others do. The US prefers other words to the besmirched term 'propaganda', including advertising, public relations, public diplomacy and marketing. All of these professional persuasion industries were conceived and developed in the US. Edward Bernays, the founder of American public relations, wrote two books about his practice, *Crystallizing Public Opinion* (1923) and *Propaganda* (1928), both of which are purported to have heavily influenced the techniques of the chief propagandist for the Third Reich, Joseph Goebbels.[4]

Several myths permeate the American system of P-word denial: (1) that the US resorts to the use of propaganda in wartime; (2) that totalitarian regimes engage in propaganda endlessly through lies and deceit; and (3) that while totalitarian governments lie to their people, democratic governments always tell the truth. The reality isn't black and white, but democratic heads of state often paint these pictures in such duo chrome.

WHITE HOUSE PROPAGANDA

Consider the example of Ronald Reagan, the late 20th-century president dubbed 'the Great Communicator' for his legendary ability to sway the masses. Reagan is credited with having shepherded the end of the Cold War in many respects through words alone. On 8 June 1982, 20 years before the Axis of Evil speech by his 21st-century Republican successor, Reagan spoke these words in an address before the British Parliament later dubbed by some as the 'original' Evil Empire Speech, or more commonly known as the Westminster Speech:

> We see around us today the marks of our terrible dilemma – predictions of doomsday, antinuclear demonstrations, an arms race in which the West must, for its own protection, be an unwilling participant. At the same time we see totalitarian forces in the world who seek subversion and conflict around the globe to further their barbarous assault on the human spirit. What, then, is our course? Must civilization perish in a hail of fiery atoms? Must freedom wither in a quiet, deadening accommodation with totalitarian evil?[5]

Reagan proposed a global campaign for American-style democracy over dictatorship. Anticipating critics that might be put off by this new cultural offensive, Reagan said: 'this is not cultural imperialism; it is providing the means for genuine self-determination and protection for diversity.'

Reagan followed this speech ten months later, on 8 March 1983, with a further Evil Empire Speech to the 41st Annual National Association of Evangelicals in Orlando, Florida. This was forcefully directed at communism and America's ideological archenemy, the Soviet Union:

> Yes, let us pray for the salvation of all of those who live in that totalitarian darkness. Pray they will discover the joy of knowing God. But until they do, let us be aware that while they preach the supremacy of the State, declare its omnipotence over individual man, and predict its eventual domination of all peoples on the earth, they are the focus of evil in the modern world.[6]

As these speeches indicate, Reagan was the first Cold War president to fully engage media and information strategies relative to the promotion of national security objectives overseas, in particular, the ideological overthrow of the Soviet Union. Two months before his Evil Empire Speech in Florida, the President signed National Security Directive 77 'Management of Public Diplomacy Relative to National Security' to establish a Special Planning Group (SPG). This group included a committee on international infor-mation 'to assume the responsibilities of the existing "Project Truth" Policy Group', and an international political committee that would coordinate outreach with foreign policy sectors (military, diplomatic, economic) as well as domestic sectors (universities, philanthropy, political parties, press) in order 'to build up the US Government's capability to promote democracy ... furthermore, this committee will initiate plans, programs and strategies designed to counter totalitarian ideologies and aggressive political action moves undertaken by the Soviet Union or Soviet surrogates'.[7] *New York Times* columnist William Safire wrote that the creation of the SPG proved that the role of the United States Information Agency (USIA) 'in ideological warfare had shifted from mouthpiece to policy participant'.[8]

DEMOCRATIC PROPAGANDA AND TRUTH

Embedded in the philosophy of American public diplomacy (especially when linked to national security) is that when the US Government engages in psychological warfare, government-sponsored broadcasting and media management, it is with the intention of spreading truth and democracy. In 1950, another American Cold War President Harry S. Truman proposed a 'Campaign of Truth' to challenge 'imperialistic communism' and 'to promote the cause of freedom against the propaganda of slavery'.[9] Three decades later, Reagan's own propaganda campaign 'Project Truth' was challenging Cold War communism through CIA-backed financing of anti-communist insurgency groups across the globe. Project Truth – later renamed Project Democracy – was run by ex-CIA agent Walter Raymond Jr, who was directed by his former boss CIA Director William J. Casey, to mount a strategic communications strategy against the communist threat coming from the leftist Sandinista government in Nicaragua and Marxist rebels in El Salvador.

The Reagan administration was worried that the Soviets were trying to gain a foothold in Central America, just a day's drive from the American South. President Reagan backed the Contras (from the Spanish term *La Contra*, short for 'movement of the *contrarrevolucionarios*') and identified them as 'freedom fighters' and 'the moral equivalent of our Founding Fathers' while the Sandinistas were painted as terrorists.[10] Raymond was hand picked to offer a 'hands off' approach to the propaganda operation, since the CIA is prohibited from influencing domestic public opinion on foreign policy. Raymond would later describe his efforts as 'gluing black hats on the

Sandinistas and white hats [on the Contras]'.[11] To help the Nicaraguan rebels, Project Democracy set up an unauthorised Office of Public Diplomacy for Latin America and the Caribbean in the US State Department. Headed by an ardent anticommunist Cuban American consultant Otto Reich, the office engaged in illegal practices, including leaking classified information that supported the Contras' rebel cause as well as preparing news stories that demonised the Nicaraguan government and idealised the Contras. A team of psychological warfare specialists was brought in to exploit news media themes, including spreading false accounts of Sandinista prostitutes being procured for US reporters covering the Central American conflict and stories of Sandinista commandants living the high life that was dubbed 'Sandinista chic'.[12] By spring 1986, $100 million in aid to the Contras was approved by the US Congress and the Iran-Contra scandal would not come to light until a November report in a Beirut newspaper *Al-Shiraa* revealed an elaborate Iranian-arms-for-hostages scheme that financed the Contras' efforts.

Project Democracy's efforts may have been sidelined by the Iran-Contra Scandal of 1987, but a formal defence of democracy was in place with the creation of the National Endowment for Democracy (NED), a bipartisan organisation founded in 1983 in response to Reagan's Westminster Speech. A quarter of a century later, in June 2007, President Bush singled out NED as an instrument in his administration's fight to end tyranny and promote democracy. A White House fact sheet notes that the

> United States has nearly doubled funding for democracy projects since 2001. The President's FY 2008 budget requests nearly $1.5 billion in funding for Democracy, Governance and Human Rights – up from less than $700 million in 2001. In addition, funding for the National Endowment for Democracy has more than doubled from $31 million to $80 million since 2001.[13]

MANICHEAN DESTINY

The National Endowment for Democracy utilises emotionally and significantly meaningful symbolic words like 'democracy' to allow propaganda to thrive and prosper in a more open society. Democracy is a word so cherished in American society and culture that it is easily converted into a world view that is distinctly Manichean, dominated by what Alex Carey called 'powerful symbols of the Satanic and the Sacred (darkness and light)'.[14] In the US, democracy represents all that is sacred, even though its attributes are rarely detailed or made specific. It is often linked to an evangelical religiosity, not surprising for the most religious democratic republic in the world. The Gallup organisation reports that one third (31 per cent) of Americans believe in the literal interpretation of the Bible and another 47 per cent believe that the Bible is the inspired word of God.[15] Nearly 80 per cent believe that

God exists, while only 1 per cent is 'convinced' that God does not exist.[16] While belief in God and church attendance has dropped off since the 1960s, the rise of evangelical faith mixed with political and social control and expression has increased. Though John F. Kennedy promised an anxious nation that he would vehemently separate his Catholic faith upbringing from government rule, all the late 20th and early 21st-century American presidents have openly expressed faith in God, although none more vocally than George W. Bush (a topic Wilfred McClay discusses in the next section of this volume).

President George W. Bush emphasises his fundamentalist Christian faith in God and credits it with having turned his life around at age 40 after years of alcohol abuse. His faith also directs his foreign policy:

> I am driven with a mission from God. God would tell me, 'George go and fight these terrorists in Afghanistan'. And I did. And then God would tell me 'George, go and end the tyranny in Iraq'. And I did. And now, again, I feel God's words coming to me, 'Go get the Palestinians their state and get the Israelis their security, and get peace in the Middle East'. And, by God, I'm gonna do it.[17]

It is not such expressions of Heaven and Hell or Good and Evil which always dominate propaganda rhetoric but their secular equivalents: The American Dream, American Way of Life, Spirit of America, America's Purpose in the World, and American Values. These 'God terms' are contrasted with 'Devil terms' like Communism during the Cold War or Islamofascism and Militant Islam during the War on Terror. Islamofascism is not just counter to transcendent American values but also threatening to America's way of life and freedom.

Less than two weeks after 9/11, President Bush told the nation and a joint session of Congress why the leading Islamofascist terrorist organisation al-Qaeda attacked the World Trade Center and the Pentagon:

> Americans are asking, why do they hate us? They hate what we see right here in this chamber – a democratically elected government. Their leaders are self-appointed. They hate our freedoms – our freedom of religion, our freedom of speech, our freedom to vote and assemble and disagree with each other.[18]

Any society so oriented toward fear appeals (loss of freedom and a particular way of life) is more susceptible to powerful propaganda symbols like the promotion of democracy that serves as a method of social control. Add the inclination that the US has toward taking action over contemplative reflection, then all the ingredients are in place for non-questioning of fundamental premises. These premises include the unexamined truth that democracies are good and any methods that enhance democracies are okay as long as the intended goal is noble.

ADVOCATING AMERICA'S STORY

Reagan's ideological efforts to advance democracy and counter communist appeal were shepherded along by his close friend, former Hollywood producer and bandleader Charles Z. Wick, under whose eight-year tenure from 1981–8 the United States Information Agency (USIA) budget doubled.[19] Wick was accused of keeping a blacklist of banned Americans like well-known liberals Walter Cronkite, Coretta Scott King, David Brinkley and the more radical MIT professor Noam Chomsky, all considered undesirable representatives of the US to those seeking to strike a delicate rhetorical balance between the Evil Empire rhetoric and 'trust, but verify' stance toward the Soviet Union. The US media, including the venerable *New York Times*, made much hullabaloo of 'the list' that Wick initially defended in the spirit of partisanship but then distanced himself from when legislators who held the purse strings for his agency made charges of censorship.[20]

Wick was famous for his 'Z-grams' (from his middle initial) to staff that expressed his zealous ideas to merge propaganda activities from USIA with White House directives, including a more confrontational stance in government broadcasting against the Soviet Union. He visited more overseas USIA posts (known as USIS, for United States Information Service) than any other director, four of which were in the Soviet Union.[21] Other than the brief tenure of acclaimed broadcast journalist Edward R. Murrow as USIA director during the Kennedy years, the propaganda agency would never have such an activist director whose background was tailor-made for the marketing and selling of America's story to the world. Wick's former director of Worldnet Television, Alvin Snyder, referred to the Reagan-Wick duo as 'commander in chief and the supreme commander in the war of propaganda', who oversaw their share of foot soldiers in the American propaganda effort, including Snyder. Snyder says of his USIA tenure:

> I had no problem with practicing advocacy journalism, because I felt we were transmitting 'good' propaganda; an exaggerated version of the truth, perhaps, but still fundamentally the truth. I would later learn that many of us at the USIA were often duped by government officials from the intelligence community, the White House, the State Department, and the Pentagon into transmitting lies – Disinformation – without realizing it at the time. We became unknowing warriors of disinformation, and then we became knowing ones.[22]

Al Snyder still acknowledges Charles Wick as the most successful open propagandist in USIA's 50-year history.

PROPAGANDA, INC.

When Bill Clinton was elected President in November 1992, I was one month into a two-year Presidential Management Fellows (PMF) programme at the United States Information Agency. Every day I traversed the entrance of an independent federal agency whose motto was displayed prominently on its facade: 'Telling America's Story to the World'. In the context of American propaganda, this motto became heavily infused with marketing the nation in a post-Cold War environment. Clinton had won the presidency on his 'it's the economy, stupid' mantra of his campaign staffers like James Carville and George Stephanopoulos. The new buzzword 'globalisation' was entering the psyche of the American public and Clinton utilised the propaganda of the deed through transforming a former Cold War agency into a quasi-Commerce Department.

USIA leadership at the time knew that the Agency was on life support. It had no domestic constituency to lobby on behalf of the Agency's interests, due in part to antiquated Smith-Mundt legislative prohibitions from the 1940s banning the distribution of overseas propaganda (films, pamphlets and programmes) to the American people. Global media organisations like Ted Turner's Cable News Network or CNN (founded in 1980), which had earned legendary status for leading the first 'television war' during the Gulf War, and the World Wide Web (launched in 1992), electronic technology instrumental in the first 'Internet war' in the former Yugoslavia, were eclipsing the ability of government propaganda efforts to manage global information efforts. USIA elected to get involved where it was needed, including areas deemed important to the Clinton Doctrine that promoted the enlargement of economic ties between the US and other countries.

Telling America's story was now 'selling' America's story through promotion of the World Trade Organization and the pro-free trade North American Free Trade Agreement (NAFTA) legislation.[23] Foreign policy crises did elevate foreign propaganda, albeit briefly. In April 1999, Clinton issued a Presidential Decision Directive (PDD 68) that created an International Public Information Committee (IPI) to counteract the bad press the administration was receiving in US military operations in Kosovo and Haiti. Once again, propaganda was tapped in the service of national security objectives as stated in the IPI charter: (1) assist US Government efforts in defeating enemies; (2) identify hostile foreign propaganda and deception that targets the US; (3) enhance US security, bolster America's economic prosperity and to promote democracy abroad; and (4) control international military information to influence the emotions, motives, objective reasoning and ultimately the behaviour of foreign governments, groups, and individuals.[24]

The IPI charter included a caveat addressing possible blowback in foreign media manipulation. While all IPI activities 'are overt and address foreign audiences only … since foreign media reports are frequently reflected in American news media, it will be impossible to entirely preclude a backwash of the IPI-generated information into America'. Despite efforts to co-ordinate international propaganda efforts, the face of white propaganda efforts, the US Information Agency, was shuttered as an independent agency in autumn 1999. A hoped-for peace dividend and a super bubble on Wall Street carried the sentiment of the day before the millennium. Looming beneath the surface was growing anxiety of a 'clash of civilizations' to use Samuel Huntington's term (as David Ryan discusses in this section) that could spoil everything and cause many to wax nostalgic for an official propaganda agency. A short 24 months later, the US would emerge on a path with the most sophisticated propaganda machinery in its history.

PROPAGANDA TODAY: MATCHING REALITY TO RHETORIC

The events of Tuesday, 11 September 2001 were the ultimate 'propaganda of the deed' that caused more immediate loss of life in a series of surprise terror attacks than in previous US history. Within hours of these attacks, President Bush declared war on the terrorists responsible for training the suicide-attackers and those nation states that harboured them. No state had declared war on the US, but within weeks of 9/11 the first target in the War on Terror, Afghanistan, was held responsible for harbouring al-Qaeda terrorists responsible for 9/11. On 4 October 2001, just days before the US attacked Bin Laden's hideout in Afghanistan, the London-based *Economist* wrote that

> another sort of war is already under way, one in which journalists are already playing an important role as a conduit or filter, though not just the scribblers and broadcasters from the West. It is the propaganda war. That word has come to have a derogatory meaning, of the dissemination of untruths. In this case, America's task is (in truth) to disseminate truths, about its motives, about its intentions, about its current and past actions in Israel and Iraq, about its views of Islam. For all that, however, this part of the war promises to be no easier to win than the many other elements of the effort.[25]

At the onset of the US-led war on terrorism, both propaganda and public diplomacy emerged as significant conceptual frames of reference. Public diplomacy was used to refer to the US efforts to win hearts and minds in the global War on Terror. In particular, a new public diplomacy czarina was named in 2001, Undersecretary of State for Public Diplomacy and Public Affairs Charlotte Beers, who within a year of 9/11 rolled out a much anticipated campaign known as 'Shared Values' to attempt to communicate effectively with Muslims overseas.

In the immediate post-9/11 environment, American propaganda had taken on a Terrorism, Inc. sheen whereby global public relations and advertising techniques were being applied to the War on Terror in an effort to shift US foreign policy from a focus that was self-reflective and problem-based ('Why do they hate us?') to one that was externally oriented ('How do we reposition Brand USA?').

Charlotte Beers was not the first to attempt to reposition Brand America from a country known for its aggressive military and economic posture to one known for religious freedom and appreciation of non-Christian religions like Islam. Her tenure was marred by an expert background in advertising that was globally suspect. The Shared Values Initiative was perceived as nothing more than an advertising programme for how happy Muslim Americans were in America. What were identified by the US as televised 'mini-documentaries' that ran from October 2002 to January 2003 in parts of the Middle East and Asia were actually 90-second infomercials. Designed to illustrate free speech, entrepreneurialism, and other important cultural values of the US through personal narratives told by actual Muslim Americans, they were delivered in an environment of a drumbeat for war in Iraq and a reduction in US credibility in the world. Global public opinion surveys from the Pew Global Attitudes Survey showed that much of the world was already quite familiar with how well Muslim Americans were living. The contentious issue remained specific US policies in the Muslim and Arab world, which Shared Values, a product of the State Department, chose not to address.

The Shared Values campaign of winter 2002–3 was rolled out prominently during the holy month of Ramadan as a symbol of goodwill and acknowledgment of appreciation of religious differences. Its cultural sensitivity to the timing of the presentation did not produce any measurable improvement in how global publics perceived US foreign relations.

PROPAGANDA FOR PEACE

Propaganda is generally used as a pejorative concept in US circles, particularly given its 20th-century associations with Nazi Germany and Stalinist Russia. It wasn't until 21st-century events renewed scholarly and public interest in the topic of propaganda – 'ours versus theirs' – that many of the old negative associations were being replaced with a more balanced or at least neutral use of the term. Robert Gass and John Seiter identify five key characteristics associated with propaganda:

(1) It has a strong ideological bent and therefore does not serve a purely information 'just the facts, ma'am' function;
(2) It is agenda-driven and purposive; propagandists are not trying to be strictly neutral or objective;
(3) It is institutional in nature; practiced by organized groups like

corporations or government agencies, religious groups, terrorist cells, social movements;

(4) It involves mass persuasion campaigns and targets a mass audience and, therefore, relies on mass media to persuade audience;

(5) Its 'bad image' is based mostly on the ethics involved with mass persuasion methods used: the end results are primary and ethics merely secondary.[26]

The first four characteristics position propaganda very much within the realm of advertising, public relations, and strategic communication attempts to influence a target group. The last characteristic is what gives propaganda its bad name. Propagandists will always favour the side of the sponsor, even if that position puts the sponsor in the most favourable light vis-à-vis the target.

Debates across the political spectrum and inside and outside government circles have emerged to identify, measure, and critique what both the government and its surrogates are engaged in to inform, influence, and engage international publics. The Pentagon, not the State Department, has emerged as the leading agency in the propaganda wars. Defense Secretary Rumsfeld told the Council on Foreign Relations in February 2006 that

> for the most part, the U.S. Government still functions as a 'five and dime' store in an E-Bay world. Today we're engaged in the first war in history – unconventional and irregular as it may be – in an era of E-mails, Blogs, Cell phones, Blackberrys, Instant Messaging, Digital cameras, a global Internet with no inhibitions, Hand-held video cameras, Talk radio, 24-hour news broadcasts, Satellite television. There's never been a war fought in this environment before.[27]

Secretary of Defense Donald Rumsfeld personally authorised an information operations roadmap in 2003 to elevate the status of psychological operations, or psyops (a term linked to Cold War covert operations), in the War on Terror.[28]

While the Smith-Mundt Act prohibits foreign psyops from being operated on the American people, this prohibition on paper has led to a puzzling paradox in reality. The Bush administration very successfully used a form of domestic psyops to market the invasion of Iraq as a front in the global War on Terror. A majority of Americans polled in August 2003 believed that Saddam Hussein had taken a personal role in the attacks on 9/11.[29] To this day, some Americans still believe that Saddam had some responsibility in 9/11, but now a majority believes that the war in Iraq was not worth it, even if part of a global fight against terror. A global military strategy to 'defeat' terror is viewed increasingly as counter-intuitive to restoring America's prestige and reputation in the world as a leading light in human rights and democracy promotion. A prominent belief now in the US, widely held across the globe, is that Saddam Hussein was used as a scapegoat in the War on Terror when Bin Laden proved elusive, but this domestic conclusion followed after years of failure to find any missing weapons of mass destruction in Iraq or any intelligence that directly linked Saddam to al-Qaeda. It also followed the re-election of President Bush in 2004.

The American President, the country's chief persuader, chose to use moral legitimacy to position the superiority of the universal appeal of the American way of life and American freedom in contrast to the enemies of both led by followers of militant Islam or violent extremism:

> To confront this enemy, America and our allies have taken the offensive with the full range of our military, intelligence, and law enforcement capabilities. Yet this battle is more than a military conflict. Like the Cold War, it's an ideological struggle between two fundamentally different visions of humanity. On one side are the extremists, who promise paradise, but deliver a life of public beatings and repression of women and suicide bombings. On the other side are huge numbers of moderate men and women – including millions in the Muslim world – who believe that every human life has dignity and value that no power on Earth can take away ... The most powerful weapon in the struggle against extremism is not bullets or bombs – it is the universal appeal of freedom. Freedom is the design of our Maker, and the longing of every soul. Freedom is the best way to unleash the creativity and economic potential of a nation. Freedom is the only ordering of a society that leads to justice. And human freedom is the only way to achieve human rights.[30]

So far, the communication gap between these competing sides of humanity is growing larger, in part because what the US professes *it is* to the world does not match what *it does*. There is no question that terrorism is a threat, but it is a global threat that impacts all nations. Islam and terrorism are not integrated at the core as all the world's major religions have used terrorist tactics and as Harvard professor Louise Richardson notes, many terrorist groups have no particular religious identification. She suggests a more sensible approach to combating terrorism through recognising the 'three Rs' of terrorism: revenge, renown, and reaction. The terrorist attacks of 11 September achieved the first two, revenge and renown, by making al-Qaeda and Osama Bin Laden the Cold War equivalents of the Red Scare. The US response – military overreaction – was a terrible blunder. In declaring war on al-Qaeda, 'Americans opted to accept al-Qaeda's language of cosmic warfare at face value and respond accordingly, rather than respond to al-Qaeda based on an objective assessment of its resources and capabilities'.[31]

Al-Qaeda now overwhelms the world's leading superpower's foreign and military policies. Though al-Qaeda's core was taken out in Afghanistan and its leadership secreted to the hinterlands of Pakistan, politically it has inspired others to use similar terror tactics and empowered al-Qaeda's reputation in the propaganda wars. Instead of addressing any of the underlying motives for anger against the US that lead to such violent tactics, the President stated at the National Endowment for Democracy in 2005: 'In fact, we're not facing a set of grievances that can be soothed and addressed. We're facing a radical ideology with unalterable objectives: to enslave whole nations and intimidate the world.'[32] So far the propaganda war is favouring those radical ideologies advanced by al-Qaeda, despite US efforts to wage a war of ideas based on moral superiority.

The United States continues to set itself apart as an exemplar of human freedom but at what cost to global peace and non-violence? On 31 May 2007 the *Los Angeles Times* published a two-inch column wire report that the US 'is among the least peaceful nations in the world, ranking 96th between Yemen and Iran, according to an index of 121 countries'.[33] The Global Peace Index consists of 24 indicators of peace such as involvement in wars, access to small arms weapons, military expenditure as percentage of gross domestic product, global arms sales, and rates of incarceration – in all the US takes a leadership role. More peaceful countries show higher levels of democracy, open and more transparent governments, and higher levels of education and material well-being. One report states that

> while the US possesses many of these characteristics, its ranking was brought down by its engagement in warfare and external conflict, as well as high levels of incarceration and homicide. The nation's rank also suffered due to the large share of military expenditure from its GDP, attributed to its status as one of the world's military-diplomatic powers.[34]

How then do we reconcile the propaganda of American rhetoric with the reality of the nation's – or, at least, the government's – deeds? Lamis Andoni proposes a full inventory-taking of the place of the US in the world:

> The collision of the hijacked planes with the twin towers was an ugly metaphor of how violent confrontation has substituted for dialogue and meaningful communication. Public policy, at least in theory, is presumed to enable such communication. Yet, unless the United States reexamines its foreign policies and goals, public policy will have been reduced to propaganda that marginalizes and dehumanizes 'the other', consequently precluding meaningful dialogue and communication.[35]

A fundamental error of attribution drives much of the propaganda rhetoric of the United States, particularly from its government leaders. It is a widely held belief that non-US citizens who wish to live like Americans think as they do. In other words, the world wishes to be more like the US than not. With this comes a driving impetus, the nation carries out propaganda campaigns that include sponsoring more favourable news stories in Iraqi media sources, as if amplification of pro-US policies in a conflict region would alone turn public opinion to its favour. In essence, what results is a sentiment that the US must resort to undemocratic means (government-sponsored media) in order to promote its democracy-building agenda in Iraq. This fundamental attribution error led to the naive display that was the Shared Values Initiative. It drives much of the Al Hurra and Radio Sawa broadcasting to the Middle East where pop music and softer news are used as a backdoor means to support US policies in the region. Global communication is not just about advocating one side in a debate or delivering the best spun message of the day to a target market overseas. It is also about what the best of higher learning purports to be: to understand, to inform and to educate.

NOTES

1. Available at www.ohchr.org/english/law/pdf/ccpr.pdf.
2. As reported in the *New York Times*, 23 March 1991, A4; quoted by Herbert Schiller, in Hamid Mowlana, George Gerbner and Herbert Schiller (eds), *Triumph of the Image* (Boulder, CO: Westview Press, 1992), p. 27.
3. Available at http://www.whitehouse.gov/news/releases/2002/01/20020129-11.html.
4. Karen S. Johnson-Cartee and Gary A. Copeland, *Strategic Political Communication* (Lanham, MD: Rowman and Littlefield, 2004), p. 195.
5. Ronald W. Reagan, Address to British Parliament, 8 June 1982.
6. Reagan address to the Annual Convention of the National Association of Evangelical, 8 March 1983, http://www.ronaldreagan.com/sp_6.html.
7. Ronald W. Reagan, National Security Directive 77, 14 January 1983.
8. Cited in Wilson P. Dizard Jr, *Inventing Public Diplomacy* (Boulder, CO: Lynn Rienner Publishers, 2004), p. 201.
9. Harry Truman, Speech before the annual convention of the American Society of Newspaper Editors, April 1950.
10. Ronald W. Reagan, Address to the Nation on United States Assistance for the Nicaraguan Democratic Resistance, 24 June 1986, http://www.reagan.utexas.edu/archives/speeches/1986/62486b.htm.
11. Cited in Robert Parry, 'The Advertising Agency: how the CIA flouted the law using Madison Avenue techniques to arm-twist for the contras', *Washington Monthly*, 24, 11 November 1992.
12. Ibid.
13. http://www.whitehouse.gov/news/releases/2007/06/20070605-6.html.
14. Alex Carey, *Taking the Risk Out of Democracy* (Urbana, IL: University of Illinois Press, 1997), p. 15.
15. Frank Newport, 'One-third of Americans believe the Bible is literally true: high

inverse correlation between education and belief in a literal Bible', *Gallup News Service*, 25 May 2007.

16. Albert L. Winseman and D. Min, 'Americans have little doubt God exists: belief strong, but not monolithic', *Gallup News Service*, 13 December 2005.

17. Cited in Ewen MacAskill, 'George Bush: "God told me to end the tyranny in Iraq": President told Palestinians God also talked to him about Middle East peace', *The Guardian*, 7 October 2005.

18. George W. Bush, Address to a Joint Session of Congress and the American People, 20 September 2001.

19. Dizard, *Inventing Public Diplomacy*, p. 200.

20. Editorial, 'U.S.I.A.'s Little List', *New York Times*, 20 February 1984.

21. Dizard, *Inventing Public Diplomacy*, p. 201.

22. Alvin A. Snyder, *Warriors of Disinformation: American Propaganda, Soviet Lies, and the Winning of the Cold War* (New York, NY: Arcade Publishing, 1995), p. xiv.

23. For a history and critique of the US Information Agency, see Nancy Snow, *Propaganda, Inc.: Selling America's Culture to the World*, 2nd edn (New York, NY: Seven Stories Press, 2002).

24. William Jefferson Clinton, International Public Information (IPI) Presidential Decision Directive 68, 30 April 1999.

25. Unsigned Editorial, 'The Propaganda War', *The Economist*, 4 October 2001.

26. Robert H. Gass and John S. Seiter, *Persuasion, Social Influence and Compliance Gaining* (Boston, MA: Allyn and Bacon, 2003), pp. 11–12.

27. Donald Rumsfeld, Speech Delivered to the Council on Foreign Relations, Harold Pratt House, New York City, 17 February 2006.

28. For a background on psyops, see the online report by Major Ed Rouse (retired U.S. Army) at http://www.psywarrior.com/psyhist.html.

29. Max Rodenbeck, 'How Terrible is it', *The New York Times Review of Books*, 53(19), 30 November 2006, 3.

30. George W. Bush, Remarks at Conference on Democracy, Security in Prague, Czech Republic, 5 June 2007.

31. Rodenbeck, 'How Terrible is it', p. 6.

32. George W. Bush, Keynote Address at the National Endowment for Democracy, 6 October 2005.

33. 'America ranks low in "Peace Index"', Times Wire Reports, *Los Angeles Times*, 31 May 2007.

34. 'First Global Peace Index ranks 121 countries: Norway tops list, U.S. comes in at 96', *PR Newswire*, Washington, DC, 30 May 2007.

35. Lamis Andoni, 'Deeds speak louder than Words', *The Washington Quarterly*, Spring 2002, 86.

PART 2
SOCIETY

7. CONTEMPORARY SOCIAL CRITICISM

Elisabeth Lasch-Quinn

Alexis de Tocqueville, whose great work *Democracy in America* (1835–40) captured with such intricacy and eloquence the hopes and dreams of the new Republic just a generation after its founding, defined democracy as 'a habit of the heart'.[1] Despite their important differences and shortcomings, the founders' communal spirit breathed life into the laws, governmental structures, and social forms of the new nation, thus affecting the social, cultural, political and intellectual experience of Americans down to the early 21st century. Including, but not reducible to, a particular political system or set of social arrangements – from enfranchisement and representative government to rights, freedom, and justice – the notion of a democratic republic involved a sensibility, a disposition, or, one might say, a pre-disposition.

Concerns arise daily from across the political spectrum about how predisposed Americans remain to democracy. Observers point to a widening gap between rich and poor unheard of since the Gilded Age, corporate dominance of political campaigns and the airwaves, low levels of voting and civic engagement, an ethos of extreme individualism that values self-gratification over commitments to others, corruption in government and business, the decline of the family and civil society institutions, a crisis of morality and civility, and many other symptoms of a society at the breaking point. What is more, while once reformers might have interpreted these problems as cause for a renewal of ideals and efforts, many contemporary thinkers, critics and commentators – and politicians – raise more funda-mental questions about the ideals themselves. They ask: are we witnessing the fall from greatness of this country and its aspirations? The perception of political exhaustion is palpable. Some conservatives raise doubts about democracy itself and even on the political left – traditionally the party of the common person – a sense of despair is apparent in the grumblings about whether an elite might be necessary after all, given the political climate of the early 21st century.

One cannot help but wonder whether the sense that the nation has exhausted all possibilities is inextricably linked to the contemporary state of American intellectual life. As other authors in this volume note, including Kevin Mattson and Martin Halliwell, the crisis in contemporary intellectual circles has been widely noted. Are we missing some crucial ingredient – a particular voice or set of voices – that might help us face our current crises and envision new, more promising ways to move on from here?

Russell Jacoby's *The Last Intellectuals: American Culture in the Age of Academe* (1987) argued most definitively in the mid-1980s that such was the case. In this influential book, Jacoby raised a loud alarm over the failure of American life to yield a generation of writers who had as much intellectual heft and inclination to attend to issues of broad public concern as the one that had come of age in the early and mid-20th century. Jacoby's book has recently drawn renewed attention as a flurry of commentators have addressed the issue of whether we have lost touch with a vital tradition in the intellectual culture of the United States.

GOLDEN AGE THINKING

Outrage, concern, alarm – these can be easily dispatched today, nearly regardless of the subject, often with charges of nostalgia. Even a hint at what was valuable about an earlier practice gets summarily dismissed as 'golden age' thinking. Perceptions of moral or community decline, and other worries about contemporary life, draw invective by those across the political spectrum who cannot abide the idea that the current way of American life may not represent progress. The charge of nostalgia defuses much current social criticism by making it look the quaint and irrelevant musings of a curmudgeon.

One of the more thoughtful salvos into the debate over the current state of social criticism was a July 2004 essay 'The democratization of cultural criticism' in *The Chronicle of Higher Education* by the intellectual historian George Cotkin. While worth taking seriously, his approach risks discounting the very tradition he celebrates, thus raising some questions about the best-intentioned defenses of the contemporary scene.

In this essay, which garnered much attention, Cotkin portrays critics of the state of contemporary intellectual life as standing in a 'line of true designated mourners pining for the glory days of criticism'.[2] Putting aside Wallace Shawn's 1997 play *The Desingated Mourner* to which the article refers, even the most finely wrought arguments appear to Cotkin as merely more stock

American 'narratives of declension'. He calls such arguments 'misplaced, self-serving, and historically inaccurate' and concludes that they are 'difficult to prove'.[3]

Unfortunately, things that are difficult to prove can also be difficult to disprove. Cotkin takes up this task anyway, mainly by mentioning the names of prominent writers like Harold Bloom, John Updike and the late Susan Sontag as well as still extant publications and forums, including Internet blogs. This approach adds to the examination of the issue at hand by providing a much-needed reminder that intellectual life continues, albeit often in the interstices of the mainstream culture. Literary and political reviews and magazines like *The New Republic*, *The New York Review of Books*, *Salmagundi*, *Commentary*, *Dissent*, *First Things*, *Raritan*, *Wilson Quarterly* and several others continue in the tradition of serious public discussion and engaged debate. But their continued contemporary relevance often seems in spite of the larger culture. The loss of the *Partisan Review* (1934–2003), for instance, an organ of nearly unparalleled significance in the history of the nation's intellectual life, gives one pause, as does the closing of the shorter-lived *Public Interest* (1965–2005). But here Cotkin thinks a longing for the dynamism and community represented by the *Partisan Review* editors and regular contributors simply marks one as hopelessly retrograde. He faults the illustrious writers and critics gathered around that magazine for failing to recognise 'what was new and exciting on the culture horizon in the 1960s and after', becoming defensive and irrelevant in the face of new trends arising in the 1960s such as Pop Art and happenings. In place of decline, Cotkin sees democratisation, with new voices and intellectual energy in abundance.

The most glaring problem with this tack is that it does not engage the points made by the original arguments Cotkin seeks to refute. Those who lament the current state of intellectual life have clarified up front that they do not mean there is no worthwhile intellectual work going on, but rather that the larger framework of understanding in which the social critic's vocation made sense has nearly vanished. Changes have clearly occurred. The rise of celebrity culture has altered notions of achievement as the legitimate source of fame. Such developments in popular culture have tarnished attempts to appeal to standards of morality and aesthetics as elitist. An orientation toward self and individual identity lends much writing an overly idiosyncratic or personal inflection, which often leads to writers sidestepping issues of public relevance and importance.[4] Academic and public policy culture encourages hyper-specialisation, mystification and an arcane prose style. Niche marketing – the desperate urge to sell anything, anywhere, to anyone – appeals to all possible media consumers, no matter how abhorrent the sought after content might be. Postmodern relativism, for many, makes attempts to cultivate taste and judgment appear suspect or impossible.

CRITICAL CONDITIONS

In *The Last Intellectuals*, Russell Jacoby wrote that 'the proposition of a missing generation [of intellectuals] does not malign individuals'.[5] Rather what concerns him is tracing the variety of factors that compromised the 'vitality of a 'public culture' that gives public intellectuals a sense of vocation and the basis of a relationship to readers. Suburbanisation, the expansion of colleges and universities, and the rise of an obfuscating academic prose style separated writers from a shared intellectual world rooted in a particular place and cordoned off intellectuals from the public. Likewise, Sven Birkerts is concerned with broad developments affecting intellectual life apart from the achievements of particular writers. In a spring 2004 *Bookforum* article, 'Critical Condition', Birkerts refers to *Partisan Review* as an 'emblem of the kind of intellectual/cultural cohesion that was once possible', but he also detects in the early 21st century a 'whole systemic ecology of things, by which I mean the connections among writers, publishers, and readers, not to mention the vast influence systems of academia on the one hand and entertainment media on the other'.[6]

By offering up names of writers who today still uphold ideals and practices we associate with earlier intellectuals like Lionel Trilling, Irving Howe and Hannah Arendt, Cotkin bypasses these deeper critiques of the changed structures and tone of intellectual life. One interesting dimension of this approach is that it must ignore the actual views expressed by some who function as exemplars in his happy tale. For instance, Harold Bloom offers a drastically different rendition of the state of things when he writes of 'the shocking process of dumbing down our cultural life'.[7]

Taking the debate as more than a shell game immediately raises two issues which it might help us to separate, although they are fused in both Cotkin's essay and those he seeks to refute: intellectual community, institutions and structures on the one hand, and the tone of criticism or nature and quality of writing itself on the other. Briefly, it seems worth asking why there is an outcry about the decline of intellectual community at this time. It is of at least passing interest that Birkerts, contributor of scores of reviews in prominent journals over the last 30 years, speaks of many intellectuals' 'terrible vacuum feeling of not mattering, not connecting, of not being heard' and 'a dispiriting sense of isolation'.[8] Serious intellectuals are practically gasping for air, living on the margins of academia or edged out altogether, often lacking engaged editors who are interested in their books for more than potential profits, falling between the cracks of the pre-programmed ideological perspectives of various periodicals, or into the chasm between high-stakes entertainment markets and esoteric special-interest scholarship. What Birkerts describes as the lack of 'a sense that there is any gathering place' affects more than writers' morale. The absence of a realm in which independent standards of judgment might flourish apart from bureaucratic or market imperatives influences the whole culture. The university, at its best, has traditionally provided such an alternative, but intellectual life within universities has been compromised by the institutional capitulation to business models, together with pressures for intellectual conformity (one way or another) in an increasingly polarised political scene. Other such traditions historically provided a counterweight to outside pressures, from salons and lyceums to urban bohemias and private households – and today some Internet publications and informal communications spring from this urge. But the lack of face-to-face contact limits the degree to which the Internet can stand in for a real community.

Regarding the tone or quality of intellectual production, Cotkin has little to say. He does finally point to one small blemish on his otherwise rosy portrait, when he points to the confession of overly personal details by recent commentators. Cotkin grants that 'there are excesses aplenty today', but to see such confessional writing as a slip or an excess is far fetched.[9] Interestingly, this propensity for first-person digression is one of the major points novelist and critic Dale Peck levels at Sven Birkerts. In 'Critical Condition' Birkerts delivered a piercing critique of the tone of much social criticism today, drawing an especially compelling contrast between an older mode of writing about books and ideas – the 'plain style' in writing, 'narrative confidence', 'steady assertion of judgment' – and the newer irony of postmodernism that makes 'straightforward declaration' seem old-fashioned and 'exposed'.[10] Birkerts weakens what is otherwise a strong case for the style of the literary moderns when he obsesses about what he thinks is a central problem of criticism today, the gratuitous insult or 'snark'. For one thing, as Cotkin rightly points out, the New York Intellectuals of the mid-20th century were hardly immune from harsh judgment and pointed attack – to say nothing of vicious infighting. For another, Birkerts has in mind Dale Peck, graciously admitting in the *Bookforum* piece that he had heard that Peck had a searing attack on him in the works. Peck's word choice is clearly excessive but it is surely as much in the service of reading, writing and thinking as Birkerts's argument. As Peck points out in his book *Hatchet Jobs* (2004), the most passionate criticism often originates from a basic level of respect, from the notion that a work is worth taking seriously: 'Thus my sharpest barbs and most inhospitable *ad hominems* tend to be directed at writers I genuinely admire'.[11]

ENGAGED CRITICISM

While Birkerts explains away open insult in psychological terms (the rage of not mattering) and economic ones (a desperate bid for attention and thus sales), it is also important to recall that great criticism comes in many forms and in the most engaged work passions run high. The loss of the art of argument, as social critic Christopher Lasch pointed out in *The Revolt of the Elites* (1994), means that it is increasingly impossible to disagree and debate.

Genuine attempts to put forth points of view that differ with the received orthodoxy – or even with our friends in casual conversation – can draw anything from defensiveness and ire to stony silence. We have lost the sense of argument as something good. While *ad hominems* and other outright insults should be ruled out of order in most civil and friendly debates (although such insults have been common in the culture wars since the early 1990s, as Kevin Mattson discusses in this volume), and it would be a tremendous boon to contemporary intellectual exchange to retrieve the lost art of argument, if forced to choose, Peck's searing assessment of the state of letters in this country is preferable to nothing at all.

One last matter nearly always falls by the wayside in discussions of the changed institutions and tone of intellectual culture: content. Here Cotkin captures something troubling about the elegiac reminiscence – its tendency to cast the problems of intellectual life as inevitable, the result of a permanent change. On his side though, the dismissal of concern speaks of a similar inexorability. Both points of view show signs of complacency. On the one hand, we get a sense of how writers used to gather and write in more fruitful ways, and on the other, we learn that intellectual life is alive and well. Neither is a call to action.

We could leave the debate at this point if it really did not matter – or if it only mattered to intellectuals themselves. But if we believe that the work of social critics has broader public relevance, it becomes clear how pressing are the issues involved. In the mid-1960s, Philip Rieff spoke of culture as the system of symbols, held together by a common commitment and faith, that makes our way of life intelligible to ourselves.[12] If intelligibility was ever needed, it is now. One of the most glaring differences between the *Partisan Review* writers and so many contemporary critics is the current tendency to shy away from the largest questions of politics and meaning. Part of what made, and still makes, those 20th-century writers so compelling is that the content of their work was irresistibly interesting and significant, having ramifications for the understanding of issues beyond any one empirical setting or individual. What was ultimately most distinctive about them was not so much how they lived and wrote, but *what they said*. They are responsible for taking a bold, dissenting stand against Stalinism before most people were at all aware of why that was needed. Many of them continued to hold to principle on other major issues, even when unpopular. This willingness to be unpopular, to stand out, to be a lone wolf howling at danger, to dissent – not to be contrarian for its own sake but to dissent out of heartfelt conviction based on observation – is the very foundation of genuine intellectual activity. Intellectual courage is the only thing that can restore credibility to a much-distrusted vocation. The triumph of advertising and public relations, identity politics and narcissistic confession – to name just a few factors involved – have not only helped erode the art of argument and the public's trust in writers, but the very language itself.

The readers, finally, are a crucial part of the story. Public intellectuals absolutely rely on an interested public. The readership for earlier writers was comprised of educated individuals across the political spectrum and from every walk of life, from law and medicine and beyond. The crisis in the humanities means that college graduates have no longer read anything in common. Some kind of shared body of knowledge or familiarity with works and questions is an essential prerequisite for a public intellectual culture. The increased dominance of the market in all aspects of life has brought a fragmentation of the reading public. An ethic of individual self-interest and emotional expression prevails and, as philosopher Alasdair MacIntyre demonstrates, this means that the only claim to an argument's validity is personal inclination.[13] No common culture is possible under conditions in which every statement is taken – and meant – personally.

Strangely, Cotkin reads a remarkably optimistic message into Wallace Shawn's play, *The Designated Mourner* (1997), suggesting that it is not all lamentation, for 'not all of what has been lost is to be mourned'.[14] Even taking Shawn's play (adapted for film by the British dramatist David Hare in 1998) completely at face value shows us a terrifying scenario in which a way of life characterised by intellectual sociability around the household of a revered literary figure gives way to what appears to be government-sanctioned violence and terror of such a magnitude that private life – as well as the life of the mind – is abolished. The only mitigating source of hope is to be found at very end of the play. The designated mourner realises that a 'whole tribe' had vanished: 'everyone on earth who could read John Donne was now dead'.[15] Yet, the designated mourner revels in what is left, from the light and the flowers to the sky and the breeze. It is an eerie celebration indeed given what appears to be the total collapse of the social world.

'Narratives of declension', yes, have been around since the Puritans. Far from some kind of dispensable complaint, however, they have offered some of the most piercing, sustained and heartfelt (one could say loving) critiques of American ways. Against Cotkin, it could be argued that they are all that has separated the nation from total collapse so far. Intellectual work matters; ideas have consequences and live on in culture. In Cotkin's terms, they may be what help us rein in our worst excesses. Rather than calling on us to throw up our arms in despair, they may be our only source of hope, the sole indication that our ideals have not died.

Of the many problems faced by the nation, the loss of hope may be its greatest. It is worth remembering Benjamin Franklin's caustic reply to the question of what kind of government we were to have: 'A republic, if you can keep it'. Together with their revolutionary ideals, the framers of the Constitution expressed many reservations, worries and doubts. Their enthusiasm was tempered by humility and awareness of human limitations. In their notion of republicanism, self-government entailed active participation, virtue and vigilance against corruption and tyranny. Franklin went so far in 1787 (just before the signing of the final draft of the US Constitution) as to warn that the tendency is that 'the people shall become so corrupted as to need despotic Government, being incapable of any other'.[16]

A PUBLIC PHILOSOPHY

Social critics have played a crucial role thus far in this larger task of keeping the American Republic. At their best, they tap into the practice of publicly engaged scholarship in their dedication both to academic excellence and innovative study and to outward-looking engagement in the public realm. This interlacing of the high standards of intellectual activity and consideration of matters of broader public concern characterises both the prodigious contribution of the founding generation and the tradition of the public intellectual, particularly in the 20th century, including thinkers such as John Dewey, Walter Lippman, Lionel Trilling, Reinhold Niebuhr, Alfred Kazin, Ralph Ellison, Daniel Patrick Moynihan and Hannah Arendt, to name just a few examples. Several late 20th-century trends, including the tendency of many academic scholars to address just one small professional subfield, worked against this tradition, but there are many signs of a resurgence of interest in the vital connection between scholarship and broader public questions.[17]

The émigré intellectual Hannah Arendt wrote in 1951 that 'the perplexity of laws in free societies is that they only tell what one should not, but never what one should do'.[18] Only by keeping alive the tradition of free and open inquiry and deep learning, the ideal of the liberal arts education, can we call on the cultural tradition as a resource to help us discuss, debate and deliberate over the multitude of issues that we face. The larger question – how we live together, broadly speaking – is the question of the public philosophy. In *Democracy's Discontent: America in Search of a Public Philosophy* (1996), the political philosopher Michael Sandel has written: 'By public philosophy, I mean the political theory implicit in our practice, the assumptions about citizenship and freedom that inform our public life'.[19] Sandel and others worry that the loss of a sense of the nation's underlying commonalities makes disagreement threatening rather than fruitful. Mary Ann Glendon, Amitai Etzioni and Jean Bethke Elshtain, among others, have made a compelling appeal for moving beyond a rights-based ethos that emphasises individual differences and entitlements to one based on a sense of common commitments and shared principles.[20] Their work is properly seen as social criticism as well as public philosophy.

The richest works to appear in the last 20 years are those written by critics whose ideas are not just billed as new and fresh, as per so many jacket cover blurbs, but are in fact new and fresh. Writers such as Philip Rieff and Wendell Berry, for instance, have offered sustained examinations of our times that fail to fall neatly into the polarised, predictable, and simplistic left/right divisions that are such a glaring fact of today's political discourse. Perhaps their work will inspire others to take on the kind of perspective that is at once more nuanced and more all-embracing than most recent writing about society.

A revived social criticism is not a luxury but a need. Only the trenchant work of serious intellectuals who devote themselves to appraising our times in all of their complexity and import has the potential to renew the discussion of the American public philosophy, resuscitate democratic politics and public discourse, and retrieve – as well as newly formulate – the ethical foundations of the nation's common life. It can potentially nurture independence of mind, classical standards of excellence, interdisciplinary collaboration, and broad-minded perspectives and become a significant presence, and even a force, in American intellectual and public life.

Here and there, even with just a small percentage of the ink being spilled, there is piercing work going on in the early 21st century within and outside of academe in many fields and on many topics. A vast resurgence of interest in the Republic's founding in particular and the meaning of democracy in general has surrounded the heated debates around a range of issues, from the concern over the proper role of the Supreme Court, originalism versus the notion of a living constitution, the role of religion in the polity, communitarianism versus liberalism to immigration and Americanisation, and many others. The time is ripe for a renewal of social criticism as many seek a renewal of the republican principles on which the nation was founded and a revitalisation of democratic politics toward a sense of common purpose and dedication to the decent and open society and the common good.

EL-Q

*   *   *

As one of the earliest and most influential European commentators on American thought and customs, Alexis de Tocqueville wrote with real excitement about the prospects of democracy in the new nation. Recent commentators have tried to rescue the democratic possibilities that Tocqueville detected – both from the threat of postmodern relativism and increased national security after 9/11. For example, in *The American Evasion of Philosophy* (1989), the African American scholar Cornel West traces a tradition of intellectual thought back to Ralph Waldo Emerson (who wrote contemporaneously with Tocqueville) in West's attempt to revive American public philosophy at a moment of 'widespread disenchantment with the traditional image of philosophy as a transcendental mode of enquiry'.[21] In the same year that Francis Fukuyama expounded his 'end of history' thesis, West argued passionately for the need to write history and the subject back into public discourse; the re-establishment of 'an Emersonian culture of creative democracy' might be a utopian goal, but West argues that it is one that should stimulate us to rediscover moral and social value at a time when public philosophy is in jeopardy.[22] West saw himself as writing in 'the

American grain', as did the late Richard Rorty who, three years before September 11, in *Achieving Our Country* (1998) identified a similar need for the renewal of public thought as a form of self-reflexive 'national pride': a necessary ingredient if the promises of the early Republic are ever to be fulfilled.[23]

As Wilfred McClay argues in the next essay in this section, another late-20th-century thinker, Robert Bellah, revived Tocqueville's phrase 'habit of the heart' in the mid-1980s to renew moral vitality at the intersection of civic and religious life. Within the context of 'post-secular America', McClay explores both the possibilities and problems of civil religion in the last few years, at a time when the separate functions of church and state have become increasingly blurred. These secular trends are nowhere more apparent than in debates about globalisation, as Howard Brick demonstrates in the third essay of this section. Brick argues that globalising trends have been on the rise since the 1970s, but it is only since 9/11 that the threat of globalisation to national and local customs has been keenly felt. Debates about the benefits and ills of globalisation shift our perspective on American social thought onto a world stage, helping us to look beyond the nation state to broader principles of cosmopolitanism and humanitarianism which cannot be territorialised. While globalisation may have opened the door to a postnational world, as both McClay and Brick demonstrate the rise of nationalism – in both its good and bad forms – is a defining condition of early 21st-century life.

The other three essays in this section turn our attention to the place of science in contemporary American society, particularly debates about whether science plays too large or too little a role in shaping political policy and social values. George W. Bush's opposition to the development of stem cell research, deriving from his Christian pro-life convictions, is explored in Christopher Thomas Scott's essay on medical science. Scott looks to recent medical trends in which ethical, scientific and civic threads have become intricately woven, arguing that the price of halting medical research might be a huge one. However, the risk that scientific breakthroughs can never be unlearnt leads us to think about the place of technology as both the bane and blessing of contemporary American life. In the last two essays in this section, Carroll Pursell investigates these tensions between technology as an agent of destruction – dramatically illustrated in the multiple aerial attacks on 9/11 – and the preserver of life as clean technologies counteract the pollution and detritus that, as novelist Don DeLillo detected as early as 1984, are the 'dark side of consumer consciousness'.[24] As John Wills elaborates, if there is one pressing issue which stresses the need for a renewed public philosophy it is the environment. Global warming is a planetary concern – evident in the devastation of the tsunami in the Indian Ocean in December 2004. But it is also a problem in the American grain, with violently erratic weather conditions across the Atlantic and Gulf of Mexico – none more so than

Hurricane Katrina in September 2005 – calling both for long-term national strategies and a series of hard international choices on fossil fuel and carbon emissions. If American social criticism is under strain in the early 21st century, this section indicates that in the fields of religion, globalisation, medicine, technology and the environment are a set of contemporary concerns that require our serious attention.

MH/CM

NOTES

Parts of this essay initially appeared in the State of American Intellectual Life, response to George Cotkin's 'The democratization of cultural criticism', H-IDEAS Virtual Symposium, 28–9 April 2005.

1. Robert Bellah used Tocqueville's phrase 'habit of the heart' for the title of his widely read exploration of late 20th-century American values: see Robert N. Bellah, *Habits of the Heart: Individualism and Commitment in American Life* (New York, NY: Harper and Row, 1985).
2. George Cotkin, 'The Democratization of Cultural Criticism', *The Chronicle of Higher Education*, 50(43), 2 July 2004, B8, http://chronicle.com/free/v50/i43/43b00801.htm.
3. Ibid.
4. In literary terms, shortly after 9/11, James Woods criticised American writers for abandoning their historical roots in social commentary. For Woods, what was lacking in contemporary American writing in 2001 was the grander ambition of the novel: the recording, extrapolation and diagnosis of social reality. This tentativeness, an unwillingness to make up what cannot be known or felt directly, might, suggested Woods, be forced into more combative open ground by the events of September 11 through the recognition that 'whatever the novel gets up to, the "culture" can always get up to something bigger': James Wood, 'Tell me how does it feel?', *Guardian Unlimited*, 6 October 2001, http://books.guardian.co.uk/departments/generalfiction/story/0,,563868,00.html.
5. Russell Jacoby, *The Last Intellectuals: American Culture in the Age of Academe* (New York, NY: Basic Books, 1987), p. 4.
6. Sven Birkerts, 'Critical Condition. Reading, writing and reviewing – an old schooler looks back', *Bookforum*, Spring 2004, http://www.bookforum.com/archive/spr_04/birkerts.html.
7. Harold Bloom, 'Dumbing down American Readers', *Boston Globe*, 24 September 2003, http://www.boston.com/news/globe/editorial_opinion/oped/articles/2003/09/24/dumbing_down_american_readers/.
8. Birkerts, 'Critical Condition'.
9. Cotkin, 'The democratization of cultural criticism'.
10. Birkerts, 'Critical Condition'.
11. Dale Peck, *Hatchet Jobs* (New York, NY: The New Press, 2004), p. 219.
12. See Philip Rieff, *The Triumph of the Therapeutic: Uses of Faith after Freud* (New York, NY: Chatto and Windus, 1966).

13. See Alasdair MacIntyre, *After Virtue* (Notre Dame, IN: University of Notre Dame Press, 1981) and *Ethics and Politics: Selected Essays*, Vol. 2 (Cambridge: Cambridge University Press, 2002).
14. Cotkin, 'The Democratization of Cultural Criticism'.
15. Wallace Shawn, *The Designated Mourner* (New York, NY: Dramatist's Play Service, [1996] 2003), p. 99.
16. Benjamin Franklin, 'On the Federal Constitution', 17 September 1787, http://www.usconstitution.net/franklin.html.
17. For a discussion of the development of humanities scholarship since World War II see David Hollinger (ed.), *The Humanities and the Dynamics of Inclusion since World War II* (Baltimore, MD: Johns Hopkins University Press, 2006).
18. Hannah Arendt, *The Origins of Totalitarianism* (New York, NY: Schocken, [1951] 2004), p. 467.
19. Michael Sandel, *Democracy's Discontent: America in Search of a Public Philosophy* (New York, NY: Belknap Press, 1996), p. 4.
20. See, for example, Mary Ann Glendon, *Rights Talk: The Impoverishment of Political Discourse* (New York, NY: Free Press, 1993); Amitai Etzioni, *The New Golden Rule: Community and Morality in a Democratic Society* (New York, NY: Basic Books, 1998) and *The Common Good* (Cambridge: Polity, 2004); and Jean Bethke Elshtain, *Who Are We? Critical Reflections and Hopeful Possibilities. Politics and Ethical Discourse* (Grand Rapids, MI: Eerdmans, 2000).
21. Cornel West, *The American Evasion of Philosophy* (Madison, WI: University of Wisconsin Press, 1989), p. 3.
22. Ibid., p. 239.
23. See Richard Rorty, *Achieving Our Country* (Cambridge, MA: Harvard University Press, 1998).
24. Don DeLillo, *White Noise* (London: Picador, 1984), p. 258.

8. RELIGION IN POST-SECULAR AMERICA

Wilfred M. McClay

As with so much else in American society at the outset of the 21st century, what one thinks about the present and future status of religion in American life depends a great deal on what interpretive stance or narrative framework one brings to the subject. Who would have imagined, even two decades ago, the kinds of debates we would see roiling the post-9/11 world, at a moment when the immense motivational power of religion has roared back into view, as potent as a force of nature? At the dawning of the 21st century, the secular worldview, whose triumph once seemed so inevitable, now seems stalled, and even to be losing ground, or being superseded. Religion, in forms both traditional and novel, both quietly civil and wildly revolutionary, seems resurgent. The dream of a fully secularised public life, a condition that Richard John Neuhaus memorably labelled as 'the naked public square', seems to have lost whatever slender claims it may have had on the American imagination.[1]

To provide a full account of the range of reasons for this 'post-secular' direction in American religious sensibility and commitment would take us far beyond the concerns of this essay. It should be stated, however, that for many western European observers the continuing American commitment to religion is a matter of great perplexity, running counter to so many of the most powerful secularising trends around the world. Perhaps, as the American intellectual historian David Hollinger has suggested, this is one sense – in its ongoing commitment to religious belief and practice – in which the United States *is* unarguably an exceptional nation.[2] But certainly one central cause of the persistence of religion has been the perceived failure of secularist modernism, specifically its inability to provide an adequate framework for the great mass of Americans to lead meaningful, morally coherent lives.[3] It is not just a matter of religion's stubborn unwillingness to go gentle into secularism's good night. Religion's new lease of life stems from the inability of its would-be displacers to fill its shoes.

Of course, merely to mention the events of 9/11 is, for many Americans and Europeans, to present in the most vivid way possible the reasons to fear this development, and seek to reverse it. The recent flood of polemical popular works advocating an exuberant and unapologetic 'new atheism', produced by writers such as Christopher Hitchens, Richard Dawkins and Sam Harris, certainly are indicative of a counter-current to post-secular developments.[4] The critiques are nothing if not sweeping. Religion, declared Hitchens, 'poisons everything'. But for all the relative marketing success of these pro-atheism tracts, they seem to have had only limited influence, preaching to the already converted while stimulating a whole new generation of Christian apologetics.[5] For better or worse, they do not speak for or to the outlook of the overwhelming majority of Americans, whose views and commitments seem, for better or worse, to be far more tangled, ambivalent and confused.

Indeed, one could make a far stronger case that in America it is secularism, rather than religion, whose power is ebbing away – and that this development should not be regarded, *prima facie*, as a bad thing. Religious liberty, after all, was the very first of the liberties enumerated in the Constitution's Bill of Rights. Small wonder, then, that religion has responded to the challenge of secularism with a vigorous defence of its place in life both public and private – a role that, whatever one thinks of it, shows no sign of going away quietly. The militant secularists appear to have overreached. Atheists have always had a compelling case to present to the American people when they argue from the priority of the old Baptist commitment to 'soul liberty', meaning individual freedom of conscience, over and against the coercions of any religious establishment, formal or informal. 'Freedom from religion' in *that* sense is widely accepted. But when they take matters further, and insist that because religion 'poisons everything' its public expression should be discouraged and ridiculed, if not actively suppressed, then their position becomes eccentric and marginal, and pushes the mainstream back toward a more religion-friendly centre.

But that is not all. There is a growing sense that religion may have new roles to play in the years to come. In this view, it has become an indispensable force for the upholding of human dignity and moral order in a postmodern world dominated by voracious state bureaucracies and sprawling trans-national business corporations, which are neither effectively accountable to national law nor effectively answerable to well-established codes of behaviour. In a word, it is a necessary corrective to the dehumanising effects of technocratic modernity, an avenue of escape from the iron cage. As the sociologist Jose Casanova argues, modernity runs the risk of being 'devoured by the inflexible, inhuman logic of its own creations', unless it restores a 'creative dialogue' with the very religious traditions it has so successfully challenged.[6] Perhaps no event in the past quarter-century has given more credibility to this view than the profound influence of the Roman Catholic Church in promoting the downfall of Soviet Communism in parts of the former Soviet empire; and no modern religious leader was more keenly alert to the public uses of his faith than the late Pope John Paul II.[7] But even on strictly American grounds, there is plentiful evidence that publicly vigorous religious beliefs and practices have survived all efforts to suppress or supersede them, and are now in the ascendant.

One can gauge the extent of this shift not only by recourse to Gallup, Roper and Barna polls but by examining shifts in public discourse. Ever since the election of Jimmy Carter as President in 1976, the taboos on public expression of religious sentiments by American political leaders seem to have been steadily eroding. The signs of desecularisation are amply reflected, too, in a long list of developments in the realms of law and governance, too many to rehearse for this occasion. The overwhelming support accorded the Religious Freedom Restoration Act (RFRA) of 1993, although it would later be overturned by the Supreme Court, was highly significant in this regard. So too was the landmark 1996 welfare-reform legislation during the Clinton presidency, which includes an option for 'charitable choice', permitting the contracting-out of public social-welfare services to openly religious organisations. As always, a significant proportion of flashpoints have clustered around issues relating to schooling, where there has been some levelling of the playing field as regards the competition between religious and non-religious schools – and, as in the current court cases regarding posting of the Ten Commandments or the sanctioning of student-led prayers at graduations and football games, there has been movement toward a reassertion of religious expression in public institutions. Not all these measures succeeded. But the trend seems unmistakable.

And some things have never changed, even with secularism's impressive victories in the federal courts and halls of government and academe. Prayers are still uttered at the commencement of Congressional sessions. God's name appears on American currency and in the oaths Americans take in court. Religion chaplains are still employed by the Congress and the armed services. The tax-exempt status of religious institutions remains intact. Avowed belief in God remains astonishingly pervasive, and church and synagogue attendance rates remain high, at least relative to other Western countries. Whatever one makes of these phenomena, the point is that the United States is very far from being an entirely secular country, one sanitised of any form of public sanction for religion.[8]

RELIGIOUS QUESTIONS AFTER 9/11

This does not mean that Americans have come to any kind of agreement about what forms of public expression they endorse. That fact became clear in the immediate wake of the terrorist attacks of 9/11, when Americans suddenly found themselves faced with an unexpected choice between radically different perspectives on the proper place of religion in modern Western society. The alternative perspectives were not new. But the urgency with which they were felt, and the intensity with which they were articulated, were. Coming at a moment when Americans had been gradually rethinking many settled precedents regarding religion and public life, the 9/11 attacks seemed to give a sharper edge to the questions being asked.

For many observers, there was only one logical conclusion to be drawn from these horrifyingly destructive acts, perpetrated by fanatically committed adherents to a militant and demanding form of Islam: that *all* religions, and particularly the great monotheisms, constitute an ever-present menace to the peace, order and individual liberty of modern Western civil life. Far from embracing the growing sentiment that the US government should be willing to grant religion a greater role in public life, such observers took 9/11 as clear evidence of just how serious a mistake this would be. The events of 9/11 seemed to confirm the contention that religion *per se* is incorrigibly toxic, and that it breeds irrationality, demonisation of others, irreconcilable division and implacable conflict. If we learned nothing else from 9/11, in this view, we should at least have relearned the hard lessons that the West learned in its own bloody religious wars at the dawn of the modern age. The essential character of the modern West, and its greatest achievement, is its secularism. To settle for anything less is to invite disaster. If there still has to be a vestigial presence of religion here and there in the world, let it be kept private and kept on a short leash. Is not Islamist terror the ultimate example of a 'faith-based initiative'? How many more examples are needed?

To be sure, most of those who put forward this position were already predisposed to do so. They found in 9/11 a pretext for restating settled views, rather than a catalyst for forming fresh ones. More importantly, though, theirs was far from being the only response to 9/11, and nowhere near being the dominant one. Many other Americans had a completely opposite response, feeling that such a heinous and frighteningly nihilistic act, so far beyond the usual psychological categories, could only be explained by resort to an older, pre-secular vocabulary, one that included the numinous concept of 'evil'. There were earnest post-9/11 efforts, such as the philosopher Susan Neiman's thoughtful book *Evil in Modern Thought* (2002), to appropriate the concept for secular use, independent of its religious roots.[9] But such efforts have been largely unconvincing. If 9/11 was taken by some as an indictment of the religious mind's fanatical tendencies, it was taken with equal justification by others as an illustration of the secular mind's explanatory poverty. If there was incorrigible fault to be found, in this latter view, it was less in the structure of the world's great monotheisms than in the labyrinth of the human heart – a fault about which those religions, particularly Christianity, have always had a great deal to say.

Even among those willing to invoke the concept of evil in its proper religious habitat, however, there was disagreement. A handful of prominent evangelical Christian leaders, notably the late Jerry Falwell and Pat Robertson, were unable to resist comparing the falling towers of lower Manhattan to the Biblical towers of Babel, and saw in the 9/11 attacks God's judgment upon the moral and social evils of contemporary America, and the withdrawal of His favour and protection.[10] In that sense, they were the mirror opposites of their foes, seizing on 9/11 as a pretext for re-proclaiming the toxicity of American secularism. But their view was not typical, and in fact, was so widely regarded as reckless and ill-considered that, despite their later apologies, its expression permanently damaged their credibility.

In any event, the more common public reaction in America was something different from either side's declaration of toxicity. It was something much simpler and more primal. Millions of Americans went to church, searching there for reassurance, for comfort, for solace, for strength, and for some semblance of redemptive meaning in the act of sharing their grief and confusion in the presence of the transcendent. Both inside and outside the churches, in windows and on labels, American flags were suddenly everywhere in evidence, and the strains of 'God Bless America' wafted through the air, along with other patriotic songs that praised America while soliciting the blessings of the Deity. There was nothing gimcrack or phony about this outpouring of sentiment.[11] For most Americans, it was unthinkable that the comforts of their religious heritage and the well-being of their nation could be in any fundamental way at odds with one another. Hence, it can be said that 9/11 produced a great revitalisation, for a time, of the American civil religion, that strain of American civic piety that bestows many of the elements of religious sentiment and faith upon the fundamental political and social institutions of the United States.

CHURCH AND STATE

Such a tendency to conflate the realms of the religious and the political has hardly been unique to American life and history. Indeed, the achievement of a stable relationship between the two constitutes one of the perennial tasks of social existence. But in the West, the immense historical influence of Christianity has had a lot to say about the particular way the two have interacted over the centuries. From its inception, the Christian faith insisted upon separating the claims of Caesar and the claims of God – recognising the legitimacy of both, though placing loyalty to God above loyalty to the state. The Christian was to be *in* the world but not *of* the world, living as a responsible and law-abiding citizen in the City of Man while reserving ultimate loyalty for the City of God. Such a separation and hierarchy of loyalties, which sundered the unity that was characteristic of the classical world, had the effect of marking out a distinctively secular realm, although at the same time confining its claims.

For Americans, this dualism has often manifested itself as an even more decisive commitment to something called 'the separation of Church and State', a slogan that is taken by many to be the cardinal principle governing American politics and religion. Yet the persistence of an energetic American civil religion, and of other instances in which the boundaries between the two becomes blurred, suggests that the matter is not nearly so simple. There is, and always has been, considerable room allowed in the American regime for the *conjunction* of religion and state. This is a proposition that a great many committed religious believers and committed secularists alike find deeply worrisome – and understandably so, since it carries with it the risk that each of the respective realms can be contaminated by the presence of its opposite number. But it is unlikely that in America the proper boundaries between religion and politics will ever be fixed once and for all. Instead, their relationship evolves out of a process of constant negotiation and renegotiation, responsive to the changing needs of the culture and the moment.[12]

The US seems to be going through just such a process at present, as the renegotiation of boundaries continues fast and furious. Consider, for example, the case that has come before the Supreme Court involving whether the words 'under God' in the Pledge of Allegiance violate the establishment clause of the First Amendment.[13] Or the many similar cases, most notoriously that of Judge Roy Moore in Alabama, involving the display of the Ten Commandments in courthouses and other public buildings.[14] Or the work of Bush's faith-based initiative, which extended an effort begun in the Clinton administration to end discrimination against religious organisations that contract to provide public services. Or the contested status of the institution of marriage, which has always been both a religious and a civil institution, a process that could lead not only to same-sex marriages but to the legalisation of polygamous and other non-traditional marital unions – a development that would, in light of the religious pluralism of America, be of far more than merely theoretical importance. A multitude of issues are in play, and it is hard to predict what the results will look like when the dust settles, if it ever does.

Experience suggests, however, that Americans are disposed to steer between two equally dangerous extremes, which serve as negative landmarks in their deliberations about the proper relationship between American religion and the American nation state. First, they are likely to continue to reject total identification of the two, which would in practice likely mean the complete domination of one by the other: a theocratic or ideological totalitarianism in which religious believers completely subordinated themselves to the apparatus of the state, or vice versa. But second, and equally important, they are not likely to aspire to a total segregation of the two, which would in practice bring about unhealthy estrangement between and among Americans, leading in turn to extreme forms of sectarianism, otherworldliness, cultural separatism and gnosticism. Religion and the American nation are inevitably entwined, and Americans have always been comfortable with some degree of entwining, and even regard it as a good thing within limits.

THE ROLE OF CIVIL RELIGION

Perhaps we can shed further light on the matter by taking a closer look at the concept of 'civil religion'. This is admittedly very much a scholar's term, rather than a term arising out of general parlance, and its use seems to be restricted mainly to anthropologists, sociologists, political scientists and historians, even though it describes a phenomenon that has existed ever since the first organised human communities. It is also a somewhat imprecise term, which can mean several things at once. Civil religion is a means of investing a particular set of political/social arrangements with an aura of the sacred, thereby elevating their stature and enhancing their stability. It can serve as a point of reference for the shared faith of the entire state or nation, focusing on the most generalised and widely held beliefs about the history and destiny of that state or nation. As such, it provides much of the social glue that binds together a society through well-established symbols, rituals, celebrations, places and values, supplying the society with an overarching sense of spiritual unity – a sacred canopy, in Peter Berger's words – and a focal point for shared memories of struggle and survival.[15] Although it borrows extensively from the society's dominant religious tradition, it is not itself a highly particularised religion, but instead a somewhat more blandly inclusive one, into whose highly general stories and propositions those of various faiths can read and project what they wish. It is, so to speak, a highest common denominator.

The phenomenon of civil religion extends back at least to classical antiquity, to the local gods of the Greek city-state, the civil theology of Plato, and to the Romans' state cult, which made the emperor into an object of worship himself. But the term itself appears in recognisably modern form in Jean-Jacques Rousseau's *Social Contract* (1762) where it was put forward as a means of cementing the people's allegiances to their polity.[16] Rousseau recognised the historic role of religious sentiment in underwriting the legitimacy of regimes and strengthening citizen's bonds to the state and their willingness to sacrifice for the general good. He deplored the influence of Christianity because of the way that it divided citizens' loyalties, causing them to neglect worldly concerns in favour of spiritual ones.

Rousseau's solution was the self-conscious replacement of Christianity with 'a purely civil profession of faith'. Since it was impossible to have a cohesive civil government without some kind of religion, and since Christianity is inherently counterproductive to or subversive of sound civil government, he thought the state should impose its own custom-tailored religion, which provides a frankly utilitarian function. That civil religion should be kept as simple as possible, with only a few, mainly positive beliefs – the existence and power of God, the afterlife and the reality of reward or punishment – and with only one negative dogma: the proscribing of intolerance. Citizens would still be permitted to have their own peculiar beliefs regarding metaphysical things, so long as such opinions were of no worldly consequence.

Needless to say, such a nakedly manipulative approach to the problem of socially binding beliefs, and such dismissiveness toward the commanding truths of Christianity and other older faiths, has not attracted universal approval, in Rousseau's day or since. In the 1950s, the American sociologist Will Herberg lambasted civil religion as 'the sanctification of the society and culture of which it is the reflection', and 'a spiritual reinforcement of national self-righteousness.'[17] But it also had its defenders. One of them, the sociologist Robert Bellah, put the term on the intellectual map, arguing in an influential 1967 article called 'Civil Religion in America' that the complaint of Herberg and others about this generalised and self-celebratory religion of 'The American Way of Life' was not the whole story.

American civil religion was, Bellah asserted, something far deeper and more worthy of respectful study: a body of symbols and beliefs that was not merely a watered down Christianity, but possessed a 'seriousness and integrity' of its own. Beginning with an examination of references to God in John F. Kennedy's inaugural address, Bellah detected in the American civil-religious tradition a durable and morally challenging theme: 'the obligation, both collective and individual, to carry out God's will on earth'. Hence, Bellah took a much more positive view of that tradition, though not denying its potential pitfalls. Against the critics, he argued that 'the civil religion at its best is a genuine apprehension of universal and transcendent religious reality as seen in or ... revealed through the experience of the American people.'[18] It provides a higher standard against which the nation could be held accountable.

For Bellah and others, the deepest source of the American civil religion is the Puritan-derived notion of America as a New Israel, a covenanted people with a divine mandate to restore the purity of the early apostolic church, and thus serve as a godly model for the restoration of the world. John Winthrop's famous 1630 sermon to his fellow settlers of Massachusetts Bay, in which he envisioned their 'plantation' as a 'city upon a hill', is the *locus classicus* for this idea of American 'chosenness'. It was only natural that inhabitants with such a strong sense of historical destiny would eventually come to see themselves, and their nation, as collective bearers of a world-historical mission. What is more surprising, however, was how persistent that self-understanding of America as the Redeemer Nation would prove to be, and how easily it incorporated the secular ideas of the Declaration of Independence and the language of liberty. The same mix of convictions can be found animating the rhetoric of the American Revolution, the vision of Manifest Destiny, the crusading sentiments of antebellum abolitionists, the benevolent imperialism of fin-de-siècle apostles of Christian civilisation, and the fervent idealism of President Woodrow Wilson at the time of World War I.

American civil religion also has its sacred scriptures, such as the Mayflower Compact, the Declaration, the Constitution, the Bill of Rights, the Gettysburg Address, the Pledge of Allegiance. It has its narratives of struggle, from the suffering of George Washington's troops at Valley Forge to the gritty valour of John McCain and Jeremiah Denton in Hanoi. It has its special ceremonial and memorial occasions, such as the Fourth of July, Veterans Day, Memorial Day, Thanksgiving Day, and Martin Luther King Day. It has its temples, shrines and holy sites, such as the Lincoln Memorial, the National Mall, the Capitol, the White House, Arlington National Cemetery, Civil War battlefields, and a great natural landmarks such as the Grand Canyon. It has its sacred objects, notably the national flag. It has its organisations, such as the Veterans of Foreign Wars, the American Legion, the Daughters of the American Revolution and the Boy Scouts. And it has its dramatis personae, chief among them being its military heroes and the long succession of presidents. Its telltale marks can be found in the frequent resort to the imagery of the Bible and reference to God and Providence in speeches and public documents, in the inclusion of God's name in the national motto ('In God We Trust') on all currency, and in the patriotic songs found in most church hymnals.

The references to God have always been non-specific, however. Since the early days of the Republic the nation's civil-religious discourse was carefully calibrated to provide a meeting ground for both the Christian and Enlightenment elements in the thought of the Revolutionary generation. One can see this non-specificity, for example, in the many references to the Deity in the presidential oratory of George Washington, which are still cited approvingly today as civil-religious texts. There is really nothing specifically Christian about such references, though they are entirely compatible with Christianity. Civil-religious references to God have evolved and broadened since the founding from generic Protestant to Protestant-Catholic to Judeo-Christian to, in much of President George W. Bush's rhetoric, Abrahamic (that is Muslim-inclusive) and even monotheistic in general. But what has not changed is the fact that such references still always convey a strong sense of God's providence, God's blessing on the land, and of the Nation's consequent responsibility to serve as a light unto the nations.

Every American president and serious presidential candidate, from Jimmy Carter to Barack Obama to Ron Paul, has felt obliged to embrace these sentiments and expresses them in oratory. Some are more enthusiastic than others. As political scientist Hugh Heclo has recently demonstrated, Ronald Reagan's oratory was especially rich in such references. But President Bush surpasses even that standard, and puts forward the civil-religious vision of America with the greatest energy of any president since Woodrow Wilson. He echoed those sentiments in 2005 when he declared, speaking to the National Endowment for Democracy, that

> the advance of freedom is the calling of our time; it is the calling of our country. From the Fourteen Points to the Four Freedoms, to the Speech at Westminster, America has put our power at the service of principle. We believe that liberty is the design of nature; we believe that liberty is the direction of history. We believe that human fulfillment and excellence come in the responsible exercise of liberty. And we believe that freedom – the freedom we prize – is not for us alone, it is the right and the capacity of all mankind ... And as we meet the terror and violence of the world, we can be certain the Author of freedom is not indifferent to the fate of freedom.[19]

In another speech to the Coast Guard Academy, Bush declared that 'the advance of human freedom' is 'a calling we follow', precisely because 'the self-evident truths of the American founding' are 'true for all'.[20] Anyone who thinks this aspect of the American civil religion has died out has simply not been paying attention.

That does not mean, however, that there is universal assent to such sentiments. Precisely because George W. Bush has been, arguably, the most evangelical president in American history, his use of such oratory has both inspired and discomfited many – sometimes even the same people. For Herberg's general critique of civil religion still has considerable potency. It is clear, given the force-field of tensions within which civil religion exists, that it has an inherently problematic relationship to the Christian faith, or to any other serious religious tradition. At its best, as Bellah noted, it provides a secular grounding for that faith, one that makes political institutions more responsive to calls for self-examination and repentance, as well as exertion and sacrifice for the common good. At its worst, it can provide divine warrant to unscrupulous and aggrandising acts, cheapen religious language, turn clergy into robed flunkies of the state and the culture, and bring the simulacrum of religious awe into places where it doesn't belong.

Indeed, if one were writing this account before 9/11, one might emphasise the extent to which there has been a growing disenchantment with American civil religion, particularly in the wake of the Vietnam conflict. Robert Bellah himself has largely withdrawn from association with the idea, and even seems to be slightly embarrassed by the fact that his considerable scholarly reputation is so tied up in this slightly disreputable concept. For many serious and committed Christians, there has been a growing sense that the American civil religion has become a pernicious idol, antithetical to the practice of their faith. This has been true not only of, say, liberal Christians who have opposed American foreign policy in the Middle East and Asia and Latin America or changes in American social-welfare policy, but also of highly conservative Christians who have grown startlingly disaffected over their inability to change settled domestic policies on social issues such as abortion and gay rights. On the religious right as well as the religious left, the question was being posed, with growing frequency, of the compatibility of authentic Christianity with the American regime.

Such multipolar disaffection found expression, for example, in the remarkably wide influence of a 1989 book called *Resident Aliens: Life in the Christian Colony*, by theologians Stanley Hauerwas and William Willimon.[21] As sophisticated liberal Methodists writing in a broadly Anabaptist tradition, the authors articulated a starkly separationist position that was strikingly consonant with the current mood of many in the Christian community at the end of the 1980s. The title came from Philippians 3:20: 'We are a commonwealth [or colony] of heaven', and the authors urged that churches think of themselves as 'colonies in the midst of an alien culture', whose members should think of themselves as 'resident aliens' in that culture – in it, but not of it. The culture-war aspects of the Clinton impeachment only accentuated this sense among conservative Christians that the civil government had nothing to do with their faith, and the President of the United States, the high priest of the civil religion, was just another un-redeemed male, indeed rather worse than the norm. The combination of Clinton's moral lapses with his conspicuous Bible-carrying and church-going seemed proof positive that the American civil religion was not only false but genuinely pernicious. With the controversial election of 2000 leaving the nation so bitterly divided, with the eventual victor seemingly tainted forever, the prospects for the civil religion could hardly have looked bleaker. Just before the attacks occurred, *Time* magazine anointed Stanley Hauerwas as America's leading theologian, a potent sign of the state of things, *ante bellum*.[22]

RE-EMERGING DIVISIONS

The attacks of 9/11 changed all of that decisively, though how permanently remains to be seen. The initial reactions of some religious conservatives to the attacks, seeing them as a divine retribution for national sins, were reflexive and unguarded expressions of the 'resident alien' sentiment. But they were out of phase with the resurgent civil religion, and their comments viewed, fairly or unfairly, as a kind of national desecration.

Indeed, it is remarkable how quickly the ailing civil religion seemed to spring back to new life, expressed especially through a multitude of impromptu church services held all over the country, an instinctive melding of the religious and the civil. Perhaps the most important of these was the service held at the National Cathedral on 14 September 2001, observing a National Day of Prayer and Remembrance, where President Bush spoke to virtually the entire assembled community of Washington officialdom – Congressmen, judges, generals, cabinet officials, and the like – and delivered a speech that touched all the classic civil-religious bases. America had a 'responsibility to history' to answer these attacks. God is present in these events, even though His 'signs are not always the ones we look for' and his purposes 'not always our own.' But our prayers are nevertheless heard, and He watches over us, and will strengthen us for the mission the lies ahead. And, directly invoking Paul's Epistle to the Romans, Bush concluded:

> As we have been assured, neither death nor life, nor angels nor principalities nor powers, nor things present nor things to come, nor height nor depth, can separate us from God's love. May He bless the souls of the departed. May He comfort our own. And may He always guide our country. God bless America.[23]

The speech was widely admired, but not by Robert Bellah. It was, he told a reporter from the *Washington Post*, 'stunningly inappropriate', little more than a 'war talk' designed to whip up bellicose sentiments. 'What', he complained, 'was it doing there?'[24] Such a comment is indicative of the fact that the civil-religious firmament was not quite so firm as it might have seemed. Such a dissenting reaction was a clear indication that the initial surge of civil-religious sentiment would not last, and the confusions and divisions of the American populace would re-emerge, as they most certainly have.

Even years after the 9/11 attacks a substantial flow of visitors continues to make pilgrimages to the former World Trade Center site in lower Manhattan, now known forever as Ground Zero. It remains an intensely moving experience, even with all the wreckage cleared away and countless pieces of residual evidence removed or cleaned up. One still encounters open and intense expressions of grief and rage and incomprehension, in the other visitors and perhaps in oneself. It has become a shrine, a holy place, and has thereby become assimilated into the American civil religion. Yet the single most moving sight, the most powerful and immediately understandable symbol, are the famous cross-shaped girders that were pulled out of the wreckage, and have been raised as a cross. What, one wonders, does it mean to the people viewing it, many of whom, one presumes, are not Christians and not even Americans? Was it a piece of nationalist kitsch or a sentimental relic? Or was it a powerful witness to the redemptive value of suffering – and thereby, a signpost pointing toward the core of the Christian story? Or did it subordinate the Christian story to the American one, and thus traduce its Christian meaning?

Much of what is powerful about civil religion, and much of what is dangerous about it, even at its best, is summed up by the ambiguity of this image. Yet 9/11 reminded us of something that the best social scientists already knew – that the impulse to create and live inside of a civil religion is an irrepressible human impulse, and that this is just as true in the age of the nation state. There can be better or worse ways of approaching it, but the need for it is not to be denied. As Bellah had always insisted, following in the Durkheimian sociological tradition, the state itself is something more than just a secular institution. Because it must sometimes call upon its citizens for acts of sacrifice and self-overcoming, and not only in acts of war, it must be able to draw on spiritual resources, deep attachments, reverent memories of the past, and visions of the direction of history to do its appropriate work.

The trouble, of course, comes when there is no consensus about what deserves to be remembered, and when the civil religion is no longer sufficiently coherent and cohesive to command widespread respect. In the 1940s and 1950s, differences were downplayed, and the American civil religion saw to it that there was a powerful sense of the nation's fundamental meaning – its legitimating myth, as sociologist Robert Wuthnow puts it. Wuthnow has cogently argued that now the United States has not one but two legitimating myths in its civil religion: one to which conservatives appeal, and one to which liberals appeal.[25] Religious conservatives are likely to point to the providential destiny of America, its special place in human history and the divine order, as validation of traditional American values and institutions. Religious liberals are more likely to disparage patriotism, and to speak in broad, universalistic tones of the country's moral responsibility to use its wealth to make the world a more just and equitable place; and they point for justification not only to biblical sources but also to the egalitarian rhetoric of the Declaration of Independence and the language of universal human rights.

The emergence of this reflected a profound shift in the larger structure of American religion. For most of American religious history, the chief lines of division had been denominational and confessional: Congregationalists versus Anglicans, new lights versus old lights, Protestants versus Catholics, and so on. But for Wuthnow, one new factor seemed more important than all others in explaining the evolution of post-war American religion: the steady growth of the state. Most of the controversial issues that have roiled this country's spiritual politics in the past several decades – school prayer and other forms of public religious expression, abortion, tax-exemption for religious organisations, the proper provision of social welfare, military strategy – have been responses to actions of the state, and have revolved around the increasingly problematic boundary between church and state.

Hence, the crucial divisions in American religion are no longer denominational ones; nor are they the divisions among Protestant, Catholic, and Jewish identities once posited by Herberg. They are essentially political divisions: conservative versus liberal, or, as James Davison Hunter phrased it, orthodox versus progressive.[26] Hence the frequently encountered phenomenon that, say, a conservative Methodist may feel and have far more in common with a conservative Catholic, or even a conservative Jew, than with a liberal of his own denomination. Three decades ago such experiences were exceedingly rare; now they have become commonplace. In the past, denominationalism correlated neatly with ethnicity, region and class; today the crucial distinctions are increasingly political, they exist within and across denominations, superseding those former points of divisions to an extent that takes one's breath away.

THE FUTURE OF POST-SECULAR AMERICA

So we return to where we began, to the lack of consensus about the larger picture of American religion and about what the future may hold. This lack of confidence is something new. For many years, the regnant assumption among scholars was that the core achievement of modernity was the triumph of instrumental rationality and the consequent disenchantment of the world, which would entail the gradual disappearance of religion as a serious moral or social agent. Such secularisation was viewed as an inevitable consequence of the rise of modern science, the 'higher criticism' of sacred texts, the general decline of institutional authority and the rise of social equality, the erosion of tradition, and other such 'acids of modernity'.

Hence the dominant way of reading American religious history envisioned it as a process of steady accommodation, in which the Puritan-Protestant hegemony of the seventeenth and eighteenth centuries gradually gave way to a variety of challengers: first to more Arminian and evangelical forms of Protestantism, then to an uneasy entente with Roman Catholicism, then to the Judeo-Christian tradition of the mid-20th century, and finally to a sort of quasi-Abrahamic theism, and even to the full range of theistic and non-theistic faiths celebrated in the radically pluralistic ideal of scholars such as Diana Eck.[27] The evolution of religious thought and practice was seen as a process of opening outward, moving steadily in the direction of more tolerant, more inclusive and more theologically undogmatic practices.

But of course, as Wuthnow's thesis indicates, that has not been what has happened. Or rather, it has not been *all* that has happened, for surely some part of that unfolding vision has in fact been realised. But it has been accompanied at every step of the way by an equal and opposite development, well anticipated by Dean Kelley's important 1972 book *Why Conservative Churches are Growing*.[28] The liberalising mainline Protestant denominations have suffered catastrophic losses in membership and attendance, while evangelical, fundamentalist and Pentecostal churches have grown by leaps and bounds. Issues such as abortion and homosexuality have galvanised a set of responses from the state that reinforce the left-right polarisation that Wuthnow described. Hard as it is to imagine now, it is not ridiculous to conjecture that even the social conservatism of Islam may eventually play a role in fostering and extending this left-right division. Such a development would not be much more historically surprising than the remarkably easy alliance of evangelical Protestants and Catholics that makes up much of the present-day 'religious right'.

Will this division continue and even deepen? That is not clear either. Further complicating the picture with regard to Christianity, which remains culturally dominant in America, is the fact that the left-right conflicts have increasingly spilled into the international arena, where they have become involved in the deep divisions between the prosperous modernising North and the impoverished global South. Perhaps the most fascinating example of this change is the 77-million-member worldwide Anglican Communion, in which the huge and very conservative churches of Africa and Asia, which have come to dwarf the relatively tiny churches of the UK, Canada and United States, are attempting to force a reversal of the Communion's drift toward acceptance of homosexuality and other departures from orthodox moral and theological norms. Fascinatingly, a sizable number of American Anglican churches, particularly in the American South, have put themselves under the authority of African and Asian bishops rather than accept such changes, an alliance that has no precedent in Anglican church history.[29]

Whether this surprising development is just a fluke of history or a leading indicator for some more profound restructuring is impossible to know for sure. But it is yet another indication of the many reasons one has for being modest in predicting what will become of American religion in the years ahead. The spirit bloweth where it listeth, and the paths taken by religious faith are not always obvious ones. The only conclusions in which we can be entirely confident of our extrapolations are conclusions that warn us of the dangers of extrapolation. The prophets of inevitable secularism were wrong. So may be the prophets of religious restoration. The rise of militant Islam was anticipated by almost no one in the West. Neither was the role played by the then-seemingly moribund and powerless Catholic Church in the overthrow of Soviet hegemony in Eastern Europe. These developments should remind us that, whatever some individual Americans may think, *religion* remains a powerful force that is not leaving the stage anytime soon.

NOTES

1. Richard John Neuhaus, *The Naked Public Square: Religion and Democracy in America* (Grand Rapids, MI: Eerdmans, 1984).
2. David Hollinger, 'Jesus matters in the USA', *Modern Intellectual History*, 1(1), 2004, 135–49.
3. For a secular agnostic perspective on this matter, see Guenther Lewy, *Why America Needs Religion: Secular Modernity and Its Discontents* (Grand Rapids, MI: Eerdmans, 1996).

4. See, for example, Christopher Hitchens, *God Is Not Great: How Religion Poisons Everything* (New York, NY: Hachette Book Group, 2007); Richard Dawkins, *The God Delusion* (Boston, MA: Houghton Mifflin, 2006); Sam Harris, *The End of Faith: Religion, Terror, and the Future of Reason* (New York, NY: Norton, 2004); and Christopher Hitchens (ed.), *The Portable Atheist: Essential Readings for the Nonbeliever* (New York, NY: Da Capo Press, 2007).

5. See, for example, Alister McGrath, *The Dawkins Delusion? Atheist Fundamentalism and the Denial of the Divine* (Wheaton, IL: IVP, 2007).

6. Jose Casanova, *Public Religions in the Modern World* (Chicago, IL: University of Chicago Press, 1994), pp. 3–39.

7. George Weigel, *The Final Revolution: The Resistance Church and the Collapse of Communism* (New York, NY: Oxford University Press, 2003).

8. 'Among wealthy nations, the United States stands alone in its embrace of religion', Pew Global Attitudes Survey, 2002, http://pewglobal.org/reports/display.php?ReportID=167.

9. Susan Neiman, *Evil in Modern Thought: An Alternative History of Philosophy* (Princeton, NJ: Princeton University Press, 2004).

10. See http://archives.cnn.com/2001/US/09/14/Falwell.apology/.

11. A striking exemplification is found in the title essay in Todd Gitlin, *The Intellectuals and the Flag* (New York, NY: Columbia University Press, 2005), especially pp. 125–30.

12. For a multipronged exploration of contemporary American religion and politics see R. M. Griffith and M. McAlister (eds), Special Issue of *American Quarterly*, 59(3), September 2007.

13. *Elk Grove Unified School District* v. *Newdow*, case no. 02-1624.

14. *Glassroth* v. *Moore*, 229 F. Supp. 2d 1290, 11th Circuit 2003, http://www.ca11.uscourts.gov/opinions/ops/200216708.pdf.

15. See Peter Berger, *The Sacred Canopy: Elements of a Sociological Theory of Religion* (New York, NY: Doubleday, 1967).

16. I have used the 1967 Washington Square Press translation by Lester G. Crocker, pp. 136–47.

17. Will Herberg, *Protestant Catholic Jew: An Essay in American Religious Sociology* (New York, NY: Doubleday, 1955), pp. 254–72.

18. Robert Bellah, 'Civil Religion in America', *Daedalus*, 96(1), 1967, 1–21.

19. See http://www.ned.org/events/anniversary/20thAniv-Bush.html.

20. See http://www.whitehouse.gov/news/releases/2003/05/20030521-2.html.

21. Stanley Hauerwas and William H. Willimon, *Resident Aliens: Life in the Christian Colony* (Nashville, TN: Abingdon Press, 1989).

22. See *Time* magazine, 17 September 2001.

23. See http://www.whitehouse.gov/news/releases/2001/09/20010914-2.html.

24. 'War Cry from the Pulpit', *Washington Post*, 22 September 2001, B09.

25. Robert Wuthnow, *The Restructuring of American Religion: Society and Faith Since World War II* (Princeton, NJ: Princeton University Press, 1988), pp. 244–57 and *The Struggle for America's Soul: Evangelicals, Liberals, and Secularism* (Grand Rapids, MI: Eerdmans, 1989).

26. James Davison Hunter, *Culture Wars: The Struggle to Define America* (New York, NY: Basic Books, 1992).

27. Diana Eck, *A New Religious America: How a 'Christian Country' Has Become the World's Most Religiously Diverse Nation* (New York, NY: HarperCollins, 2001).

28. Dean Kelley, *Why Conservative Churches Are Growing: A Study in Sociology of Religion* (New York, NY: Harper, 1972).

29. A useful introduction to this subject is in Philip Jenkins's extremely important book *The Next Christendom: The Coming of Global Christianity* (New York, NY: Oxford University Press, 2002), especially pp. 191–220. Also see Miranda K. Hassett, *Anglican Communion in Crisis* (Princeton, NJ: Princeton University Press, 2007).

9. THE US AND GLOBALISATION

Howard Brick

The theme is centuries old and it has risen to consciousness at several points over the course of US history, but the precise term 'globalisation' crystallised at the centre of American consciousness in the mid-1990s. Globalisation concentrated the elements of a discourse that had been thickening since the late 1970s, forming those elements into a kind of master concept that has now largely supplanted such predecessors as 'post-industrial society' or 'postmodernism'. The claims adhering to the term are diverse, and even the simplest definition is bound to be very partial; basically, it asserts that the bonds of world connection have grown dramatically in range and depth over recent decades and that all societies are now, to a large extent, shaped by their embeddedness in a global context. The events begun on 11 September 2001 brought about a brief pause in globalisation talk, for it was hard to say whether terror and war ruptured the drift toward world connection or demonstrated the extent of global reach in startlingly perverse ways. Soon, however, the discourse of globalisation picked up again, and it has continued to yield a mounting body of books and articles throughout the first decade of the new century.

Nonetheless, globalisation and its penumbra of meanings and connotations have taken on a new cast since the election of George W. Bush, the 2001 terrorist attacks, and the 2003 invasion of Iraq. However varied were the meanings and evaluations of globalisation, its centre of gravity in the 1990s lay in some proximity to Francis Fukuyama's famous forecast of an 'end of history' – a long-awaited resolution of historic conflicts and a settlement on the universal applicability of liberal democratic capitalism.[1] It implied a convergence of world societies that, even amidst the somewhat-unanticipated burst of ethnic, civil and sectional strife in places like the

Balkans and Rwanda, sustained expectations that general standards of political morality would come to prevail in world affairs. Moves toward organising social and political affairs not merely in 'international' but in 'supranational' terms appeared to have momentum in the late 1990s, suggesting the diminishing sway of nation states. Yet, by a sharp turn, events following 2001 have once again brought the state back in. Now, any venture in global analysis must address somehow the position of the US in the world, the character of its world leadership, and the question of its rising or falling fortunes. Today, imperial force, resistance and retaliation, crisis and chaos appear just as potent as the themes of growing global coherence appeared merely a decade ago. In other words, not only the trends toward global integration but also the forces and relations that striate and disturb world contexts demand attention. The latter call into question neither the reality nor the salience of a new range of world connections among peoples, nations, economies and cultures; rather, they cast doubt on whether there is in fact a single, whole process that guides the making of those connections and determines their effects.

THE ROOTS OF GLOBALISATION

The proximate sources of globalisation discourse are recognisable in the late 1970s and early 1980s, when social, economic and political thought in the US started to undergo a wide-ranging reorientation. Increasingly, writers claimed, issues facing these fields could no longer be adequately understood within national boundaries; instead, relations stretching across the surface of the world set the unavoidable frame of analysis. Over two decades, these convictions mounted and shaped a widespread sensibility, broader than advocacy of any particular policy or analysis, that accepted 'globalisation' as the name for a state of affairs deemed profoundly new.

How new was this trend from the 1970s to 1990s? From the early Republic on, tension between insularity (an exceptionalist claim for utterly unique national traits, neatly coinciding with the practical avoidance of 'foreign entanglements' with the great powers of the Old World) and a cosmopolitan appeal to the world had marked American culture. The growth of American power, particularly in the wake of 1898, was registered conceptually by more explicit attention to world contexts, even an eagerness to understand the American experience in terms more alike than different from that of other peoples and countries.[2] There may be no better expression of this mood than W. E. B. Du Bois's claim that 'the problem of the Twentieth Century is the problem of the color-line' – a world problem, that is, of which American Jim Crow was only one instance, a manifestation of that 'crazy imperialism of the day' which treats people as resources.[3] Successive intellectual 'turns' toward global awareness kept coming: after World War II, political scientist Louis Hartz claimed the 'happy arrogance' shared by the US and Europe alike was bound to end 'when the big wide world rushes in' on them.[4] Worldwide events of 1968 gave a strong impression of simultaneity. Around that time, a few post-industrial prophets, radical internationalists, and liberal theorists of global conflict-resolution recognised a new age and a new consciousness marked by declining powers of the nation state or a new form of social analysis investigating the nature of 'world systems.'[5] Yet the conditions of the Cold War and the power of the US in a bipolar world never let thought stray too far from the primacy of the nation state and the projection of force by self-interested governments.

A distinctive world turn in thought – whereby the press of global contexts was perceived to cut into the privileged terrain of the national state and nationally distinct societies – commenced after political setbacks to American power (most notably in Vietnam) and the economic crisis of the mid-1970s revealed some slippage of American geopolitical and market standing.[6] To be sure, responses to this slippage took varied, contradictory forms: the Reaganite reply was to reinvigorate the Cold War, hike old-fashioned patriotism to shrill levels, while also claiming to whittle away at the strong state. It was the alternative pole – the liberal 'industrial-policy' writers – who made some of the most vigorous early globalising arguments: that a new order of multipolar worldwide competition thrust the hitherto shielded American economy into a new framework requiring a global consciousness as well as a reinvigoration of state activism.[7] Thus Robert Reich followed up his diagnosis of the 1970s economic shift, *The Next American Frontier* (1983), with his 1991 book, *The Work of Nations*, which cleverly alluded to Adam Smith's more famous title while examining the status of labour, the pressure of world economic imperatives and the enduring need for macroeconomic management by nation states. The last claim would not have been necessary had the mounting clamour in favour of a global free market not suggested that national economic regulation had lost its *raison d'être* or its efficacy.

Left-wing social and cultural theory also moved toward a broad trans-national perspective in the 1980s. In a widely discussed 1984 essay, Fredric Jameson attributed the mood of disorientation and the method of 'pastiche' in postmodern arts to the rise of a 'multinational capitalism', whose social relations, splayed out over the globe, eluded our critical grasp.[8] His call for new 'cognitive maps' to navigate this terrain was one of the early signals of the world turn in American thought. Similarly, David Harvey's *The Condition of Postmodernity* (1989) argued that the development of a 'global capitalism' had forced a quantum leap in 'space-time compression' that paradoxically both brought the world closer together and made it more elusive than before, experienced more as fragmentation than wholeness. Harvey's emphasis on the contrariety within 'space-time compression' – the odd combination of organisation and communication, on the one hand, and incoherence on the other – emphasised the intrinsically contradictory character of these phenomena, which later disputes over globalisation often failed to grasp.[9]

Still, the term globalisation and the debates associated with it did not emerge fully into visibility until the early and mid-1990s. The collapse of the East European Communist bloc in 1989 and the effective 'end of the Cold War' with the demise of the Soviet Union in 1991 – celebrated by Fukuyama as the achievement of a world-historical plateau in universal human reason and followed in the same spirit by George H. W. Bush's declaration of a 'new world order' – gave a needed boost to the idiom. At the same time came a heightened emphasis on dramatically reducing tariffs, from the 1986 commencement of the 'Uruguay round' of negotiations widening the General Agreement on Tariffs and Trade (GATT) to the emblematic organisation of the World Trade Organization (WTO) in 1995. Three other trends contributed as well:

(1) The advance of environmentalism from local, regional, and national concerns with pollution to more world-oriented perspectives, in quasi-mystical, holistic conceptions of Earth as 'Gaia', or in the identification of large-scale issues such as ozone depletion or the 'greenhouse effect'.

(2) The trend of multiculturalism moving (a) beyond concerns with intranational racial and ethnic diversity to address experiences of cross-border, cross-cultural experiences defined in terms of postnational or hybrid identities, and (b) to embrace indigeneity, a generic stance of 'fourth world' peoples defending traditional cultures against encroachment by Euro-American industrial and post-industrial ways.

(3) Growth in nongovernmental organisations (NGOs) around the world, best symbolised by the explosion in the early 1990s of new national affiliates of the French service organisation Médecins Sans Frontières (Doctors without Borders), signalling a new wave of humanitarianism.

Such diverse moves in thought and practice fostered an image of the world remade as one.

A quick look at catalogues and bibliographies reveals a sudden spike by the mid-1990s of publications devoted explicitly to globalisation. One of the early noted contributions to its discussion (at least in American academic circles) dwelt not primarily on free trade but on the experience of cultural hybridity and new, transnational worldviews in Arjun Appadurai's *Modernity at Large: Cultural Dimensions of Globalization* (1996). Still, free trade was bound to become a keynote of globalisation, especially after President Clinton's endorsement of the North American Free Trade Agreement (NAFTA) drawn up by his predecessor's administration, making neoliberalism the consensus of the American political establishment.[10] Meanwhile, popular counter-movements emerged to challenge the free-trade agenda and the force of economic integration. Global indigeneity made itself known with the counter-commemoration by native peoples of the Americas amidst the Columbus quincentenary in 1992. In 1995, the campaign slogan 'Fifty Years is Enough' united groups opposed to the policies of the International Monetary Fund and the World Bank. Founded in 1945 as liberal institutions intended to secure the international stability of markets and promote economic development, both agencies were now assailed as a financial establishment that worsened living conditions in poor countries by imposing policies of privatisation and social service cuts as preconditions for re-scheduling onerous Third World debt.

The late 1990s boom, coming after more than 20 years of economic malaise, was the final ingredient needed to seal the conviction that a new age had opened in human history: globalisation, pictured either as a triumphant achievement or pervasive threat.[11] Impulses to herald (or decry) the new age helped obscure the sheer multiplicity of thoughts and experiences that had contributed to this mounting world-oriented sensibility. Indeed, the discussion of globalisation from this time onward was to become so troubled and so confusing because the term meant many different things to different people. It denoted a *programme* or *policy* in terms of free trade or neoliberalism, which could be promoted or criticised, advanced or reversed. It implied a *process*, more or less given, that added to degrees of interconnection among different societies, states and regions, whereupon one might debate whether the trend was really new or whether a recent qualitative change in such developments really altered human experience. And it simply identified a range of diverse *phenomena* that highlighted one way or another 'the perspective of the world'.[12] In 1992, National Public Radio reviewed a new four CD set of music entitled *Global Meditation*, recording the sounds of religious traditions – notably non-Western and indigenous traditions – around the world. Such field recordings had been the province of ethnomusicologists for over a century.[13] Did the intention to bring all these sounds together in one popular compilation mark an innovation creating a field now to be called 'world music'? How meaningful would it be to ask whether one was pro world music or anti world music?

GLOBALISATION BEFORE 9/11

The literature of globalisation blossomed, particularly from 1995 to 1999, the latter date marking a culmination in some sense. The American boom and stock-market bubble reached new heights, while the financial upheaval of the East Asian currency crisis in 1997–8, however devastating on the ground, was apparently contained without a catastrophic breakdown in world trade. The deposition of Indonesia's Suharto in its wake offered further evidence of a global march toward democracy, and the brief Kosovo war (March–June 1999) took shape as an international venture in so-called humanitarian intervention. The year ended with the vast surprise of massive demonstrations in Seattle (29 November–2 December), disrupting the annual World Trade Organization meeting and marking the coming out of an anti-globalisation movement. By then globalisation was on almost everyone's lips. The first major academic survey in the field, *Global Transformations* by British political theorist David Held and his collaborators, appeared then too.[14]

Quickly apparent in the popular literature on the topic, however, was a keen sense of unease accompanying the announcement of a new age. For the fundamentals that kicked off the new sensibility – the end of the Cold War, the ascent of a neoliberal consensus, the onset of the 1990s boom – had not in fact issued in an end of history, a plateau of achievement, a new era of worldwide stability and collaboration. For most of the Western world, the new Balkan wars signalled an unanticipated phenomenon: the resurgence, once bipolar geopolitics loosened its grip, of apparently old national and ethnic conflicts that could be vastly destructive. If, in turn, the Rwandan genocide of 1994 failed to engage the attention of the West as the Bosnian War had, it remained a blot on the modern cosmopolitan conscience, a lesson that excited anxiety and stimulated calls for a greater degree of global humanitarian vigilance.

Two bellwethers of US globalisation discourse in this first period – Benjamin Barber's *Jihad vs. McWorld* (1995) and Thomas Friedman's *The Lexus and the Olive Tree* (1999) – were both preoccupied by this paramount indicator of strain and disproportion in the new order: the tension between integrative and fissile forces at large in the world. Both chose to frame their sense of the strain by reference to the Middle East. Barber's decision to name localist, traditionalist or nationalist movements by allusion to *jihad* in the Muslim world was a misleading and unfortunate one. The most salient example of the forces Barber regarded as intolerant, reactionary and exclusivist was Bosnian Serb nationalism, and the root of his allusion to Islam (a reference to Iranian fundamentalism) did not in fact suggest to Barber that there existed a generic Islamic threat to Westernisation. His main point was the incompatibility of either of the main trends he saw – border-crossing global business summed up as 'McWorld' and regressive ethnic, religious and nationalist inwardness – with the need for better forms of genuinely democratic governance in a 'global' world. Barber had long been an advocate of robust civic engagement and thus a kind participatory democracy: 'strong democracy' in an earlier formulation. The globetrotting managements of large corporations, intent on evading economic regulation, eviscerated true civic politics, and so did the traditionalists who, as they sought to escape modernist intrusions, could never imagine an inclusive and diverse political community. There was no question Barber was a 'strong state' advocate, though he recognised the limited purview of nation states in dealing with both world business and ethnic rivalries. His was a kind of classic liberalism, not in the neoliberal vein of deregulated economic

practices but in the modernising sense that hailed an increasingly cosmopolitan field of action. The blunt contradiction between the antithetical
forces of business and ethnos called for new innovations in transnational
forms of governance that engaged and protected the free citizen.[15]

Thomas Friedman, on the other hand, was a tireless advocate of free trade
as a brave new world of economic growth and material prosperity for all,
in the mould of Bill Clinton's moderate liberalism. Here was the key theme:
the move away from the strong state of New Deal liberalism, welcomed by
these new Democrats, should not evacuate all the capacities of national
government. A *New York Times* reporter who had graduated from Middle
East correspondent to foreign-affairs commentator and then to jet-setting
coverage of global business, Friedman remained both an American patriot
insistent on US leadership in world affairs and a self-professed religious man
conscious of the need for traditions that gave individuals a place at home
in the world. He admired the Japan-made Lexus automobile that rich
entrepreneurs in India's computing industry drove (while discounting all
arguments that free international trade weakened developing economies)
even as he recognised the appeal of home (that is, the olive tree), which
might, but need not, be a divisive localising force. With such economic
confidence and disarming piety, Friedman ended with vague appeals to
balance and proportion between the global and the local, while voicing
no doubt about the beneficence of worldwide economic flows in goods,
services and investment.[16]

This first phase of globalisation discourse raised the question of what
place and function the national state had in an emerging order of global scale.
The more conservative American policy-makers advocating free trade never
doubted that economic deregulation fit perfectly well with assertive US
power on a world plane, just as everyone knew in the nineteenth century
that free trade was the policy of the dominant force, Britain. Meanwhile,
American liberals, who were eager to maintain some kind of active
government, presented themselves as far-sighted modernisers open to the
world at large. When pressed, the liberals were ready to accommodate new
initiatives in multilateral international institutions, but they were no more
eager to see the decline of the nation state than their partisan opponents.
Nonetheless, the new global discourse had come to contemplate just that,
whether in fear (as when critics of laissez-faire and free trade claimed these
trends dismantled the civic obligations of national regulatory regimes) or in
anticipation (as exponents of the new humanitarianism argued that
traditional definitions of national sovereignty ought to give way before a
growing cosmopolitan consciousness of human rights). To be a citizen of
the world – the old ideal of universal human ethics, perpetual peace and
world federalism – stirred a measure of idealism among a wing of American
intellectuals, especially those who considered themselves most open to
European trends, manifested in the NGO image of Médecins Sans

Frontières and in the steady moves toward transnational organisation in the European Union.

Globalisation was to become a hot issue in more ways than one. Insofar as free-trade advocates adopted the term as a flag for their neoliberal assumptions, the word named a programme that could be debated as its consequences were deemed beneficial or injurious. As part of a broad world turn in consciousness, however, globalisation always suggested something more than those specific policies. Perhaps it said too much and thus too little, for while it might have indicated merely the appearance of any particular phenomenon on a world scale (for example, the globalisation of AIDS), turning it into a self-standing substantive noun – globalisation conceived as a process working on unidentified objects – skirted hard questions of what exactly had changed and precisely which causal elements explained the change.[17] Nevertheless, theorists went to work trying to determine whether or not some generic heightening of world-spanning relations, interactions, exchanges and resemblances had in fact recently emerged, either as a wholly new stage of development or a qualitatively new step forward in long-term changes that now reached a critical stage. David Held and his collaborators summed up the debate as one between 'hyperglobalizers' who insisted that the world frame of social, economic, political and cultural relations had entirely eclipsed prior divisions, particularly of the national sort, and 'sceptics' who denied that any profoundly new trend had ruptured prior practices and the conduct of affairs.[18] For the latter, the current keen enthusiasm (or anxiety) amounted to 'globaloney'.[19] The sceptics had a number of arguments to mobilise, including the claim that trends toward integration had been growing steadily rather than by sudden rupture, that old and resilient modes of local, regional and national difference showed no near prospect of withering away, or that older concepts for grasping worldwide ties such as capitalism, modernisation, imperialism or cultural diffusion worked just as well if not better to capture events.[20]

These analytical disputes seemed tame compared to the public uproar that hit the headlines in Seattle and stayed there as large street protests at the sites of international economic and diplomatic meetings continued to mount until the Genoa G-8 summit in summer 2001. These unwieldy demonstrations, lacking clear steering committees, platforms or lists of demands, befuddled most observers. Newspapers assumed the dissenters' distaste for globalisation (in this context, usually taken to mean neoliberalism and corporate leadership of international exchange and investment) implied a preference for old-fashioned nationalism and protectionism, as when American steelworkers marched to save their jobs. The same could not be said about the world-minded environmentalists who campaigned against maritime practices endangering sea turtles. Strident defenders of neoliberalism responded simply by denouncing both sorts, steelworkers and friends of sea turtles, as Luddites, backward-looking opponents of economic growth and modernisation. Very shortly, however, a respectable critique emerged as former World Bank officer Joseph Stiglitz penned a sharp rejoinder to those IMF programmes that demanded fiscal austerity and financial deregulation in all its recipient countries, under the title *Globalization and Its Discontents* (2002).[21] Now the issue was rendered legitimately debatable.

About the same time, hyperglobaliser discourse received a shot in the arm from an unlikely source: a book published to much acclaim in 2000 called *Empire*, written in an idiosyncratic Marxist and postmodern vein by the imprisoned Italian revolutionary Antonio Negri and his young American colleague, comparative literature professor Michael Hardt. The title referred to a new kind of sovereignty, beyond nation state and old-style imperialist power, that had begun to show itself in a distended and inchoate form of supranational authority. Taking their distance from anti-globalisation forces in the streets who may have favoured the virtues of small communities and traditional cultures, Hardt and Negri seemed almost to welcome the new order. Yet they regarded this peculiarly amorphous and decentred form of world power as the ultimate postnational form of hierarchical government, doomed to face an equally amorphous and decentred popular revolt Hardt and Negri identified with 'the Multitude'. There stood an increasingly mobile, variegated and plastic body of the world's peoples whose power was evident in transnational labour migrations and bold new forms of communication and empathy; they possessed the capacity to create a genuinely world-spanning, post-industrial communism of popular and stateless self-government. In a new 'smooth-surfaced' world of fluid interactions, the struggle between traditional sovereignty and communal self-rule became acute.[22]

GLOBALISATION IN THE NEW CENTURY

Suddenly, however, the attacks on US targets by al-Qaeda operatives in the fall of 2001 changed a great deal. Among other things, the wave of anti-globalisation protests more or less abruptly ended. The grand violence of taking down skyscrapers made publics nervous about even the traffic disruptions and petty property damage wrought by Seattle and Genoa protesters; at least, the current anxiety gave governments a pretext for cracking down on street crowds. Of course, the 9/11 events could be another sign of a postnational world: the attackers were stateless terrorists whose animus appeared aimed broadly at the global system. A few voices held on to cosmopolitan, humanitarian and supranational principles of the late 1990s in arguing that terrorism must be addressed by some sort of world police force and judiciary, an endeavour to be understood as crime-fighting instead of President Bush's 'War on Terror'. They carried little weight. Pundits, most notably Thomas Friedman, rushed to declare the onset of World War III, portrayed as a blunt conflict between modernity and fanatical wreckers, or as the conservative political scientist Samuel Huntington had earlier called it, a 'clash of civilizations' between the West and a medieval Islam.[23] Yet the most evident blow struck by al-Qaeda was to the pre-eminence of globalisation as such, not only because 'terror' became an issue more pressing than the terms of international trade, but also because the War on Terror (even if it were viewed as a supranational civilisational struggle) brought the state back into the frame. National security, national powers of military defence and offence, tightened borders, suspicion of foreigners, and new modes of surveillance and control achieved a renewed, nearly absolute priority in public discourse. That the events coincided with the bursting of the 1990s economic bubble and emboldened the Bush administration in its disinclination to take part in international multilateral agreements, meant that globalisation had to be rethought all over again.

Much of the world, not to speak of American citizens, accepted the US definition of national defence as justification for an attack on the al-Qaeda-allied Taliban government of Afghanistan. Yet the rapid slide from that venture to the US invasion of Iraq, notwithstanding loud worldwide opposition, reinforced the rapid shift in public discourse away from prospects of building one world toward attempts at understanding the meaning and scope of US coercive power. By 2003 and 2004, a good deal of scholarship turned to address the history of American foreign relations and the US projection of force. Was the new Bush unilateralist doctrine of pre-emptive war an epoch-making break in American foreign relations, or was it consistent with practices since the inception of the Cold War of wielding preponderant power on the world stage, with or without the consent and support of allies?[24] Was promotion of democracy a valid exercise of the humanitarian intervention only yesterday legitimated by the Kosovo War or had disregard for sovereignty taken a dangerous new turn? What aspects of the current crisis had been established by the practices of old empires – the Ottomans and British – and were American practices understandable as imperial themselves?

Not a few proponents of the war made themselves known as advocates of imperial power, which cast a new world order of global governance in the shade – unless it was understood that the great empire was the legitimate face of global governance. Critics, of course, complained that US national arrogance as global policeman had refurbished old imperialist projects with a new degree of recklessness or revealed an unexampled form of single-power hegemony. In any case, the globalisation debate had shifted radically. By the time Michael Hardt and Antonio Negri published their anticipated sequel to *Empire*, the counterpart volume focused not on the ultimate system of hierarchical sovereignty but on the forces that emerged as its popular reflection and antithesis, *Multitude* (2004), the issue of concerted violence had risen to prominence. The authors acknowledged that 'big government is back' and their prescription for a popular struggle against war had a clearly defined target in a particular state, namely the US engaged in an endless avenging of 9/11.[25]

The collapse of the stock market bubble and economic slump that followed closely on the heels of 9/11 led to two years of declines in world trade and investment, compounding the sense that the globalising tide was running out.[26] Nonetheless, after a breather (and an economic rebound in world trade and investment by 2004), the globalisation discourse resumed in robust fashion. Whatever names are applied, it is clear that many forms of global economic interaction have shown dramatic growth since the 1980s, indicated by the dispersion of industrial production; the enormous volume of money channelled around the world in investment and currency exchanges; the proportion of economies devoted to manufacturing and export trade in those 'developing' countries that have experienced growth; the vast extension across the world of chain merchandisers such as McDonald's in just the past fifteen years; the logistics revolution that has made far-flung manufacturing facilities and fleets of container ships into highly rationalised global supply chains feeding Wal-Mart and other chain retailers; and the speed and scope of communications that facilitate the movement of money, goods, business information and services. One scholar in the field of global studies, Manfred Steger, now claims the breach between 'hyperglobalizers' and 'sceptics' has been overcome in common recognition of globalisation's reality, a process crossing boundaries and making communication and exchange much more fluid. That is surely going too far; sceptics continue to argue, at a minimum, about whether particular transnational phenomena indeed add up to genuinely global formulas having some degree of integral unity. Yet the discourse has indeed developed apace. Radical critics of neoliberalism, for the most part, no longer describe themselves as anti-globalisation; by and large they have adopted different locutions, such as the 'anti-corporate globalisation movement', affirming their attempt to locate alternative principles of global organisation and development, signalled by the annual World Social Forum, usually convened in Porto Alegre, Brazil.

At the same time, *New York Times* columnist Thomas Friedman returned in 2005 with a new instalment in his world economic reportage, entitled *The World is Flat: a Brief History of the 21st Century*. He claimed to have discovered that 'while I was sleeping' (a coy reference to his preoccupation with World War III, which ended in the disgrace of a messy, prolonged US occupation of Iraq that he repudiated in summer 2006), globalisation had taken a new leap forward. The epoch of 'Globalization 3.0' had begun, in which fibre-optic communication channels and software for shared projects established a new platform for work and innovation that was genuinely dispersed across multiple sites around the globe.[27] As software development and call centres boomed in Bangalore, India, Friedman trumpeted the confidence of post-colonial entrepreneurs convinced that the field of competition in production, exchange and innovation had been radically levelled or 'flattened'. Now the whole world was engaged in mutual interaction, and the speed of change and demand for adaptability left no secluded space; primarily, the job of governments was to prepare their citizens to make the most of opportunities for personal advancement and leave no one outside the private race for wealth. In Friedman's view, steeling the competitive individual for the unending race (and hence perpetual insecurity) appeared as a profoundly liberating move toward a world of steady economic progress. The 'flattening' of the world was a thesis much like the Hardt and Negri claim that the Earth had become 'smooth-surfaced'. For them, the claim seemed to mean that no non-capitalist sectors remained unincorporated in the world market, but in their own way, they too dwelled in the romance of the whole world imagined as a grand post-industrial idyll. Obscured by this image is the practical matter of how industrial operations have spread to far-flung locations, whether Bangladeshi ship-breaking yards or low-wage (and low-tech) Chinese electrical appliance assembly plants, leaving behind deadly swaths of dirty work and refuse, and belying the portrait of ever-widening circles of qualified workers in Web-based services.[28]

Some of the current debate remains focused on the virtues of reduced trade barriers and estimating the aggregate statistics of economic growth as evidence of progress in 'reducing poverty'. Jagdish M. Bhagwati, a colleague of Joseph Stiglitz in Columbia University's Economics department and clearly a humane man, wrote *In Defense of Globalization* (2004) as if the key question is: are you for or against it?[29] No matter that yet another Columbia professor, Thomas Pogge, could easily document the appalling rise of global inequality over centuries and with no sign of abating: an ever-growing gap between the world's richest and poorest that shames any simple defence of globalised modernity.[30] Meanwhile, the sense that globalising developments are not merely subject to opposed assessments but carry within themselves conflicting meanings is lost on all too many observers. The popular left-wing Canadian journalist Naomi Klein, an early supporter of the anti-globalisation demonstrators at the turn of the millennium, has captured this aspect of its character well when she notes simply that the reduction of tariff 'walls' dividing nations has been often allied with the ongoing privatisation of public resources that erects new 'fences' between the rich and the poor.[31]

The best scholarship regarding globalisation has indeed reached a new level of sophistication, recognising that not only is a simple yea or nay response infeasible but also that the phenomena of global reach are not all one. 'Multi-scalarity' is the term some observers use to capture this theme: that is, that in different places and different endeavours, social practices unfold on a local, regional, national or world scale; that these varied contexts overlap with each other, yielding a range of cumulative or contradictory effects. The most successful figure in this vein is the University of Chicago sociologist Saskia Sassen, who cogently argues that new world-spanning processes have indeed emerged in recent decades to mark a qualitative change in social affairs, while those processes intersect with, and cannot be put into effect without, resources and commitments made at the national level. Thus it is far from clear that 'the ascendance of a new order necessarily means the end of the old order'.[32] Once this kind of complexity comes into view, it becomes evident that the surface of the world as a social field is far from 'smooth-surfaced' or 'flat' but instead profoundly uneven, and as a result a range of globalising tendencies do not necessarily assume the shape of a single or holistic process. Indeed, some of the best new work in the field surrenders generalisations about globalisation and settles for the more modest and unfinished notion of ubiquitous 'global connection'. Thus anthropologist Anna Tsing has written an extraordinary ethnography of foraging peoples in the Kilamantan region of southern Borneo, who are locked in struggle with foreign and Indonesian investors intent on plundering their forests. They are aided by a group of Jakarta-based nature lovers whose cosmopolitan environmentalism is equally alien to the locals' traditionalism. In such awkward encounters of global connection the watchword for Tsing is 'friction'.[33]

This simple word insists that profound degrees of unevenness, inequality and conflict are unlikely to depart the field of global relations very soon. All the familiar issues remain painfully present on the global terrain: the vying for hegemony on the world stage, the persistence of economic competition and its geopolitical echoes (including US anxiety over the rise of China), yawning gaps of wealth that have consigned much of sub-Saharan Africa – globalising trends notwithstanding – to the status of forgotten and receding economic wastes.[34] Devising a viable world programme for the achievement of peace, justice and shared prosperity will remain a daunting task. In this pursuit, the inadequacy of the modern nation state – too small to address problems that cross borders, too large to satisfy popular demands for cultural belonging and political self-determination – will remain as evident as it has been to far-sighted analysts for over a century.[35] Perhaps the theme of globalisation, measuring the acceleration of trends that both integrate and fracture experiences in the world, reminds us that the demand for a world programme of radical change seeking peace, justice and prosperity remains inescapable. But any reification of globalisation as a single, coherent and internally uniform process, bringing the world inexorably together, is never likely to help much in fashioning such a programme or in realising it.

NOTES

1. Francis Fukuyama, 'The End of History?', *National Interest*, 16, Summer 1989, 3–18.
2. Thomas Bender, *A Nation among Nations: America's Place in World History* (New York, NY: Hill and Wang, 2006), pp. 11–13.

3. W. E. B. Du Bois, *The Souls of Black Folk* (New York, NY: NAL, 1969), pp. xi, 69.
4. Louis Hartz, *The Liberal Tradition in America* (New York, NY: Harcourt Brace Jovanovich, 1955), p. 27.
5. See Zbigniew Brzezinski, *Between Two Ages: America's Role in the Technetronic Era* (New York, NY: Viking Press, 1970), pp. 3–8; George Modelski, *Principles of World Politics* (New York, NY: Free Press, 1972); Immanuel Wallerstein, *The Modern World-System* (New York, NY: Academic Press, 1974).
6. See Robert Brenner, *The Economics of Global Turbulence: The Advanced Capitalist Economies from Long Boom to Long Downturn, 1945–2005* (London: Verso, 2006).
7. See Lester Thurow, *The Zero-Sum Society: Distribution and the Possibilities for Economic Change* (New York, NY: Basic Books, 1980); Robert Reich, *The Next American Frontier* (New York, NY: Penguin, 1983); Lester Thurow, *The Zero-Sum Solution: Building a World-Class American Economy* (New York, NY: Basic Books, 1985); Robert Reich, *The Work of Nations: Preparing Ourselves for 21st Century Capitalism* (New York, NY: Vintage, 1991).
8. Fredric Jameson, 'Postmodernism, or the cultural logic of late capitalism', *New Left Review*, 146, July–August 1984, 53–92.
9. See David Harvey, *The Condition of Postmodernity* (Oxford: Blackwell, 1989).
10. Michael H. Hunt, *The American Ascendancy: How the US Gained and Wielded Global Dominance* (Chapel Hill, NC: University of North Carolina Press, 2007), pp. 289–92.
11. See Robert Brenner, *The Boom and the Bubble: The US in the World Economy* (London: Verso, 2002).
12. I borrow the phrase from that hallmark of the initial 'world turn' circa 1980, Fernand Braudel, *Civilization and Capitalism, 15th–18th Century*, vol. 3: *The Perspective of the World*, trans. Siân Reynolds (Berkeley, CA: University of California Press, 1984).
13. See Philip V. Bohlman, *World Music: A Very Short Introduction* (Oxford: Oxford University Press, 2002).
14. See David Held *et al.*, *Global Transformations: Politics, Economics and Culture* (Stanford, CA: Stanford University Press, 1999).
15. See Benjamin R. Barber, *Jihad vs. McWorld* (New York, NY: Times Books, 1995).
16. Thomas Friedman, *The Lexus and the Olive Tree*, rev. edn (New York, NY: Anchor Books, [1999] 2000), pp. 433, 468–73.
17. See Justin Rosenberg, *The Follies of Globalisation Theory: Polemical Essays* (London: Verso, 2000).
18. Held *et al.*, *Global Transformations*, pp. 3–7.
19. See Michael Veseth, *Globaloney: Unraveling the Myths of Globalization* (Lanham, MD: Rowman and Littlefield, 2005).
20. Grahame Thompson, 'The Limits to Globalization: Questions for Held and Wolf', in Anthony Barnett *et al.* (eds), *Debating Globalization* (Cambridge: Polity, 2005), pp. 52–8. Michael Mann, *Incoherent Empire* (London: Verso, 2003), pp. 49–79.
21. See also Dani Rodrik's, *Has Globalization Gone Too Far?* (Washington, DC: Institute for International Economics, 1997).
22. See Michael Hardt and Antonio Negri, *Empire* (Cambridge, MA: Harvard University Press, 2000).

23. See Thomas L. Friedman, 'World War III', *New York Times*, 13 September 2001.
24. See Melvyn P. Leffler, *A Preponderance of Power: National Security, the Truman Administration, and the Cold War* (Stanford, CA: Stanford University Press, 1992) and Michael H. Hunt, *The American Ascendancy: How the US Gained and Wielded Global Dominance* (Chapel Hill, NC: University of North Carolina Press, 2007).
25. Michael Hardt and Antonio Negri, *Multitude: War and Democracy in the Age of Empire* (New York, NY: Penguin, 2004), pp. 176–7.
26. David Held and Anthony McGrew (eds), *Globalization Theory: Approaches and Controversies* (Cambridge: Polity, 2007), p. 3.
27. Thomas L. Friedman, *The World is Flat: A Brief History of the Twenty-First Century*, rev. edn (New York, NY: Picador, [2005] 2007), p. 9.
28. See the work of Canadian photographer Edward Burtynsky in the film *Manufactured Landscapes* (Jennifer Baichwal, Canada, 2006).
29. See Jagdish Bhagwati, *In Defense of Globalization* (Oxford: Oxford University Press, 2004).
30. See Thomas Pogge, *World Poverty and Human Rights: Cosmopolitan Responsibilities and Reforms* (Cambridge: Polity, 2002).
31. Naomi Klein, 'Fences of enclosure, windows of possibility', in David Rothenberg and Wandee J. Pryor (eds), *Writing the World: On Globalization* (Cambridge, MA: MIT Press, 2005), pp. 195–200.
32. See Saskia Sassen, *Territory, Authority, Rights: From Medieval to Global Assemblages* (Princeton, NJ: Princeton University Press, 2006).
33. See Anna Lowenhaupt Tsing, *Friction: an Ethnography of Global Connection* (Princeton, NJ: Princeton University Press, 2005).
34. See John Mearsheimer, *The Tragedy of Great-Power Politics* (New York, NY: Norton, 2001).
35. This problem of scale has been noted by 20th-century writers as diverse as Leon Trotsky and Daniel Bell.

10. THE FUTURE OF MEDICINE

Christopher Thomas Scott

Ailing President George W. Bush to undergo stem cell therapy in London

Daughter Jenna donates cells in hopes of curing his deadly disease

CHRISTOPHER THOMAS SCOTT
London Correspondent, World Press International
August 9, 2016

British authorities, including former Prime Minister Tony Blair, greeted a gravely ill George W. Bush, aged 70, as he arrived on a hospital gurney to a subdued gathering at Heathrow International Airport. Bush suffers from Guillain-Barré (ghee-yan bah-ray) Syndrome (GBS), an immune system disorder that mercilessly attacks the body's nervous system.[1] In its severe form, it causes paralysis of the legs, arms, breathing muscles and face. GBS affects thousands of Americans every year. In acute cases such as Mr. Bush's, the pulmonary complications can be deadly.

Bush's sickness came on suddenly after suffering a bout of flu at his ranch in Crawford, Texas. As his condition worsened, family members consulted with specialists at Washington's newly rebuilt Walter Reed Medical Center. Within hours, he was rushed to London on a specially equipped plane staffed with medical personnel. He entered the prestigious King's College Stem Cell Therapy Institute, where treatments for auto-immune diseases such as type I diabetes, rheumatoid arthritis and GBS show great promise.

A Grim Anniversary

The news comes exactly fifteen years after Bush's controversial proclamations on embryonic stem cell research. From his Texas ranch on 9 August 2001, he announced that from that day forward, not a single dollar from the $28 billion budget of the National Institutes of Health (NIH) could be used to make new embryonic stem cell lines (some funding was still possible for research with a handful of pre-existing embryonic cell lines). His pronouncement prompted outrage from scientists, citizens, doctors and patients, who objected to a policy based on the beliefs of a powerful political minority. Advocates stepped into the breach, supporting a handful of private and state-funded programmes, including California's multibillion-dollar bond measure for embryonic stem cell research, which awarded its first grants in 2007. Congress scrambled to write, and then successfully voted to enact laws to overturn his policy.

But the legislative efforts were in vain. In 2006, Bush scuppered the first Congressional action – his first veto ever. In conservative quarters, his open religious views and uncompromising moral certitude prompted other political gambits, including the passage of the Embryo Protection Act, authored by then-senator Sam Brownback, a religious conservative. Under the sweeping provisions of the Act, any American scientist, clinician or patient found using stem cells made from unwanted, two-day-old frozen embryos obtained from *in vitro* fertilisation (IFV) clinics is subject to criminal penalties of $1 million and ten years in prison.[2]

The result of the embryo legislation was swift and immediate. Senior biomedical stem cell researchers abandoned their laboratories. Young university scientists, who use government funds to establish their research programmes, chose other careers. A chill descended on American capital markets, which rely on steady and unencumbered transfer of technology and talent from academic and non-profit institutions into the for-profit sector. A new term entered the investment lexicon: 'founder flight'. American inventiveness, long a trademark of NIH investment in frontier medicine, began to slow. Countries such as England, Norway, Israel, Australia, China and Singapore stepped into the breach, developing novel therapies to benefit their citizens. The result: an epidemic of offshore interventions as sick Americans travelled abroad for embryonic stem cell treatment, risking imprisonment once they returned home.

A Bitter Irony

The therapy sought by Bush began its journey in the United States. Researchers announced in 2002 that they could cure mice mimicking human forms of autoimmune disease using embryonic stem cells.[3] Fine-tuning the treatment came thanks to a second type of laboratory mouse with a brain partially comprised of diseased human neurons. Thousands of drug candidates were screened in these animals. One of these compounds will be administered to Mr. Bush.

Use of the special mice, called neural chimeras, is also illegal in the US. After they were first developed in California, Bush stated in his 2006 State of the Union address: 'Tonight I ask you to pass legislation to prohibit the most egregious abuses of medical research: human cloning in all its forms, creating or implanting embryos for experiments, creating human-animal hybrids, and buying, selling, or patenting human embryos'. Brownback's embryo protection act also outlaws neural chimeras.[4] As a result, the valuable rodents were smuggled to Singapore, where they are used to discover drugs for a wide range of dementias, including Parkinson's and Alzheimer's.

A DNA Donor: Don't Leave Home Without One

Bush's treatment is becoming standard care for Europeans but is virtually unknown in America. Clinicians will begin by using a technique called nuclear transfer – also known as therapeutic cloning. Using a very fine glass needle, the nucleus – containing genetic material or DNA – is gently suctioned from a skin cell donated by Bush's daughter, Jenna. The nucleus is transferred into a human egg stripped of its DNA. A small pulse of electricity prompts the egg to divide. After a few days, a clump of cells from the inside of the egg are removed and put into a plastic dish where they begin to multiply, forming an immortal line of embryonic stem cells.

The cells made from his daughter's DNA, while not genetically identical, must be used because the elder Bush's cells are defective. Doctors first will attempt to fix his faulty immune system by replacing his rampaging white blood cells with healthy, specialised stem cells made from the 'Jenna line'. The procedure involves a mild dose of chemotherapy and drugs to prevent rejection of the new cells. Once he has stabilised, a different chemical cocktail will induce the embryonic line to produce a fresh supply of neural stem cells. They will be injected into his brain to replace motor neurons damaged by the disease. Drugs discovered using the outlawed chimeric mice will stabilise Bush while he recovers. Thanks to the new technologies, thousands of patients suffering from autoimmune disease now lead vastly improved lives.

Banishment

News of Bush's sickness and treatment sent shock waves through Washington. Religious conservative Pat Robertson, the keynote speaker at a Tennessee conference for geologists studying intelligent design, called for Bush's immediate imprisonment upon his return to Texas. Former senate majority leader Bill Frist, now president of a health management company, said he had reviewed a video feed of Bush shortly after he arrived in London. Frist, a heart surgeon and social conservative, enraged moderate voters in 2005 with his push for federal intervention to maintain life support for Terri Schiavo, a brain-damaged Florida woman. 'As a medical doctor, I see nothing wrong with him', he declared. 'It's clear that his facial expression and labored breathing is just excitement at the prospect of seeing his old friend Tony Blair'.

Meanwhile, Congress called a special session to discuss the issue of a pardon for the former President. When asked, after considering Bush's grave condition, if the cloning act ought to be amended to allow therapies using embryonic stem cells, Senate Majority leader Brownback said: 'No. God is punishing him for the sins he committed during college. His family can be forgiven for trying to make him well. But we must think of all the cloned human beings – the walking, talking embryos reaching out to us with their little hands – that were murdered as a result of this therapy. We must respect their lives more than the life of suffering humans, even humans that are former American presidents. I wish him good luck during his long convalescence in England'.

How likely is this drama that befalls a fictional American president? The events recounted up until the present day are true. Routine cures or treatments for diabetes, dementias and spinal injuries may be years away, but researchers have cured mice mimicking a form of diabetes with stem cells and tissue transplants.[5] In other experiments, spinal injured rats can walk again after given a transplant made from human embryonic stem cells. A clinical trial using the method in human subjects is planned for 2008 (the research has had to be funded by private sources).[6] In an experimental trial in Oregon, children with a deadly neurodegenerative disease are being injected with stem cells taken from foetal brain tissue.[7] Mice with brains partially comprised of human neural cells may help companies discover new drugs for dementias. But nuclear transfer, a method that might one day produce custom-matched lines of cells, tissues and rudimentary organs for the sick and infirm (including future statesmen and women), has not yet been successfully developed using human cells.

While the science struggled, the political winds were momentous. To the outrage of the scientific and medical communities, Kansas Senator Sam Brownback introduced legislative acts that would criminalise the use of embryonic stem cells (hESCs) for research and medical use, along with mice made with bits of human brain tissue. The legislation contained a particularly onerous provision, mandating the same penalties for researchers on any American who *provides* or *receives* medical treatments developed in another country. It also meant that patients and doctors could go to jail, too. The consequences of the legislation raised the mind-bending prospect that American parents travelling to the UK (or anywhere else where the research was permitted) to treat a diabetic child with an embryonic stem cell therapy would risk the family's imprisonment once they attempted to return home.

Yet Bush was steadfast. Eight months after his 9 August 2001 pronouncement that no federal funds could be used for any research using stem cell lines made from newly destroyed embryos, he said:

> I strongly support a comprehensive law against all human cloning. And I endorse the bill – wholeheartedly endorse the bill (S. 658) – sponsored by Senator Brownback and Senator Mary Landrieu. This carefully drafted bill would ban all human cloning in the United States, including the cloning of embryos for research.[8]

In a 2006 State of the Union address, he painted animal-human chimeras with the same moral brush: 'Tonight I ask you to pass legislation to prohibit the most egregious abuses of medical research: human cloning in all its forms, creating or implanting embryos for experiments, creating human-animal hybrids, and buying, selling, or patenting human embryos.'

Bush neatly seized a rhetorical trick used early on by religious conservatives, a triangulated moral position atop which the debate pivoted. At base level, everyone agreed that any attempt to clone a human being (so-called reproductive cloning) was abhorrent. But to Bush and his supporters, cloning cells for research and medicine was portrayed as equivalent to cloning human beings. Intersecting cloning was another trope with a long and fractious political history. Neoconservatives had declared an embryo 'proxy' war: a conflagration encompassing the issues of abortion, *in vitro* fertilisation and embryo research. To them, the embryo is a human being, and destroying it is murder.

The first embryo war began in 1973. The Supreme Court ruling in *Roe* v. *Wade* legalising abortion in the first two trimesters of pregnancy opened a Pandora's Box of worst-case scenarios. Religious leaders and a vigorous anti-abortion movement claimed the decision would result in the black-market sale or barter of fertilised eggs and indiscriminate use of embryos for laboratory experiments. Even more worrisome to the pro-life supporters was the possibility of the unregulated use of aborted foetal tissue. An alarmed Congress halted federally funded embryo research until guidelines could be established. The 1974 action had surprising staying power. With one short-lived exception, the 'temporary' moratorium has passed its 30th anniversary – no government funds are allowed for embryo research, a policy that swept essential questions about infertility, reproductive medicine, prenatal diagnosis and embryonic stem cell research beyond the reach of most American clinicians and scientists. Bush's 2001 policy tightened the noose, and Brownback's bill upped the ante: use any embryo, donated or otherwise, and go to jail.

The actions boiled over a long-simmering controversy about embryo research and the spectre of human clones. Eighty Nobel Prize winners, led by Stanford University's Paul Berg, wrote a letter to the President condemning his policy and the actions of Congress, arguing that it was crippling their research. Others pointed out the moral inconsistency of a policy that permits thousands of unused *in vitro* fertilisation embryos to be dumped down the drain yearly while disallowing their use to treat disease. Berg, a man who has spent a career at the forefront of science policy, understands how important it is to measure words. He described how he felt when he first read the legislation: 'I couldn't believe the arrogance of a bunch people in Congress saying to 290 million Americans, sorry folks, you're not going to have the therapies to cure your disease because we are offended by this technology.'[9] Two of Brownback's bills passed the House of Representatives by wide margins but never came before the Senate. Countermeasures to overturn the Bush policy were passed by the House and Senate in separate sessions of Congress, but neither vote was enough to override a presidential veto. In the end, Bush's tenure was marked by his uncompromising moral stance: he vowed to fight any threat that would kill Americans – foreign terrorists flying planes into buildings or scientists destroying embryos for research. In late 2006, Bush's final veto count: one against withdrawing troops from the Iraq War; two against embryonic stem cell research.

NOW AND THEN

The stem cell debate is perhaps the most visible fracture between religious and social conservatives and the scientific community, yet the fault lines reach deep into the natural sciences, touching genetics, evolution, reproductive biology and climate change. Taking their cues from Bush (and vice versa), neoconservative commentators regard science, scientists and academics with suspicion, calling into question the foundations of empirical thought laid out by Aristotle and Thomas Aquinas. The scientific method and hard evidence was out. Metaphysics and argument for argument's sake was in.

Nowhere was this more apparent than the ruckus about creationism and its sidekick, intelligent design. Conservatives jettisoned the notion that in order to compete as a credible theory, intelligent design should have scientific merit. In a nod to discourse as an academic value, teaching creationism and intelligent design alongside evolution seemed only fair. Every idea was worth debating, proof or no. As the literary theorist Stanley Fish notes, intelligent designers lifted a page out of liberalism (and empiricism) to make their case.[10] The nineteenth-century philosopher John Stuart Mill insisted that knowledge is nothing without repeated challenge – the process of debate is more important than the end product itself. 'Teach the controversy' became the battle cry. Bush echoed this position at a White House roundtable: 'Part of education is to expose people to different schools of thought ... you're asking me whether or not people ought to be exposed to different ideas, and the answer is yes.'[11] This 'academic cross-dressing', as Fish acerbically puts it, subverts the values of truth and accuracy for a supposedly nobler cause of public and political debate.

The conservative push against science moved deep into secondary education. *The New Republic* asked *Weekly Standard* editor William Kristol if he believes in evolution and whether it should be taught in public schools. He said, 'I'm not a scientist ... It's like me asking you whether you believe in the Big Bang ... I managed to have my children go through the Fairfax, Virginia, schools without ever looking at one of their science textbooks.'[12] Kristol and other conservative commentators know the American cultural winds favour scepticism of science, especially in the American South. Movie theatres there, fearing backlash from conservative Christians, refused to show the IMAX film *Volcanoes of the Deep Sea* (2003) because of a brief mention of evolution. In Tennessee, a new creation museum asks its employees to sign a statement of faith that says they believe dinosaurs and man once co-existed. The $27 million, 60,000 square foot facility, built by a Christian publishing company called Answers in Genesis, establishes the earth's age as 6,000 years and depicts dioramas of humans ambling alongside dinosaurs.

Public acceptance of evolution in the United States is among the lowest in the world. A true or false answer to the question 'Have human beings, as we know them, developed from earlier species of animals?' ranks America 32 out of 33 countries in making a false claim; Iceland, Denmark, Sweden, France, Japan and the UK round out the top six. Digging deeper into the reasons for the opinion, researchers correlated pro-life, fundamentalist religious and conservative partisan views with the low score.[13] A 2006 poll of Americans shows only a third believe that evolution is supported by hard evidence. Half believe in the biblical account of creation, and that creationism should be taught in science class. A recent study by the National Science Teachers Association finds that three out of ten teachers feel pressure from students and parents to include non-scientific alternatives to evolution in the classroom.[14] And in a case that garnered international attention, the Kansas Board of Education approved standards critical of evolution-based science in 2005, after considering 23 pages of revisions from the state's intelligent design chapter. The vote was an embarrassment for Kansas, which repealed the guidelines in 2007. But the conservative state wasn't alone: during 2005 and 2006, 18 other states considered anti-evolution legislation.

The conservative-driven anti-science backlash is not just limited to stem cells and teaching evolution. Scientific journals, newspapers and legislators published essays and reports detailing political interference in a number of science agency appointments, including the NIH, NASA, EPA and the FDA. The most damning of these came from the 200,000-member Union of Concerned Scientists, an advocacy organisation based in Washington. In early 2004, it issued a report backing a statement signed by over 60 scientists, including Nobel laureates and National Medal of Science recipients. The statement accused the Bush administration with widespread and unprecedented 'manipulation of the process through which science enters into its decisions'. The document contained a litany of abuses, including manipulation of scientific data, suppression of evidence about climate change, and stacking advisory committees with political appointees.[15]

The meddling was especially acute on the Council on Bioethics, an appointed commission advising the President on ethics and science policy. Accusations abounded that the administration used political litmus tests to screen prospective commissioners. After the council's deliberations on stem cell research, members opposing the Bush policy were fired or asked to resign. The eighteen-member group produced four major reports, consistent with longstanding opinions of the council's conservative majority. The recommendations overwhelmingly reflect the 'Brave New World' philosophy: left unchecked, big science, stem cell research and biotechnology threaten the humanity of Americans. One of the sacked councillors, Elizabeth Blackburn – an award-winning and internationally known cancer expert – remarked that Leon Kass, the first council chair and Bush appointee, had a 'nausea for diversity' and added later that she considered her removal a result of 'Bush stacking the council with the compliant'.[16]

This isn't the first time Americans have fretted about science run amok. The world faced a similar quandary 30 years ago amid widespread concerns about the dangers of recombinant DNA research. The federal government came breathtakingly close to criminalising biomedical research in those days, too. Finally, on the heels of a meeting held by 150 scientists, government officials and others in a sun-drenched retreat in Asilomar, near Monterey, California, the National Institutes of Health adopted a framework that included regulation, oversight and review by the newly formed Recombinant DNA Advisory Committee. This body monitored laboratory research that was recognised for transforming science and creating a new industry. The policy became an example of how scientists put the brakes on an area of research with unknown consequences, and how the recommendations were embraced and promulgated by a national agency.

There are important differences between the recombinant DNA story of the 1970s and now. Concerns then were primarily focused on environmental safety. The worry was that unethical or inattentive genetic engineers would release mutant organisms into the environment, which could infect humans, disrupt ecosystems or destroy agricultural crops. The Asilomar meeting produced a series of rationally conceived checks and balances to prevent these hazards and other abuses. In contrast, embryonic stem cell research invokes individual and cultural values: both non-rational constructs. Values can be based on deeply held moral beliefs. A rational approach, such as the use of unwanted frozen embryos for research purposes, can be challenged by a person's moral belief. For example, in a clinical setting, an ethics committee, along with the treating physician, can recommend that a dying woman in an intensive care unit be removed from costly, sophisticated equipment that will not save her and instead be made as comfortable as possible during her final days. These are carefully reasoned arguments, based on an application of ethical theory and a history of similar medical cases. But the family, when confronted with the decision, may believe in miracles. The discussion can proceed no further. The moral arcs of the stem cell debate produce the same irresolvable conflict. Though a numerical minority, many Americans believe the obligations to an embryonic iota of 100 cells trump the obligations to living persons.

The second difference is the steady erosion of public trust in science and medicine. 'Scientists are no longer perceived exclusively as guardians of objective truth but as smart promoters of their own interests', argue one pair of commentators.[17] The academy itself has come under attack from watchdog groups and its own members. Two books from 2003, Sheldon Krimsky's *Science in the Private Interest: Has the Lure of Profits Corrupted Biomedical Research?* and Jennifer Washburn's *University Inc.: The Corporate Corruption of Higher Education*, enumerate the ways in which biomedical scientists and their institutions have become hostage to the filthy lucre offered by the private sector. And even a past president of Harvard University frets about how the drive to find money to expand biomedical research has eclipsed the more noble pursuits of academic inquiry and teaching the liberal arts.[18]

The fears are not limited to the US. In 2000, a House of Lords select committee confirmed a 'crisis of trust' in science after polling 1000 citizens, especially with respect to gene therapy, genetically modified food, animal experimentation and xenotransplantation.[19] The stateside crisis is in part due to a growing disinterest in science education. Bush's verbal slip to school-children about the 'nerd patrol' – those unpopular kids adept in science and mathematics – betrays a conspicuous, postmodern slide towards anti-intellectualism. 'Rigor, thoroughness, a commitment to consistency, intellectual honesty, exactness, or a sensibility to small differences are all generally undervalued' in this milieu, warns one political philosopher.[20] But a rigorous education does not always translate into a keen appreciation of evidence and argument. We believe things because we trust experts – including religious authorities, politicians and parents – who say it is true. In this way, intuitive pseudoscientific or metaphysical explanations can clash with the long-held doctrines of the biological sciences.

As if on cue, this mistrust turned into an unwavering 'I told you so' by stem cell opponents during the early days of 2006, when two papers published by a team of South Korean embryonic stem cell researchers were revealed to be fakes. The discoveries were considered the first important step – called nuclear transfer – to produce custom therapies like the one described above for our fictional and suffering former President. When the dust settled, the scandal went down as the worst scientific fraud in recent memory.

Destined for textbooks, it featured a basketful of misdeeds, ranging from venal sins, shameless falsehoods, and treading on the rights of women researchers who donated their eggs for the research.

While media coverage of the fraud was brief, the South Korean event bolstered the moral high ground seized by opponents: scientists can't be trusted – and scientists who work on embryos commit murder. Embryos made by transferring a nucleus and then destroyed to make specialised, compatible cells for a sick person through therapeutic cloning (even a former president) was as wrong as embryos destroyed to investigate, say, the developmental complexities of infertility. Political conservatives used the event as a new weapon in old armamentarium that had successfully interfered with three decades of embryo research. In 1979, one year after the UK announced the birth of Louise Brown, the world's first test tube baby, a national ethics advisory board recommended that federal dollars be spent investigating the safety of assisted reproductive technologies. But because of political wrangling, no authority was ever granted to review research proposals, and few laws were written to oversee the procedures in private clinics.

Predictions are that stem cell research will eclipse by orders of magnitude the impact of recombinant DNA. What would the world be like if the US government had banned recombinant DNA research back in 1976? Assuming the prohibition persisted during the subsequent decades, and no other research filled the void, the world would be without the Human Genome Project, without the identification of 1,500 disease genes, and without DNA fingerprinting. The US would also be $16 billion poorer in research and investment, $35 billion poorer in revenue and lacking some 200,000 jobs. In addition, 325 million people would not benefit from over 130 drugs, including vaccines for influenza and hepatitis B.[21]

NATIONAL FRACTURE

What has this moral fracture wrought for America? For research and medicine, the impacts are profound.

US stem cell policy is oddly incoherent when compared to other countries that support embryonic stem cell research. Though a presidential procla-mation is not law, it carries the force of law. Bush's mandate prohibiting funding of new lines of embryonic stem cells – delivered from his ranch in Texas – was never debated or voted on by Congress. Conservative lawmakers linked bans on reproductive cloning (on which there was unanimous agreement among scientists, lawmakers and citizens) to bans on embryonic stem cell research. The hybrid bills divided the Senate and were never passed. The result: America has no laws banning human cloning. Because of the federal government's regulatory silence, the research community turned to other institutions for guidance. The National Academy of Science's *Guidelines for Human Embryonic Stem Cell Research* (2005) is used at both the state and local levels.[22]

The federal vacuum has prompted a patchwork of state legislation. About a dozen states expressly encourage the research, including California, New Jersey and Wisconsin. But in 2006, South Dakota criminalised it. In Michigan, researchers must contend with laws that would jail scientists for up to 10 years and fine them $10 million for using embryos to make cell lines. In Virginia, the stem cell statute is so obscurely written that it isn't clear if using an embryo made by nuclear transfer is legal or not. But two dozen states are silent on the issue, meaning embryonic stem cell lines might be made there, but only with non-federal dollars.

Funding follows the same pattern, with a half-dozen states putting their money on the table. Chief among these is California, which in 2004 passed a $3 billion, ten-year measure to support all types of stem cell research. The sheer size of the California initiative not only sends a message about the promise of embryonic stem cells but also underscores how expensive biomedical research can be and how distant therapies are from human use. The measure is designed to outlast several administrations and to insulate California from the vagaries of Congressional politics, but the money only began to flow in the summer of 2007.

The legislative thicket and spotty funding could cause a perilous backwash. Interstate and international collaboration may be thwarted, hamstrung by discontinuities in law and resources. Capital markets, sensitive to risks both scientific and political, are reluctant to venture into territory darkened by political whim and uneven sources of intellectual capital. Sensing an opportunity to trump a technological colossus, other countries aggressively recruit senior American researchers. One study finds senior American stem cell scientists are more than five times more likely to receive international job offers than those in other fields.[23] In another, the US rate of publishing seminal embryonic stem cell papers in peer-reviewed journals has begun to slow, while other countries step up the pace.[24] In a foretelling of America's place in a global race for the first tools and treatments, embryonic stem cell lines made here are shipped offshore more often than they are used in our own laboratories.[25] Nobel Prize winner Berg complains that 'America will become experts in mouse stem cell biology.' Irving Weissman, an internationally recognised stem cell biologist who has testified in front of Congress echoes the sentiment: 'America may very well buy the first stem cell treatments from China.'[26]

There is hand wringing in Washington too. A National Science Foundation executive said:

Collectively, India, China, South Korea, and Japan, have more than doubled the number of students receiving bachelor's degrees in the natural sciences since 1975 and quadrupled their number earning engineering degrees. Since the late 1980s, the EU has produced more natural science and engineering PhDs than the US.[27]

Others maintain the US faces a 'Sputnik moment' similar to the fears engendered by the space race of 50 years ago. They warn that globalisation threatens its technological dominance. Americans have become users, not inventors, of new technology.

INTERNATIONAL HEALING?

In *Rising Above the Gathering Storm* (2007), a report commissioned by the US Congress, a committee of leading engineers, scientists and educators warns: 'Thanks to globalization, driven by modern communications and other advances, workers in virtually every sector must now face competitors who live just a mouse-click away in Ireland, Finland, China, India, or dozens of other nations whose economies are growing.'[28]

Until now, there has been little challenge to American biomedical hegemony. But the moral fissures caused by the debate have forged a new global socio-political landscape. Does it matter that the US takes a central role in the discovery and development of new medicines? Can we settle as a bit player in the stem cell supply chain? What is more important: American technological dominance or a speedy route to a treatment for the world's infirm? After all, discovery and development of biotechnology is modular and decentralised, linking together like a chain of toy beads. It is quite possible that countries – and their governments, scientists and institutions – will figure out which link they can most readily provide. The markets for that technology, product or service will surely follow. Will the globalisation of medicine, exemplified by Thomas Friedman's flattened earth, be more saviour than villain, helping to span what has become this century's greatest moral divide? Or will it produce a new set of ethical concerns? Answering these questions demands a closer look at the national actors in the race for the world's first new medicines made from embryonic stem cells.

Consider Singapore. This tiny Asian nation is a financial juggernaut, luring Western pharmaceutical companies to the Pacific Rim by fronting a third of their building costs. At least thirty companies have taken the government up on the offer, building research facilities at Biopolis, a glistening new $8 billion research park. The country also has recruited a well-regarded contingent of American and British stem cell scientists with hefty salaries and lavish new laboratories. Singapore was among the first countries to forge guidelines for embryonic stem cells so the research could move quickly.

Across the Bay of Bengal lies India. Its pharmaceutical industries are among the biggest in the world. A large and sparsely monitored assisted reproductive technology industry with political clout means it has eggs and embryos – scarce resources required for stem cell research. There is also human capital – willing subjects to enrol in experimental clinical trails. But there are concerns about the country's ethical readiness: 'As stem cell science moves from the laboratory into the clinic and the experimental treatment of patients, it does so in a governance vacuum', states one report.[29] India's clinical trials expertise is underdeveloped, and the agency in charge of oversight, The Drug Controller General, is reported as understaffed and overly influenced by the country's pharmaceutical industry. Western companies remain wary about locating there, because of patent infringement.

China, an economic giant with a massive workforce and market, could take a deep bite out of Western dominance in high technology. Its manufacturing and technical strengths are seemingly limitless. However, its reputation for playing fast and loose with intellectual property, human rights and experimental medicine cause concern that it will become the Wild, Wild East of modern medicine. Safeguards for the use of embryos and human research subjects are largely missing and poorly enforced.[30] Part of China's approach is due to its cultural norms: the embryo does not have a significant moral status, the root cause of ethical rupture in the West. The 'regulatory gradient' between overly permissive and non-permissive jurisdictions has caused some Americans to travel long distances to China to undergo risky and expensive treatment for maladies such as spinal cord injury and ataxia.

But China has a way to go before it can assert itself in any meaningful way in one of the most complicated and fraught fields of modern biology. Its commitment to stem cell research is small, only $2 million per year from 2000–5.[31] Like India, China trains thousands of its scientists in American and European laboratories. But nearly three quarters of them never return, surpassed only by India's chronic brain drain.

Finally, note the country treating our ersatz President. In contrast to the US, the UK's Human Fertilisation and Embryology Authority (HFEA) oversees IVF clinics, and laboratories making embryonic stem cells may only do so under a government licence. In contrast to the US, the British government fully embraces the future possibilities of the science. In 2005, the UK's Stem Cell Initiative set out a ten-year strategy for research and development, raising the government's commitment of $100 million per year.[32] London is home to the UK Stem Cell Bank, a facility that catalogues, stores, characterises and distributes hESC lines to researchers around the world. In the future, the bank will likely serve as a source of cells for therapies. The cultural differences between the two nations on this issue are profound. The former head of HFEA, Baroness Ruth Deech, remarked during a recent speech in the US that the British seem mystified that frozen embryos are given so much religious and political importance.[33]

But like California, the UK sits in isolation to some of its EU neighbours. The production of human embryonic stem cells is a punishable offence in Germany, though lines made prior to 2002 may be imported into German laboratories. Joining Germany, restrictive countries include Ireland, Austria,

Denmark, Italy and France. Reflecting an opposed set of national values, permissive nations include Sweden, the Netherlands, Finland and Greece.

The moral wrangling across the EU has produced a peculiar pairing, one with staggering consequences for stem cell research: patent law and ethics. In 1998, the European community adopted the European Directive on the Legal Protection of Biotechnological Inventions to remove legal obstacles arising from differences in national law among the EU member states.[34] Deep within the directive lies a list of technologies to be excluded from patentability on the grounds of *ordre public* or morality. This has led to the rejection of crucial embryonic stem cell patents – the coin of the realm for any company hoping to commercialise medicines for human use – for moral, rather than technical reasons. The directive's interpretation has caused legal gridlock among European member states, which attempt to reject or accept patents based on national ethical norms. The evidence so far is that the focus on the moral exclusion policy on uses of human embryos by the European Patent Office (EPO) is thwarting the ability to patent at the national level. Germany overturned a stem cell patent granted to a German neuroscientist on the grounds it was immoral.[35] The dithering in other jurisdictions means that the EU isn't the safe haven for stem cells it was thought to be. In fact, it is possible the morality clause might be invoked for *any* technology using *any* kind of cell made from embryonic stem cells, turning entire stretches of the EU into a wasteland for companies and capital markets with expertise in regenerative medicine.

BORDER LINES, CELL LINES AND THE FUTURE OF MEDICINE

As the Bush legacy ends in 2008 so the Bush administration's restrictions will likely end too and religious conservatives will lose the political clout to pass laws that would imprison a suffering American president – or any other citizen – trying to return home from an offshore treatment. However, it is far from certain whether globalisation can work with morality guarding the borders. But globalisation may make the difference between having some new therapies or none at all. A future therapy for an autoimmune disease such as GBS or diabetes, rather than developing naturally and swiftly among those nations most qualified, may instead have to navigate a torturous, inefficient and expensive route – consequences borne from politics claiming the moral high ground.

The human costs of a world fractured by religion and politics are ethical as well as economic. Political, legal and moral gradients among nations now mean increases in medical tourism for untested stem cell treatments. Clinical trials initially deemed too risky (or too politically fraught) have moved into countries with lower regulatory thresholds. In one case, stem cell injections in humans with heart disease started in South America, Thailand and Asia before being rigorously tested in Europe. Only then was the first US trial approved. Years later, a public registry lists dozens of such clinical trials worldwide.

In our future scenario, the therapy sought by Mr Bush could have been first tested on humans in China. With its porous regulatory framework and plentiful research subjects, China may indeed find a place in translating discoveries made elsewhere into clinical practice. The company developing the technology could be Singaporean, bankrolled by a government-backed venture capital firm. A similar treatment for diabetes would yield a multi-billion dollar blockbuster for the company and for Singapore, which would use the money to lure more investment and more Western-trained re-searchers to the island. The human egg into which daughter Jenna's DNA was transferred might have been procured from a woman frequenting an in vitro fertilisation clinic in rural India. The company may have emerged from a costly set of lawsuits with Saudi investors backing a competing group of scientists and entrepreneurs working in Germany. Because patents on embryonic stem cell therapies are not enforced there, Germany could become home to biotech pirates, infringing on inventions claimed and practiced elsewhere in Europe and the US. The costs of winning the suit would be passed along to patients and to the healthcare system, providing such a system even paid for such early-stage therapy.

Shortly after the 2001 Bush proclamation, National Medal of Science winner Robert Weinberg wrote:

> In the end, politics will settle the debate in this country about whether human therapeutic cloning is allowed to proceed. If the decision is yes, then we will continue to lead the world in a crucial, cutting edge area of biomedical research. If it is no, US biologists will undertake hegiras to laboratories in Australia, Japan, Israel, and certain countries in Europe – an outcome that will leave American science greatly diminished.[36]

Politics could settle the debate in a very different way, after the first cures using embryonic stem cells are discovered and made available on a distant shore. No American politician can defend a position that would place political expediency above the medical needs of his or her constituents. No politician would dare refuse a sick or suffering person care and treatment.

The vote will be swift and the message clear: let science proceed.

NOTES

1. This is a hypothetical scenario set in 2016. Everything referenced prior to the publication date is based on reported events and published research.
2. Brownback introduced legislation in 2002 and 2005 that would criminalise use of embryos for research and for using human stem cells to make animal models of disease; the penalties: $1 million fine and up to ten years in prison for

scientists, caregivers and patients. Neither bill has passed.

3. Recent research foreshadows a time when embryonic stem cells may treat diabetes, multiple sclerosis and rheumatoid arthritis, among them: see Yuichi Hori *et al.*, *Proceedings of the National Academy of Sciences*, 99, 2002, 16105–10.

4. A mouse with 1 per cent human neural cells was produced at the Salk Institute in 2005: see A. R. Muotri *et al.*, *Proceedings of the National Academy of Sciences*, 102, 2005, 18644–8.

5. See J. A. Shizuru *et al.*, 'Prevention of type 1 diabetes in nonobese diabetic mice by allogeneic bone marrow transplantation', *Diabetes*, 54(6), June 2005, 1770–9.

6. Human embryonic stem cell-derived oligodendrocyte progenitor cell transplants remyelinate and restore locomotion after spinal cord injury: see H. S. Keirstead *et al.*, *Journal of Neuroscience*, 25(19), 11 May 2005, 4694–705.

7. Stem Cells Inc., a biotechnology company based in the San Francisco bay area, is developing a treatment for Batten Disease. The first clinical trial commenced in 2006.

8. See White House press release, 'President Bush calls on Senate to back human cloning ban', http://www.whitehouse.gov/news/releases/2002/04/20020410-4.html.

9. Christopher Thomas Scott, *Stem Cell Now: A Brief Introduction to the Coming Medical Revolution* (New York, NY: Plume, 2006), p. 165.

10. Stanley Fish, 'Academic Cross-dressing: how intelligent design gets its arguments from the left', *Harper's Magazine*, December 2005, pp. 70–2.

11. A transcript of Bush's remarks can be found at: http://www.washingtonpost.com/wp-dyn/content/article/2005/08/02/AR2005080200899_5.html.

12. Ben Adler, 'Conservatives and Evolution: The Evolutionary War', *The New Republic*, 7 July 2005, https://ssl.tnr.com/p/docsub.mhtml?i=w050704&s=adler070705.

13. J. Miller *et al.*, 'Public acceptance of Evolution', *Science*, 313, 11 August 2006, 765–6.

14. National Science Teachers Association, 'Survey indicates science teachers feel pressure to teach nonscientific alternatives to evolution', 24 March 2005, http://www.nsta.org/pressroom&news.

15. 'Scientific integrity in policymaking: an investigation into the Bush administration's misuse of science', Union of Concerned Scientists, March 2004, http://www.ucsusa.org/.

16. See Timothy Noah, 'Leon Kass, you silly ass: please stop denying you tilted the Bioethics Panel', *Slate*, 8 March 2004, http://slate.msn.com/id/2096848/; and Rick Weiss, 'Bush ejects two from Bioethics Council: changes renew criticisms that President puts politics ahead of science', *Washington Post*, 28 February 2004.

17. B. Haerlin and D. Parr, 'How to restore public trust in science', *Nature*, 400, 5 August 1999, 499.

18. Sheldon Krimsky, *Science in the Private Interest: Has the Lure of Profits Corrupted Biomedical Research?* (Lanham, MD: Rowman and Littlefield, 2003); Jennifer Washburn, *University Inc.: The Corporate Corruption of Higher Education* (New York, NY: Basic Books, [2003] 2006); and Derek Bok, *Universities in the Marketplace: the Commercialization of Higher Education* (Princeton, NJ: Princeton University Press, 2003).

19. See http://www.parliament.the-stationery office.co.uk/pa/ld199900/ldselect/ ldsctech/38/3801.htm.

20. M. North, 'Chastened, not Stirred: The secret agents of literature departments reap what they sow', *Telos*, (37)1, 118–39.

21. Christopher Thomas Scott and Thomas Maeder, 'The consequences of the restrictions of human stem cell research', *Acumen Journal of Sciences*, 1(1), 2003, 36–45.

22. National Research Council, *Guidelines for Human Embryonic Stem Cell Research* (2005).

23. A. D. Levine, 'Research policy and the mobility of US stem cell scientists', *Nature Biotechnology*, 24(7), 2006, 865–6.

24. J. Owens-Smith and J. McCormick, 'An international gap in embryonic stem cell research', *Nature Biotechnology*, 24(4), 2006, 391–2.

25. Preliminary data gathered by the author's research at Stanford University.

26. Personal communication, August 2004 and September 2005.

27. See http://www.nsf.gov/news/speeches/olsen/05/ko051009_pkal.jsp.

28. *Rising Above the Gathering Storm: Energizing and Employing America for a Brighter Economic Future* (Washington DC: National Academies Press, 2007), p. 1.

29. B. Salter *et al.*, 'Stem cell science in India: emerging economies and the politics of globalization', *Regenerative Medicine*, 2(1), 2007, 75–89.

30. B. Salter *et al.*, 'China and the global stem cell bioeconomy: an emerging political strategy?', *Regenerative Medicine*, 1(5), 2006, 671–83.

31. F. Murray and D. Spar, 'Bit player or powerhouse? China and stem cell research', *New England Journal of Medicine*, 355(12), 21 September 2006, 1191–4.

32. Report and Recommendations of the UK Stem Cell Initiative, November 2005, http://www.dh.gov.uk/en/Policyandguidance/Healthandsocialcaretopics/ Stemcell/index.htm.

33. Ruth Deech, 'Women, Ethics and Embryos', unpublished talk at Stanford University, 2 May 2007.

34. Downloadable directive at: europa.eu.int/eur-lex/pri/en/oj/dat/1998/l_213/ l_21319980730en00130021.pdf

35. See Aurora Plomer *et al.*, 'Challenges to embryonic stem cell patents', *Cell Stem Cell*, 2, January 2008, 13–17.

36. Robert Weinberg, 'Of Clones and Clowns', *Atlantic Monthly*, June 2002, http://www.theatlantic.com/doc/200206/weinberg.

11. TECHNOLOGY IN THE 21st CENTURY

Carroll Pursell

Any attempt to discuss the technology of the 21st century, based on the record of the first five to ten years, demands a caveat. Futurology, so popular 30 years ago, has all but disappeared, perhaps because in so much of the United States fortune telling is illegal. Even the easy prediction that change, however unclear in its details now, will continue, is no doubt true but misleading. Technologies change, but not because they must. Technologies change because people with the power to make it happen want it to.

While change will no doubt take place over the remainder of the century, many technologies will not change at all. In his important book *The Shock of the Old* (2007), David Edgerton asserts that 'time was always jumbled up, in the pre-modern era, the post-modern era and the modern era.' In what he calls 'use-centered history technologies do not only appear, they also disappear and reappear, and mix and match across the centuries.' He also calls attention to what he terms 'creole' technologies, those 'transplanted from their place of origin finding uses on a greater scale elsewhere.'[1] As in the past, old technologies and those transplanted will continue to be at least as important as those newly invented and rushed to market.

Over the years, those who have yielded to the temptation to predict the future on the basis of those new technologies seem always, as Joseph Corn has pointed out, to make the same mistakes: what he calls 'the fallacy of total revolution, the fallacy of social continuity, and the fallacy of the technological fix', all of which contribute to 'the extravagant and often utopian tone of technological prediction.'[2] The first of these errs in believing that the new wipes out the old and sweeps all before it. At the same time, the second fallacy mistakenly believes that when a new and improved technology replaces an old and inferior one, the social context remains the same: an autogiro may replace the car for taking commuters to work, but it will still be Dad making the trip while Mom and the kids stay at home and await his return. And finally, the last fallacy assumes that new technologies only fix things, they never create new problems or make existing situations worse.

If we try to avoid these fallacies then, and keep in mind Edgerton's notion of creole technologies and the persistence of the old mixed in with the new, what can we guess as to the shape of 21st-century technology? And here it is helpful to keep in mind another of Edgerton's admonitions: 'stop thinking about "technology", but instead think of "things". Thinking about the use of things, rather than of technology, connects us directly with the world we know rather than the strange world in which "technology" lives'.[3]

9/11 AND THE TECHNOLOGICAL FIX

The continuity of technologies is well demonstrated in the specific reactions to the destruction of New York's World Trade Center on 11 September 2001. For one thing, the technologies involved perfectly reflect the technological vanguardism and hubris of 20th-century America. The hijacked Boeing 767 used in the attack was designed to carry up to 255 passengers and to fly as far as from New York City to Beijing. Fully loaded it carried 23,980 gallons of aviation fuel. Like all Boeing civilian jetliners, its design had evolved in close conjunction with decades of military aircraft development and was the direct descendent of the bombers that had carried out the terror bombings of German and Japanese cities during World War II. The simple box cutter, the hijackers' weapon of choice, had been used in perhaps most American homes for generations. The skyscraper, probably the architectural signature of New York City, has been a fixture of the skyline for a century.

Even the nightmare of American vulnerability had been a feature of American Cold War popular culture since 1945, when the US used atomic bombs, those most dramatic of 'Weapons of Mass Destruction', against Hiroshima and Nagasaki, killing over a hundred thousand people, nearly all civilians including women, children and the elderly. Only a few years into the 'Atomic Age' the major powers, including the US, had written off their own civilian populations as essentially unsaveable in a nuclear exchange. There is every reason to believe that the American people knew that they were helplessly vulnerable, despite backyard bomb shelters and 'duck-and-cover' instruction for school children.

It hardly comes as a surprise that the terrorist attacks of 9/11 have attracted no single, fixed meaning. Perhaps in part this was because it was all so familiar, as a part of Edgerton's 'Shock of the Old'. Not only were the jetliner, the skyscraper and the box cutter all perfectly familiar, but even the dramatic image of the 9/11 destruction, that played endlessly on more than 30 television channels, was already old. Scores of motion pictures since 1945 had staged something similar. A whole genre of entertainment had been created around the spectacle of great structures collapsing into themselves through the technology of controlled implosion. Indeed, the implosion of the Pruitt-Igoe public housing complex in St Louis in 1972 is often heralded by architectural critics such as Charles Jencks as the start of the postmodern era, and members of the demolition firm most responsible for implosions sometimes referred to themselves (pre-9/11) as 'terrorists'.[4] The date of 11 September had itself marked an earlier (though largely unacknowledged) dark moment in American history when, in 1973, General Augusto Pinochet, with the tacit support of the US government, overthrew the democratically-elected President Salvador Allende of Chile, with the killing of many more than three thousand civilians.

The twin World Trade Towers themselves were showcases of aggressive American capitalism. The Japanese designer of what were then the world's tallest structures was specifically instructed to emphasise sheer scale and the result was what he called a 'swagger building'.[5] The towers were a success not only as beacons of American capitalism's global reach but also in terms of maximising profit within its own bounds. In response to cost pressures, a series of construction techniques and materials were used to free-up an unprecedented 75 per cent of each floor for office rentals. The techniques, in at least some cases untested, included a curtain of exterior steel columns, cutting the number of vertical girders, supporting the floors on bridge-like trusses rather than steel beams, and an innovative elevator plan which cut the number of shafts that ran through all 110 floors. Additionally, elevator shafts and stairwells were enclosed with wallboard rather than concrete. The aggregate cost-saving and profit-maximising measures helped turn the towers into a death trap for its thousands of employees.[6]

The reaction to these events, at the time of writing, tells us a great deal about the ways in which technologies are human intentions made material. The twin towers are to be replaced with a Freedom Tower 1,776 feet tall, a height dictated by the desire to build patriotism (the date of American independence) into the very dimensions of the building. The construction design for the new building includes air intakes with chemical and biological filtering systems; a central core with water-resistant elevators; pressurised fire-escape stairs and a separate staircase for emergency workers; extra-strong concrete casings for the core, sprinklers and emergency risers; multilayered glass curtain walls; and setback from the sidewalk to protect against car bombs. In a final act of bravado, the structure will be 408 feet higher than the towers destroyed on 9/11.[7]

The technological fix was applied to airplanes as well. Cockpit doors were immediately reinforced to prevent forced entry and in 2006 the SAFEE (Security of Aircraft in the Future European Environment) Project unveiled plans for the terror-proof plane of the future. In this plan, the cockpit door will be fitted with a fingerprint reading device and any unauthorised entry will activate a computer that will fly the plane away from 'sensitive targets'. Hand-held sniffer devices will check passengers at the door for dangerous chemicals, recording devices in toilets will listen for 'questionable noises', and tiny cameras will scan passengers' faces for nervous tics.[8]

GREEN TECHNOLOGIES

A much more significant example of the technological fix is provided by attempts to produce 'clean' energy in the face of a now acknowledged and rapidly worsening environment of global warming. The basic problem is that the burning of fossil fuels, whether coal to produce electricity, petroleum to power cars or any other such activity, produces greenhouse gases. A wide range of technologies, from wood-burning fireplaces to jet engines, are employed in producing the problem, and an equally wide range of technological alternatives are available to help relieve it. The choices made by governments, corporations and individuals in the United States are instructive.

The 'cleanest' technologies are probably those which are hardly seen as technologies at all. Wearing warmer clothing in winter and cooler in summer, for example, or double-glazing windows, planting shade trees and insulating the walls and roofs of buildings would all contribute to a diminution of energy consumption, as would a greater use of bicycles and public transportation.

Next might be the technologies of solar and wind power production. These were widely publicised in the US, especially in California, during the 1970s as part of the Appropriate Technology Movement but largely abandoned once energy prices dropped following the end of the OPEC fuel crisis. A generation later they are being touted again, but again mainly in California. Such technologies which require a change in 'lifestyle' or might challenge entrenched economic interests (and their political allies) are the least likely to become public policy and therefore be made available to citizens at large in forms both economical and convenient.

Instead, panaceas both old and new have been put forward. Nuclear power, with its potential for catastrophic accidents and certain problems of decommissioning and waste disposal, has been reborn in the new millennium as 'clean and green'. The administration of George W. Bush, while opposing increasing standards for automobile fuel efficiency, and even siding against California regulations being challenged in court by automobile manufacturers, committed itself in 2003 to spending $1.2 billion to help the auto industry develop hydrogen fuel-cell technology for powering cars. Such cars, it was agreed, would produce only water as exhaust.

But technologies exist in systems, not in isolation. Fuel cells would be clean only if the hydrogen they used were itself produced in a clean manner: using solar energy for example would keep hydrocarbon production to a minimum. The Bush administration however declared that 'America's abundant coal resources offer an attractive mid-term option for producing the large quantities of hydrogen that will be required to fuel the nation's energy needs.'[9] Indeed, the administration's National Hydrogen Energy Roadmap drafted in 2002 projected that 90 per cent of all the necessary hydrogen would be extracted from oil, natural gas, coal and other fossil fuels. The remaining 10 per cent would be produced using nuclear energy.[10]

Early in 2007, President Bush travelled to Detroit to join car manufacturers in touting 'flexible fuel' vehicles that could run on either ethanol or biodiesel blends. The manufacturers claimed they could have half their production converted to 'flexible' engines by 2012, although it was noted that only 1,100 of the nation's 170,000 fuelling stations offered ethanol blends. The chairman and CEO of General Motors admitted that they and the President spent 'very little time' talking about increased fuel efficiency, perhaps the technology which would make the greatest and fastest impact on petroleum consumption.[11]

Those countries, like Australia and the US, which have large reserves of coal, have looked to 21st-century technologies to help avoid the necessity of damaging the mining industry in the drive to combat global warming. The American industry-sponsored group CARE (Coalition for Affordable and Reliable Energy) predicted that the demand for electricity would go up 53.4 per cent in the first 25 years of the new century, and that since 'coal will remain the largest single source of electricity', 65 coal-fired power plants each generating 300 megawatts would need to be built in each of those years. It was claimed this could be done with zero emissions if the plants used the electricity to produce hydrogen and at the same time 'sequestered' their own greenhouse emissions.[12]

The US Department of Energy's Office of Fossil Energy in January 2006 was managing over 500 research projects, including 90 that were perusing the most publicised of the potential new technologies, carbon sequestration, the object of which is to capture and permanently store the greenhouse gases produced when coal is burned.[13] Bush's President's Committee of Advisors on Science and Technology (PCAST) called for a large programme to 'provide a science-based assessment of the prospects and costs of CO_2 sequestration. This is very high-risk, long-term R&D [research and development] that will not be undertaken by industry alone without strong incentives or regulations'. The cost at the time was between $100 and $300 for treating a tonne of coal but the goal was to get that cost down to $10 per ton by 2015.[14]

Despite the high cost, high risk and long time-frame, sequestration – along with hydrogen (equally high cost, high risk, and also with a long time-frame) – seemed to be Bush's favourite technology. During his campaign for the presidency in 2000 he pledged to commit $2 billion over ten years to develop clean coal technology. In June 2001 he singled out 'carbon capture, storage and sequestration' as particularly promising, and in February 2003 announced that he would spend $1 billion on FutureGen, slated to be 'the world's first coal-fueled prototype power plant to incorporate carbon sequestration technologies'.[15] Six years later, the international coal lobby group, the World Coal Institute, estimated that even if the nine sequestration experiments underway around the world 'stay on schedule, they will only be able to dispose of carbon generated from the equivalent of about four large coal-fired power plants'.[16]

Yet another favourite 'clean' energy source is ethanol to be used as a fuel additive for internal combustion engines. This technology had been advocated in the US since the 1930s, in part because ethanol is made from corn and its mandated wide use would be economically attractive to farmers and politically attractive to their Congressional representatives. In his 2007 State of the Union address, Bush called for 'a mandatory fuels standard to require 35 billion gallons of renewable and alternative fuels in 2017' and mentioned ethanol specifically. However, studies dating back as far as 1980 by President Carter's Department of Energy Gasahol Study Group estimated that a gallon of ethanol took more energy to produce than it provided. In 2001, the former chair of that group revisited the subject and figured that it took 131,000btu (British thermal units) to produce a gallon of ethanol, which then gave about 77,000btu in fuel energy. The study was attacked by the industry, which claimed that the energy used to grow the corn should not be counted in the equation, because the residue, after the starch had been removed, was fed to livestock.[17]

A truly speculative technology surfaced in January 2007 when the Bush administration, responding to a draft United Nations climate change document, advocated the importance of undertaking research and development on methods of reflecting sunlight back into space. 'Modifying solar radiance', it stated, 'may be an important strategy if mitigation of emissions fails. Doing the R&D to estimate the consequences of applying such a strategy is important insurance that should be taken out'. The methods suggested to deflect sunlight were giant orbiting mirrors, releasing thousands of tiny, shiny balloons, or pumping microscopic sulphate droplets into the high atmosphere. The response of the UN's Intergovernmental Panel on Climate Change was that such schemes were 'speculative, uncosted and with potential unknown side-effects'.[18]

While the Bush administration cast about for long-range, expensive, and sometimes far-fetched technological fixes, other nations were surging forward to become providers of more proven green technologies. In 1992, a report by the Office of Technology Assessment urged American manufacturers to design their products and production methods in such a way that environmental protection was a goal rather than a constraint and cited cases of profitable results flowing from such a priority. Perhaps inevitably the National Association of Manufacturers reaffirmed its belief that 'regulatory programs tend to stifle innovation'.[19] Two years later it was charged that the growing need for environmentally friendly technologies amounted to a 'second Industrial Revolution', but that because in America both the federal government and major corporations continued to see environmental constraints as a problem to be avoided rather than an opportunity to be seized, the country had lost its leadership in the area. According to this argument, the country's decades of spending on defence and space technologies has produced an impressive array of devices that were finding civilian application by the late 1980s. A 1994 book charged that 'the world's best gas turbines, wind turbines, solar cells, fuel cells, and antipollution scrubbers – everything from on-board car computers to advanced light bulbs was housed in America's technological arsenal'.[20] Instead of making these and similar technologies the basis of American industrial innovation and leadership into the 21st century, they were frittered away, picked up especially by Japan and Germany.

In 2005, the Japanese firm Sharp produced 27 per cent of the world's photovoltaics, making it the world leader for the fifth year in a row. Second in terms of production was the Japanese firm Kyocera. Photovoltaic cells were first developed by Bell Laboratories in New Jersey. Toyota, which was poised to pass General Motors as the world's leading automobile maker, was a leader in producing clean cars, with its hybrid gasoline/electric Prius consistently surpassing other regular production models in terms of both low emissions and high mileage per gallon.[21]

It is precisely in the area of global warming, and attendant technologies, that American science has most come under pressure in the new century – a topic that John Wills develops in the next chapter. As policies shifted from pollution abatement to pollution prevention, some chemists sought recognition as 'environmental chemists'. Not surprisingly scientists within the chemical industry, which was hit during the 1980s by such public disasters as Union Carbide's Bhopal gas leak (1984) that killed thousands and the discovery of the hole in the ozone layer over the Antarctic (1986), were marshalled to help the industry literally clean up its act. At the same time, academic chemists, who tended to see environmental 'science' as rather soft and not quite 'academic' enough, were slow to respond.[22]

Even when science was focused on these new problems, the results were often contentious, not least because careers, reputations and large sums of money invested in older technologies were at stake. In 1998, the government classified CO_2 as a pollutant and therefore subject to provisions of the Clean Air Act. In 2003, the Bush administration reversed that decision, thus lifting the obligation of mitigation by automobile manufacturers and power plant operators. The justification was that CO_2 was a naturally occurring gas necessary for plants to carry out photosynthesis. Indeed one lobby group, The Greening Earth Society, sponsored by the Western Fuels Association, went so far as to claim that data in a National Oceanic and Atmospheric Administration (NOAA) report on increased levels of CO_2 supported the notion that this was making the world's plants grow better.[23] The propensity of the Bush administration to muzzle government scientists and edit scientific reports to support administration policies and protect old technologies led to the issuance of a statement, signed by 10,000 scientists (including 52 Nobel Laureates) protesting political interference.[24]

MILITARY TECHNOLOGIES

If the US was slow off the mark with green technologies in the 21st century, it continued to follow the familiar path of innovation in military hardware. Indeed, in 1991, after its apparent success in the first Iraq War, the Pentagon announced a 'revolution in military affairs' (RMA) based on the creation of 'massive technologically-oriented support structures' which would allow it to establish dominance over the enemy with fewer troops in the field. The result is part of the reason that, between 2003 and 2005, the US spent an annual $466 billion on defence, almost seven times as much as its nearest rival, China.[25]

Among the backers of RMA there are different schools of thought, which emphasise different technologies. As identified by one scholar, the 'system of systems' group concentrates on computers and communications systems as well as 'smart' weapons. The 'dominant battlespace knowledge' school of thought builds onto this the extensive use of sensors to create a 'tactically transparent' battlefield. The 'global reach, global strike' group emphasises new ships, aircraft and space weapons capable of quickly projecting American dominance anywhere in the world. Finally, the 'vulnerability' school worries most about protection rather than projection, and seeks new technologies to provide better defence to American forces.[26]

Critics of RMA, including current and former military officers, identify four reasons why it is, in the words of one, 'doomed to fail': first, because the chosen technology is focused only on a narrow range of missions, none of which are typical of those most commonly undertaken; second, because the technological infrastructure of any system of computers and other electric devices, including sensors, is vulnerable to ordinary breakdowns, let alone to enemy action; third, because countermeasures can easily be undertaken, even by less technically sophisticated enemies; and, lastly, because of institutional impediments, including sheer inertia, which often are highly resistant to change.[27] In 2002, some two-thirds of the Army's Special Forces were distributed between more than 85 countries around the world. Concern was voiced that the Pentagon 'visions of empire' were focusing attention on new technologies while any real 'empire-building' required more personnel instead, and a greater emphasis on people rather than machines.[28]

Nevertheless, Iraq, like the late 20th-century wars before it (Vietnam, Grenada, Panama, Somalia, the former Yugoslavia and Kosovo, Haiti, Sudan, and Afghanistan, for example) was a proving ground for new or improved weapons. The 21,500-pound Massive Ordnance Air Blast super-bomb (MOAB) arrived too late to be part of the 'Shock and Awe' campaign against Baghdad and the giant Bunker Buster was not due for testing in Nevada until mid-2006. Some other weapons designed in part for use in Iraq were also in the testing stage. Since very few American troops could speak Arabic, a Voice Response Translator (VRT) was developed that could be attached to a megaphone to translate a prescribed set of English phrases into Arabic: examples cited included 'Thank you for cooperating' and 'We have to detain you'. Early in January 2007 a 'ray gun' was demonstrated on volunteers that, while 'not painful', emitted 130° Fahrenheit radiant heat that penetrated garments and made the targets think their clothing was on fire. It was said to be a non-lethal crowd-control device that would be ready for production by 2010. Development of cyborg insects (implanted with a tiny microcomputer system when they are still pupa) to gather battlefield data was being forwarded by DARPA (the Defense Advanced Research Projects Agency). By 2006, robot soldiers (Special Weapons Observation Recon-naissance Detection Systems, or SWORDS) were thought to be already under test in Iraq and it was planned to replace the computer screens, joysticks and keypads with 'Gameboy-style controlled and virtual-reality goggles'.

More importantly, the development of the Predator, a drone aircraft used already in the Balkans during the mid-1990s to collect information, was continued in both Afghanistan and Iraq. From 2001 on, it not only collected information but acted on it, being equipped with Hellfire laser-guided missiles. In 2002, one famously searched out, discovered and destroyed a vehicle travelling in Yemen with six occupants, identified by the US as al-Qaeda terrorists.

GLOBALISATION AND EMPIRE

Immediately after World War II, the American federal government created a complex and well-funded system to foster technological progress through the support, in both public and private venues, of technical and scientific research and development. Based on the putative success of such efforts during the war itself, the nation took enormous pride in what it took to be American leadership in such activities. From Nobel prizes to a cornucopia of new military and civilian technologies, American science and technology was the world standard, leading European nations to decry a 'technology gap' and developing countries to worry about the 'brain drain' of their brightest and best.

At the beginning of the 21st century, that leadership was a critical underpinning of US global hegemony. As David Harvey observed, 'much of the world's research and development is done in the US. This gives it a sustained technological advantage, and biases the global paths of technological change towards its own interests (particularly those centered in the military-industrial complex)'. Furthermore, 'it generates a flow of technological rents from the rest of the world into the US economy'.[29]

From the mid-20th century on, however, voices in the country raised periodic concern that this proud vanguardism was threatened both by progress being made abroad and by alleged lack of support at home. The Soviet success in building an atomic bomb much earlier than expected, and beating the US into space with an orbiting satellite, the famous Sputnik 1, were worrisome but so was the rapid recovery of its former enemies Germany and Japan, which, having been 'disarmed', were free to devote all of their technical and scientific resources to meeting civilian needs and desires.

This anxiety has continued into the 21st century. In 2007, a report by the World Economic Forum found that by its 'Networked Readiness Index', the United States has slipped from first to seventh place among nations, trailing such countries as Denmark (the new leader), Sweden, Singapore, Finland and Switzerland in its ability to 'participate in and benefit from developments in information and communication technology'. Such American groups as the American Electronics Association confirmed the perception, blaming a host of factors including falling numbers of engineering graduates, insufficient funds for research and development, and a general low level of numeracy and scientific literacy generally. Other critics pointed to the fact that the technologies of information and communication were firmly in the hands of large corporations in the cable and telecom industry, which were more interested in protecting their market shares than in pushing new technologies.[30]

The 2006 report of the National Science Foundation on science and engineering showed a mixed picture. The European Union's dominance in high-technology manufacturing between 1980 and 1995 had been turned around in 1996 and figures for 2003 showed that the US produced 40 per cent of global value added in high-technology, compared with only 18 per cent from the EU and 12 per cent from Japan. The US continued to be a strong exporter of 'manufacturing technological know-how sold as intellectual property', the 'technological rents' to which Harvey referred. On the other hand, in 2002, for the first time, American imports of advanced technology products exceed exports with the deficit growing to $37 billion in 2004.[31] In an attempt to keep the good times rolling, a White House press release titled 'The United States and the European Union Initiative to Enhance Transatlantic Economic Integration and Growth' (20 June 2005) listed twelve initiatives in the area of technological innovation, designed to 'increase synergies across the Atlantic as we become more knowledge-based economies'.

Europe, however, was not content simply to integrate its efforts with those of the US. In 2005, the EU launched its first satellite for its own Galileo global-positioning system, designed to make it independent of the American system and therefore more sensitive to European military needs. That same year the EU moved to end the long-time American control of the Internet. Perhaps more importantly, the EU parliament began discussions of establishing a European Institute of Technology in a clear effort to match the potential for technology and science innovation demonstrated by the Massachusetts Institute of Technology (MIT). The reality of American dominance was joined, in the planners' mind, by the rising spectre of Indian and Chinese competition. Already in 2006, China was producing each year more graduates in technology, science and mathematics than all the countries of the EU combined.

The problem is as serious at the worksite as it is in the laboratory. The doctrine of 'Globalization through Free Trade', which has driven American economic policy for the past generation, was based on the faith that it would produce a win-win outcome. What is becoming increasingly apparent, however, is that the out-sourcing of not only American investment but cutting-edge technologies is producing gains overseas in the very labour efficiency that was largely responsible for American prosperity in the first place. A Chinese or Indian worker with a shovel does not need an engineering degree to become more productive; he or she needs a backhoe instead.

In the 'homeland' itself, American technological prowess is often eccentrically applied and unevenly enjoyed. The tendency to 'save' old technologies by inventing specific fixes for specific problems can be seen in small as well as large instances. If automobile congestion continues in the 21st century, robot garages will help ease the problem. Increasingly popular in other countries, the US got only its second early in 2007 when one opened in New York City's Chinatown. Cars driven onto a pallet are then auto-matically moved vertically and horizontally into vacant spaces. When checked out by their drivers, they are retrieved and presented always facing the exit door. In this garage, the new system allows 67 cars to be parked in a space that would normally accommodate only 24.[32]

At MIT a 'One Laptop per Child' project is trying to develop a cheap laptop computer (the price was down to $150 each in 2007) that could be distributed to all poor children around the world. Its sponsors were said to believe that 'allowing poor children access to modern technologies … would give those who don't have access to teachers and schools the ability [to] teach themselves'.[33] And this is despite the fact that the appalling conditions under which many of those children live hardly seem to provide the necessary environment for such high-tech fixes.

Even within the US, the adoption of electronic gadgets was less than one might have expected. In 2006, for example, mobile phone use was well behind the world leader, Hong Kong, where there were 1,184 phones for every 1,000 people. The US, with 630 Internet users per 1,000 people, trailed

Australia, which had 646. New Zealand, Iceland, Sweden and Malta were also more networked than the US. The giddy elaboration of picture phones and iPods, and computer games as alternative worlds continues apace however, and the only surprise would be if it suddenly stopped.

At the same time, the American space programme, that technological icon of the 1960s, had apparently lost its power to stir the hearts of the American public (and the purse strings of Congress). A survey conducted in 2006 found 'high levels of indifference among 18-to-25 year olds toward manned trips to the moon and Mars'.[34] NASA was properly alarmed of course, realising like any great industrial corporation, that it made little sense to proceed with technological products that it could not sell.

Just as World War I had been called the 'chemists' war', World War II had made heroes out of the physicists, who along with electrical engineers had played a major role in developing some of the most spectacular new weapons of the conflict: radar, proximity fuses, jet propulsion, and of course the atomic bomb itself. During the years of the Cold War, physicists continued to play a leading role in setting technological (especially military) priorities and generally advising the federal government on matters of what was called 'science policy', but was mostly about which technologies should be pursued with research and development spending.

Before the end of the century, however, the life sciences had begun to forge past physics as the glamour field, and while the latter continued to get and spend a very large part of the nation's science budget, biotechnology was increasingly the area where bold new breakthroughs were expected. The description of the fundamental structure of DNA by Watson and Crick in 1953 is a convenient marker for the beginnings of this change and, during the 1960s, three universities in the San Francisco Bay Area (the University of California at Berkeley, the UC San Francisco medical school and Stanford) led in converting a swelling stream of federal research funds in the life sciences first into a rapidly growing body of fundamental knowledge about the 'science of life', then, with additional help from academic entrepreneurs and venture capitalists, into what is now called the biotechnology industry, encompassing such marvels as genetic engineering, recombinant DNA, cloning and stem cell research.

Although agriculture in the US did not experience its 'Industrial Revolution' until well into the 20th century, in the years after World War II it had largely accomplished the ideal advocated decades before of having 'Every Farm a Factory'. At the turn of the 21st century, such military technologies as the Global Positioning System (GPS) were being applied by farmers to pinpoint areas under cultivation that needed particular applications of fertilizers or pesticides as well as to map terrain prior to laying out dikes for flooding fields. Tractors equipped with lasers were used to help level land for the same purpose.

More dramatically, however, the new century saw the adoption of spin-offs from the 'science of life' research and development, first with the introduction of genetically modified (GM) crops. GM soy beans and corn, for example, were spreading at a rapid rate around the world, marketed to increase yields and cut the need for pesticides, but also useful for concentrating the world supply of seed crops in the hands of a few large American corporations. The inclusion of a new 'suicide gene' made such crops suitable for food stock, but incapable of growing the next crop when planted and thereby requiring farmers to buy new seeds each year. Health concerns joined with fears of economic peonage and the endangerment of biodiversity to fuel worldwide protests against such GM crops.

Similarly, 'designer hens' and new ways of 'pharming' have been introduced, again in the face of protest. The hens were given human genes that made them capable of laying eggs with anti-cancer proteins in their whites, thus making possible the more efficient and cheaper production of a wide range of drugs. In another laboratory, tobacco has been genetically modified to produce a protein that fights HIV. This last example of 'pharming', especially, also raises the spectre of such genes escaping into the 'natural' gene pool of the country and producing unanticipated, but potentially devastating, effects. There can be little doubt that with the potential of 'miracle cures' for a whole range of diseases, not to mention enormous profits, there will continue to be great pressure to expand this area of technological development.

The eclipse of the American Empire (as critics such as Tom Engelhardt and Niall Ferguson are calling it) in the 21st century is perhaps more likely than not, and technology will be a critical element of that decline. Overblown, overpriced and morally dubious weapons that do not, in the end, serve the purpose will be one factor. A mismatched set of government priorities, incentives and no-go zones in research and development will be another. The wholesale export of jobs to overseas workers, along with the technology to increase their efficiency, will make its own contribution. For a nation that relies so heavily on its supposed technological vanguardism for not only its prosperity and global reach but its very self-definition as well, the prospect is fraught.

NOTES

1. David Edgerton, *The Shock of the Old: Technology and Global History since 1900* (New York, NY: Oxford University Press, 2007), pp. x, xii.
2. Joseph J. Corn (ed.), *Imagining Tomorrow: History, Technology, and the American Future* (Cambridge, MA: MIT Press, 1986), p. 219.
3. Edgerton, *The Shock of the Old*, p. xv.
4. Charles Jencks cited in David Harvey, *The Condition of Postmodernity: An Inquiry into the Origins of Cultural Change* (Oxford: Blackwell, 1989), p. 39.
5. Quoted in Michael Adas, *Dominance by Design: Technological Imperatives and*

America's Civilizing Mission (Cambridge, MA: Harvard University Press, 2006), p. 390.

6. Ibid., pp. 389–91.
7. Rebecca Morelle, 'Building a skyscraper after 9/11', BBC News, 9 April 2006.
8. Molly Moore, 'Future aircraft designed to put terrorists out of action', *Sydney Morning Herald*, 18 January 2007, reprinted from *The Washington Post*.
9. 'Hydrogen & clean fuels research', US Department of Energy, http://fossil.energy.gov/programs/fuelss/index.html.
10. Barry C. Lynn, 'Hydrogen's dirty secret', *Mother Jones*, May–June 2003, http://www.motherjones.com/cgi-bin/print_article.pl?url+http.
11. CNN.com, 27 March 2007.
12. CARE, 'Cleaner environment', http://www.careenergy.com/cleaner_environment/clean-coal-technology.asp.
13. US Department of Energy, http://www.fossil.energy.gov/fred/feprograms.jsp?prog=Carbon+Sequestration.
14. US Department of Energy, 'Carbon sequestration R&D overview', http://www.fossil.energy.gov/programs/sequestration/overview.html.
15. US Department of Energy, 'Clean coal technology and the President's clean coal initiative', http://www.fossil.energy.gov/programs/powersystems/cleancoal/. US Department of Energy, 'Key R&D programs and initiatives', http://www.fossil.energy.gov/programs/sequestration/index.html.
16. Wendy Frew, 'Slow burn for carbon capture technology', *Sydney Morning Herald*, 2–3 December 2006.
17. Farhad Manjoo, 'Ethanol guzzles gas, study says', *Wired News*, 2003, http://www.com/news/politics/0,1283,46045,00.html.
18. Quoted in David Adam, 'US answer to global warming: smoke and giant space mirrors', *The Guardian*, 27 January 2007.
19. Quoted in 'Manufacturers urged to make environmentalism a goal', *New York Times*, 29 September 1992.
20. Curtis Moore and Alan Miller, *Green Gold: Japan, Germany, the United States, and the Race for Environmental Technology* (Boston, MA: Beacon Press, 1994), pp. 1, 2, 11.
21. 'Japanese firms embrace green technology', *Taipei Times*, 6 April 2005. Deborah Cameron, 'Rising sun turns green', *Sydney Morning Herald*, 22–23 October 2005.
22. Ivan Amato, 'The slow birth of green chemistry', *Science*, 259, 12 March 1991, 1538–41.
23. Roberta C. Barbalace, 'CO_2 pollution and global warming: when does carbon dioxide become a pollutant?', 7 November 2006, EnvironmentalChemistry.com, http://environmentalchemistry.com/yogi/environmental/200611CO2global warming.html. Roberta C. Barbalace, 'Sorting out science from junk science: is it really science?', 3 August 2006, http://environmentalchemistry.com/yogi/environmental/200608junkscience.html.
24. Jonathan Amos, 'US scientists reject interference', BBC News, 14 December 2006.
25. John A. Gentry, 'Doomed to Fail: America's blind faith in military technology', *Paramaters*, 88, Winter 2002–3. *Sydney Morning Herald*, 11–12 February 2006.
26. Taken from Michael O'Hanlon, 'High technology and the defense budget', *The Chronicle of Higher Education*, 14 February 2003, B12.

27. Gentry, 'Doomed to Fail', pp. 88–9.
28. Jason Vest, 'The army's empire skeptics', *The Nation*, 276, 3 March 2003, 27.
29. David Harvey, *The New Imperialism* (Oxford: Oxford University Press, 2005), p. 221.
30. SFGate.com, 29 March 2007.
31. National Science Foundation, *Science and Engineering Indicators 2006*.
32. 'Pack 'em in – New Yorkers get a robotic garage', http://www.cnn.com/2007/TECH/01/30/robotic.garage.ap/index.html.
33. *The Age* (Melbourne), 12 January 2007.
34. See http://www.cnn.com/2006/TECH/space.youth.apathy.ap/index.html.

12. AMERICA AND THE ENVIRONMENT

John Wills

'Thank God men cannot fly, and lay waste the sky as well as the earth', Henry David Thoreau pondered at his Walden retreat near Concord, Massachusetts in the late 1840s. The rise of industrialisation, commerce and materialism offended the sensibilities of a man dedicated to intellectual contemplation and transcendental nature. Thoreau struggled with the enterprise of nation-building going on about him. On some days, the sounds of the Fitchburg Railroad penetrated his forest surroundings, an 'iron horse' that made 'the hills echo with his snort like thunder, shaking the earth with his feet, and breathing fire and smoke from his nostrils.' On other days, Thoreau managed to sit in his 'sunny doorway from sunrise till noon, rapt in a revery, amid the pines and hickories and sumachs, in undisturbed solitude and stillness, while the birds sang around or flitted noiseless through the house.'[1] One hundred and fifty years on air flight is a common practice, with the waste products of the aviation industry a growing contributor to global warming, and industrialisation, commerce and materialism continue to shape American priorities at the beginning of the 21st century. At the same time, the United States is regarded by many as the birthplace of the national park idea, and respected for its history of environmental activism and legislation. Thoreau's beloved rural idyll of Walden Pond has been designated a National Historical and Literary Landmark and entertains thousands of visitors each year. No longer a perfect place of solitude, Walden is nonetheless protected.

This sense of America as a place of extremes and contradictions provides the inspiration for this chapter. Especially in terms of its international reputation, the country desperately lacks green credentials. Due to the failure of the Bush administration to ratify the Kyoto Protocol, an international framework designed to combat climate change, America is oft considered one of the countries least likely to endorse global environmental law. According to popular hyperbole, the USA represents a nation of gas-guzzling automobiles, oil magnates-cum-politicians, and a McDonald's-like 'supersize' greed when it comes to consumption. America serves as the world's new eco-villain. Yet this harsh stereotype ignores the diversity of opinion held across the nation. Many citizens support environmental causes by recycling, contributing to wildlife charities and attending annual Earth Day events. States (such as California) continue to pioneer green technology initiatives and enact strict pollution legislation. The four sections in this chapter provide an insight into recent environmental dilemmas, disasters and challenges in the United States. There are stories of green optimism and green pessimism. Hurricane Katrina and global warming are discussed, along with the California energy crisis, going green as a mainstream agenda, and shifting notions of what nature means in contemporary American culture. Collectively, these discussions posit the idea of a nation with a choice at the beginning of the 21st century: to continue to react with ambivalence to an unfolding climate crisis or aspire to a new position in the world as a green republic.

HURRICANE KATRINA AND GLOBAL WARMING

In late August 2005, just four years after the 9/11 terrorist attack, another unexpected disaster hit the United States. A category-5 hurricane moved into the Gulf of Mexico. Storm surges devastated the Louisiana coastline. Worst hit was New Orleans. Hurricane Katrina caused a surge of water that breached several canal banks on the morning of 29 August. Lower Ninth Ward, St Bernard Parish, City Park and Lakeview immediately flooded. Over 50 levee breaches followed. Within two days, approximately 80 per cent of the city had flooded. Routes out of New Orleans disappeared amidst water and wreckage. Over 700 people lost their lives.[2]

In the light of 9/11, the United States was meant to be capable of responding effectively to any new catastrophe on home soil. Hurricane Katrina suggested otherwise. Events had initially proceeded smoothly. Louisiana Governor Kathleen Blanco announced a state of emergency on the Friday before Hurricane Katrina hit. The same weekend, city mayor C. Ray Nagin issued a mandatory evacuation of New Orleans. By Monday morning, 80 per cent of residents had left the city. However, adequate plans had not been made for those unable to flee due to travel costs or ill health. Some 26,000 huddled in the Louisiana Superdome, a huge sports facility in the Central Business District set aside as a 'refuge of last resort' for those who could not leave. While the city flooded, federal authorities downplayed the catastrophe, and proved slow to commit resources. The Superdome suffered roof damage and supplies failed to reach refugees in sufficient quantities. Elsewhere, survivors struggled to find assistance. Growing cases of dehydrated and stranded residents pointed to broad mismanagement of the relief effort. In particular, the work of the Federal Emergency Management Agency (FEMA) and the Bush administration received widespread criticism, with the predictable epithet of 'Katrinagate' entering the popular lexicon. Heavily televised, the incident shocked the world. National confidence was fractured by stark images of urban poverty and floating dead bodies, disorganised relief efforts, and instances of looting (poor social behaviour proved especially significant given the portrayal of American heroes in 9/11). More akin to a city in a Third World country, the devastated New Orleans seemed out of place in 21st-century America's affluent, middle-class landscape. Long-term problems included one million homeless and an $80 billion price tag, placing Hurricane Katrina as the costliest natural disaster in America on record.

The racial dynamics of the story proved hard to avoid. New Orleans denoted a troubled city. As historian Kent B. Germany explained: 'in the mid-1960s, this city of almost 650,000 residents was one of the most impoverished, most unequal, most violent, and least educated places in the United States.'[3] By the 1970s, War on Poverty programmes and Total Community Action (TCA) had partially rectified a historic, Jim Crow-fostered imbalance in the city, but economic decline, the withdrawal of federal support, and an exodus of white and black middle classes left the place vulnerable by the late 1980s. During the course of Katrina, television cameras elucidated the dramatic urban poverty and ethnic inequality that haunted the city. The high number of destitute, homeless African Americans indicated that not all of America lived the American dream. Lack of progress in the post-civil rights era suggested that black Americans continued to represent third-rate citizens. World Watch journal reported: 'Poor and black = low, wet, and maybe dead'.[4] The slow response of FEMA and President Bush was taken by some as proof of institutional racism still at work in America. How would federal authorities have responded to a hurricane hitting a rich, white and Republican city, rather than a poor, black and Democratic one? Internet sites aired a photograph of African Americans 'looting' supplies from flooded stores, leading to accusations of racial bias in the media (by comparison, white residents were merely 'finding' supplies in another captioned image).[5] While the National Guard and federal troops did move in to patrol streets, onsite reports of murders and rapes were later discredited. Many elements of media coverage failed to portray the scene with accuracy. Claims that white residents lived only in higher elevations and thus avoided catastrophe proved erroneous. Environmental analyst Richard Campanella suggested that Katrina had a roughly proportional impact on black and white residents. Of the population of New Orleans, 67 per cent was black, with 76 per cent affected by the disaster. White residents accounted for 28 per cent of the city population, and 20 per cent emerged as flood victims. However, Campanella remained adamant that 'those who were stranded in the inundated city and suffered excruciatingly long lays in rescue were overwhelmingly African American and poor'.[6] Media attention noticeably shifted away from New Orleans in the months that followed. The hopes of President Bush that 'we will not just rebuild, we will build higher and better' may not be easily fulfilled.[7] Land-use wrangles, threats to historic neighbourhoods, problems of homelessness and a questionable market-driven approach to urban renewal suggest a slow recovery for the beleaguered city.

The environment proved the other obvious story of Hurricane Katrina. Natural sediment levees dating back millennia provided the material foundations for New Orleans. The course of the Mississippi River gave the city its bowl-like shape. Engineered canals, artificial levees, pumping stations and reclaimed wetlands all facilitated urban growth in the late 19th and early 20th centuries. By the time of Katrina, nearly 50 per cent of streets were below sea level. While usually strong enough to withhold stormy weather, water defences failed on several occasions in the 20th century. In 1927, New Orleans flooded due to drainage problems, while in 1965 Hurricane Betsy caused a storm surge that overwhelmed parts of the city for seven days. The building of New Orleans on a floodplain ultimately made it vulnerable to water fluctuations, regardless of whatever technological fixes came along.[8]

Some media commentators interpreted the scale of disaster at New Orleans as a sign of dramatic climate change ahead. The *Boston Globe* connected Katrina with a spate of other ecological events around the world, from wildfires in Spain to torrential rain in Bombay. The newspaper declared the 'real name' of Katrina to be 'global warming' and recommended that Americans make themselves familiar with the term.[9] ABC News reported that global warming had increased the intensity of major storms in the recent period, claiming: 'if Katrina had struck the Gulf Coast just three decades earlier, the results might have been quite different'.[10] Scientists wrangled over the root cause of stronger, more frequent hurricanes. A record 33 hurricanes in the Atlantic basin between 1995 and 1999 seemed connected to rising global temperatures and heat-trapping pollutants, but some climatologists claimed a natural climatic cycle to be the principal culprit.[11]

Scepticism over the relationship between Hurricane Katrina and global warming reflected broader US doubts over climate change. The Bush administration proved consistent in its opposition to labelling global warming a manmade malady. Chief reservations included the reliability of scientific data, the prospect of significant damage to the national economy by enforcing strict pollution targets, and the need to involve China and India in global environmental legislation initiatives. Despite early declarations of a willingness to work on the issue (Bush noted in a speech in June 2001 how 'the earth's well-being is also an issue important to America'), the government compromised international strategies for change. Most cited was the failure of the United States to ratify the Kyoto Treaty.[12] Along with involvement in the Iraq conflict, US reticence over global warming significantly contributed to a decline in prestige for the country on the world stage. Contributing 5 per cent of the world population, but 25 per cent of world carbon dioxide production, America remains a necessary player in debates over world pollution targets. Any serious attempt to combat climate change will depend on a more positive relationship between future American presidents and world leaders.

The reticence of the Bush administration to combat global warming nonetheless galvanised individual states to act on the issue. In August 2006, Arnold Schwarzenegger, Governor of California, met with British Prime-minister Tony Blair to agree to share scientific research and economic mechanisms designed to curb global warming. Schwarzenegger committed California to stringently cutting its greenhouse gas emissions. The Anglo-American relationship no longer depended on world leader-to-leader dialogue. At the beginning of 2008, *USA Today* reported a boom in state legislation designed to reduce global warming by the implementation of greenhouse-gas reduction targets. Seventeen states also set about suing the Environmental Protection Agency and the Bush administration over a controversial veto of state-led strict car emissions standards (the targets proved considerably tighter than those set out in the federal energy bill of 2007).[13] Frustration over the lack of leadership on the global warming issue heralded from all sides, including business. As the *LA Times* reported in 2006, 'the United States, which has always risen to scientific and technological challenges, is in danger of sitting this one out'.[14]

SUPERSIZE KILOWATTS

While animal and human power, firewood and coal provided the United States with energy in the 19th century, by the 20th century fossil fuels dominated the energy market. In particular, national growth became strongly associated with petroleum use. Throughout the period, demand for petroleum rose as the automobile became the favoured mode of transport. During the 1950s, America found itself unable to meet fuel needs from internal sources. Importing oil became a necessity. In the 1970s, US dependence on foreign energy reserves was brought home with dramatic effect during the OPEC crisis. The mainly Arab-based Organization of Petroleum Exporting Countries punished the Nixon administration for US backing of Israel in the Yom Kippur War. OPEC banned shipment of oil to America as a response. Soon after, barrel prices rose 400 per cent. Fuel shortages left Americans queuing at the pumps. Conservation measures included national 55mph speed limits to increase car engine economy and rationed fuel sales for odd-numbered last-digit licence plates on odd days of the month, even numbers for even days. The OPEC crisis highlighted the globalisation of the fuel industry and the precariousness of oil dependency. However, in the long term, it failed to result in significantly better fuel consumption rates in American-produced vehicles or a clear long-term strategy for energy conservation. If anything, by the 1990s, gasoline seemed a cheap commodity again. The popularity of the Sports Utility Vehicle (SUV) encouraged mass acceptance of poor fuel efficiency. The Hummer, a large 4×4 vehicle employed by military personnel in the 1990–1 Gulf War and promoted for sale to the rich and famous from 1992, averaged just ten miles per gallon. It served as a suitable symbol of US decadence, everyday environmental ignorance, and a 'supersize me' attitude to consumption. At the close of the century, the US imported a record 11 million barrels of oil every day.

Confirming this idea of the United States as a foremost 'oil nation', the Bush administration of 2001–8 garnered a reputation as a strong ally of the petroleum industry. In part, this reflected personal links with energy providers. National Security Advisor (later Secretary of State) Condoleezza Rice had an oil tanker named after her in recognition of her directorship at Chevron. Several attempts to open the Arctic National Wildlife Refuge (ANWR) in Alaska to oil drilling were narrowly seen off. As oil supplies diminish over the course of the 21st century, further pressure will come on remaining national reserves. The escalation in gasoline prices from just over $1 per gallon in 1998 to over $3 per gallon in 2008 suggests a crisis ahead.

Meanwhile, problems in electricity supplies have already had dramatic effect in the opening years of the 21st century. Long considered a pioneer in energy production thanks to technological innovation, the state of California underwent dramatic power outages in 2000–1. The first blackouts hit San Francisco in June 2000. During the winter, operating reserves regularly fell below just 5 per cent. Worrying over the power consumed on the Capitol Christmas tree, beleaguered Governor Gray Davis turned the lights off early. To make matters worse, the major state provider, Pacific Gas and Electric Company (PG&E), filed for bankruptcy. California's energy crisis was brought on by a number of factors: (1) poorly thought out restructuring and deregulation of state energy provision in the 1990s; (2) rising natural gas prices; (3) out-of-state supply problems (including price manipulation); (4) environmental factors, including storm damage to production facilities; and (5) old, and maintenance heavy, facilities. PG&E (along with other state providers) was capped on its charges to consumers, but suddenly found itself unable to meet the costs of buying in power and fixing plants. The market experiment in state energy proved disastrous. At root, however, it all came down to the demands put on the energy landscape. The population of California had risen from 10.5 million in 1950 to 33.9 million by 2000. State growth proved similarly impressive. No governmental authority, corporation or citizen group had really thought out a sustainable plan on how to meet the rise of the Golden State.[15]

Crises unfolding in both oil production and electrical supply threaten to undermine historic associations of the United States with abundance. Ever since European settlement, America has been cast as a bounteous landscape capable of fuelling myriad economic enterprises. The sheer scale of the country aided visions of limitless wealth, resources and land on the 19th-century trans-Mississippi frontier before it closed in 1890. Unfettered capitalism and materialism shaped the mindset of the 20th-century entrepreneur. This heady myth of abundance cannot automatically survive the 21st century. The United States might not be able to compete with India or China in terms of economic growth or energy resources. Green, virtual and high technology businesses may succeed, while large scale, traditional industries flounder. A 'supersize' mentality might prove neither feasible nor desirable in the decades ahead. Losing competitiveness and targeted by health groups, McDonald's phased out its supersize meal options in 2004. The wise option may be to follow in the footsteps of Ronald McDonald.

A GREEN REPUBLIC?

Although a radical proposition, the notion of a 21st-century green republic is firmly rooted in American soil. President Thomas Jefferson proved a great advocate of a green and agrarian nation. Writers such as Ralph Waldo Emerson, Henry David Thoreau and John Muir connected cultural nationalism with American wilderness. Ignoring for the moment Native American earth practices, modern conservation dates back over one hundred years. The Sierra Club, a gentleman's hiking club founded in 1892, championed the preservation of national park landscapes, in particular Yosemite in northern California. In the 1960s and 1970s, citizens embraced a new environmental consciousness, and hosted the first national display of environmental concern, Earth Day, on 22 April 1970. In the later decades of the 20th century, the environmental movement broadened to include social justice campaigns and urban reform movements. While successes proved rare in the so-called 'anti-environment' climate of the Bush administration (and some animal rights protesters and eco-radicals found themselves branded eco-terrorists), activism remained strong on behalf of the planet.

Annual Gallup polls from 2000 to 2007 indicated that around 60 to 70 per cent of Americans either felt sympathetic towards green issues or actively participated in the environmental movement.[16] Many US citizens considered themselves to be 'green' on some level, whether by virtue of their home recycling efforts, support for national parks, or purchasing of organic food. In a phone survey by GFK Roper conducted in December 2007, 49 per cent of those interviewed announced that their new year's resolution for 2008 was to 'be greener', with especially the younger generation eager to commit to lifestyle changes. Being 'green' seemed eminently fashionable.[17] *Elle* magazine carried a green issue in May 2006. Guest edited by Laurie David, green activist (and wife of *Curb Your Enthusiasm*'s Larry David), the women's magazine included features on 'The Hot Environmentalist' Robert F.

Kennedy Jr, how to go about a 'green detox', eco-friendly celebrity advice and fashion tips. *Vanity Fair* published a similar green issue the same month. In it, Editor Graydon Carter declared, 'Green is the new black'.[18]

The rising popularity of green-branded commerce attested to this new fashion trend. Purveyor of premium natural and organic foods, Whole Foods Market first opened in Austin, Texas in 1980 and seven years later Wild Oats Market, another organic food chain, started life in Boulder, Colorado. By acquiring smaller independent stores and expanding into new markets, both Whole Foods and Wild Oats grew rapidly in the 1990s. On merging in 2007, the companies boasted a combined total of over 250 stores across 38 states. Green supermarkets gained a reputation for ethical, rewarding employment schemes. However, the retail prices of some eco-friendly products dictated a level of exclusivity, with unintended ethnic and class repercussions. Few people on low incomes could afford a $7.99 takeaway salad.

Green branding also expanded beyond its traditional fold of organic food and small-scale, localised production. Large multinational corporations embraced ecological sensibilities. Japanese automakers found a new market for their economical vehicles in the USA during the 1970s OPEC crisis. At the outset of the 21st century, the Toyota Prius became a green status symbol in America. Capable of between 50 and 60 miles per imperial gallon, the Prius marked a fresh direction for the automobile in smog-heavy locations such as Los Angeles. Sales rocketed thanks to escalating oil prices and Hollywood celebrity endorsement (Leonardo DiCaprio and Cameron Diaz proved speedy converts to hybrids). The Prius also benefited from an early lead in the eco-car market. According to 2007 press reports, sales slowed a little as other 'clean' cars, including BMW's MINI and Honda's Civic Hybrid, increased competition.[19]

The commitment of all major auto manufacturers to green technology suggests a major revolution in transport is emerging. Cognisant of growing pressure from consumers and legislators alike for maximum highway miles, Ford and General Motors both recently committed to alternative fuels. Ford announced at the Los Angeles Auto Show in November 2007 its 'blueprint for sustainability' featuring smaller but more powerful engines and new technological developments.[20] Critics might argue this is merely a resurgence of 'green-washing' tactics dating back to the environmental revolution of the 1970s. While the Sierra Club rated British Petroleum a 'top of the barrel' performer in January 2007 for, amongst other things, promising an $8 billion investment in alternative energy, has the oil corporation advanced its 'Beyond Petroleum' agenda significantly enough when hydrocarbon revenues hit over $285 billion in 2004 alone?[21] Produced in a hasty fashion for the very first Earth Day, *The Environmental Handbook* (1970) included a chapter entitled 'Eco pornography or how to spot an ecological phony'. The opening paragraph read: 'Now that the environmental crisis is in the daily news and maturing in political sex appeal, panaceas are coming from curious sources – the ad agencies of the major industries that created the crisis.' The article highlighted in its discussion green advertisements by motor manufacturer Ford and the Shell Oil Company.[22]

The green revolution of the 1970s also had an impact on national politics. Congress passed the National Environmental Policy Act (1969), a revised Clean Air Act (1970) and the Endangered Species Act (1973), but in the 1980s the Reagan administration resisted environmental pressure for more reform. Secretary of the Interior James Watts had few qualms over putting economic development before wilderness protection on public lands. In both the 2000 and 2004 presidential elections, candidates shrank from green campaigning. Democratic hopefuls with eco-credentials shied from environmental debate for fear of alienating corporate America. Advisors for 2000 hopeful Al Gore, author of green tome *Earth in the Balance* (1992), recommended that he play down his ecological sympathies. That said, in 21st-century California, Republican Governor Arnold Schwarzenegger demonstrated that 'going green' could serve as a vote winner. An early fan of the Hummer, Schwarzenegger converted his 4×4 to run on bio-fuel, and called for the green movement to beef up its image and get 'environmentally muscular' (an apt phrase given Schwarzenegger's muscle-building background). With issues of climatic change and resource scarcity likely to increase in severity, the broad political spectrum needs to embrace green issues to win votes in the 21st century. As Schwarzenegger warned any politician who failed to 'go green': 'You will become a political penguin on a smaller and smaller ice floe, drifting out to sea. Goodbye, my little friend.'[23]

NATURE THREATENED

Such images of shrinking ice caps borrowed from the hugely successful documentary on global warming, *An Inconvenient Truth* (2006), presented by Al Gore. For his efforts, Gore won the Nobel Peace Prize and the film received a Hollywood Oscar. If *An Inconvenient Truth* emerges as the production to springboard a new level of mass consciousness over climate warming in the United States, the movie follows in the footpath of an earlier work that revolutionised American attitudes toward the environment, *Silent Spring* (1962) by Rachel Carson. Former US Fish and Wildlife Service (at that time the Bureau of Fisheries) biologist, Carson challenged the unquestioned dominance of chemical-based pesticides such as DDT in the post-war era, or as she put it at the time: 'the current vogue for poisons'. Rather than a mark of technological progress and sophistication, Carson presented widely popular agricultural control programmes of the 1950s and 1960s 'as crude a weapon as the cave man's club'.[24] While facilitating a rise in crop manufacture, pesticides contaminated the environment. Carson documented a range of follies, including milk poisoning in Long Island (1957) and birdlife losses in Duxbury, Massachusetts (1958). *Silent Spring* proved a damming indictment of the corporate-scientific elite behind the large-scale use of pesticides. The strong backlash against the title proved remarkable by its fervour. The agri-chemical industry spent hundreds of thousands of dollars in character assassination bids and legal claims. One *Newsweek* editor described the scene: 'thanks to a woman named Rachel Carson, a big fuss has been stirred up to scare the American public out of its wits.'[25] Historian Paul Brooks contended that 'perhaps not since the classic controversy over Charles Darwin's *The Origin of Species* just over a century earlier had a single book been more bitterly attacked by those who felt their interests threatened.'[26]

A nationwide bestseller, *Silent Spring* remains for many the title that sparked the modern environmental movement in the United States. In 1992, Al Gore provided an introduction to the 30th-anniversary edition of the book. Gore remarked how '*Silent Spring* could not be stifled. Solutions to the problems it raised weren't immediate, but the book itself achieved enormous popularity and public support'.[27] The title prompted a Science Advisory Committee (set up by President John F. Kennedy) to investigate pesticide use, and DDT was banned from domestic application in 1972. More importantly, many people spoke out about environmental problems for the first time. Carson highlighted growing concern over invisible manmade threats to the environment. 'A fable for tomorrow', the opening chapter of *Silent Spring*, described fictional small-town America silenced by a mystery force, later revealed as pesticides, but equally referencing the atomic threat in Cold War America. Ultimately, the chain of living organisms seemed at risk from all kinds of pollution, atomic fallout and chemical pesticides included. Carson worried over the irresponsibility of industrial society, calling for more democratic, popular input into science and technology. On a more philosophical level, she fretted over the control over nature exercised by modern man: 'only within the moment of time represented by the present century has one species – man – acquired significant power to alter the nature of his world.'[28] Gore raised a similar mixture of science and sentiment in *An Inconvenient Truth*. On a basic level, both *Silent Spring* and *An Inconvenient Truth* succeeded in 'getting the message out.' Gore explained, after several decades of eco-talk, that 'I think I'm finally getting a little better at it'.[29] Critics disagreed, portraying his film as more a disaster movie than a documentary. Along with questions over scientific accuracy, debates ran over its appropriateness as an educational tool in schools.[30] Despite the popular appeal of *An Inconvenient Truth* (as the following chapter on 'Contemporary American Culture' discusses), whether the movie can become the *Silent Spring* for its generation remains open to conjecture.

The 'invisible threat' that Carson documented did not end with the banning of DDT. In the 1990s, concerns grew over genetically modified crops and genetic mutation. An even greater doomsday seemed on the horizon. American eco-journalist Bill McKibben's bestseller *The End of Nature* (1989) captured such alarm. In it, McKibben described the sense of reassurance in knowing that one creosote plant in the American Southwest, 11,700 years old, continued to thrive as if nature remained immutable. McKibben went on to detail the impact of carbon dioxide gases, ozone holes, acid rain and global warming on the natural world, leading to his prediction that no part of nature could escape the coming storm. The ancient creosote bush seemed in imminent danger of keeling over. Nature, as something distinct from man's influence, no longer existed.[31]

Despite the warnings of Carson and McKibben, experimentation with nature proved irresistible in the 21st century. The British cloned a sheep in 1996 that they nicknamed Dolly after the country singer Dolly Parton. Relatively harmless experiments included allegedly engineering the first hypoallergenic cat by genetic screening and selective breeding. Allerca, a California biotechnology company, released kittens for sale from 2006 at a cost of $3500 each.[32] The pet Glofish, a fluorescent, genetically modified zebrafish caused more controversy due to the common relation between fish and human diet. Of course, humans have always manipulated nature. Native Americans employed fire to clear areas for planting. European colonists introduced exotic plants that overwhelmed native ones, reshaping the American landscape in the process. National Park Service wildlife rangers in the late 19th century shot wolves to manufacture deer havens, then in 1996 brought the animals back to Yellowstone National Park to restore a natural predator–prey alliance. And in Hollywood, celebrity Paris Hilton dutifully carries her Chihuahua, Tinkerbell, while shopping, the tiny dog a distant and very engineered cousin of the grey wolf. The scale of manipulation has increased in recent decades. On a fundamental level, nature in the 21st century is literally being remade. The temptation to tinker seems too much to resist.

At the same time, it is important to remember that ecology itself is fluid and ever changing. The discovery of wild species at landscapes long thought ruined proved one of the more exciting stories at the beginning of the 21st century. At decommissioned American nuclear sites such as Hanford, Trinity and even Nevada Test Site, all connected with US atomic bomb testing in the 1940s and 1950s, wildlife biologists discovered endangered plants and animals prospering. Areas conceived in the popular imagination as apocalyptic, irradiated and, by their sheer function, diametrically opposed to nature, were reborn as wilderness enclaves. Hanford Reach, in Washington State, where plutonium for the first atomic weapons was produced, became a registered National Monument in 2000. There is cause for optimism in the 21st century. At the very least, we should not write off the American environment for a few years yet.[33]

NOTES

1. Henry David Thoreau, *Walden* (1854), in George Palmer Blake (ed.) *Henry David Thoreau: Three Complete Books* (New York, NY: Gramercy, 1993), pp. 260, 257.
2. The total death toll for Hurricane Katrina is estimated to be over 1,000 people. See 'Katrina's official death toll tops 1,000', CNN.com, 21 September 2005, http://edition.cnn.com/2005/US/09/21/katrina.impact/.
3. Kent B. Germany, 'The Politics of Poverty and History: Racial inequality and the long prelude of Katrina', *Journal of American History*, 94(3), December 2007, 744.
4. Eric Mann, 'Race and the high ground in New Orleans', *World Watch: Vision for a Sustainable World*, 19, September–October 2006, 1.
5. Tania Ralli, 'Who's a looter? In storm's aftermath, pictures kick up a different kind of tempest', *New York Times*, 5 September 2005.
6. Richard Campanella, 'An ethnic geography of New Orleans', *Journal of American History*, 94(3), December 2007, 715.
7. 'President discusses hurricane relief in Address to Nation', Office of the Press Secretary, The White House, 15 September 2005, http://www.whitehouse.gov/news/releases/2005/09/20050915-8.html.
8. See Ari Kelman, 'Boundary Issues: Clarifying New Orleans's murky edges', *Journal of American History*, 94(3), December 2007, 695–703.
9. Ross Gelbspan, 'Katrina's real name', *The Boston Globe*, 30 August 2005.
10. ABC News, 'Did global warming boost Katrina's fury?', 14 September 2005.
11. Jeffrey Kluger, 'Is global warming fueling Katrina?', *Time*, 29 August 2005; Joseph B. Verrengia, 'Katrina reignites global warming debate', *USA Today*, 1 September 2005.
12. 'President Bush discusses global climate change', Office of the Press Secretary, The White House, 11 June 2001, http://www.whitehouse.gov/news/releases/2001/06/20010611-2.html.
13. Paul Davidson, 'States combat global warming', *USA Today*, 20 January 2008; John M. Broder and Felicity Barringer, 'E.P.A. says 17 states can't set emission rules', *New York Times*, 20 December 2007.
14. Editorial, 'Welcome hot air from Arnold and Blair', *Los Angeles Times*, 2 August 2006.
15. For more on the California energy crisis, see John Wills, *Conservation Fallout: Nuclear Protest at Diablo Canyon* (Reno, NV: University of Nevada Press, 2006), p. 183.
16. Riley E. Dunlap, 'The state of environmentalism in the U.S.', Gallup News Service, 19 April 2007, http://www.gallup.com/poll/27256/State-Environmentalism-US.aspx.
17. See 'Tiller's Nationwide Green Survey', 17 December 2007, http://www.tillerllc.com/cgi-bin/tillerinthenews.pl?record=9.
18. ABC News, '*Vanity Fair* hails green "the new black" on eco-unfriendly paper', 24 April 2006.
19. Alex Taylor III, 'The birth of the Prius', *Fortune*, 6 March 2006; Chris Isidore, 'Prius' new option: incentives for buyers', *CNN Money*, 8 February 2007.
20. Scott Burgess, 'Going green: Ford charts course for fuel efficiency as carmakers

get eco friendly', *The Detroit News*, 15 November 2007.

21. Sarah Ives and Robynne Boyd, 'Pick your poison: an updated environmentalist's guide to gasoline', *Sierra Magazine*, January–February 2007, http://www.sierraclub.org/sierra/pickyourpoison/.

22. Thomas Turner, 'Eco Pornography or how to spot an Ecological Phony', in Garrett De Bell (ed.) *The Environmental Handbook* (New York, NY: Ballantine, 1970), p. 263.

23. 'Schwarzenegger pumps up green movement', CNN.com, 12 April 2007, http://edition.cnn.com/2007/POLITICS/04/12/arnold.green/index.html.

24. Rachel Carson, *Silent Spring* (Boston, MA: Houghton Mifflin, [1962] 1987), p. 297.

25. Robert Gottlieb, *Forcing the Spring: The Transformation of the American Environmental Movement* (Washington, DC: Island Press, 1993), p. 85.

26. Paul Brooks, *The House of Life: Rachel Carson at Work* (New York, NY: Houghton Mifflin, 1993), p. 293.

27. Al Gore, 'Introduction', in Rachel Carson, *Silent Spring* 30th Anniversary Edition (New York, NY: Houghton Mifflin, 1992), text available online at: http://www.uneco.org/ssalgoreintro.html.

28. Carson, *Silent Spring*, p. 5.

29. William J. Broad, 'From a rapt audience, a call to cool the hype', *New York Times*, 13 March 2007.

30. Blaine Harden, 'Gore film sparks parents' anger', *Washington Post*, 25 January 2007.

31. Bill McKibben, *The End of Nature* (London: Penguin, 1989), pp. 3–7.

32. Penni Crabtree, 'Allerca promises sneeze-free cats', *San Diego Union Tribune*, 8 June 2006.

33. For more on the resurgence of nature at post-nuclear landscapes, see John Wills, '"Welcome to the Atomic Park": American Nuclear Landscapes and the "unnaturally natural"', *Environment and History* 7(4), November 2001, 449–72.

PART 3
CULTURE

13. CONTEMPORARY AMERICAN CULTURE

Martin Halliwell

Late 20th-century American culture is often characterised in terms of its plurality and eclecticism. The diversification of cultural forms, particularly in visual and digital media, and broader horizons about what constitutes cultural production have contributed to an environment in which being black, poor, female or gay (at least in theory) no longer stands in the way of talent or strength of vision. Young graduates are finding showcases for low-budget movies in the burgeoning film festival circuit; many new authors are being published, helped by the promotion of new fiction on the *Oprah Winfrey Show*, particularly writing by young black women; and multimedia performance and installations have extended the boundaries of what art is able to represent. Although the attempt to link cultural production to national politics can often be reductive, one framework for understanding cultural diversity in the 1990s is in terms of President Clinton's final State of the Union address. In January 2000, Clinton stressed that 'never before has our nation enjoyed, at once, so much prosperity and social progress with so little crisis and so few external threats'.[1] Clinton's vision was both pluralist and centrist: he saw 'enormous potential of communities from Appalachia to the Mississippi Delta, from Watts to Pine Ridge Reservation', but wanted to link this closely to a restoration of 'the vital center, replacing outmoded ideologies with a new vision anchored in basic, enduring values'. In early 2000, Clinton called for the 21st century to be one of 'big dreams', driven by an 'American revolution' of 'opportunity, responsibility and community'.

As the essays in the third section of this book demonstrate, diversification of cultural forms is still very much part of American and global culture. But

Clinton's predictions ('we will make America the safest big country on earth'; 'we will reverse the course of climate change'; 'we must strengthen our gun laws') have to be set alongside an ossification of ideological, economic and cultural lines after 9/11, as evident in Clinton's Dimbleby Lecture of December 2001 where he worried about the marriage of 'ancient hatreds and modern weapons' and barely spoke about culture, aside from the Internet revolution.[2] The culture industry in the US has been expanding for 60 years, with national and international agendas becoming ever more closely intertwined and a global market blurring the demarcation between national cultures. Despite suspicions from the left that big business in America controls filmmaking, publishing and broadcasting, no longer is the culture industry the monolith that Theodor Adorno and Max Horkheimer detected in 1944. But, equally, in the climate of the years following 2001, no longer is the commercial undertow of American culture offset by the nation being held in high esteem across the globe.

Indeed, one might argue the reverse. Although American Ivy League universities consistently top opinion polls as the world's best, the Public Policy expert Richard Florida has posited that over the last few years the 'creative class' has been leaving the US in a global talent flow to countries with stable or shrinking populations.[3] Contrary to Clinton's 'twenty-first century revolution' serving 'to open new markets, start new businesses, hire new workers right here in America – in our inner cities, poor rural areas, and Native American reservations', the outsourcing of labour to Asian and South American countries and the attractiveness of job opportunities for US college students in Europe and Australasia have coincided with the intensification of wealth in the North East and on the West Coast and a closing of minds to both home-grown and immigrant talent. Added to this is a widespread suspicion that in the years after 9/11 any cultural expression that does not tally with core national values is in danger of being seen as subversive. Rebecca Tillett argues in the next essay that these fears are not new, but a term that many thought had been consigned to Cold War history – 'un-American' – has re-emerged alongside the national trauma of 9/11. The fact that Democrat John Kerry was vilified by Republicans during his 2004 presidential campaign for 'flip-flopping' on crucial issues, and for being a 'commie' in respect of his anti-Vietnam stance during his student days, led Kerry to be treated with suspicion by some voters and the negative counterpart to President Bush's homely values.

INTELLECTUALS AND THE CULTURE WARS

As Elisabeth Lasch-Quinn argues in the opening essay of Part 2, one of the most significant trends in recent and contemporary cultural thought is the decline of potent intellectual voices in America. The death of two generations of intellectuals, including Jacques Derrida, Gilles Deleuze and

Jean Baudrillard in France and Arthur Schlesinger Jr, John Rawls, Edward Said, Susan Sontag and Richard Rorty in America, and the waning of interest in 'theory' in the academy has led to what many are calling an intellectual impasse in the US and Europe. Perhaps the flourishing of postmodernism in the 1980s and 90s, and with it the weakening of grand narratives that can explain historical and cultural phenomena, has led to a fragmentation of the 'vital center' that Schlesinger was recommending in the late 1940s. Twenty years later, amidst the student protests of the late 1960s, a transatlantic cross-section of thinkers – Derrida and Sontag amongst them – were calling for the decentralisation of culture, fearing that Schlesinger's 'vital center' could easily degenerate into a 'dead center' presided over by a power elite. While Schlesinger was worried early in the Clinton presidency that pluralism had actually led to a 'disuniting' and 'decomposition' of national identity, there is a sense that without a firm critical position the public intellectual has lost direction in a late-capitalist global landscape, or has been made obsolete through the growth of mass media.[4]

It is the loss of an intellectual community that worried the Penn National Commission on Society, Culture and Community, which first convened in 1996. The Commission concluded three years later that the 'thinning' of public discourse was getting worse, wedded to the suspicion that universities since the late 1960s have been aiding and abetting 'the breakdown of precisely those notions of community that have justified the university's existence as the model for the larger community'.[5] The Commission's recommendation was to 'thicken' and 'widen' public debates, bringing into dialogue 'museums, libraries, schools, colleges and universities, professional sports, the military, and even the Internet'. But the contributors added a note of pessimism, commenting that professionals and leaders of these institutions 'are unprepared for their new civic responsibilities'.[6]

Perhaps, then, it is to individuals rather than institutional structures to which we should look for intellectual hope – 9/11 saw the public re-emergence of the Canadian political theorist Noam Chomsky, while the likes of Fredric Jameson, Martha Nussbaum and Cornel West continue to refine their cultural perspectives at the interface of the academy and public life. Nonetheless, the dearth of strong public voices outside of party politics has left journalists and television pundits to fill the void. Attacks on the academy are frequent, such as David Horowitz's attempt in *The Professors: the 101 Most Dangerous Academics in America* (2006) to unearth, to his mind, potentially subversive thinkers in universities and talk-show host Laura Ingraham's assault on 'the old left-wing guard' at elite universities.[7] And it is not just professional thinkers that have come under fire. Intellectual politicians have long been vulnerable for being too cerebral, such as Democrat candidates Adlai Stevenson in the 1952 and 1956 presidential elections, Al Gore in 2000, and John Kerry in 2004. The upshot is that the loss of intellectual bite in the academy and public life has led to a restricted culture in which journalists and pundits are taking the lead on the issues of leadership, immigration and climate change.

The left continues to accuse the right of abdicating responsibility for dealing with contemporary affairs outside narrow self-interest and for cosying up to big business, even abusing political power in the name of self-aggrandisement, while the right accuse the left of treason and siding with the nation's enemies. As Dominic Sandbrook notes in the opening essay of Part 1, the 'culture wars' are often traced back to Pat Buchanan's speech at the 1992 Republican National Convention in which Buchanan identified 'a cultural war as critical to the kind of nation we shall be as the Cold War itself, for this war is for the soul of America'.[8] Although Buchanan framed it in religious terms, 'culture wars' became a touchstone for public debate in the 1990s, with the left and right at loggerheads with each other – a struggle which, as Kevin Mattson discusses, continues into the current decade. The aggressive voices of Ann Coulter, Russ Limbaugh, Michelle Marvin and Bill O'Reilly on the right criticise the left for being un-American and even treasonous, to take the title of Coulter's 2003 book *Treason: Liberal Treachery from the Cold War to the War on Terrorism*. Always a polemicist, Coulter has even tried to rescue the 'indispensable' Joseph McCarthy as a responsible conservative during the early Cold War, but her real goal is to attack liberal mythmaking and deceit, while talk-radio host Michael Savage calls liberalism a 'mental disorder'.[9]

Coulter and Savage are extreme cases, but the problem with the culture wars is that, rather than constructing debates across political lines, the warring factions often resort to the kind of propaganda which recalls the anticommunist strategies of the 1950s, demonising the opposition before accusing them of 'sedition and immorality'.[10] Responses from the left can be equally extreme, with conspiracy theories rife about the Bush administration colluding with al-Qaeda ahead of 9/11 and being partly responsible for the World Trade Center attacks, such as the claims made by the 9/11 Truth Movement and the Internet film *Loose Change* (2006).[11]

This is not so much a symptom of the loss of the political centre, or a debate about where arts funding should go (with heated arguments about who should be awarded National Endowment for the Arts grants in the 1990s), but a divided political landscape where debates about the country's role in global affairs have split the nation. Two film comedies, *Meet the Fockers* (2004) and *The Break-Up* (2006), use this idea that political outlooks have irreversibly diverged to emphasise rifts between families. In *Meet the Fockers*, Greg Focker (Ben Stiller) suffers at the hands of an oppressive ex-CIA soon-to-be father-in-law who resorts to surveillance to investigate Greg's past, played by Robert De Niro as the Republican counterpoint to Greg's Jewish parents (Dustin Hoffman and Barbara Streisand) with their new age philosophy and hippie passion for meditation and massage. And *The Break-Up* stages a scenario where the effete brother of art gallery curator Brooke

Myers (Jennifer Aniston) launches into a hilariously camp acapella version of rock band Yes's 1983 song 'Owner of a Lonely Heart' at the dinner table, deeply disturbing her fiancé Gary Grobowski (Vince Vaughan) and his blue-collar family.

Despite the appealing snapshots that these two films offer of families riven by irreconcilable belief systems, there is more substance to it than that. A book such as *Letters to a Young Conservative: the Art of Mentoring* (2002) by Bombay-born Dinesh D'Souza, for example, tries to rescue one version of classical liberalism – concerned with 'social and civic virtue' – from the liberal politics of the late 1960s that 'attacked the moral consensus as narrow and repressive'.[12] While D'Souza (former policy advisor for President Reagan) sees some overlap in the 'moral vocabulary' of liberal and conservative views – they both speak of 'equality' and 'morality' even though they mean different things by each – he returns to classical political theory in believing that the fundamental rift revolves around opposite notions of 'human nature'. Side-stepping the postmodern argument that 'human nature' is just another cultural construct, D'Souza concurs with other conservatives like Francis Fukuyama in *Our Postmodern Future* (2002) in basing his philosophy on the essentialist notion that human nature is fixed and immutable.

Against what D'Souza sees as the naive liberal belief in inherent human goodness, he outlines a 'realistic' conservative understanding of the warring factions of good and evil in individuals, nation states and governments alike, leading him to endorse 'personal responsibility' and the use of force in international relations to keep at bay those destructive or evil impulses. Written in reasonable and dispassionate language in the form of a series of letters to Chris, a 'young conservative', D'Souza still falls into the trap of the culture wars. He ends his first letter to Chris by claiming:

> liberalism has become the party of anti-Americanism, economic plun-der, and immorality. By contrast, conservative policies are not only more likely to produce the good society, they are also the best means to achieve liberal goals such as peace, tolerance, and social justice.

A book that begins by promising the reader a nuanced account of political and cultural identity in the 21st century, ends up driven by the same polemic that inspires Coulter and Savage, and concludes with the reminder to all young conservatives that 'truth is on our side and that it is a very powerful weapon. With truth as our guide and courage in our hearts, we will not only endure, we will prevail'.[13]

Another book that takes the form of letters offers a neat counterpart to D'Souza's conservative lessons. Written as a collective, *Letters from Young Activists* (2005) offers a very different cultural vision, not in terms of a political ideology of truth, right or force but the complex intersections of the children of the 1960s generation united by concerns about the early-century climate. The writers included in the volume are not professional authors or thinkers; selected only by their youth (between the ages of 10 and 31), by their transnational diversity ('we are Black, Puerto Rican, Chicana/o, Salvadoran, Palestinian, White, Haitian, Chinese, Indian, Tamil, and Native American'), and their discovery of politics at a young age 'through friends and music scenes; our negative experiences with politics, parents, or teachers; or because we couldn't stand by and watch the injustices that surround us'.[14] Seeing themselves in a movement that is inclusive and transcends national and ethnic boundaries, the contributors pitch themselves against the 'neo-conservative imperial project' they identify with the Bush administration, but they don't wish to replace it with polemic or antagonism.[15] Rather, through a series of letters addressed to the past, present and future, the 48 contributors attempt to bridge the generational gap by carving out identities in which diversity and value are not opposing terms and where celebration and critique can function dialectically.

Given the youthful age of the contributors, it is not surprising that some of the responses are limited by personal experience, but the book provides evidence that grassroots cultures – from college campus activism, to the revival of the radical spirit of the Students for a Democratic Society, to global anticapitalist protests – are stimulating meaningful responses to international pressures and perceived inequalities at home.[16] While these two books indicate that cultural thought is most obviously embodied in written form, it is also useful to trace these ideas through other cultural modes. In music and film – two 20th-century cultural forms – political battle lines have been clearly demarcated in the first decade of the 21st century.

MUSICAL PROTEST

One pressing dilemma for socially conscious musicians is how to counter the growth of music corporations since the 1980s that have the financial weight to determine both sales and substance. The popularity of reality television and talent competition shows such as *American Idol* and *The Swan* (both hits shows on Fox) are evidence that the media space in which ideas can flourish has been restricted by the entertainment demands of network radio and television. The public forum for debate is also severely limited, with channels focusing only on headline news or offering skewed debates, and chat shows such as advertising executive Donny Deutsch's *The Big Idea* on CNBC promising topical discussion but invariably delivering lifestyle interviews. The erosion of public debate is bemoaned by Al Gore, among others, in his 2007 book *The Assault of Reason*, and there is some truth in it, with Edward R. Murrow's claim in 1958 that television often serves to insulate the viewer from the surrounding world. Potentially the most democratic of media has, in an age of massive cable choice, been compromised by corporate ownership and the flattening of cultural value.

But this theory about the decline of a democratic culture overlooks the way in which music continues to be used in agonistic and questioning ways, particularly since the outbreak of war with Iraq in spring 2003. The support for John Kerry in the run-up to the 2004 presidential election was very strong within the music fraternity. The result, the Vote for Change concerts that took place in October 2004, was a series of inter-generational events held in strategic states across the country that brought the established voices of Bruce Springsteen, Jackson Browne, John Mellencamp, Michael Stipe and James Taylor together with younger groups such as The Dixie Chicks. The twin aims of the concerts were to heighten public awareness of politics and to raise money for widespread voter education in swing states. But despite raising nearly $10 million for America Coming Together – a 'get out and vote' organisation funded by labour unions – the fact that none of the states in which the concerts took place were actually lost by the Republican Party in the 2004 election suggests an unbridgeable divide between culture and electoral politics, or a climate in which this kind of protest is now ineffectual.

The Vote for Change concerts were an attempt to revive the spirit of the 1960s counterculture and the way in which people's songs were mobilised by the Civil Rights Movement, but critics would argue that cultural expression should never be wedded so closely to political campaigns. Charity music events that began in the mid-1980s with 'Live Aid' and 'USA for Africa' continue to have currency, such as the series of 'Concerts for Darfur' since February 2005 to raise money for humanitarian crisis in Sudan, the Hurricane Katrina relief concert 'From the Big Apple to the Big Easy' held in Madison Square Gardens in September 2005, and the transcontinental 'Live Earth' events in July 2007. While the connections between the charitable causes of the mid-1980s and the present are evident in the U2 and Green Day collaboration 'The Saints Are Coming' – the two groups perform in a spoof video in which US troops mobilised in Iraq come to the aid of Katrina victims – there is also a clear link between the 1960s counterculture and the present moment. Stars of the mid-1960s Simon and Garfunkel reformed to play at the 'From the Big Apple to the Big Easy' concert, Bob Dylan's 2006 tour had a distinctly anti-war sensibility with a new arrangement of his 1963 song 'Masters of War', and Joni Mitchell's multimedia 'Flag Dance' exhibition in winter 2006–7 had an anti-war theme. While the reformation of the late 1960s supergroup Crosby, Stills, Nash and Young for their 'Freedom of Speech' tour of 2006 could be seen as jumping on the political bandwagon, it is better understood as a realisation that the icons of the 1969 Woodstock Festival were once more living through a seismic moment of change.

This direct repoliticisation of music was also a feature of albums written by two stalwarts of the music scene: Neil Young's 2006 release *Living With War* and John Mellencamp's 2007 album *Freedom's Road*. Even though Young appeared to endorse Bush policy straight after 9/11, *Living With War* captured the widespread feeling five years later that war had become a permanent condition.[17] But Young faced a great deal of criticism for his single 'Let's Impeach the President' largely because Young is Canadian (despite living in California) and his lyrics are too direct: 'Lets impeach the President for lying / And misleading our country into war / Abusing all the power that we gave him / And shipping all the money out the door'.[18] *Living With War* was joined a year later by The Eagles' first album for nearly three decades, *Long Road Out of Eden* (2007); both albums bemoan the loss of 'the garden', a 1960s ideal of innocence and freedom quashed by a climate of suspicion and fear. In contrast, Bush's voice is incorporated in 'Let's Impeach the President' as a series of sound-bites, espousing views on Saddam Hussein, September 11, Iraq and US intelligence, while The Eagles on the title track of their album lament the 'bloody, stupid waste' of taking the political highway to empire.

After suffering a brain aneurysm in Spring 2005, Young wrote *Living With War* swiftly and angrily – an embattled mood on display in a CNN interview of April 2006 where Young charged Bush of robbing a '9/11 mentality' from American people. It is also an explicitly anti-consumerist album: first released in a free downloadable format and presented in a grungy brown paper cover in its CD form, many of the tracks use heavy guitars to attenuate Young's critique of consumerism, political mismanagement and loss of leadership. Although its political theme is constant and didactic, musically it is eclectic: for example, Young's use of a gospel choir and an elegiac bugle on 'Shock & Awe' inflects the needless waste of life that war has precipitated: 'Thousands of bodies in the ground / They're holding boxes to a trumpet sound'. 'Shock & Awe' considers the way that historical lessons of the past have been overlooked in favour of power politics; history has become 'the cruel judge of overconfidence' and the hard-nosed militarism that followed 9/11.

But it was not just established voices that were producing musical messages. The patriotic and militaristic sentiments of country singer Darryl Worley's 2003 hit 'Have You Forgotten?' (in which 'those towers', 'Bin Laden' and 'our Pentagon' are all name-checked) led to massive radio airplay; Detroit rapper Eminem joked about the search for Bin Laden in his 2002 video 'Without Me'; the non-partisan punk band Bad Religion's 2004 album *The Empire Strikes First* targeted ire at the Bush administration; and, in the UK, Radiohead's 2003 *Hail to the Thief* album was a direct attack on Bush's narrow election win three years earlier. Even though the appearance of Barbara Bush at a New York Radiohead gig in 2006 complicates the neat battle lines of the culture wars, the biggest furore in the music industry in recent years occurred when, ten days before the deployment of US troops in Iraq in March 2003, singer Natalie Maines of The Dixie Chicks announced in a London concert that she was ashamed to come from the same state as President Bush. Rather than just annoying fellow Texans, the band received hate mail, long-term fans boycotted their gigs, and they were dropped from radio playlists across the country. Despite being snubbed by the Nashville country music awards, ironically this incident helped to propel The Dixie Chicks to a broader international audience and gave them subject matter for their 2006 single 'Not Ready to Make Nice' about the band's unwillingness to compromise. The direct sentiment of 'Not Ready to Make Nice' mirrored other bands, both young and old, in an indignant response to what many perceived as the oligarchy of the White House. The neo-punk band Green Day, for example, had a hit with 'American Idiot', from their eponymous 2004 album, which featured on its cover a hand clutching a grenade-cum-bleeding heart. On first listen, the title track seems little more than a rant against Bush's 'redneck agenda', oppression of gay rights and media control, but there is a subtlety to the lyrics, offsetting the ennui of an 'alien nation' with a bleak vision of 'idiot America'.

The Iraq War and the 2004 election were not the only events that marked a musical sensitivity to social issues or an attempt to impose a meaningful symbolic pattern – a new grand narrative – on contemporary events. For this we have to go back to 9/11 and the *America: Tribute to Heroes* telethon (organised by George Clooney) of 21 September 2001 and the 'Concert for New York City' of 20 October (organised by Paul McCartney) for the New York Fire and Police Departments. Neil Young's version of John Lennon's 'Imagine' on *Tribute to Heroes* and McCartney's anthemic song 'Freedom' encapsulated the need to cut through the ideological complexities of 9/11, but also a transatlantic sympathy with the plight of the US in the immediate aftermath of the attacks on the World Trade Center.

Arguably the most sensitive response to 9/11 came in the guise of Bruce Springsteen's 2002 album *The Rising*. This was seen by many as Springsteen's return to form, in terms of its musical range, the reformation of the E Street Band, and its aim to deal with the heightening of national identity in the aftermath of 9/11. However, it is easy to skew a reading of the album through this prism and forget that its most evocative song 'My City of Ruins' was written the previous year about Asbury Park in New Jersey, evoking the title of Springsteen's first album *Greetings from Asbury Park, N.J.* (1973). The elegiac tone of the song is offset by the use of a black gospel backing-group; the intonation on the repeated refrain 'with these hands' evokes both working-class solidarity (recalling the 1950 union film *With These Hands*) and multicultural striving. In shifting the topography from New Jersey to Manhattan, 9/11 provided a fresh context for 'My City of Ruins', and Springsteen appropriately used the song to open the *Tribute to Heroes* telethon ten days after the World Trade Center attacks. Loss, pain and emptiness are constant themes on the album: the chasm between lovers separated across ethnic lines in 'Worlds Apart'; the void of 'Empty Sky' in which the songwriter wakes up 'one morning to an empty sky' that eerily echoes the loss of blood in the streets; 'Into the Fire' told from the perspective of an unnamed fire-fighter;

and in the last track on the album the sense that 'Paradise' itself is empty.[19]

Critics applauded the album for its depth of tone, linking the despair of 9/11 to a collective 'rising', countering grief with optimism on tracks like 'Into the Fire' with its gospel choir: 'May your strength gives us strength. / May your faith give us faith. / May your hope give us hope.'[20] A review in *Time* magazine points out, though, that despite the liberal humanism and cross-faith spirituality of the album, it lacks an authentic political voice, favouring an emotive rather than an explanatory register.[21] Despite his endorsement of John Kerry in 2004, Springsteen's defence is based on the nature of the musician's art; he claimed in a *Nightline* interview of August 2004 that 'I stayed a step away from partisan politics because I felt it was always important to have an independent voice. I wanted my fans to feel like they could trust that' – perhaps leading him to deal with political themes at a further remove on his 2007 album *Magic*.[22] Artistic independence has arguably been jeopardised by recent social trends, but it is affirmed in the ways that music continues to cut between debates and to reconnect people in disparate places and with differing belief systems.

HOLLYWOOD RECONNECTED

Like the music industry, the most significant year for the re-emergence of a socially conscious film culture was 2004, the year in which Michael Moore's *Fahrenheit 9/11* won a Palme d'Or and an Academy Award, and in which George Clooney's film *Good Night, and Good Luck* symbolised what many liberal journalists were calling the 'New McCarthyism' of that year. In revisiting CBS journalist Ed Murrow's successful campaign in early 1954 to expose Joseph McCarthy, *Good Night, and Good Luck* also tapped into the threat of censorship from the Federal Communications Commission that followed the exposure of Janet Jackson's breast whilst performing live with Justin Timberlake at the Houston Superbowl earlier that year. The reaction to this climate of censorship was stridency, particularly among film actors. But there were earlier signs that Hollywood was reconnecting with broader social issues: Halle Berry and Denzel Washington had won best female and male lead roles at the Academy Awards in 2002, the first time that two black actors had done so; the release of a host of feature-length documentaries dealing with contemporary issues from 9/11 to the Iraq War to the fast food industry; and the increasing popularity of grassroots film festivals such as Sundance, Sansevieria, Austin, Ann Arbor, Portland and Seattle.

But if one takes a brief look at the highest-grossing films of the early 21st century there is scant evidence of change; the world market was saturated by US products and there is very little variation of the Top 20 films in terms of North American and global box-office successes.[23] In the world box-office Top 20 in 2006 there were fourteen US films; the other six were US co-productions. The top ten films in this list are dominated by Hollywood sequels: *Pirates of the Caribbean: Dead Man's Chest* at number one, and *X-Men: the Last Stand*, *Mission: Impossible III* and *Superman Returns* at six, seven and eight, with Buena Vista, Sony Columbia, 20th Century Fox and Warner Brothers dominating production and distribution. Only Martin Scorsese's Oscar-winning *The Departed* (fourteen in the world list, sixteen in the North American list), a reworking of the Hong Kong crime thriller *Internal Affairs* (2003), could be said to be an art-house product, and even that had the major box-office draws of Leonardo DiCaprio, Matt Damon and Jack Nicholson in the lead roles. The phenomenal success at the box office of the DreamWorks animation *Shrek The Third* in its first weekend in May 2007 (taking $122 million in North America), following *Spider-Man 3* three weeks earlier, which took $148 million nationally and $227 million globally in its first weekend, reveals a market driven by precisely targeted products with lucrative spin-off franchises.

These statistics do little to shake the perception that Hollywood is decadent, wedded to advertising, fashion and cosmetic industries and stimulated only by the dollar. However, there is a different story to tell, which suggests a more creative synergy between business and culture. Undoubtedly, 2006 was a good year for film business; 599 films were released in the US, up 64 from 2005, but, of these, 396 were independent films. This coincided with a significant increase in cinema attendance, moving back to the level of 2000, and revealing a market in which the distinction between 'independent' and 'Hollywood' film has become increasingly blurred. Filmmakers such as Martin Scorsese, Joel and Ethan Coen, David Lynch, Richard Linklater, Steven Soderburgh and Quentin Tarantino quite often work on the margins between studios and independents, while, as Peter Biskind argues, the rise of Miramax and the success of Robert Redford's Sundance Festival have created a more variegated film culture than in previous decades.[24] Only first-time, non-narrative, 'underground' or extremely experimental films can be seen to occupy a truly independent space, such as Jonathan Caouette's *Tarnation* (2003), using Super-8 film, answer-machine messages and video-diary footage on a $218.32 budget to document the story of his schizophrenic mother, and *Me, You and Everyone We Know* (2005), marking the directorial and acting debut of art school student Miranda July. Such young talent – Caouette was born in 1973, July in 1974 – reveals a grassroots movie culture far away from the media glare of Beverly Hills, with films echoing the style and interests of established indie directors Todd Solondz and Gus van Sant who work at arm's length from the industry.

The realignment of film culture has coincided with Hollywood becoming a place where left-liberal politics sits easily alongside big business. In his 2006 Academy Awards speech, George Clooney proclaimed he was proud to be part of an industry self-consciously 'out of touch' with dominant social values and committed to explore the complexities of current issues. While some films are explicitly politicised in drawing parallels between the present and earlier cultural moments, many try to avoid the simplistic 'heroes and villains' view of history to which Hollywood is prone. For example, rather than CBS journalist Ed Murrow simply vanquishing the corrupt Joseph McCarthy in *Good Night, and Good Luck* the moral polarities are not that clear: Murrow is in danger of losing his professional objectivity and McCarthy is left to undermine himself through the use of extensive archival footage.

Questionable heroes, ambiguous morality and lack of neat resolutions were all common in feature films released between 2004 and 2006: from the troubled superhero of the *Spiderman* films (played by Tobey McGuire) to Steven Spielberg's *Munich* (2005), which examines the aftermath of the Munich Olympic bombings of 1972 when eleven Israeli athletes were killed. Leading a team of Mossad agents hired by the Israeli government to avenge the athletes' murderers, the family man Avner (Eric Bana) becomes corrupted by the seemingly endless series of killings that ensue. While Spielberg and screenwriters Tony Kushner and Eric Roth wanted to critique the dangers of all forms of extremism in *Munich*, its layering of stories suggests a world without resolutions in which plots and plotting are inseparable, as novelist Don DeLillo detected in his novels *Libra* (1988) and *Mao II* (1991). This interconnected (sometimes described as 'hypertextual') linking of stories and lives was a strong feature of films, both on the local level – as for the Oscar-winning film *Crash* (2004) which exposes prejudice and racism on all social levels in Los Angeles – or on a global level – in the case of *Syriana* (2005) and *The Kingdom* (2007), which focus on CIA and FBI agents respectively to explore the many levels in which stories, beliefs and political interests come into friction within US-Middle East relations. Using a global cast of actors and striving for cultural accuracy, director Stephen Gaghan stated that his intention in *Syriana* was to reflect the visceral 'complexity' of the contemporary world and 'to embrace it narratively', explaining: 'there are no good guys and no bad guys and there are no easy answers ... the stories don't wrap up in neat little life lessons, the questions remain open'.[25]

Open questions within wider narrative patterns are also explored by eco-conscious films, such as *Sunshine State* (2002) which examines the clash between ordinary lives and business opportunities in northern Florida and, on a global scale, in the Oscar-winning documentary *An Inconvenient Truth* (2006), which has become the third-highest grossing documentary in the US. The figurehead of *An Inconvenient Truth*, Al Gore, is a long-term advocate of ecological causes, whose extended lecture mixes hard scientific data, satellite photography and audience-friendly visual technology to push home his message about the reality of global warming and the need to change habits. Criticised for being aloof and impersonal during his 2000 election campaign, *An Inconvenient Truth* shows the former Vice-President in a more relaxed mood, joking with his audience and displaying a very personal connection to the natural world. Viewed by some critics as a cynical attempt to re-engage with the public before the run-up to the 2008 election campaign (even though he declared early on he would not be running in the Democrat primaries), Gore is careful in the film not to play party politics. It would have been easy to target the eco-sceptics or wag his finger at the Bush administration for ignoring environmental threats (or bungling the federal response to Hurricane Katrina, as Spike Lee does in his 2006 documentary on the devastation in New Orleans, *When the Levees Broke: a Requiem in Four Acts*), but the global issues addressed by Gore are seemingly more important to him than jostling for the political high-ground. Pointing out that US carbon emissions have been higher than those of any other nation for decades, Gore's call is for all Americans to be personally responsible for environmental issues.

This call for action was taken up in 2007 – the year in which Gore was the co-recipient of the Nobel Peace Prize for his environmental work – but with more urgency. This urgency was stimulated by scientific claims that the next ten years are critical for radically reducing carbon emissions, and industry player Lawrence Bender (producer of *An Inconvenient Truth*) has claimed that global warming is the 'greatest issue facing us in our lifetime'.[26] In response, Warner Brothers released *The 11th Hour* which examines the state of current ecosystems and future prospects, using for its publicity an image of a big footprint deeply impressed on the globe. Starting life as a small-scale independent film, directors Leila Conners Peterson and Nadia Conners worked with A-lister Leonardo DiCaprio, who part-financed the project, to balance a critique of corporate effluence with a strident proposal about the reduction of the carbon footprint. The film assembles a mixture of experts to analyse the extreme weather conditions experienced since the Boxing Day 2004 tsunami in the Indian Ocean. Focusing only partly on Hurricane Katrina, *The 11th Hour* aspires to be a transnational film that prompts all viewers to become eco-activists. Narrated by DiCaprio, *The 11th Hour* is another example of a movie-length documentary that tries to offset what a panel of directors at the 'Greening of America' talk at the Cannes Film Festival in 2007 see as the failure of television to give an adequate public forum for discussing environmental change. The difference between a film like *The 11th Hour* and other 'state of the nation' films, is that it does not just deal with national conditions, but balances these with a global sensibility and an emphasis on the importance of local and personal politics.

*   *   *

Although a number of films released in autumn 2007 that dealt directly with global terrorism and the Middle East (*The Kingdom, In the Valley of Elah* and *Rendition*) received a lukewarm reception from American audiences (perhaps because they were too close to the bone), the links between politics and culture appear to be stronger than ever in the first years of the 21st century.[27] This is in part due to the cultural vanguard that has formed in response to the Bush presidency, but it also cuts across ideological lines in the wake of

9/11. If cultural thought appears to be in crisis because of the lack of public intellectuals in the early century, then American cultural practice is nevertheless vibrant and, in many ways, ahead of cultural thought in its assessment of the contemporary world.

In early 2008, it seems that the protest culture of the last few years might well ebb following the autumn 2008 presidential election, whilst environmental and demographic themes are liable to become stronger as the years go by. Some current cultural practitioners may seem in a few years unfashionably earnest, such as Michael Moore, who has faced unbounded criticism (not only from the right) for exaggeration in his social critiques of gun culture, the Bush presidency and medical insurance companies in his trio of documentaries *Bowling for Columbine* (2002), *Fahrenheit 9/11* (2004) and *Sicko* (2007). While the culture wars of the 1990s were still strong in 2004, battle lines have started to blur in the second half of the decade. A glimpse of this is evident in Matt Groening's *The Simpsons Movie* of 2007, which lampoons both the right (the residents of Springfield face the bullying tactics of Hometown Security and a malicious presidential advisor) and the left (Maggie Simpson presents a talk in the town hall with the parodic title 'An Irritating Truth'), but the film still manages to deal with serious environmental and social issues.

Richard Crockatt has recently argued that the 'discussion of culture in relation to politics is bedevilled by a preoccupation with polarities … conflicts are driven either by dimly remembered but highly potent and symbolic historical memories or by urgent present needs'.[28] It is easy to duplicate these polarities either by eliding culture too readily with party politics, or by focusing on culture as responding only to present economic or political needs rather than a driving force in its own right. As the following five essays demonstrate, a cultural perspective is as crucial for understanding the contemporary nation – and trends that go beyond the nation state – as the two other sections of this volume. In the next essay, Rebecca Tillett provides a historical context for understanding the issues surrounding immigration, ethnicities and the 'clash of civilizations' (earlier discussed in this volume), while the other essays focus on specific cultural forms.

Catherine Morley looks at the way in which words and narratives have become fraught with meaning following 9/11: a worry that stimulated Toni Morrison in her memorial poem 'The Dead of September 11' (2001) to claim: 'I have nothing to say – no words stronger than the steel that pressed you into itself'.[29] This blurring of boundaries between words and images is a theme within photojournalism following 9/11 as Liam Kennedy develops in his essay on American 'ways of seeing'. Lynn Spigel and Max Dawson follow this by exploring the ways in which television and digital media complicate notions of cultural production, while Paul Wells concludes the section by discussing the re-emergence of animation as a cultural bridge between old and new media. It is tempting to see contemporary cultural production as a stark rupture with the past, but these essays also reveal clear lines of development from 20th-century cultural trends.

NOTES

1. President Clinton's State of the Union address, 27 January 2000, www.washingtonpost.com/wp-srv/politics/special/states/docs/sou00.htm.
2. Bill Clinton, 'The Struggle for the Soul of the 21st Century', BBC Richard Dimbleby Lecture, London, 14 December 2001.
3. See Richard Florida, *The Flight of the Creative Class: The New Global Competition for Talent* (New York, NY: HarperCollins, 2007).
4. See Arthur M. Schlesinger Jr, *The Vital Center: The Politics of Freedom* (New Brunswick, NJ: Transaction, [1949] 1998) and *The Disuniting of America: Reflections on a Multicultural Society* (New York, NY: Norton, [1991] 1992).
5. Don M. Randel, 'The Myth of the Academic Community', in Judith Rodin and Stephen P. Steinberg (eds), *Public Discourse in America: Conversation and Community in the Twenty-First Century* (Philadelphia, PA: University of Pennsylvania Press, 2003), p. 227.
6. Rodin and Steinberg (eds), *Public Discourse in America*, p. xiv.
7. Laura Ingraham, *Shut Up and Sing: How Elites from Hollywood, Politics and the Media are Subverting America* (Washington, DC: Regnery Publishing, 2003), p. 16.
8. Pat Buchanan, 1992 Republican National Convention Speech, 17 August 1992.
9. See Ann Coulter, *Treason: Liberal Treachery from the Cold War to the War on Terrorism* (NewYork, NY: Crown Forum, 2003) and Michael Savage, *Liberalism is a Mental Disorder: Savage Solutions* (New York, NY: Thomas Nelson, 2005). For a discussion of the revisioning of 1950s thought in the early 21st century see Martin Halliwell, *American Culture in the 1950s* (Edinburgh: Edinburgh University Press, 2007), pp. 225–44.
10. Richard Bolton (ed.), *Culture Wars* (New York, NY: New Press, 1992), p. 15.
11. Christopher Hayes, '9/11: the Roots of Paranoia', *The Nation*, 25 December 2006, 11–14.
12. Dinesh D'Souza, *Letters to a Young Conservative* (New York, NY: Basic Books, 2002), pp. 5, 4.
13. Ibid., p. 223.
14. Dan Berger *et al.*, *Letter from Young Activists: Today's Rebels Speak Out* (New York, NY: Nation Books, 2005), p. xxvi.
15. Ibid., p. xxxi.
16. See Christopher Phelps, 'The new SDS', *The Nation*, 16 April 2007, 11–14.
17. Reebee Garofalo, 'Pop goes to war, 2001–2004: U.S. popular music after 9/11', in Jonathan Ritter and J. Martin Daughtry (eds), *Music in the Post 9/11 World* (New York, NY: Routledge, 2007), p. 9.
18. See Neil Young's CNN interview on 18 April 2006.
19. Springsteen has become closely linked to 9/11 as evidenced in Mike Binder's film *Reign Over Me* (2007). The film's protagonist Mike (Adam Sandler) is suffering from post-traumatic stress disorder five years after his wife and daughters were killed aboard one of the planes that crashed into the World Trade Center. Retreating into a childlike world of denial, Springsteen's 1980

album *The River* is a touchstone for both Mike's retreat into the past and an inter-textual reference to the events of 9/11.

20. See Kevin M. Cherry, 'Come on up for the Rising', *National Review Online*, 29 July 2002, http://www.theaustralian.news.com.au/story/0,20867,21800832-1702, 00.html.

21. Josh Tyrengiel, 'Bruce Rising', *Time*, 5 August 2002, 52–9.

22. Bryan Garman, 'Models of Charity and Spirit: Bruce Springsteen, 9/11, and the War on Terror', in Ritter and Daughtry (eds), *Music in the Post 9/11 World*, pp. 71–89. Bruce Springsteen in conversation with Ted Koppel, *Nightline*, ABC News, 4 August 2004, http://www.moveleft.com/moveleft_essay_2004_08_ 07_bruce_springsteen_supports_john_kerry.asp. Springsteen's song 'The Rising' was used in the presidential nomination campaigns for both Barack Obama and Hillary Clinton, with Springsteen endorsing Obama in April 2008.

23. Statistics taken from *Focus 2007: World Film Market Trends* (Paris: Marché du Film, 2007), pp. 9, 39.

24. See Peter Biskind, *Down and Dirty Pictures: Miramax, Sundance and the Rise of Independent Film* (London: Bloomsbury, 2004).

25. Stephen Gaghan, Final Production Notes for *Syriana*, Warner Brothers Press Pack, 2005.

26. 'The Greening of America', American Pavilion, Cannes Film Festival, 20 May 2007.

27. Ann Donahue, 'Don't mention the war', *Los Angeles Times*, 7 November 2007.

28. Richard Crockatt, *After 9/11: Cultural Dimensions of American Global Power* (London: Routledge 2007), p. 49.

29. Toni Morrison, 'The Dead of September 11', in Judith Greenberg, *Trauma at Home* (Lincoln, NB: University of Nebraska Press, 2003), p. 1.

14. CULTURAL PLURALISM AND NATIONAL IDENTITY

Rebecca Tillett

Fundamental concerns about cultural pluralism are evident in America's continued emphasis upon the principle of *e pluribus unum*. The notion of 'one nation under God, indivisible' remains a crucial aspect of a united American identity, with ethnic and cultural differences assimilated to ensure a homogeneous 'Americaneity' based primarily on the enduring worldview and ideologies of the original white, Anglo-Saxon, Protestant pilgrims. In the context of immigration, the primary source of American cultural pluralism, this remains of extreme importance in the 21st century, as millions continue to emigrate to the US each year. While immigration numbers rose so that 10 per cent of all Americans are 'foreign-born' at the turn of the millennium,[1] projections for 2007–60 suggest that immigration figures could rise by a further 63 per cent or 105 million.[2]

Yet in the wake of 9/11, both public opinion and government policy has begun to react not only to external attacks upon and criticisms of American national identity, but also to the rise in the numbers of immigrants to the US and their ability and/or desire to assimilate to a single homogeneous American identity. The result has been a tightening not only of America's national borders but also of the boundaries of national cultural identity, evident in the passing of legislature such as the Patriot Act of 2001. Responding to the need for greater national security after 9/11, the very name of the Patriot Act suggests America's increasingly nationalist focus, and responds to widespread anxieties over ever more diverse definitions of American cultural identity. As a result, what it means to be American is becoming inextricably entwined with concepts of nationalism and 'patriotism', and with the re-assertion of a universal 'Americaneity', while cultural pluralism is being viewed with greater suspicion and mistrust. In both national and international contexts, such developments are potentially far-reaching.

EARLY CULTURAL ANXIETIES

While the events of 9/11 are clearly unprecedented, it is significant that the reassertion of a universal Americaneity in response to a perceived 'foreign threat' has a very lengthy history, during which it has played a decisive role in defining American national identity. Indeed, the reaction to cultural pluralism after 9/11 can only be fully understood within the historical context of a long philosophical and political debate. However, it is a debate that is highly complex and often deeply paradoxical and self-contradictory, displaying what Eric Kaufman has identified as a 'pervasive dualism'.[3] America is, therefore, celebrated for its ethnic and cultural diversity, particularly in terms of freedom, religion and tolerance, often in direct comparison to the oppressive climate of Europe, and yet also bitterly and even fearfully critiqued for the very same reasons. In 1782, the naturalised American J. Hector St John de Crèvecoeur celebrated America as a receptacle for 'that strange mixture of blood, which you will find in no other country',[4] while some 50 years later, in 1835, Alexis de Tocqueville compared America favourably to Europe and praised

> a society formed of all the nations of the world ... people having different languages, beliefs, opinions: in a word, a society without roots, without memories, without prejudices, without routines, without common ideas, without a national character, yet a hundred times happier than our own.[5]

What is remarkable in these comments is that both writers also paradoxically suggest the *lack* of any hegemonic national American character in the early years of the new Republic, deriving primarily from the diversity of immigrant cultures. From its emergence as an independent nation, America was thus interpreted as a 'the world's first universal nation'.[6] While this concept continued to be applauded by American citizens, it also caused them increasing concern and contributed to the expression of a range of deep-seated fears about the loss of an essential European heritage evident in a range of 'Anglo-Saxon' cultural markers such as language, customs and cultural values. Notably, such fears and concerns were fed by an increasing public perception of the apparent contradictions between cultural homogeneity and the compelling notions of American freedom and individualism. As a result, America's engagement with cultural pluralism has long been a cause for comment if not apprehension, especially from an Anglo-American perspective.

Alongside the positive interpretations of Crèvecoeur and Tocqueville, concern was therefore also publicly expressed over the ability of recently arrived immigrants to assimilate and even their intentions regarding assimilation. In his essay 'Observations Concerning the Increase of Mankind' (1751), Benjamin Franklin queried the reluctance with which German immigrants adopted the English language, and expressed what he considered to be justified Anglo-Saxon fears over the increasing 'Germanification' of Pennsylvania:

> Why should the Palatine Boors [Germans] be suffered to swarm into our Settlements ... herding together [to] establish their Language and Manners to the Exclusion of ours? Why should Pennsylvania, founded by the English, become a Colony of Aliens, who will shortly be so numerous as to Germanize us instead of our Anglifying them.[7]

Franklin's choice of terminology exposes a response to cultural hegemony that continues to pervade the national and international debates on cultural pluralism in the 21st century. Accordingly, the newly arriving German immigrants are suspected not only of having little inclination to assimilate, but of actively establishing German cultural customs and language as a viable alternative to the traditional 'Anglification' of immigrant groups. A crucial problem is clearly the sheer weight of numbers: by the 1750s, mass immigration caused the German-speaking population of Pennsylvania to rise to between 60,000 and 100,000, or between one-third and three-fifths of the total population of the colony.[8] This mass migration (paralleled in the 21st century by increasing concerns over Spanish-speaking immigrants) is clearly interpreted as one of the dangers of cultural pluralism.

Franklin's concerns over American culture and the effects of cultural pluralism illustrate internal tensions within American cultural thought, which became more fully expressed in the early 19th century by the 'Nativist' movement. What is perhaps most significant are the ways in which previously sociocultural and even philosophical responses were actively translated into the political arena, both in terms of national debates and of specific policies and legislation. Notably, such political developments occurred alongside America's growing economic power, and mounting popular interest in Social Darwinism, eugenics and 'scientific' discourses on race.

LEGISLATING AGAINST 'UNWELCOME STRANGERS'

Similar reactions were equally evident within the US legislature. Congress responded to popular concerns by regulating immigration and, in 1875, passed legislation that effectively excluded specific lower-class social groups, including convicted criminals and prostitutes. As David M. Reimer argues, these immigrant groups became identified as 'unwelcome strangers', and were soon joined by other social and racial groups popularly considered to be exerting a damaging moral and cultural influence upon American society.[9] In this context, the vast growth in numbers of Chinese immigrants after the Californian Gold Rush of 1849, followed by a sudden influx of non-Anglo-Saxon Europeans in the latter years of the nineteenth century, caused a series of social upheavals and, in turn, provoked a range of oppressive legislation that attempted to control the social, national, ethnic and racial origins of immigrants to America.

If, as Daniel J. Tichenor suggests, 'nations define themselves through the official selection and control of foreigners seeking permanent residence on their soil', then perhaps the single most significant piece of American immigration legislation was the 1882 Chinese Exclusion Act, which excluded Chinese (and later wider Asian) immigration to the US for over 60 years.[10] The Exclusion Act is momentous: an instance of 'unprecedented regulatory authority' that 'linked national state-building to the preservation of existing orders of ethnic, racial and religious hierarchy'.[11] Indeed, the act marks the beginning of an era of increasingly punitive immigration legislation based upon race, ethnicity and political ideology, evident in the subsequent 1907–8 'Gentleman's Agreement' which restricted Japanese immigration.[12] Such exclusion was considered warranted in racial terms: in 1909, Theodore Roosevelt commented that, not only would Americans 'not permit the Japanese to come in large numbers among them', but that such 'opposition' was 'entirely warranted, and not only must be, but ought to be, heeded by the national government in the interest of our people and our civilization'.[13] Accordingly, ever increasing restrictions to wider Asian immigration became evident in the first half of the 20th century, with the introduction of further legislation including the 1921 Emergency Quota Act (limiting immigration numbers) and the 1924 Immigration Act, which identified specific racial and ethnic groups as 'undesirable', particularly those from Asia, and from Southern and Eastern (non-Anglo-Saxon) Europe.[14] As a result, the act reflected not only popular fears concerning race but also those concerning religion, and clearly acted to forestall cultural diversity by reinforcing a homogeneous Americaneity.

RENEWED DEBATE IN THE 20TH CENTURY

The early years of the 20th century saw a renewal of the philosophical debate surrounding cultural pluralism. Popular nativist opinions were crystallised in Israel Zangwill's 1908 play *The Melting Pot*, which asserted that 'America is God's Crucible … the fusion of all races', drawing a response in Horace Kallen's influential essay 'Democracy Versus the Melting Pot' (1915).[15] Kallen proposed that the key paradox at the heart of American concepts of democracy and equality was a mistaken belief that 'only things that are alike in fact … and only men that are alike in origin and in spirit … can be truly "equal"'. Kallen's alternative was 'harmony' and a 'democracy of nationalities' where, as Sidney Ratner suggests, 'Americanization ... involved not the destruction of all the distinctive cultural group traits' but rather 'the cherishing and preserving of every ethnic group's cultural heritage'.[16]

Kallen's direct challenge to popular concepts of immigration and assimilation sparked further debate. In 1916, Madison Grant's *The Passing of the Great Race* clearly laid out widespread popular fears and provided the single most influential nativist viewpoint. Grant's approach illustrated developments both in scientific racism and in eugenics, an increasingly race- and class-centred discussion of genetics.[17] As Grant's title suggests, his concern was the degeneration and disappearance of an 'authentic' American culture due to the proliferation of cultural pluralism. By contrast, Randolph Bourne's essay 'Trans-national America' (1916), responded to Kallen in a much more positive manner, proposing a radical reinterpretation of American freedom and arguing that all immigrants come to America with an identical purpose: 'to get the freedom to live as they wanted'.[18] Significantly, enforced assimilation overrode those same desires and needs. What is especially notable about this re-emergence of the debate on cultural pluralism is the ways in which polarised viewpoints became inflected within American immigration policy throughout the rest of the century.

As with American reactions to 9/11, American fears over cultural pluralism in the early 20th century also responded to the outbreak of a series of external political hostilities. With increasing German immigration throughout the 19th century, a proliferation of German language schools, churches, publications and communities, and the outbreak of World War I in Europe, many German Americans began to progressively identify themselves with Germany and German concepts of nationalism. The involvement of the United States in the war from 1917 caused the loyalties of German Americans to be called into question and identified as a cause for concern. Indeed, Theodore Roosevelt's 1915 speech demonstrates that the concerns expressed by Franklin more than 150 years earlier remained at the forefront of national anxieties:

> There is no room in this country for hyphenated Americanism ... a hyphenated American is not an American at all ... Americanism is a matter of the spirit and of the soul. Our allegiance must be purely to the United States.

For Roosevelt, cultural pluralism threatened national ruin: American society as 'a tangle of squabbling nationalities ... each preserving its separate nationality' that would 'preven[t] all possibility of its continuing to be a nation at all'.[19] Roosevelt's concern was subsequently reflected by American internment policies during World War II when Japanese immigrants and naturalised citizens alike were forced into internment camps and imprisoned if they refused to 'prove' their allegiance to the US. Significantly, the experiences of both German and Japanese Americans prefigure the immigration and security policies that resulted from fears over national security after 9/11.

A More Liberal Era

While events of the early 20th century bear an uncanny resemblance to those of the early 21st century, American ideas about and responses to cultural pluralism did change throughout the later years of the 20th century, resulting in the eventual repeal of the restrictive legislation of 1924. Although restrictions on Asian immigration were relaxed by the Chinese Exclusion Repeal Act of 1943, immigration controls were subsequently reiterated by the 1952 Immigration and Nationality Act, which established new restrictions based upon labour requirements, and responded to the popular fears and concerns over communism by enabling 'subversive' behaviour and allegiances to be identified as a reason for exclusion. Significantly, as with earlier immigration policy, public fears and concerns over cultural pluralism informed this legislation: a key feature of the act was the identification of communist ideology as specifically 'un-American'. However, the far less exclusionary amendments of 1965 relaxed restrictions on 'undesirable' countries of origin and enabled much wider immigration into America, notably from Asia and Eastern Europe. In this context, the 1965 Immigration Act responded to a much more liberal era and changing popular perceptions of cultural pluralism in the wake of the Civil Rights Movement.

Prominent African American political activists such as Martin Luther King and Malcolm X, and Mexican American labour rights activists such as César Chávez had achieved unparalleled success in making 'minority' cultures highly visible to Anglo-America, with the result that popular responses to cultural pluralism and to concepts of American identity acknowledged greater diversity and so became far more inclusive. Again, popular opinion was clearly reflected in the legislature: the 1965 act removed restrictions on immigration for the purposes of family reunion, and heralded an unprecedented rise in immigration figures. In spite of Lyndon B. Johnson's assertion that '[the] bill ... [would] not affect the lives of millions', the act prefigured a mass immigration that would transform American society through the introduction of multiple diverse cultures.[20] Ultimately, the 1965 Immigration Act would cause both consternation and a further reassertion of a homogeneous Anglo-Saxon Protestant Americaneity.

Campaigns for civil rights in the 1960s had seen a range of wider successes: non-Anglo-Saxon cultures had become more visible and exposed the diversity and plurality of American culture; the processes and even the desirability of assimilation had been thrown into doubt; and the failure to apply cultural ideals such as democracy and equality to all American citizens had been critiqued and interrogated. However, in the wake of unprecedented and unanticipated mass immigration, popular opinion and legislation again became more reactionary and restrictive. Once again, politics, popular opinions and philosophical debates converged with the result that restrictions were evident not only within conceptions of American culture, but also within immigration policy. The 1986 Immigration Reform and Control Act criminalised Americans who knowingly employed illegal immigrants. While the legislation attempted to curb illegal migration to the US, it also gave illegal aliens within America the chance to apply for naturalisation. Significantly, this legislation dealt with a new and increasing problem: immigration and migration from within the Americas. Increasing public concern over the matter, especially in those states bordering Mexico, influenced the creation of a Task Force on Immigration, and marked the beginning of growing hostility towards and punitive policies directed at Spanish-speaking migrants and immigrants.

While the 1990 Immigration Act allowed larger numbers of immigrants into the US, more restrictive measures were introduced. As with the policies of many previous administrations, legislation engaged with popular opinion and ongoing debates surrounding the increasingly inseparable issues of immigration and cultural pluralism. As a result, the 1996 Illegal Immigration Reform and Immigrant Responsibility Act responded to a 'resurgence of nativism in California' that Michael Alvarez and Tara L. Butterfield suggest is evidence of the 'cyclical' nature of American nativism.[21] Additionally, the pervasive dualism within both philosophical debates and government policies was demonstrated by two specific policies: the 'One America' Initiative (1997) and 'Operation Gatekeeper' (1994). On the one hand, the 'One America' drive actively and publicly embraced growing diversity by advocating bilingual education, promoting better race relations, and ensuring the appointment and visibility of culturally diverse individuals at the heart of American government. Yet, simultaneously, 'Operation Gatekeeper' responded to illegal immigration by transforming the US-Mexico border into a militarised zone, by doubling the Border Patrol, and by fortifying the area with a high steel fence, now popularly referred to as the 'Tortilla Curtain'.[22]

CONTEMPORARY DEBATES AND CONTROVERSIES

Reflecting the events of almost a century earlier, contemporary government policy and public opinion has engaged with the ongoing philosophical debate surrounding cultural pluralism. American intellectuals at the end of the 20th century have increasingly begun to publicly debate not only the threats posed to homogeneous Americaneity by immigration, but also the inability and unwillingness of immigrants to assimilate to, or even recognise, a homogeneous Anglo-Saxon American culture. As a result, the contemporary philosophical debate has increasingly tended to reiterate Roosevelt's 1915 criticisms of 'hyphenated Americans'. It is notable that two of the main theorists in question – the late Arthur Schlesinger Jr and Samuel Huntington – served as presidential advisors (to Presidents Kennedy and Johnson), and so combined their role as leading academics with the direct shaping of government policy. Both were/are also respected Harvard academics, adding weight and influence to their opinions. Significantly, both have also been the most vocal critics of mass immigration and cultural pluralism in recent years, and the most active proponents of contemporary nativism, publishing best-selling books on the topic that demonstrate their engagement with popular opinion: Schlesinger's *The Disuniting of America* (1991), and a series of critiques from Huntington including *The Clash of Civilizations* (1996), 'The Hispanic Challenge' (2004) and *Who Are We? The Challenges to America's National Identity* (2004).

For Schlesinger, the threat is clearly to a white, male, heterosexual, Protestant, capitalist America; he argues that 'when … a visible minority pledges primary allegiance to their groups … it presents a threat to the brittle bonds of national identity'.[23] The dangers posed by cultural pluralism are therefore multiple, and the threat evident not only from many established immigrant and settler groups but also from those formerly forcibly relocated. Schlesinger's perceived 'threat' includes African America's drive for civil rights, increased immigration from Asia and the Hispanic world, and the rising power of non-Christian religions such as Islam. Huntington, by contrast, is more focused on specific examples: the cultural threat posed by Spanish-speaking immigrants, the religious threat of Islam, and economic and political threat of China. For both Schlesinger and Huntington, however, the threat has been worsened by America's liberal immigration laws after 1965 and by the refusal of newly arrived immigrants to assimilate to traditional notions of American identity. The dangers of cultural pluralism are clearly laid out in Huntington's work; his concern is not only with the threat posed to American national identity, but also with challenges to America's status as the sole global economic superpower and its role as a profoundly Christian nation. As a result, Huntington anticipates that all future national conflicts will be driven by cultural interests, that cultural differences 'will be the battle lines of the future'.[24]

Huntington's theories have proved both influential – he is widely credited with having 'predicted' the events of 9/11 – and highly damaging to popular understandings of American cultural pluralism.[25] Clearly, popular and political discussions of concepts such as national culture and 'citizenship' have become increasingly evident in many Western countries since 9/11, and so the debate over terrorism has become inextricably linked to culture and culture clash. Contemporary popular, political and philosophical questions regarding cultural pluralism are increasingly re-focusing upon the ability and desire of immigrants to adopt the culture and cultural values of their new countries of residence. This is a key problem that Huntington identifies among Spanish-speaking migrants and immigrants at the start of the 21st century, who pose 'special social and cultural problems'. For Huntington, the major threat to American identity is the massive growth in numbers of Spanish-speaking immigrants: identified as the largest 'minority' group in 2005 with 14.5 per cent of the population (compared to 12.8 per cent for the former largest group, African Americans).[26] In this context, Huntington's concern is that the 'persistent inflow' of these new groups is effectively transporting entire communities and social groups, resulting in a segregation of immigrant groups into Spanish-speaking Catholic areas where there is no need to learn English.

To Huntington's mind, this represents 'the most serious cleavage in American society' of recent years, problematised by the high 'fertility rates' of such social groups. Huntington argues that a 'contempt of [American] culture' demonstrates 'irreconcilable [cultural] differences' and can lead only to 'the end of the America we have known for more than three centuries'. His solution is not only blunt, but also intolerant of cultural pluralism:

> There is no Americano dream. There is only the American dream created by an Anglo-Protestant society. Mexican Americans will share in that dream only if they dream in English.[27]

This is clearly also the public perception of the situation; a series of interlinked articles for the *Washington Post* on 'The myth of the melting pot' (1998) presented a snapshot of immigrant America and suggested a rise in a 'white flight', the migration of Anglo-Americans, from areas so inundated with Spanish-speaking immigrants that they seem like another country. Presenting a deeply critical portrait of Miami, which is described as having an 'exotic, foreign feel' and where white Americans are in 'the minority' as a result of massive Cuban immigration, this piece suggests that American cultural hegemony is not merely under attack but perhaps already defeated.[28]

Significantly, Huntington's two-pronged attack also identifies Islam as damaging to concepts of American national cultural identity, and specifies Islam as one of 'the battle lines of the future'. Written in the wake of the first Gulf War (1990–1), Huntington's thesis on the clash of American and Islamic cultural values is perhaps not so dramatically prescient, yet the problem is complicated by a growth in the numbers of Muslim Americans at the end of the 20th century, and by fears of further terrorist activity since 9/11. Like concerns over Japanese Americans during World War II, the popular concern has become one of loyalty, and Muslim Americans are increasingly questioned as to whether they place loyalty to their country above that for their religion and culture. Problematically, Huntington's thesis extends the range of the external cultural threat to ally the Islamic world with China, to predict 'the next pattern of conflict', and to play on popular fears of China's communist regime, growing economy and population, emergence as a new superpower, and the long-established tensions over

America's Asian immigration legislation.[29]

Given the perceived external threat since 9/11, Huntington's nativist argument has become part of the public debate and, more problematically, has fed into government policy. The implications of this translation of a philosophical debate into actual legislation after 9/11 are far-reaching, primarily because an academic thesis is only an intellectual theory, and one of many. One of the key aspects of Huntington's popular success has been his active engagement with deeply held public anxieties. As Amitai Etzioni argues, this is 'best characterized as a theory of fear'.[30] This clearly has been more profoundly influenced both by the events of 9/11, and by the subsequent policies of the Bush administration such as the 2001 Patriot Act and the 2005 Border Protection, Anti-Terrorism, and Illegal Immigration Control Act. What has become more evident are the ways that American cultural perception has been reoriented: how immigration control has been transformed into 'border protection', and how illegal immigrants have merged with and become inseparable from popular constructions of terrorism and terrorists. Congress has also, in the years after 9/11, begun investigating higher education policy, and questioning whether the teaching of Middle East Studies is itself 'un-American', with the result that Middle East Studies in America has identified itself as 'under siege'.[31]

Perhaps the most significant recent addition to the debate in the 21st century is Walter Benn Michaels's *The Trouble With Diversity* (2006). Michaels argues that the overwhelming nature of identity politics in the 21st century has effectively erased social and economic inequalities. The problem, as Michaels sees it, is simply economic: 'differences between us present a problem: the need to get rid of inequality or to justify it'.[32] For Michaels, cultural pluralism has emerged as a justification of social inequality, where the concept of social class is transformed into 'a version of race', and rich and poor are conceived of as 'different races'.[33] The crux of Michaels's argument is that, while 'race' as a category has long been scientifically disproved, our reliance upon the concept of cultural pluralism ensures that we can continue to think (and act) in terms of 'race', with cultural pluralism adopted as the easiest route to a 'colour-blind' society ('colour-blind' was a term frequently used, sometimes ambivalently, to characterise the tone of Barack Obama's presidential campaign of 2008, perhaps prompting Obama to make his 'A More Perfect Union' speech in Philadelphia on 18 March in which he explicitly framed the 21st-century race debate).

Michaels's argument is highly significant, not only because it addresses the extreme economic differences within contemporary America and seeks to produce a class-based assessment, but also because he argues that we have learnt to 'think of inequality as a consequence of our prejudices rather than as a consequence of our social system'.[34] However, Michaels's argument not only over-simplifies a highly complex issue but is, in places, deeply self-contradictory. The definition of 'cultural pluralism' as either socially constructed or based on actual biological distinctions is highly simplistic. More problematically, Michaels's either/or argument – either culture/race or economics – fails to identify or fully discuss the links *between* social categories such as race, culture, poverty and/or wealth. This contradiction is most evident when Michaels speaks specifically of the legacy of the slave trade – where 'we can't plausibly deny that the economic circumstances of African Americans today are importantly a consequence of slavery and past racism' – but then paradoxically suggests that the 21st-century world is one in which 'most of us are not racist … [and] where, on the humanities faculties of our universities, we might more plausibly say not that racism is rare but that it is extinct'.[35] As a result, although Michaels raises a range of highly pertinent questions about the relationships between contemporary social inequality and cultural pluralism, his contention that racism has been eliminated is, as Scott McLemee comments, simply 'bewildering'. In this context, Michaels's premise that cultural pluralism is itself an 'obstacle to pursuing the real politics of social justice' is an interesting development in the ongoing philosophical debate.[36]

RECENT CHALLENGES TO AMERICAN NATIONAL IDENTITY

The ongoing tensions between cultural diversity and national identity are, perhaps appropriately, best illustrated by a recent case from the second Gulf War: the media interest in and frenzy surrounding Private Jessica Lynch. Lynch was one of a group captured by Iraqi forces in March 2003 during an ambush of an American military convoy. Lynch subsequently became a symbol both of American identity and of the American struggle in Iraq. Accordingly, much media attention was devoted to the plight of 'the blond 19 year old from Palestine, West Virginia', with the effect that the story took on the heroic elements of the colonial captivity narrative, complete with a growing equation of Lynch with American national and cultural identity.[37] This equation of individual and nation is of crucial significance: as Stacy Takacs comments, the 'vested interests of the military and commercial media coalesced around the need for a good story to clarify the moral stakes of the war in Iraq'.[38] Accordingly, the subsequent media focus on Lynch's survival in spite of her own feminine physical frailty, her gallant attempts to fight her attackers in spite of her wounds, her abuse (reportedly both physical and sexual) at the hands of her Iraqi captors, her mistreatment while lying defenceless in an Iraqi hospital, and her filmed rescue by American troops, all acted to emphasise Lynch's newly pivotal role as an icon of American national and cultural identity. This pivotal role is perhaps most evident in the number of documentaries that subsequently emerged, all of which focused on Lynch's 'pioneering American spirit', while stripping away her military status to present a highly feminised vulnerability.

Private Lynch was thus effectively transformed into a global media phenomenon. However, in the months that followed it became clear that Lynch's story was far less heroic and far more mundane than the publicised version: Lynch was not wounded in action, never managed to fire a shot at enemy forces, and was treated well by Iraqi doctors. In this context, Lynch's mythologising as an American icon exposes the complex relationships between cultural and national identity. Quite simply, Lynch is physically representative of the kind of American national identity that the US wanted to promote: she is young, blonde and white. Indeed, the debate surrounding the Lynch affair has raged around the specific choices made by the Bush administration as to which captured American soldiers within Lynch's group were representative of American nation and culture. Significantly, Lynch was not the only choice available, there were two further wounded female American soldiers in the unit: Specialist Shoshana Johnson, who was wounded in action and became America's first black female prisoner of war, and Private Lori Ann Piestewa, a member of the Hopi nation who was the first Native American woman to die in combat for her country. Notably, neither Johnson nor Piestewa matched the desired criteria for American cultural and national identity: both were single mothers; both were wounded in combat, with Piestewa later dying from her wounds; and, most importantly, neither fitted into the heroic American 'captivity narrative' either as it has traditionally been constructed or as it was reconstructed around Lynch's experiences. Moreover, although both were awarded Purple Hearts, neither was white.

As John Howard and Laura Prividera argue, the pervasive cultural forces that structure Lynch's story also therefore act upon the stories of Johnson and Piestewa, reducing them to 'secondary characters ... in terms of their relationship to Private Lynch'.[39] This reduction in cultural and national status is equally evident in the events since Lynch and Johnson's return to the US. Lynch returned to a hero's welcome from a crowd of thousands in West Virginia, was awarded an honourable discharge and a substantial disability pension, and benefited financially from a book deal. By contrast, the honouring of Piestewa's memory has been left primarily to local tribal groups, who campaigned successfully for a local Arizona peak to be renamed in her honour; and, ironically, to Lynch who has devoted time and energy to emphasising Piestewa's pivotal role in her own survival. Johnson's experience has been perhaps even more complex and controversial, and debate has been exceptionally fierce since it was revealed that her disability pension (for wounds suffered in combat) had been set at a fraction of the disability pension awarded to Lynch (for wounds suffered in an accident). Given the absolute emphasis placed by both the military and the media upon Lynch's own racial and cultural background, it is therefore exceptionally difficult to assess the experiences of Piestewa and Johnson outside of racial and cultural categories and their cases are, therefore, deeply significant for considerations of American cultural pluralism in the 21st century.

Such conceptions of American cultural diversity are equally significant to the events surrounding Hurricane Katrina. As John Wills discusses in this volume, in August 2005 Katrina devastated entire areas of New Orleans, causing widespread death and destruction in what was to become a globally televised humanitarian crisis. Recent figures estimate that more than 1,100 drowned, thousands more remain unaccounted for, and more than one million have been displaced.[40] The Bush administration's failure to act immediately to provide relief, coupled with the profound impact of televised images of innumerable drowned bodies and of desperate pleas from poor communities trapped in flooded areas, provoked enormous public outcry and laid bare deeply entrenched divisions within American society. While the aftermath of Katrina relates to a range of complex inter-related social issues, there is little doubt that the incident marks a crisis point in recent American social relations. In this context, Katrina exposes the ways in which popular American culture identified cultural diversity as a significant contributing factor for those most affected: the African American community of New Orleans's Ninth Ward.

Given Louisiana's history as a slave-holding state, it is not surprising that subsequent critical interpretations have traced this legacy amongst those most affected, the descendents of freed slaves who continue to earn well below the national average and to experience few chances for social or economic advancement. Estimates suggest that, at the time of the hurricane, New Orleans was the '12th poorest city' in America, with a population almost 70 per cent African American, and 30 per cent of all residents living 'below the federal poverty line'. Moreover, those areas most devastated had a '98-percent black population' and poverty and unemployment rates of over 40 per cent.[41] What was perhaps most evident from the media coverage of the Katrina disaster was the continued entrenched racism of American society. Pleas for aid from poor black communities were repeatedly ignored, as was the economic inability of the poor to actually leave the area: many poor black families simply lacked the financial means to evacuate.[42] In conjunction, the media ran 'lurid' stories (later widely disproved) of 'New Orleans blacks committing widespread murders, sexual assaults, carjackings, and terroristic shootings at rescue workers'. As Manning Marable argues, the 'racist subtext' of such news stories suggested that 'New Orleans blacks were not worthy of being saved'.[43]

While the individual costs of Hurricane Katrina continue to be counted, there can be little doubt that the institutional and cultural costs are being thoroughly assessed, with Katrina offering evidence of the inextricable links between race and class, of 'institutional discrimination [and] individual racism', and even of 'global apartheid'.[44] The lack of government action has, concomitantly, been interpreted as a complex response to race and class where, as Henry Giroux argues, the entrenched 'ideological hostility' of the Bush administration towards supporting those most socially in need exposes

239

the social crisis at the heart of American cultural diversity that can be directly related 'to a deeper set of memories of racial injustice and violence ... that suggest a link between an apartheid past and ... [an] utter disregard for populations now considered disposable'.[45] In the context of cultural pluralism in the 21st century, it is notable that the institutional response to Katrina derives directly from long-standing 'historical and contemporary orientations towards Blacks in the United States' that 'shaped responses ... without overt antipathy or intention'.[46] City decisions in the wake of the catastrophe smack of social opportunism, with the chance to rebuild New Orleans – as it could be rather than as it was – leading potentially to the permanent exclusion of poor black communities, and fuelling the ongoing debate surrounding the values and dangers of American cultural pluralism.

TRENDS FOR THE 21ST CENTURY

If, as the 2005 Census suggests, minority American cultural groups have become 'the majority in 10% of U.S. counties', then the implications for the future might suggest a cause for concern.[47] In terms of national implications, the tightening of immigration policies and borders reverses the more liberal policies of the 1960s. Additionally, the tightening of cultural boundaries reiterates a restrictive conceptualisation of American cultural identity that fails both to accommodate new immigrants, and to recognise the massive transformation of American culture through immigration in the last years of the 20th century. In this context, African American communities continue to suffer institutionalised racism even while their status as the largest minority culture is lost to growing numbers of Spanish-speaking immigrants.

In terms of international implications, the increasing polarisation of the world in terms of religion and politics is problematic and highly divisive, and the reinforcing of binary divisions between Islam and Christianity and between America and China/Asia reintroduce and rework a range of complex and negative historical relationships. With the War on Terror far from concluded, it seems safe to assume that restrictive border controls and negative attitudes towards the Islamic world are likely to remain part of American policy for some years to come. Additionally, given China's increasing economic and political power, and development of nuclear technology, it might also be reasonable to assume a transformation in American-Chinese relations in the near future.

However, the future is not all bleak. In his critique of Huntington's thesis, Edward Said commented that the 'clash of civilisations thesis is a gimmick ... better for reinforcing defensive self-pride than for critical understanding of the bewildering interdependence of our time'.[48] Said's comment, which illustrates the dangers of reactionary attitudes and suggests the need for a more engaged analysis of contemporary American identity, exposes the connections between current concepts of cultural pluralism and a very lengthy American debate dating back to the 18th century. Indeed, contemporary understandings of American cultural pluralism, along with responses to 9/11, only make sense within this lengthy cultural debate.

Nonetheless, positive interpretations of the situation are evident. In the aftermath of Hurricane Katrina, some commentators have suggested that the exposure of ongoing entrenched racism marks a 'turning point' for American cultural pluralism, with the potential for 'positive change' evident in the 'wave of activism' in New Orleans since 2005.[49] While Charles Hirschman's contribution to a series of academic articles entitled 'Border Battles: The U.S. Immigration Debates' recognises a 'deep ambivalence about future immigration' within America, he nonetheless notes that the 'demographic challenges' faced by the US in the 21st century 'are not unique'. More importantly, not only do current debates 'echo throughout American history', but Hirschman notes that 'almost all popular fears about … the negative impact' of cultural pluralism and immigration 'have been proved false by history'. American culture has, by contrast, been positively 'broadened' by pluralism.[50]

NOTES

1. Figures from 'The Population Profile of the United States: 2000', May 2002, http://www.census.gov/population/www/pop-profile/profile2000.html.
2. Steven A. Camarota, '100 Million More: Projecting the Impact of Immigration on the US Population, 2007–2060', Centre for Immigration Studies, August 2007, http://www.cis.org/articles/2007/back707.html.
3. Eric Kaufman, 'Nativist Cosmopolitans: institutional reflexivity and the decline of "double-consciousness" in American nationalist thought', *Historical Sociology*, 14(1), 2001, 48.
4. J. Hector St John de Crèvecoeur, *Letters from an American Farmer and Sketches of Eighteenth Century American Life* (New York, NY: Penguin, [1782] 1981), pp. 69–70.
5. Alexis de Tocqueville, *Democracy in America* (London: David Campbell, [1835] 1994), pp. 173–4.
6. Kaufman, 'Nativist Cosmopolitans', p. 47.
7. Benjamin Franklin, 'Observations concerning the increase of Mankind', in Leonard W. Labaree *et al.* (eds), *The Papers of Benjamin Franklin* (New Haven, CT: Yale University Press, [1751] 1999), vol. 4, p. 234.
8. John B. Frantz, 'Franklin and the Pennsylvania Germans', *Pennsylvania History*, 65, Winter 1998, 21.
9. David M. Reimer, *Unwelcome Strangers: American Identity and the Turn Against Immigration* (New York, NY: Columbia University Press, 1999).
10. Daniel J. Tichenor, *Dividing Lines: The Politics of Immigration Control in America* (Princeton, NJ: Princeton University Press, 2002), p. 1.
11. Tichenor, *Dividing Lines*, p. 88.
12. Also known as the Root-Takahira Agreement.
13. Theodore Roosevelt, 'The Threat of Japan', The Papers of Theodore Roosevelt,

http://www.mtholyoke.edu/acad/intrel/trjapan.htm.

14. Also known as the Johnson-Reed Act.

15. Israel Zangwill, 'The Melting Pot' (1908), Act I, http://beatl.barnard.columbia.edu/wsharpe/citylit/Melting1.html.

16. Horace M. Kallen, 'Democracy versus the melting-pot: a study of American nationality', *The Nation*, 25 February 1915, http://www.expo98.msu.edu/people/Kallen.htm. Sidney Ratner, 'Horace M. Kallen and cultural pluralism', *Modern Judaism*, 4, 1984, 187.

17. Grant's text is currently only available online on white supremacist websites.

18. Randolph Bourne, 'Trans-national America', *Atlantic Monthly*, 118, July 1916, http://www.swarthmore.edu/SocSci/rbannis1/AIH19th/Bourne.html.

19. For the full speech, see T. R. Theodore Roosevelt: Quotes, Sayings and Aphorisms, http://www.theodore-roosevelt.com/trquotes.html.

20. Lyndon B. Johnson, 3 October 1965 http://www.lbjlib.utexas.edu/Johnson/archives.hom/speeches.hom/651003.asp.

21. R. Michael Alvarez and Tara L. Butterfield, 'The resurgence of Nativism in California? The case of Proposition 187 and illegal immigration (1997)', *Social Science Quarterly*, 8(1), March 2000, 167.

22. See Joseph Nevins, *Operation Gatekeeper: The Rise of the "Illegal Alien" and the Making of the US-Mexico Boundary* (New York, NY: Routledge, 2002), passim.

23. Arthur M. Schlesinger Jr, *The Disuniting of America: Reflections on a Multicultural Society* (New York, NY: Norton, [1991] 1992), p. 64.

24. Samuel P. Huntington, 'The Clash of Civilizations', *Foreign Affairs*, 72(3), Summer 1993, 22.

25. See the interview with Huntington, 'Five years after 9/11: the clash of civilizations revisited', 18 August 2006, http://pewforum.org/events/index.php?EventID=125.

26. The Associated Press, 'Diversity Growing Across the U.S.', http://www.msnbc.msn.com/id/14348539/print/1/display.1098/.

27. Samuel Huntington, 'The Hispanic challenge', *Foreign Policy*, March–April 2004, 30–45.

28. William Booth, 'A white migration north from Miami', *Washington Post*, 11 November 1998, A1.

29. Huntington, 'The Clash of Civilizations', pp. 29, 22.

30. Amitai Etzioni, 'The Real Threat: An essay on Samuel Huntington', *Contemporary Sociology*, 34(5), 2005, 477.

31. Joan W. Scott, 'Middle East Studies under siege', *The Link*, 39(1), January–March 2006.

32. Walter Benn Michaels, *The Trouble With Diversity* (New York, NY: Henry Holt, 2006), p. 6.

33. Ibid., p. 9.

34. Ibid., p. 20.

35. Ibid., pp. 126, 73.

36. Scott McLemee, 'Liberty, equality … diversity?', *Inside Higher Ed*, 20 September 2006, http://www.insidehighered.com/views/2006/09/20/mclemee.

37. Stacy Takacs, 'Jessica Lynch and the regeneration of American identity and power post-9/11', *Feminist Media Studies*, 5(3), 2005, 301.

38. Ibid., p. 297.

39. John W. Howard and Laura C. Prividera, 'Rescuing patriarchy or saving "Jessica Lynch": The rhetorical construction of the American woman soldier', *Woman and Language*, 27(2), 2004, 96.

40. Kristin E. Henkel, John F. Dovidio and Samuel L. Gaertner, 'Institutional discrimination, individual racism, and Hurricane Katrina', *Analyses of Social Issues and Public Policy*, 6(1), 2006, 105; Henry A. Giroux, 'Reading Hurricane Katrina: Race, class, and the biopolitics of disposability', *College Literature*, 33(3), Summer 2006, 183.

41. Giroux, 'Reading Hurricane Katrina', p. 183; Manning Marable, 'Race, class, and the Katrina crisis', *Working USA: The Journal of Labor and Society*, 9(2), 2006, 156.

42. Henkel, Dovidio and Gaertner, 'Institutional discrimination, individual racism, and Hurricane Katrina', p. 108.

43. Manning Marable, 'Race, class, and the Katrina crisis', *Working USA: The Journal of Labor and Society*, 9(2), 2006, 155–6.

44. Henkel, Dovidio and Gaertner, 'Institutional discrimination, individual racism, and Hurricane Katrina'; Giroux, 'Reading Hurricane Katrina'; Marable, 'Race, class, and the Katrina crisis', p. 159.

45. Giroux, 'Reading Hurricane Katrina', pp. 184–5.

46. Henkel, Dovidio and Gaertner, 'Institutional discrimination, individual racism, and Hurricane Katrina', p. 100.

47. CNN, 'Minorities become the majority in 10 percent of U.S. counties', 9 August 2007, http://edition.cnn.com/2007/US/08/09/minority.counties.ap/index.html.

48. Edward Said, 'The Clash of Ignorance', *The Nation*, 22 October 2001, http://www.thenation.com/doc/20011022/said.

49. Henkel, Dovidio and Gaertner, 'Institutional discrimination, individual racism, and Hurricane Katrina', p. 119.

50. Charles Hirschman, 'The Impact of Immigration on American Society: Looking Backward to the Future', Social Science Research Council Issue Forum: Border Battles, The U.S. Immigration Debates, http://borderbattles.ssrc.org/Hirschman.

15. WRITING IN THE WAKE OF 9/11

Catherine Morley

For the literary scholar, one of the most revealing things abut 9/11 was the great public interest afterwards in what writers would have to say: how could the writer respond to such a catastrophic event, an event that seemed so cinematic that, according to Kathryn Flett in *The Observer*, it 'mocked all power of description?'[1] Yet there seemed an overriding need for words in the wake of 9/11. As Ulrich Baer has pointed out:

> In the first days after the attack, the astounding efforts by the rescue workers found a symbolic echo in the poems postered on walls and fences: first in makeshift memorials, then delivered to inboxes all over the globe. This spontaneous burgeoning of poetry responded to a need – a need for words that then took the form of written scrolls hung on fences and walls along with donated pens and markers, allowing anyone to offer the language of poetry where little could be said.[2]

Responding to this public desire for words of explanation or elucidation, in the immediate aftermath of the attacks the weekend supplements were flooded with confessions of diminished power from authors across the globe. Jay McInerney, Arundhathi Roy, Zadie Smith and Ian McEwan all wrote of their sense of the futility of the act of writing, the inconsequential nature of the writer and the inability of language to encapsulate or represent the reverberations of the attacks. One of the most interesting responses came from Martin Amis, who commented upon the figurative nature of the acts:

> The Pentagon is a symbol, and the World Trade Center is, or was, a symbol, and an American passenger jet is also a symbol – of indigenous

mobility and zest, and of the galaxy of glittering destinations … It was well understood that an edifice so demonstrably comprised of concrete and steel would also become an unforgettable metaphor.[3]

Amis's emphasis on language and symbolism aligns the terrorist with the artful, plotting writer and, as Alex Houen has pointed out in *Terrorism and Modern Literature* (2002), Osama Bin Laden also read the 11 September attacks figuratively.[4] In extracted interviews and transcripts of television messages Bin Laden described the attacks as targeted at the 'icons of military and economic power', stating that it is 'thanks … to God that what America is tasting now is only a copy of what we have tasted'.[5] Indeed, for Terrorism Studies scholars such as Houen, on many levels September 11 'amounted … to a monumental collision of symbols, metaphors and shadowy figures'.[6]

The conflation of the writer and the terrorist is taken further by Margaret Scanlan in her book *Plotting Terror* (2001), which argues that much terrorist literature presents writers and terrorists as 'remnants of a romantic belief in the power of marginalised persons to transform history' with recent fiction offering 'an increasingly pessimistic account of the novel's social power, a pessimism that some recent novelists extend to the revolutionary impulse itself'.[7] Because, as Don DeLillo's Bill Gray in *Mao II* (1991) puts it, 'writers know how reality is created', fiction that deals with terrorism elucidates the process whereby militants, the media and politicians construct terrorism as a political reality.[8] The links between television and terrorism have been well-rehearsed, but the links between the terrorist and the writer have come under much closer scrutiny in the wake of 9/11.[9] On consideration, terrorist-inspired fiction does indeed complicate the distinction between writers and terrorists, between stories and real acts of violence. After all, the fiction writer, in making use of the terrorist atrocity in the construction of fiction, is in some way channelling some of the power of the terrorist act, converting violence into a spectacle, and appropriating the narrative of the victims.[10] According to Scanlan, novels which deal with terrorism often force a writer 'to assess his or her own political commitments, actions and failures … the terrorist novel opens itself up to the more general questions about the writer's ability to understand, respond to, and influence politics.'[11] Indeed, this might account for the widespread public soul-searching of authors across the globe in the wake of the attacks.

However, few American writers have overtly addressed the figure of the 'other' or the terrorist, preferring instead to retreat to the domestic interiors of American lives. One thinks, for instance, of Ken Kalfus's *A Disorder Peculiar to the Country* (2006), McInerney's *The Good Life* (2006) or Claire Messud's *The Emperor's Children* (2006), each of which deals with the impact of the attacks on individual families and couples. There are, of course, exceptions to this. John Updike's *Terrorist* (2006) takes the reader into the mind and the world of a would-be, home-grown jihadist, Ahmad Mullaway

Mulloy. Mohsin Hamid, albeit ironically and through parodic inversion, takes on the terrorist in *The Reluctant Fundamentalist* (2006) whereby the Pakistani 'fundamentalist' resists the fundamentals of the corporate New York life-style. Needless to say, writers outside the borders of the US have taken on the Muslim subject more willingly, and according to Pankaj Mishra much more successfully, than their American counterparts.[12]

Amongst American writers, however, the themes that emerge most strongly from the literature that self-consciously responds to 9/11 are the seeming redundancy of language and the resultant possibilities for literary art, the will to understand or make sense of 'the other', and domestic discord. Although a whole raft of literature has been produced, for reasons of space this essay will focus on prose fiction, mainly the novel, rather than poetic or dramatic responses. This allows the inclusion of the work of writers like DeLillo and Updike, who have come to occupy almost titanic positions in the canon of contemporary American letters and whose responses to the September 11 events were most keenly anticipated. Emphasis on prose fiction also facilitates the inclusion of New York-based writers such as Lydia Davis and Jenefer Shute, who offer shorter, more immediate, prose responses to the events.[13]

THE DISINTEGRATION OF THE DOTCOM GENERATION

Writers such as Messud and McInerncy use New York City as a backdrop for their vast and, in the former instance, multigenerational stories of familial discord and adultery. Both, along with former brat-packer Bret Easton Ellis in *Lunar Park* (2005), use 9/11 as a means of examining the complacency of the dotcom generation and their resultant confusion in the fallout; McInerney and Ellis consider the attacks in terms of an assault upon American masculinity. Philip Roth responded with the provocatively titled *The Plot Against America* (2004), which belied its titular promise to unpick the conspiracies against the nation by presenting the plot against America as coming from within the nation itself in the historically reconfigured election of Charles Lindburgh as President in the 1940s. Rather than take on the vagaries of terrorist plotting, Roth takes the long view and presents a novel that forces Americans to address their history and, perhaps, their own complicity in the fortunes of the future. Moreover, Roth presents a wilfully playful book, a book which continually draws attention to its own status as artifice and fictional construction due to the melding of his usual perceptive historical realism with the telltale marks of Borgesian magic realism. For Roth, the terrorist attacks provoke not a sustained meditation on the status of the other, but on the self, the American self, and the processes of writing and fictional plotting.

One might argue that this is a typical reaction on the part of the American writer, a breed that has almost incessantly been obsessed with the self, the individual and the tenets of individualism, which lie at the heart of American myths of exceptionalism.[14] However, the post-9/11 meditations on the self and on the national psyche are of a distinctly different flavour from their precedents, offering less ebullience than uncertainty. Messud taps into this in her portrayal of three successful 30-year-old New Yorkers, emotionally and physically scarred by the gap in the landscape. The optimism of the dotcom generation gives way to a questioning of the self, of values and ideology, the gaping hole in Manhattan reflective of a wound in the psyche of the young Manhattanites. Ellis, meanwhile, presents a pseudo-autobiographical account of the author's descent from the glitter of his New York heyday to the freakish world of the suburbs, as well as his loss of confidence and potency as a writer.

Accompanying this psychological uncertainty, writers present a reassessment of familial and emotional ties. Most recently, Don DeLillo's *Falling Man* (2007) explores the fractured fragments of a marriage in the wake of the attacks. Messud, McInerney, Updike, Kalfus, DeLillo and Ellis all examine the theme of adultery and its repercussions for the American family. Given this intense literary focus on the American family and the consequences of the attacks for a series of white middle-class males, it might be argued that the expressions of 9/11 amplify tensions existent before the attacks. Stephen Shapiro argues that the prevailing concern of American literary fiction, which is evident in various narrative recurrences, is the de-establishment of the American middle class and the rise of poverty in the United States. For Shapiro, the imperial fantasy of American dominance is itself a fiction, a response to the fact that in the decade preceding the attacks, the middle class had been severely squeezed by economic factors such as debt and the increasing cost of higher education.[15] Total consumer debt, after all, had increased from some $797 billion in January 1990 to more than $1,000 billion five years later and a staggering $1,820 billion by September 2001: a reflection of the economic expansion of the Clinton years, no doubt, but also a considerable source of national self-searching and individual anxiety.[16]

Shapiro's thesis may not be universally applicable but it is certainly evident, for instance, in the work of Ellis whose *Lunar Park* is a novel of credit, debt and indebtedness to Robert Ellis (the father of the protagonist) who, though economically successful, dies owing millions of dollars in back taxes. Indeed, the debt to and death of the father are intricately connected to the conception of Ellis's son, Ashton (reminiscent of the ashes of New York City in the fallout), and all lead back to the empty vault at the Bank of America, to which the various debts are owed. Updike, too, picks up on middle-class anxieties and encroaching poverty in his depiction of a formerly prosperous, predominantly white, mill town, New Prospect, which rests on the outskirts of New Jersey. Now populated by the descendents of the African American mill-workers, the town has become something of a ghetto for African Americans and other racial minorities. Money (and the evaporation of it) and class also recur as anxieties throughout McInerney's novel, linked mainly (as in the cases of Updike and Ellis) with attacks upon the masculine role as provider and protector of family and nation.[17]

'WORDS FAIL ME'

In keeping with such concerns regarding economic capital and class, the widespread response to the events of 9/11, both literary and cultural, was that the attacks heralded a new political order, a different America; as Paul Auster put it: 'so the twenty-first century finally begins'.[18] Coinciding with this new millennium, this newly transfigured America, is the problem of language and linguistic response. In his essay of December 2001 'In the ruins of the future', DeLillo writes of 9/11 as contributing to the failure of metaphor, the impossibility of a figurative language which could articulate the event in all its cultural and subjective enormity. The response of DeLillo was shared by many of his contemporaries and extended beyond the borders of the US. This response to trauma is not unprecedented. After the atrocities of the Holocaust and the World War II, Theodor Adorno stated (in 1951) that he considered writing poetry after Auschwitz 'barbaric'. In later modifications of this point, Adorno stressed the necessity of literary art to avoid the aestheticisation of the horror of the camps. For Adorno, literary art after Auschwitz was faced with the problem of potentially conferring meaning upon something that was ultimately meaningless. Siri Hustvedt takes up this point in her short story 'The World Trade Center' which reminds the reader of other crimes against humanity, listing place names synonymous with massive loss of life as 'words engulfed by the unspeakable'. Hustvedt elaborates on the impossibility of matching the reality of the situation to the words that conjure the image: 'It might be easy to say, "Burning bodies fell from the windows of the World Trade Center," but it isn't easy to embrace the reality of the sentence.' For Hustvedt, the truths of the day are more subjective than language can ever be. The true manifestations of September 11 are to be found in the changed habits of New Yorkers and their children, those who have come to scream in sleep, to wet the bed or imagine skeletons in the streets of the city:

> These are the translations of horror when it enters the mind and the body, and when they seem to speak more directly to the truth than the elegant phrases we have been hearing lately, both political and literary. We have to talk, but we should be careful with our words.[19]

Freighted with meaning, yet also meaningless, the words 'World Trade Center' have become 'the unspeakable'. Hustvedt's acknowledgement that people will continue to and need to speak reminds one of DeLillo's sense of a necessary counternarrative to the attacks.

For DeLillo, the attacks on September 11 represented a seizure of the global narrative by terrorists against which the writer must pitch his narrative, must regain his power over words:

> The event itself has no purchase on the mercies of analogy or simile. We have to take the shock and horror as it is. But living language is not diminished. The writer wants to understand what this day has done to us ... But language is inseparable from the world that provokes it. The writer begins in the towers, trying to imagine the moment, desperately. Before politics, before history and religion, there is the primal terror. People falling from the towers hand in hand. This is part of the counternarrative, hands and spirits joining, human beauty in the crush of meshed steel. In its desertion of every basis for comparison, the event asserts its singularity. There is something empty in the sky. The writer tries to give memory, tenderness and meaning to all that howling space.[20]

The notion of counternarrative is not new to DeLillo. It is an approximation of a term he uses in his 1997 article 'The Power of History', in which he elucidated on the methodology informing *Underworld* (1997) as the composition of 'counter-history'.[21] Then, as now, his notion of counternarrative was that which slipped past the governing, official narrative of history, the stories that go untold, obliterated by the dominant narrative of the attack. Counternarrative is the writer's attempt, through words, to wrestle power from the actions of the terrorist. All that breaks from the overwhelming narrative of the attacks and the hole in the landscape is counternarrative: the hundreds of stories criss-crossing New York City on the day, the memories real and imagined, the photographs of missing people, the fragments and shards of strewn personal belongings. For DeLillo, the writer must seize on these smaller, multiple stories, these individual moments and possessions, and pitch them against the massive spectacle of the attacks that seems to defy normal frames of response.

Ulrich Baer's edited collection of short stories, *110 Stories: New York Writes After September 11* (2002), is a clear example of counternarrative in the DeLillo sense. A collection of subjective stories and memories in the aftermath of the attacks, the book is pitched as a 'model for New York's perpetual self-reconstitution through metaphor and language that will prove as significant as the construction in concrete and steel around us.'[22] The stories range from meditations on children through to Muslim experiences in New York after the attacks. Frequently, the book presents stories that address the inability of language to 'fit' the new world order. Avital Ronell in 'This Was a Test' scrutinises the language of George W. Bush in his statement that the attacks 'were a test', asking 'How does his language usage work here?' She questions the new 'rhetoric of justification' invented for military action and cites

Nietzsche in exploring the meaning of the word 'test' as 'a crisis in the relationship of experience to interpretation'.[23] Jane Tillman's story 'Save me from the pious and the vengeful' begins and ends with the assertion that 'Out of nothing comes language and out of language comes nothing and everything', and goes on to explore the manifold ways in which the author attempts to create a story that might in some way offer meaning to the events. Ending with recourse to Margaret Fuller, Tillman claims to leave the imagining of the newly configured America, the stories, to others.

Lydia Davis's story 'Grammar Questions' deals obliquely with 9/11 through the precise attention to the laws of grammar and language in a monologue about a dying man (the father of the narrator). Scrutinising every verb tense and grammatical configuration, the narrator is preoccupied with life, death, existence and 'the body.' In the face of death, the narrator also considers the accuracy of pronouns in describing the dying man: 'he', 'it', 'my father', 'the body'. Davis's story confronts the inadequacy of language in the face of trauma, linking the unspeakability of her impending loss with incomprehension; without the language to articulate crisis it is impossible to understand that crisis. This is connected with Hustvedt's sense of the 'unspeakable', that which is heavily burdened with meaning but also meaningless. As Davis's narrator gropes for the grammatical terminology to describe her dying father, she evades the reality of the situation – the fact of his imminent death. The direct thematic parallel to this, her failure to directly address the events of 9/11, represents a real and subjective trauma in her retreat from the gravity of the situation.

Jenefer Shute's story 'Instructions for Surviving the Unprecedented (Break Glass in Case of Emergency, if Glass Not Already Broken)' is a nineteen-paragraph, fictional protocol supposedly directed at those who live alone. Ostensibly, the various paragraphs list the actions of a traumatised New Yorker gripped with panic. But each, ultimately, is interested in the salvage of language as a means of communication and as a way to make sense of the situation. Each paragraph of the story charts the failure of language and the failure of communication, with the television stories delivering news of what is occurring just a few blocks away, with the dead phone lines, the radio reporter 'stumbling incredulously over his words', and the need of the trauma victim to 'be part of a narrative'.[24] Listing the subject's responses, Shute's 'instructions' emphasise incomprehension and disbelief, a cognitive insufficiency which, in turn, is linked with the linguistic insufficiency experienced by the subject as she is faced with composition. As the story progresses, each attempt at communication or representation fails: the elderly neighbour in shock is unresponsive, the phones remain dead throughout, as does email, and the immigrant superintendent's hanging of an American flag on the front of the speaker's apartment building seems like a misrepresentation of her feelings. These various attempts at linguistic communication culminate in the moment when the speaker is presented with the marker pen and enjoined to write a poem or a message to commemorate the victims. She writes 'Words fail me.' Finally part of a narrative, she is overwhelmed by the failure of words to articulate her trauma. The story, however, is not bleak in its final outlook. The speaker concludes in the final paragraph that words, in the coming months, will regain their redemptive, communicative power. Indeed, the text itself is testament to the survival of words.

INFILTRATING THE INFIDEL

Shute's ultimate faith in language, in the power of words, confirms DeLillo's sense of the necessity of the counternarrative – the subjective stories which diverge from the narrative inscribed by the terrorist. *Falling Man*, DeLillo's novel, deals with fragments of lives. The book opens with Keith, a man emerging from the Twin Towers on September 11 with minor injuries, who in his dazed state ends up on the doorstep of his estranged wife, Lianne. The novel cuts between their stories and impressions of events, their transitory resumption of a married existence and Keith's initiation of an affair with Florence, a fellow worker at the World Trade Center. Interspersed with the narrative of Keith and Lianne are smaller stories. Lianne, a book editor, teaches a creative writing class to Alzheimer's sufferers and their stories and memories, as well as those of Keith's poker friends, appear intermittently throughout the more dominant narrative. The eponymous Falling Man is a performance artist who stages falls in public, wearing a safety harness beneath his suit; a routine intended to remind New Yorkers of images of businessmen falling or jumping from the Twin Towers. Subjugated to shorter, peripheral sections is the story of the terrorist, Hammad, whose story enters the narrative at three stages, at the edge of each chapter. Indeed, he too is the falling man of the title, dangling dangerously at the sidelines of the narrative.

Though strongly criticised for his portrayal of Hammad and his emphasis on the local and the domestic by Mishra in his essay on 9/11 writing, the narrative's relegation of Hammad to its periphery is less a slight against the 'other' than a formal embodiment of the ostracism of minority groups in current-day America. DeLillo used the same formal strategy in bringing forgotten African American histories to the forefront in *Underworld*. There, the story of Cotter Martin and his link to a celebrated white baseball was set apart from the rest of the narrative, physically indicative of his erasure from dominant cultural history. Here, it is unclear whether DeLillo deliberately sets Hammad's story apart in a gesture at wrestling the predominant narrative of 9/11 from the terrorist or whether his intentions are to indicate the failure of American culture to integrate its citizens within the parameters of its national discourse. Bearing in mind the narrative strategy of *Underworld*, one might argue the latter. On the basis of DeLillo's depiction of terrorist factions and their antagonism of the writer in *Mao II*, as well as the author's comments throughout 'In the ruins of the future', one might argue the former. However, in the conclusion of DeLillo's 2001 essay the author relates how he recently made his way through the Canal Street area of the city, the site of Ground Zero, and came upon a Muslim woman facing east in prayer among the street vendors. DeLillo describes an epiphany of sorts, a recognition of a universal humanity, an understanding of all the 9/11 victims not in terms of nationality but as 'their own nation and race, one identity, young or old, devout or unbelieving – a union of souls.'[25]

This union of souls, the unification of victim and terrorist, is presented at the conclusion of *Falling Man*, throughout which both falling men invoked by the title, Keith and Hammad, come to resemble each other physically in the growth of their beards, psychologically in their retreat into themselves and in their admiration of male compatriots. In the weeks after the descent of the towers Keith is haunted by the phrase 'organic shrapnel', a term used to describe the means whereby the body of a suicide bomber can become lodged within the flesh of the victim. By the end of the novel, which swings back to the start of the book and to the morning of September 11, Hammad in the hijacked plane metamorphoses into Keith in the towers like a piece of organic shrapnel lodging itself within a body, intimating the relation between the terrorist and the terror survivor. While on the surface DeLillo's novel of domestic discord is a parable of wider domestic dissonance, on a deeper level it is a story of the simultaneous interconnection and disconnection of communities and ethnic groups in contemporary New York City. As the hijacked plane collides with the tower and the stories of Keith and Hammad are enmeshed, DeLillo reveals the likeness between West and East, between 'us' and 'them', and the necessary interdependence in the new globalised world of terrorist and terror-survivor narratives.

This affinity between worlds is also taken up by John Updike in *Terrorist*. Since his critically problematic portrayal of a young male African American in *Rabbit Redux* (1971), John Updike has steered clear of unknown ethnic and geographical territory, preferring instead (to invoke the title of one of his non-fiction collections) to 'hug the shore' of his commonplace terrain: East Coast, white, male mid-life and old-age crises. His latest book, however, seems to have broken the mould and Updike's much awaited post-9/11 book infiltrates the mind of a home-grown, would-be Islamic terrorist. Ahmad is the progeny of a 'freckle-faced mick' mother and a long absent Egyptian Muslim father. The setting of New Prospect, as Jonathan Raban observed in his review of the book for the *New York Review of Books*, 'shares much the same geographical coordinates as Paterson, New Jersey' where the 9/11 bombers based themselves.[26] Thus Updike, from the outset, observes that the cradle of jihad rests not in the Middle East but in those crumbling, peripheral and immigrant-laden cities of the West.

Since the age of eleven, we are told, Ahmad Mulloy has dedicated himself to the 'Straight Path of Islam' and finds friendship and refuge from the excesses of his contemporary and multicultural community in the *ummah* – the Internet-based community of the Muslim faithful. Ahmad, however, looks out on the world with distinctly Updikean eyes: his observations, his judgements and his reflective musings are those of his creator:

> *Devils*, Ahmad thinks. *These devils seek to take away my God.* All day long, at Central High School, girls sway and sneer and expose their soft bodies and alluring hair. Their bare bellies, adorned with shining navel studs and low-down purple tattoos, ask, *What else is there to see? ...*

This is about the height of Ahmad's jihadist rage against America. And, as the reviewers pointed out, if we are to consider the merits and authenticity of the portrayal, it seems too measured, too balanced and too reasoned to come from a young man whose destiny (as prescribed by both the author and his imam) is to become the terrorist of the novel's title, the man who will drive a truck laden with four thousand kilos of ammonium nitrate into Lincoln Tunnel.

In one of his discussions with his imam, Ahmad 'seeks to extract from the images in the Qur'an's Arabic some hint of the Merciful's relenting at some point in time, and calling a halt to Hutama ...' Here is the divisive seed of doubt, the hope within Ahmad that he will not have to drive to his death in a truck full of explosives. This conversation with the imam is mirrored at various stages throughout the book. Ahmad engages in a lengthy conversation on the nature of jihad and his heavenly rewards with the Lebanese American (and perhaps CIA mole) Charlie Chehab in which the latter likens Osama Bin Laden to George Washington and the mujahideen to the 1776 American revolutionaries. He attends a Christian service to hear a high-school friend sing and listens to an effusive pastor sermonise on salvation and Moses 'who led the chosen people out of slavery and yet was denied himself admission to the Promised Land.' Later still, Jack Levy (the man who thwarts the terrorist plot) likens many of Ahmad's beliefs lifted from the Qur'an with the 'repulsive and ridiculous stuff in the Torah'. When they discuss Sayyid Qutb's concept of *j-a hilliyya*, Levy describes it as 'sensible': 'I'll assign him as optional reading, if I live. I've signed up to teach a course in civics this semester'.[27] Throughout the book, Ahmad's faith in the Qur'an and his faith in God is set comparatively alongside American patriotism, secularism, Christianity and Judaism.

This alignment seems deliberately designed to highlight the comparative elements of the American and the Muslim 'other', to show us how closely aligned both really are. Levy's quip that he'll assign Qutb's *Milestones*, the primary sourcebook of the modern jihad, as optional reading on his civics course reinforces the sense, impressed at the outset by the mundane American setting, that this is now the reality of American identity; it is against this that post-Cold War Americans define themselves. Thus, Ahmad's diluted rage, his hope for the end of Hutama, is not so surprising. By choosing a jihadi foot-soldier born and raised in New Jersey, Updike seeks to make his terrorist a knowable and recognisable entity, an enemy of the state conceived and bred within it and who is not so unlike his adversaries.

Critics, of course, have found this contentious. Jonathan Raban, for instance, writes that in his portrayal of Ahmad 'Updike robs him of the last surviving shred of Islamist conviction.'[28] Writing in the *Times Literary Supplement*, Stephen Abell takes a contrary view, with the same end point, viewing Ahmad as an 'unnaturally reductive portrait ... he is allowed to stand for nothing but his religion, is no more than a Muslim metonymy'.[29] Other critics have been similarly hostile. Michiko Kakutani, in the *New York Times*, exclaims: 'John Updike writing about terrorism? The bard of the middle-class mundane, the chronicler of suburban adultery and angst, tackling Islamic radicalism and the call to jihad?'[30] But one might argue that by outlining affinities with Ahmad and comparing his fervour with that of other religious faiths, Updike, in fact, avoids the clichés and stereotypes of ranting mad suicide-bombers that abound in the American media. By empathising with Ahmad, by offering a sympathetic portrayal of faith, doubt and confusion, the keenly Protestant Updike offers his readership a more complex terrorist, and a much less reductive picture than that which the critics decry.

Levy speaks directly out of the ideology of contemporary, post-9/11 America, asking how the detonation of the bomb will be a 'glorious victory for Islam' and seeking clarification on the 'seventy-two virgins who will minister to [him] on the other side'. Levy is quick to deflate much of Ahmad's mystic, self-aggrandisement and, perhaps tellingly, it is Levy who prevails. By the end of the narrative, the young man acknowledges in mournful loss that, indeed, the devils have taken away his God. All that remains is the nothingness so feared by Ahmad as he peers upward, insect-like in the face of the godly Manhattan skyscrapers, divested of hope and power.

The struggle of words, of rhetoric, between Levy and Ahmad in the truck as they drive through New Jersey and eventually into Manhattan is clearly a battle of ideas, an exchange on the nature of life, death and faith. But it is also a struggle for power, ending, at a superficial level at least, with the ultimate victory of the white-haired sexagenarian. *Terrorist*, by extension of its dialectic on faith, explores the nature of power and the idea of the act of terror as a fictional construction: not only has Ahmad succumbed to the metaphors and symbols woven by his imam, it seems he has also been duped by a CIA trap, he has been taken in by a plot. His whole endeavour to blow up the tunnel was orchestrated not by a true believer in the Straight Path but by Charlie Chehab, an infidel, the enemy. Updike clearly conceives terrorism as a constructed phenomenon, and his role as a writer in the face of something which seeks to puncture a hole in the everydayness of existence must be to admit the futility of his enterprise or use his medium to regain some power, to reassert control over the everyday which Updike has claimed as his artistic domain.

Terrorist offers no clear-cut answers. It is an ongoing dialectic on the nature of faith, destiny and existence. It deliberately blurs the boundaries between religious denominations, and between 'us' and 'other' by presenting an American boy, naive and sympathetic, as the source of fundamentalist Islamic violence. It is perhaps telling that the potential disaster is thwarted by a typical Updike hero: Jack Levy directs Ahmad along a straight path, a path not unlike the straight path the boy thought would lead to paradise. Ironically, therefore, one might say that through Levy, an over-sexed (under-laid), white male in his 60s, a man who yearns for the 1950s and is the epitome of the quotidian banal, Updike strikes one last blow for the writer.

NOTES

1. Kathryn Flett, 'Images that mocked all power of description', *The Observer*, 16 September 2001.
2. Ulrich Baer (ed.), *110 Stories: New York Writes After 9/11* (New York, NY: New York University Press, 2002), p. 2.
3. Martin Amis, 'Fear and loathing', *The Guardian*, G2, 18 September 2001.
4. Alex Houen, *Terrorism and Modern Literature, from Joseph Conrad to Ciaran Carson* (Oxford: Oxford University Press, 2002), p. 4.
5. Quoted in Hamid Mir, interview with Osama Bin Laden, 'Muslims have the right to attack America', *The Observer*, 11 November 2001; quoted in Audrey Gillan, 'Bin Laden appears on video to threaten US', *The Guardian*, 8 October 2001.
6. Alex Houen, *Terrorism and Modern Literature, from Joseph Conrad to Ciaran Carson* (Oxford: Oxford University Press, 2002), p. 4.
7. Margaret Scanlan, *Plotting Terror: Novelists and Terrorists in Contemporary Fiction* (Charlottesville, VA: University of Virginia Press, 2001), p. 7.
8. See Don DeLillo, *Mao II* (London: Vintage, 1991), p. 41. Here, Bill Gray, the novel's protagonist elucidates further: 'There's a curious knot that binds novelists and terrorists. In the West we become famous effigies as our books lose the power to shape and influence … Years ago I used to think it was possible for a novelist to alter the inner life of the culture. Now bomb-makers and gunmen have taken that territory. They make raids on human consciousness. What writers used to do before we were all incorporated'.
9. Houen, Scanlon, Crenshaw, Douglass and Zulaika, to name but a few, spend much time on the subject.
10. Indeed, DeLillo does this quite deliberately in *Falling Man* (2007), where the eponymous performance artist, in his act, mimics the fall of a man agreed to be Jonathan Briley, who in his descent appeared to plummet straight, upside down with one leg bent and his shirt whipping in the breeze.
11. Margaret Scanlan, *Plotting Terror*, p. 7.
12. Pankaj Mishra, 'The End of Innocence', *The Guardian*, 19 May 2007. According

to Mishra, Loraine Adams's *Harbor*, Nadeem Aslam's *Maps for Lost Lovers* and Laila Lalami's *Hope and Other Dangerous Pursuits* adequately describe the divided selves of Muslims: 'There are no simple oppositions in these books between "Muslims" and the "west". They simply assume that for many Muslims the west is inseparable from their deepest sense of themselves, and that most people from societies that western imperialism cracked open long ago cannot afford to see the west as an alien and dangerous "other"; it is implicated in their private as well as public conflicts.' Also, Mishra contends that writers of non-fiction such as George Packer, Thomas Ricks and Rajiv Chandrasekaren offer more insightful glimpses into the realities of post-9/11 America.

13. I am grateful to Alison Kelly for introducing me to Shute and Davis and for ideas raised by her unpublished paper, '"Words Fail Me": 9/11 and its Aftermath in Stories by Linda Davis, Jenefer Shute and Lorrie Moore', presented at the British Association for American Studies Annual Conference, University of Leicester, 20 April 2007.

14. See, for example, Mishra, 'The End of Innocence', *The Guardian*, 19 May 2007.

15. Stephen Shapiro, 'Biopsies: the etiology of resentment in the era of middle class collapse', unpublished paper presented at British Association for American Studies Annual Conference, University of Leicester, 22 April 2007.

16. See Federal Reserve Statistical Release G.19, 7 June 2007, at http://www.federalreserve.gov/releases/g19/hist/cc_hist_sa.txt. See the Demos Report 'Generation broke' by Tamara Draut and Javier Silva (available at www.demos-usa.org), which charts the growth in credit card debt among young Americans between 1992 and 2001. See also Teresa Sullivan *et al.*, *The Fragile Middle Class: Americans in Debt* (New Haven, CT: Yale University Press, 2000).

17. Throughout the latter part of the 20th century, one observes a dramatic increase in the number of dual-income families in the United States. In 1967, the labour force participation of married mothers was 27.9 per cent; by 1997 it had reached 59.2 per cent. For statistics and overview see Mark Evan Edwards, "Uncertainty and the rise of the work-family dilemma', *Journal of Marriage and Family*, 63(1), February 2001, 189.

18. Paul Auster, 'Random Notes – September 11, 2001, 4.00 P.M.; Underground', in Baer (ed.), *110 Stories*, p. 35.

19. Siri Hustvedt, 'The World Trade Centre', in Baer (ed.), *110 Stories*, p. 158.

20. Don DeLillo, 'In the Ruins of the Future', *Harpers*, December 2001.

21. Don DeLillo, 'The Power of History', *New York Times Magazine*, 7 September 1997. Counter-history is not unlike the author's conception of counternarrative, insofar as both seek to deliver a narrative of either the past or present that deviates from the governing narrative or version of events. For DeLillo, interestingly, it is through language and words that hegemonic discourses and accounts can be dismantled: 'Language can be a form of counter-history ... Let language shape the world. Let it break the faith of conventional re-creation. Language lives in everything it touches and can be an agent of redemption, the thing that delivers us, paradoxically, from history's flat, thin, tight relentless designs, its arrangement of stark pages and that allows us to find an unconstraining otherness, a free veer from time and place and fate.'

22. Baer (ed.), *110 Stories*, p. 1.

23. Avital Ronell, 'This Was a Test', in Baer (ed.), *110 Stories*, pp. 251–3.
24. Jenefer Shute, 'Instructions for Surviving the Unprecedented (Break Glass in Case of Emergency, if Glass Not Already Broken)', in Baer (ed.), *110 Stories*, pp. 271–2.
25. Don DeLillo, 'In the Ruins of the Future', *Harpers*, December 2001.
26. Jonathan Raban, 'The good soldier', *New York Review of Books*, 53(12), 13 July 2006.
27. John Updike, *Terrorist* (London: Penguin, 2006), pp. 3, 77, 58–9, 302.
28. Raban, 'The Good Soldier'.
29. Stephen Abell, 'John Updike's simplifications', *Times Literary Supplement*, 26 July 2006.
30. Michiko Kakutani, 'John Updike's "Terrorist" imagines a homegrown threat to homeland security', *New York Times*, 6 June 2006.

16. AMERICAN WAYS OF SEEING

Liam Kennedy

In 1936 Henry Luce, the founder of *Life* magazine, famously articulated the magazine's purpose:

> To see life; to see the world; to eyewitness great events; to watch the faces of the poor and the gestures of the proud; to see strange things – machines, armies, multitudes, shadows in the jungle and on the moon; to see man's work – his paintings, towers and discoveries; to see things thousands of miles away, things hidden behind walls and within rooms, things dangerous to come to; the women that men love and many children; to see and to take pleasure in seeing; to see and be amazed; to see and be instructed; thus to see, and to be shown, is now the will and new expectancy of half mankind.[1]

The truth of Luce's emphasis on a new way of seeing and a new will to see refers to a visual history of America and of its interactions with the rest of the world that stretches well beyond the history of the picture magazines. What Luce celebrated and *Life* illustrated in the mid-20th century was an American way of seeing: that is, a way of seeing the world that is visually codified and thematised by the national concerns of the United States. This American way of seeing is at once democratic and imperial: democratic, in that it seeks to represent the diversity of humanity, to see and to show the activities, hopes and fears of ordinary peoples, and bear witness to their sufferings; imperial, in that it privileges and distinguishes an American point of view that is commensurate to America's powerful role in world affairs. The American visualisation of the nation's expansion and of its foreign relations yokes together the democratic and imperial impulses – the will to see is sublimated in a will to power – and this visualisation bears with it an epistemology of American geopolitical thinking.

The imperatives of the will to see that Luce celebrated were an important frame for American citizens' understanding of national and international concerns in the Cold War period. With the end of the Cold War and more particularly the onset of a 'War on Terror' in the 21st century, this will to see has become both attenuated ideologically (it is more difficult to identify an 'American' way of seeing) and dispersed technologically, due to the emergence of new communications technologies and the disintegration of discrete categories and genres of visual information in the digital age. There is an ongoing blurring of the boundaries between news and entertainment, between media and public diplomacy, between professional and amateur journalism, and between modes and genres of photographic representation. This blurring of boundaries characterises the instability of contemporary visual fields and also renders the visualisation of US foreign policy a more volatile representation.

American photojournalism, which bears a long and complex relationship with the production of national identity and its international extensions, provides a useful focus for analysis of the close yet shifting relationship between visual media, the mythos of the nation, and the geopolitical visions of the state. This chapter will focus on the role of photojournalism in the framing of US foreign policy, sketching the history of this framing and looking in some detail at ways in which the photojournalistic image has mutated in the 21st century to both support and challenge the state's geopolitical visions. In particular, we will consider imagery of the attacks on the World Trade Center and of the American military presence in Iraq.

PHOTOJOURNALISM AND THE END OF PHOTOGRAPHY

Photojournalism has been instrumentally involved in the visualisation of US foreign policy and more broadly the representation of America's geopolitical visions from the mid-19th century onwards. In part, this is due to the historical connection between the evolution of photography and the development of a young nation. The origins of photography in the US are tied up with the documenting of westward expansion, and with internal and external conflicts that defined the boundaries of the nation and the role of the state. From the 1840s, photographs were used to inform the public about events, people and places in the news, and the roots of modern photojournalism are evident in these uses.[2] As the nation grew, a process that was not organic but determined, political and bloody, photography recorded, documented and celebrated this growth. It developed conventions and frames, a way of seeing that conjoined the democratic and imperial impulses of an emergent American worldview.

By the end of the 19th century photography was already well established as the leading medium of national record and with the invention of the half-tone process in the mid-1880s it took on an even more prominent role in the representation of domestic and foreign news, as photographs could now be more easily produced and disseminated. The photographic roots of photojournalism were established as a key media in linking America's growing will to power to a new landscape of international relations and communication systems. In the 20th century, the triumph of American modernity on a global scale ushered in an increasingly confident perspective on international affairs, framed by domestic ideals and ideologies. The 'golden age' of American photojournalism was from the mid-1920s to the mid-1960s, a period in which picture magazines and news magazines came to the fore as the premier conveyors of photojournalistic imagery. As picture magazines such as *Life* articulated narratives of national identity, photo-journalism took on a leading role in representing the intersections of national and international affairs.[3]

Coverage of the Vietnam War is often cited as photojournalism's last great historical moment of record and relevance. During the war, photojournalists moved into a more adversarial relationship with the military, as they questioned the management of the war, and in the work of many photographers the tensions held within the conjunction of democratic and imperial impulses in the American worldview began to visually erupt. The visual legacies of the Vietnam War are still being played out within American popular culture and the myth that the imagery of the war contributed to defeat has haunted a generation of military and political leaders. The management of news media intensified during the conflicts involving the US in the 1980s – for example, there were bans on media access to the military invasions of Grenada in 1983 and Panama in 1989. The visual reportage of international affairs was also affected by the broad changes in American media production in the 1970s and 1980s as the mass circulation, general interest magazines went out of business and photojournalism lost a key foundation and forum. Television had come to dominate the visualisation of US foreign affairs and the golden age of photojournalism was at an end. Documentary and news photography was entering a period when the fracturing of the American worldview would be reflected in the fragmenting of media publics and of visual genres and stylings in American media and popular culture more generally.[4]

Since the 1970s, photojournalism has continued to dwell under a sense of diminished strength and relevance, a poor second to televised ways of seeing. What seemed a litmus test of its status and potential came with the first Gulf War, which was also a major test of the post-Vietnam relations between the military and the media. But this was not ostensibly a photographer's war. On the one hand, it was CNN's war, the first war to be covered live by satellite television feeds. On the other hand, it was a war in which visual production and representation was tightly controlled and choreographed by the

American military. For many photojournalists, the Gulf War was a major nail in the coffin of documentary photography. Fred Richtin, photo-editor at the *New York Times* during the war, wrote an article titled 'The End of Photography as We have Known It', in which he observed:

> Never has 'spin control' and 'photo opportunity' been so easily embraced in the world, nor so successfully. The tradition of the war photographers … was circumvented and very likely ended with another first – pictures seen from a bomb's point of view. The world of Robert Capa and W. Eugene Smith and Don McCullin begins to fade next to the technological wizardry of a 'smart' bomb taking its own images …[5]

A significant concomitant of this control of imagery was the near invisibility of bodily violence – during the Gulf War there were very few images of corpses or injured bodies in the American press.[6]

Richtin's polemic on 'the end of photography' as a documentary medium of warfare has proved premature but the Gulf War was certainly a turning point in the visualisation of US foreign policy. This was due in part to military news management but also to broader determinants of a new technological order in which photojournalism has struggled for relevance. There seems little doubt that in the digital age photojournalism has lost its privileged role as the definitive medium of events, understood as moments frozen by the camera. In the last fifteen years, the conception of events (already substantially ceded to television) has been supplanted by video and digital image-making and dispersal. During the same period, professional photojournalism was seriously undermined due to budget cuts and the increased media use of agency and stock images. Not surprisingly, there have been many mournful declarations about the decline or death of photojournalism in this period. But these jeremiads tend to too readily conflate aims and means and lament photojournalism's loss of status as a privileged medium of national record. Photojournalism is only in decline to the degree that it is still perceived as a late modern, pre-digital form of image-making. In truth, it too is mutating in relation to the broader conditions of globalised image warfare and in the 21st century it has begun to find some new energies and outlets.

FRAMING SEPTEMBER 11

'The most interesting, most successful, and most imaginative response to [September 11] within all the visual arts came from photojournalism', claims Peter Galassi, curator of photography at Manhattan's Museum of Modern Art.[7] Galassi's statement is something of a valedictory, acknowledging that the roles of photojournalists and photojournalism had been diminished in recent years. Through coverage of events of September 11, however, photojournalism did come to the foreground of mass visual communication in a striking fashion. Among photography professionals there was a notable concurrence that photography's documentary integrity had been significantly rejuvenated, that post-September 11 photography had 'got its job back'.[8] Such statements propose that September 11 ushered in not only a new period in American history, but also a new way of seeing and a renewed belief in the photographic image as an index of 'democratised reality'.[9]

The major photo agencies and many leading photojournalists took advantage of their renewed relevance. Magnum, Reuters and Associated Press all produced testimonial volumes, designed to display what photo-journalism can do and to advertise what their particular agency had done. The Magnum volume, titled *New York September 11*, carries the greatest weight – in terms of the legend of the agency, the fame of the photographers, and the quality of the production and design. The book references the legend of Magnum in its presentation of imagery. It is broken into sections, most of which are defined by the work of an individual photographer, signal-ling respect for auteurism. With much of the imagery elements of the photographer's style is recognisable – Susan Meiselas using trees to frame a shot of the burning towers, Larry Towell focusing on human activity and faces – and often brilliant compositions lend a compelling visual power to individual images. Steve McCurry's opening images have the greatest coherence in that they show very open vistas of the burning World Trade Center from the relatively unobstructed view on top of his apartment building and meticulously (in terms of fine detail) chart the implosion of one of the towers and the monstrous billowing smoke it emits. Thereafter, individual images strike the eye – the empty lobby of the Two World Financial Center, the statue of a man seated on a bench covered in ash and surrounded by debris, two firefighters looking disorientated as one trails an empty stretcher – not because of their relation to surrounding images but because they seem to reach beyond documentary representation to a symbolic realm, triggering connotations well beyond the subject of representation. Several images seem to make reference to the act of photography or the role of the photographer, such as an image by Larry Towell that shows a man holding a missing poster up to camera, and an image by Alex Webb that is a close up of a portion of a street memorial in which votive candles are set in front of a photograph of the pre-September 11 World Trade Center.

The weightiness of meaning in the Magnum imagery is part of the burden of representation they acknowledge through their own traditions. A note at the end of the book states that 'an idiosyncratic mix of reporter and artist ... continues to define Magnum, emphasising not only what is seen but also the way one sees it'.[10] This mix is certainly present in *New York September 11* though it is constrained in the view of Thomas Hoepker (chief editor on the project), who notes that some images under consideration 'emphasized the artistry in photography rather than telling the story. We didn't put those pictures in this book', and goes on to stress the purpose of the book is 'to bear witness'.[11] But the book does much more than this because of the 'artistry' of the work displayed and its high quality production. The artistry may at times be most marked in composition, in the scaling of human figures against brutal, devastated landscapes, but is ever-present in the use of light and colour. The admixture of sunlight, gloom and ash is used to potent visual effect in many images. Alex Webb's description of what he saw is suggestive of this:

> I meandered through the powder-filled streets of the financial district: a strange, whited out, monochromatic scene ... When Building 7 collapsed the sky turned a dark ochre. People became dusty silhouettes, the sun a dim fireball.[12]

The camerawork of the Magnum photographers inevitably aestheticises what it depicts, (re)producing an element of sublimity, of horror and beauty, in representation of the attacks and their aftermath. The artistry of these images has the viewer mentally browsing connections from distinct genres and photographic traditions, from landscape photography to street photography to war photography. This is not unusual in looking at the work of Magnum photographers. What is unusual and perhaps lends the issue of aestheticisation a new sensitivity is that the site and subject of the imagery is American.

It is not surprising that one of the bestselling tribute books based on photojournalistic imagery was produced by *Life*, entitled *One Nation: America Remembers September 11, 2001*. The events of September 11 offered *Life* an opportunity to do what it once did best, and *One Nation* offers diverse snapshots of a nation under attack and the heroism of ordinary Americans. Mayor Rudolph Giuliani's introduction spells out the key narrative component of the stories *One Nation* tells: 'We have met the worst of humanity with the best of humanity'.[13] The book's cover image is indicative of this, a photo mosaic of September 11 victims by Robert Silvers, it presents hundreds of faces on a grid pattern upon which is superimposed the image of the American flag. This is an evocative image that hints at the history of *Life*'s ideological unconscious, the conviction that 'America' represents humanity itself.

The design of *One Nation* is a curious balance of news, photo essay and magazine formats. In keeping with *Life*'s approach to communicating current history it is often educative in tone and styling, using text, imagery and graphics to inform its audience of the what and how of events though only rarely investigating the why. It begins with a photo essay on the construction of the World Trade Center, and then moves to a detailed timeline of events on September 11. The timeline runs across 59 pages, with the times and brief details of key events accompanied by images. It begins with an image of terrorists passing through an airport security check in Portland at 5.45 a.m. and ends at 10.21 p.m. with President Bush calling an end to a security meeting. The visual chronicle is striking, due in large part to the shrewd selection and editing of images, drawing on the work of leading photo-journalists such as Magnum's Steve McCurry and Susan Meiselas, but also some of the most compelling amateur photography (such as that taken by people evacuating the towers) and video footage (Evan Fairbanks's remark-able sequence of Flight 175 crashing into the south tower). The sequencing and layout lend the imagery a narrative momentum that few other visual tellings of this story have managed to present. The rest of the *Life* volume seeks to supplement this telling with a range of interpretations and presentations, including portraits of courage and heroism, reflections from leading writers, and images of Americans returning to work; it closes with a photograph of a pilot climbing into the cockpit of an F-18 as it readies for takeoff in the Arabian Sea.

The Magnum and *Life* projects seek to restore or rejuvenate their reputations for documentary integrity and their claims to 'bear witness' for a nation. But do they usher in or reflect a new way of seeing, a new role for photography? In certain respects this seems very doubtful. With the work of these photographers, as with countless others recording the events of September 11, we find the use of standard generic photographic conventions and the repetition of visual tropes and motifs. Certain scenes recur again and again: the towers burning, people running ahead of dust clouds, the remains of the tower façade still standing, rescuers at work in Ground Zero, dust-covered objects and people. Of course, the very repetition of these scenes is suggestive of the use of photography to make trauma bearable. Andy Grundberg, the *New York Times*'s photography critic, reflected that people needed to keep looking at the images because 'they freeze-frame a calamity so great that the mind struggles, even months later, to comprehend the data being sent by the eyes'.[14] The idea that people could not believe their eyes may be clichéd yet suggests that the issue of a new way of seeing goes beyond the use of genre conventions: it implicates an emergent visual culture in the wake of September 11, one that both defines and is defined by public memory and trauma.

Perhaps the strongest evidence of this was the extended functions – evidentiary, testimonial and mnemonic – the still image took on within the visual history of September 11. As well as the professional image-makers, anyone who had a camera trained it on the destruction and amateur imagery began to appear in public spaces. The *New York Times* ran a daily gallery of portraits of people dead or missing. Impromptu, makeshift shrines and memorials, many adorned with photographs, appeared throughout the city. Posters advertising 'missing' persons were pinned or plastered to street furniture – the pathos is pronounced as smiling faces look out from contexts of intimacy to one of public trauma and grief. All of these uses of the still image evidenced its instrumental role in communicating the trauma of a citizenry. A now famous example of this is the exhibition 'Here Is New York' (2004), which invited anyone with images connected to the attacks to submit them to a Soho gallery. Over 4,000 photographs were scanned and digitally printed (8×10) and taped to wire lines strung from the gallery ceiling. Charles Traub, one of the exhibition organisers, observed that people photographed the destruction of the World Trade Center 'because they needed to verify what they saw. I think they're bringing their pictures here to give testament to history …'[15] The exhibition represents democratic and therapeutic ideals long associated with the act of photography and historically resonant with the humanist core of American photography.

This intensive tribute to photography's testimonial role was remarked on by several commentators at the time. The organisers of 'Here is New York' stated their belief that 'the World Trade Center disaster and its aftermath has ushered in a new period in our history, one which demands that we look at and think about images in a new and unconventional way'.[16] Brian Wallis, Chief Curator of the International Center of Photography in New York, restated this view:

> Without question, the photographs of September 11 have changed the way we look at the world. It is imperative to examine what photography means in the wake of these seismic shifts, how what occurred … has altered or re-ignited our sense of what photography can achieve, both as document and as personal vision.[17]

Photography's elevated testimonial role in relation to 9/11 was more temporary and local than these comments suggest. Yet, there were significant features of the photographic coverage that suggest that, to the extent that documentary imagery was reanimating the democratic impulses in American photography, it was doing so beyond the usual conventions and channels of photojournalistic production and display. The amateur and vernacular surge in the photographic coverage of 9/11 has since become a common feature of the digitalised image world of the 21st century.

There is another sense in which the photographic responses to 9/11 were indicative of an emergent visual culture. Although 9/11 did not simply usher in a new way of seeing for Americans, it did disrupt the visual field and with it the correlates of national identity – it introduced a new sense of vulnerability into American culture in which the imperatives of 'precarious life' would begin to shape how Americans see themselves and others.[18]

FRAMING THE WAR IN IRAQ

The advent of digitalisation has affected the production and dissemination of war images by American media but the results, within the more mainstream media channels at least, have neither been a more plural nor a more investigative visual repertoire. In the recent wars in Afghanistan and Iraq, American photographers have had the opportunity to be 'embedded' with military forces near the front lines, a scenario that led to speculation that photographers would have access to the raw realities of warfare. But despite the claims of 'real time' and spontaneous coverage, photographs from the conflicts in Afghanistan and Iraq have been characterised by a narrow range of recurrent motifs and routinised scenarios. Several recent studies of the range of photographic imagery of the Iraq War in American newspapers and magazines show that the great majority of images fall into 'a highly restricted pattern of depiction limited largely to a discourse of military technological power and response'.[19] This was perhaps most clearly evident in the early days of the conflict when a great deal of imagery focused on military hardware and the media reproduced the 'shock and awe' produced by this hardware. But it has remained the norm of coverage even as the organising news narratives of the war have become more confused or attenuated in framing the meaning of depicted events. To be sure, the embedded photographers have produced a greater ratio of combat images than in the Gulf War but this is still a small number out of overall coverage, and photographs of wounded or dead bodies remain rare.[20]

The embedded system promises 'real time' and transparent imagery of life on the front lines of the war, but restricts the visual coverage to comply with 'security' requirements and produces an American-centred vision of the conflict. This is not to say the embedded reporters are happily complicit with the system, rather the system produces a frame that regulates their visual productions. This frame, as Judith Butler points out, is always already charged with interpretation:

> the mandated visual image produced by embedded reporting, the one that complies with state and defense department requirements, builds an interpretation ... We do not have to have a caption or a narrative at work to understand that a political background is being explicitly formulated and renewed through the frame. In this sense, the frame takes part in the interpretation of the war compelled by the state; it is not just a visual image awaiting its interpretation; it is itself interpreting, actively, even forcibly.[21]

While it is useful to consider the embedding system as a form of framing, it is also important to acknowledge that there are many other elements contributing to the sanitised imagery of the wars in Afghanistan and Iraq. The restricted visual repertoires, embargoes on images of graphic violence, and American-centred viewpoint are due to a complex mix of political, editorial and practical considerations. When editors make decisions about the reproduction of images, notions of professional ethics, public accountability, privacy and taste are invoked and sometimes intensely discussed. But these notions are inextricably tied up with political and economic motivations and considerations. Not surprisingly, this area of decision-making has become a target of political backlash as editors are charged with both doing too much and too little to censor war imagery. For all the constraints, many American photographers have been producing imaginative work, some of them pushing at the boundaries of the frame even as they work within it. However, very little of this more imaginative and investigative visual journalism has made it into mainstream American media.

While digital technology has revolutionised photographic practice, the framing devices of mainstream media remain very powerful controls on the production of imagery. However, in large part due to the effects of new digital technologies, the mainstream is becoming a more volatile and porous sphere and new sites and uses of visual journalism have emerged to challenge or supplement official modes and messages. Perhaps most significant of these are the Internet blog sites that track the mainstream news media. One of many examples is a blog titled crisispictures.org, which first became well known in late 2004, when the assault on Fallujah led to claims and counterclaims about the levels and targets of violence. The site released many striking images of life in the city; it posted many graphic shots and tended to point the finger of blame for civilian suffering at the military. Many of the photographs are far more graphic than are usually carried in newspapers, showing decapitated bodies, dead and bloodied troops, and wounded women and children.[22] It shows scenes that are more similar to what Iraqis, and many in the Arab world, see on their satellite news channels. Significantly, many of the images are drawn from the wire services, that is to say they are photographs taken by established photojournalists in Iraq, many of them with American media accreditation, but the images have not been used by the American media – a reminder that not only are the published images filtered but they are a very small number of those submitted.

Blogging by both professional and amateur photographers is an erratic business but it has opened up new possibilities for photojournalism that has not otherwise found outlets in the American media and there are signs that it is starting to shape the menus of mainstream news outlets. At the same time the very proliferation of images of global conflicts and traumas, exacerbated by digitalisation and new media, is challenging conventional visualisations of American foreign policy. Whatever the attempt to fix them as representation or evidence, images slip and slide and float in and out of contexts.[23] The promiscuity of the image can cause leaks that escape and challenge even the most powerful of political and media frames of interpretation. The most famous example of such leakage to date is the production and dissemination of images of torture and abuse in Abu Ghraib prison. More than 1,800 images were digitally produced and many of these have been circulated on the Internet, despite early efforts by the government to prohibit their publication and ongoing legal attempts to prevent more being published. The threat this leakage posed to US government and military efforts to control the visualisation of the war in Iraq was palpable in Donald Rumsfeld's comments to a Senate Armed Services Committee hearing: 'People are running around with digital cameras and taking these unbelievable photos and passing them off, against the law, to the media, to our surprise, when they had not even arrived in the Pentagon'.[24]

The Abu Ghraib photographs visualised the War on Terror as a spectacle of bare life, of bodies stripped of rights and liberties, and positioned the viewer as a complicit audience whose gaze reinforces the terror – as such, they are a visceral reflection of the biopolitical power exercised by the US in the name of national security. And yet, important as the Abu Ghraib images are to questioning US conduct of the war against terror, they are but one famous example of the visual 'blowback' emanating from Iraq and many other areas where visual technologies and techniques, crafted in and by the US, are being used to question or challenge the authority and activity of US foreign policy. This is also to suggest that the promiscuous image signifies the operations of what Walter Benjamin termed 'unconscious optics' in the act of photographic seeing. Writing about photography in 1936, Benjamin observed: 'It is through photography that we discover the optical unconscious, just as we discover the psychic unconscious through psychoanalysis'.[25] Benjamin perceived the optical unconscious as a dimension of the material world that is normally filtered out by trained ways of seeing, thus remaining invisible, but which can be made visible using techniques of photography and film. The optical unconscious refers us to the supplements of conventionalised ways of seeing or residues of alternative ways of seeing. In the digital age, the convergence of technologies (for example, of the camera and the mobile phone) extends our understanding of the optical unconscious into once hidden or barely visible areas of private and public life, of domestic and foreign environments. It is a perverse extension of what Henry Luce celebrated as the human will 'to see things thousands of miles away, things hidden behind walls and within rooms, things dangerous to come to'.

It is important to add that the optical unconscious of US foreign policy is not simply a question of what is hidden, occluded or overlooked by conventionalised ways of seeing, but also of how these conventions are redistributed by new technologies. An excellent example is the photoblogs posted by serving American soldiers in Iraq.[26] In these sites much of the content is mundane and everyday from the soldier's point of view, yet these images suggestively trace the optical unconscious of US foreign policy in the domesticated and institutionalised activities of American soldiers in foreign lands. Certain visual tropes and categories of photograph are apparent. Many images have a touristic focus on smiling soldiers posing in the desert or in front of ancient sites, others centre on military hardware and soldiers on patrol, while others depict soldiers relaxing in barracks. The everydayness of much of the imagery both belies and accentuates the extraordinary conditions being depicted, most apparent in the many images of soldiers whiling away time in barracks playing electronic games, watching DVDs, playing cards or posing in their bedrooms, often surrounded by imagery of American popular and pornographic cultures. The images have varied functions: some record army life for friends and family, others are created primarily to share among the unit in the first instance, including imagery of memorials to dead comrades. Few would seem to fit the conventional frames of visual journalism, yet the urge to document and to disseminate the material is strongly expressed by those posting the images.

These images have a distinctive visual language, blending the genres of institutional, touristic, pornographic and war photography into a very new genre of 'soldier's photographs'. This form of visual communication – in real time and communal – is new in the representation of warfare; in earlier wars soldiers took photographs, but these were not immediately shared in the way websites can disseminate images globally. Digicams, cameraphones and photoblogs are the media that have proved visually commensurate to the war in Iraq, though the visual styles and genres produced by these media are mutating at a fast pace, drawing on established analogic forms and melding them into new visual formations. These images should also be understood as part of the widespread interest in voyeuristic and documentary imaging that has millions of people photographing or filming their lives for Internet or other media dissemination. This is also to say that in creating, posing for and disseminating these images the soldiers are responding to conventions of American visual culture.

I do not mean to suggest that the soldiers' photographs and photoblogs provide us with the 'real' image of the American military in Iraq, not least because there are very serious issues of attribution and authenticity surrounding this sort of image production. For example, many of the soldiers' photoblog images reappear under different names and with alternative tags on the context of their production; in some cases soldiers have lifted professional photojournalistic images from the Internet and sought to pass them off as their own. Nor do I suggest that exposure to more and more images will guarantee any meaningful knowledge of US foreign policy or sympathy for others – if anything, the War on Terror may mark the emergence of the 'banality of images'.[27] However, the digitalisation of war imagery has introduced a fascinating uncertainty into the rationality of perception that mainstream visual media offer American audiences. And there is no doubt that the Internet is playing a role in redesigning and redistributing visual understanding about international relations and US foreign policy and that it is becoming a central battleground of information and image warfare.

Throughout much of the 20th century, American photojournalism was a privileged medium for the American worldview. It lost this privileged role in part due to the emergence of new technologies of news communication and in part because its core conventions did not keep pace with changing geopolitical concerns of the US leadership and military. However, the frequent claims that photojournalism is dead are premature. As the American worldview has shape-shifted so photojournalism has evolved. Today, its status remains somewhat diminished and yet its mutations in relation to the new technologies of seeing and the new global scenes it represents have provided the photojournalistic image with an afterlife. The advent of digital photography, of cameraphones, and of photoblogging has introduced new relations between photographers, the medium and the audience – the emerging culture of DIY media and of 'citizen journalism' is going to become more and more important in the representation and shaping of the news and of the ways in which Americans see the world beyond America.

The will to see that Henry Luce identified with growing American confidence in the mid-20th century has become a more troubled relationship with the global image world of the 21st century. It has been both exacerbated and attenuated by the visualisations of a 'War on Terror' that projects national fears and desires onto the international landscape. The democratic and imperial impulses of the American worldview remain in tension in these visualisations, echoing the historical tensions between universalism and exceptionalism at the ideological heart of the American experience. The democratic energies are recodified in the new technologies and extensions of seeing, while the imperial will to power is now so 'preponderant' that it creates a global imperium in the name of national security. It is likely these tensions will continue to characterise and to test the American will to see in the 21st century.

NOTES

1. Henry Luce, quoted in Robert T. Elson, *Time, Inc.: The Intimate History of a Publishing Enterprise, 1923–1941* (New York, NY: Atheneum, 1968), p. 278.
2. See Susan Moeller, *Shooting War: Photography and the American Experience of Combat* (New York, NY: Basic Books, 1989).
3. See Wendy Kozol, *Life's America: Family and Nation in Postwar Photojournalism* (Philadelphia, PA: Temple University Press, 1994).
4. This was a period when the status of the photographic image itself was under much intellectual and critical scrutiny; it was burdened by formal, ethical and historical questions that contributed to the crumbling authority of its evidentiary forms. Susan Sontag, in her mid-1970s writings on photography, provided what was probably the most challenging and influential critique, arguing that photographs cannot tell us political truths and that the 'humanistic' strain in American photography was exhausted. See Susan Sontag, *On Photography* (London: Penguin, 1977).

5. Fred Richtin, 'The End of Photography as we have known it', in Paul Wombell (ed.), *Photovideo: Photography in the Age of the Computer* (London: Rivers Oram Press, 1991), p. 11.

6. It was not until after the event that a few, belatedly, began to appear, perhaps the most famous of which was the photograph by Kenneth Jarecke of an Iraqi soldier inside his tank, burnt to near dust. See Kenneth Jarecke and Exene Cervenka, *Just Another War* (Joliet, IL: Bedrock Press, 1992).

7. Blake Eskin, 'Getting the Big Picture', *ARTnews*, February 2002, 101.

8. Ingrid Sischy, 'Lasting Images', http://www.abc.net.au/rn/arts/sunmorn/stories/s487406.htm.

9. See Sontag, *On Photography*, pp. 29–30 and Alberto Manguel, 'Reading pictures', *Index on Censorship*, 191, November–December 1999, 10–12.

10. Magnum Photographers, *New York September 11* (New York, NY: PowerHouse Books, 2001), p. 142.

11. Ibid., p. 67.

12. Ibid., p. 74.

13. *One Nation: America Remembers September 11 2001*, p. 6.

14. Andy Grundberg, 'Photography', *New York Times Book Review*, 2 December 2001, 35.

15. 'Creative Responses and Cautious Retractions', *Art on Paper*, January–February 2002, 24.

16. Marianne Hirsch, 'The Day Time Stopped', *Chronicle of Higher Education*, 25 January 2002, 6.

17. Brian Wallis, 'Aftermath: Photography in the Wake of September 11', http://www.icp.org/exhibitions/aftermath/.

18. See Judith Butler, *Precarious Life: The Powers of Mourning and Violence* (London: Verso, 2004).

19. Michael Griffin, 'Picturing America's "War on Terrorism" in Afghanistan and Iraq', *Journalism*, 5(4), 2004, 383.

20. While there are pictures of Iraqi dead there are very few images of dead American soldiers. A major survey carried out by the *Los Angeles Times* found that in a six-month period in which 559 Americans and Western allies died, 'almost no pictures from the war zone of Americans killed in action' appeared in the mainstream print media. See James Rainey, 'Unseen Pictures, Untold Stories', *Los Angeles Times*, 21 May 2005, http://www.latimes.com/news/nationworld/iraq/complete/la-na-iraqphoto21may21,1,5741110.story?coll=la-iraq-complete.

21. Judith Butler, 'Photography, War, Outrage', *PMLA*, 120(3), 2005, 823.

22. See www.crisispictures.org.

23. See Susan Buck-Morss, 'Visual Studies and Global Imagination', 2004, http://www.surrealismcentre.ac.uk/publications/papers/journal2/acrobat_files/buck_morss_article.pdf.

24. Robert Plummer, 'US Powerless to Halt Iraq Net Images', BBC News, 8 May 2004, http://66.249.93.104/search?q=cache:Di6Ei6P_lN0J:news.bbc.co.uk/2/hi/americas/3695897.stm+rumsfeld+people+are+running+around+cameras&hl=en&gl=uk&ct=clnk&cd=15.

25. Walter Benjamin, 'A Small History of Photography', in Edmund Jephcott and

Kingsley Shorter (trans.) *One Way Street* (London: New Left Books, 1979), pp. 240–57.

26. Photoblogs are websites on which people post and share their photographs. They emerged as a popular phenomenon around 2000 with the convergence of digital cameras and broadband, and growing access to these technologies.

27. See Nicholas Mirzoeff, *Watching Babylon: The War in Iraq and Global Visual Culture* (London: Routledge, 2005), p. 67.

17. TELEVISION AND DIGITAL MEDIA

Lynn Spigel and Max Dawson

In February 1941, when publisher Henry Luce dubbed the 20th century 'the American Century', his magazine empire was about to fall prey to an even more dazzling media attraction: television. In May of that year, the Radio Corporation of America (RCA) procured government-sanctioned technological standards for its television receivers and eagerly planned for a consumer boom. Although commercial TV was delayed by World War II, in the 1950s television would become the signature technology of the American Century that Luce described, functioning both as a central fixture in the home and as a symbol (for better or worse) of the state of American democracy and culture. The growth of the new medium at mid-century was part of, and also helped precipitate, fundamental transformations in everyday life, and it also contributed to shifts in consumer habits, political campaigns and civic engagement, and society more broadly. While sociologists have for many years debated the nature and degree of these changes, almost everyone has some opinion on just what television has done to them, their nation and the world more generally.

Television penetrated American homes faster than any previous domestic technology. While in 1948 less than 2 per cent of US homes had a television set, by 1960 almost 90 per cent of US households had one or more TV. Yet, despite its popularity, television was prone to a wide range of anxious speculation, most of which belied more profound hopes and fears about technology, culture, and the social and political uncertainties of the post-war world. Would TV destroy the literate culture of reading? Would it make children weak and husbands lazy? Would women stop doing the chores, too embroiled in the daytime soaps to get the wash done or the roast baked? Would TV interfere with romance or perhaps, on the brighter side, could it help bring the family together around a shared sense of pleasure?[1] Might it, as many African Americans hoped, allow for greater opportunities than cinema had before it by showcasing African American talent in dignified roles both in front of and behind the cameras? Or would it, as other African Americans feared, perpetuate racial stereotypes and misunderstandings? Would TV foster international peace – as NBC President Sylvester Pat Weaver suggested – or did it (as the Vietnam telecasts so dramatically demonstrated) merely document a theatre of war? Would TV offer Americans (rich and poor) opportunities to see ballet, theatre, and the visual arts in the comforts of their living rooms? Or had it, as Federal Communications Commission (FCC) Chair Newton Minow claimed in 1961, become a 'vast wasteland?'[2]

If these hopes and fears seem old fashioned today, it is nevertheless the case that television continues to be a central medium not just for entertainment or information, but also for speculations about the present state of gender roles, family life, race relations, international conflict, and the general prospects for art in media culture. At the millennium, television's future and its possible influences on social and political life are embroiled in a new set of developments related to its convergence with digital technologies, the rise of multichannel TV systems, and the growth of multinational media conglomerates like Viacom and News Corporation. Television is also responding to and helping to facilitate changing patterns of global economic and cultural flows, as well as larger transformations in work and leisure in a post-Fordist world. All of these developments have already changed the 'old' TV culture. Nevertheless, as a symbolic force for constructing an imaginary American 'public' – somewhere out there, as the saying goes, in TV Land – television still functions to define the nation, sometimes in exceedingly nationalist ways.

FROM NATIONAL BROADCASTING TO NARROWCAST NATION

At the turn of the 21st century, the ABC network, CNN and PBS offered day-long New Year celebrations featuring footage from New York's Times Square, the Eiffel Tower in Paris, the Hollywood Sign in Los Angeles and London's Millennium Dome, as well as glimpses of New Year's Eve experienced in cultures worldwide (on ABC Dick Clark's annual ball-dropping party from Times Square had a 'one world theme'). This form of televisual cosmopolitanism was an extension of century-old dreams for television's role as a unifying force among nations. Bringing the world 'live' into the living rooms across the nation, TV has historically promised to bind places together in simultaneous viewing rituals experienced by people across the globe. The world, as Marshall McLuhan put it, would be 'retribalized' and turned into a 'global village' through this new media environment.[3] Yet despite dreams of global connectivity, at the millennium, television ironically became one of the central vehicles for patriotic – and even isolationist – sentiments following the attacks of 11 September 2001.

Television's almost week-long uninterrupted coverage of the attacks reminded the nation of television's role in creating a symbolic citizenship by constructing an image of Americans as a unified national public.[4] The footage of the World Trade Center falling down, coupled with newscasts that anchored its meaning for the nation, took over the airwaves. Worried about the apparent tastelessness of movies, sitcoms, serials and advertising on these sombre days, the networks and advertisers pulled entertainment series and commercials from the airwaves. This not only meant a devastating loss of advertising revenue for the networks, it also meant that television's familiar functions in the daily routine of the nation had dramatically changed. The 'everydayness' of television, its daily rhythms and programming flows, were curtailed and replaced with 24/7 news coverage – *without* commercials. When President Bush famously instructed the nation to 'return to normal', by flying on planes and even taking their families to Disneyland, television's return to commercial entertainment and its ritualised daily programming flows became part of the national mission. In short, on television, as in the nation more generally, the return to normal meant the return to normal levels of consumption.

By 15 September, the television networks began the transition back to commercial entertainment with programmes that upheld the industry's concerns with projecting an image of 'good taste' by evoking themes of national unity and patriotism. The 'quality' series *The West Wing* devoted an entire episode to a teach-in about US-Middle-East relations that nevertheless rehearsed familiar Orientalist themes about Islam and its various 'anti-modern' customs. Meanwhile, 'event' television shows like *America: A Tribute to Heroes* in October 2001 presented a bevy of stars singing the national anthem (although many of them seemed not to know the words). Indeed, on television, grand narratives of national unity were everywhere. Americans were compelled to perform belief in these narrative myths or else be marked somehow as bad Americans. When comedian Bill Maher famously remarked on the bravery of the suicide attackers, his comments created a national uproar, resulting in the loss of sponsors for and eventual cancellation in 2002 of his programme *Politically Incorrect*.

Nevertheless, despite the nationalist sentiments, if the US was really going to return to normal, at least on television 'normal' was no longer really constituted through national unity. Whereas television was historically a three-network broadcast medium playing to large national audiences, by the millennium television had become a 'narrowcast' medium that plays to smaller niche audiences on a range of some 500-plus channels. Not surprisingly, in this respect, television's role in spreading a myth of national unity after 9/11 was very short lived. On television, as in US politics, the return to normal meant a return to the deep divisions of the red state versus blue state logics of American regionalism. In this mythos, the coasts are represented as the urbane centres of progressive liberalism (despite the many conservative sections of the regions) while the states in between are conceived as a vast wasteland of anti-modern farmers, Bible-belt hillbillies, and generally uncultured, unfashionable people. Reality television programmes like *Wife Swap* (the US version) and *The Simple Life* (with Paris Hilton) trade on this mythos while cable stations like PAX (now Ion) have organised themselves around the appeal to midwestern Christian values.[5] Other programmes, such as *Entourage, The Housewives of Orange County* and *Sunset Tan*, present spectacles of vacuous Southern California lifestyles complete with Botox injections, nasty divorces, ruthless agents and hot pink bikinis on simulated sun-toned skin. Meanwhile, news stations have divided up the pie in the red versus blue logic, with the Fox Network staking its appeal squarely on the former, so that 24/7 news now has become a matter of taste as opposed to the 20th-century ideal of 'objective' reporting.[6]

More generally, in its economic logics, the contemporary television industry thrives more on the vagaries of taste than it does on the politics of nation. In this 'post-broadcasting' system, viewers are joined together through consumer identity formations measured by market researchers in demographic profiles. In the current US cable mix, Lifetime is the 'woman's network'; Bravo is the 'gay network'; BET is the 'black network'; while other networks (such as the Food Network or the History Channel) adhere to lifestyle formations and specialised tastes. Configured as 'brands' by the media conglomerates that own them, these networks operate on what John Caldwell calls 'tiered' programming strategies, whereby programmes targeting specific demographics are aired on special, themed narrowcasting channels.[7] In large part this new TV marketplace is a function of fundamental shifts in television's political economy, particularly since the deregulation climate of the Reagan administration in the 1980s. The FCC's deregulation (or more accurately put, re-regulation) of broadcasting, which culminated in the 1996 Communications Act, loosened restrictions on station ownership. In turn this allowed media conglomerates like the Walt Disney Company and Viacom to amass greater numbers of television and radio stations, while also owning (or part owning) cable networks, newspapers, magazines, movie studios, record labels, syndication companies, search engines, and a host of other corporations. Although, as Robert McChesney notes, the Communications Act of 1996 used the rhetoric of democracy and choice to justify corporate conglomeration, by 1997 'the preponderance of US mass communication [was] controlled by less than two dozen enormous profit-maximizing corporations'.[8] In 2003, Congress and the FCC considered loosening the rules even more, resulting in a series of disputes over media ownership that now are still up for debate.[9] While media conglomerates and pro-deregulation government officials argue that the new cable marketplace has a robust diversity of channels and that media conglomerates often provide programmes or whole networks that cater to diverse tastes, critics like McChesney worry that media conglomeration leads to anti-democratic tendencies with too few companies controlling the airwaves.

To be sure, the new marketplace raises important questions about the media's role in the new century. Whereas the American broadcast system had been predicated on the 1934 FCC mandate that individual broadcast stations had to operate in the 'public interest' of their local markets, it was never exactly clear how to measure performance in that area, or even what exactly the 'public interest' was in a system that ultimately relied on the private interests of advertisers and broadcast barons. Insofar as cable stations and their parent corporations are not regulated by these same FCC standards, the problem of the public interest and television's role as public servant is evermore vexing today. As Herman Gray and Beretta E. Smith-Shomade argue, television tends to level all differences and internal struggles in communities of colour and to address racialised groups as homogeneous consumer types: for example, the African American audience is imagined as one block rather than a group composed of different social, political and class interests.[10] In the multi-channel universe, this kind of homogenisation of various publics has become a way to target smaller 'niche' demographics of cable, but the end result isn't always diversity of point of view.

Considering the entire US television landscape, Smith-Shomade observes that even though we tend to think that the current multi-channel system offers a multitude of black-cast programmes, this 'perceived abundance' is not borne out by the numbers, which demonstrate (percentage-wise) an 'actual lack' of people of colour both in front of and behind the camera.[11] Meanwhile, according to a study recently conducted by the UCLA Chicano Research Center, the statistics are particularly skewed when it comes to Latino populations. Latinos make up only 4 per cent of regular prime-time characters on network television, even though they are the largest minority group in the US.[12] While by no means endorsing media monopolies or the lack of diversity on television, other critics point to some inroads that new cable channels can make. For example, Charlotte Brunsdon shows how reality lifestyle programmes in Britain opened up new representations of gay and lesbian partners sharing households, something not previously seen (at least as 'ordinary') on television, and a trend that also appears in the homemaking shows on US cable networks. Similarly, Lisa Parks observes that the Oxygen Network (which uses interactive digital platforms) was not only founded by women (including Oprah Winfrey) but also addresses female audiences as technologically savvy viewers who can use the Oxygen website to search for information on healthcare, legal aid and other issues affecting women's lives.[13]

To compete in the new media marketplace, the old broadcast networks have turned to new genres and formats – most vividly with the introduction of 'Reality' programmes. First associated in the late 1980s and early 1990s with magazine-format programmes like NBC's *Unsolved Mysteries*, CBS's *Rescue 911* or Fox's *Cops*, and then mutating into 'docu-soaps' like MTV's *Real World* and the BBC's *The Living Soap*, Reality television is now a broad generic label used to describe unscripted (although edited-for-drama) programmes that recombine the old genres of broadcast television (from game shows to soaps to beauty pageants to documentaries) into a relatively low cost, high rating, and internationally marketable alternative to traditional prime-time series. Although some advertisers have been reluctant to associate their products with them, Reality programmes often outperform traditional fiction series and news magazines, at least among the much-desired 18–49 and 18–34 demographics.[14]

Immediately upon its inception (particularly with the success of *Survivor* in 2000), Reality television spawned a new series of debates about the state of American culture. Did millions of Americans flock to see people eating worms (*Fear Factor*) because our culture had finally plummeted to its 'fall of the Roman Empire' decline? What did it mean that just as many (if not more) well-educated high-income groups chose *Joe Millionaire* over *Masterpiece Theater*? Who could predict the state of things to come when more people voted for their favourite wannabe on *American Idol* than they did for George W. Bush in the last election? Is Reality television, as Laurie Ouelette has argued, the epitome of a neoliberal culture where TV magistrates like Judge Judy and self-help gurus like Dr Phil give dime-store advice to people (many of whom are struggling single moms or out-of-work dads) at a time when social welfare programmes that might actually benefit these people have all but disappeared? Or is Reality television, as Henry Jenkins claims, proof of the media's participatory and democratic potential as people converse about the shows (and also make media productions of their own) on Internet chat rooms, blogs, websites, YouTube and the like?[15]

As Jenkins and other critics also point out, the culture of media convergence is not limited to entertainment; it is also changing political life as both grassroots groups and elected politicians now use a combination of old media (like TV) and newer media (like blogs and websites) to get their message out. Most dramatically, in this regard, after HBO aired its much-awaited final episode of *The Sopranos*, Hillary and Bill Clinton offered up a parody of it on Hillary's 2007–8 presidential campaign website. In a playful spoof on Carmela and Tony Soprano, the celebrated politicians restage the last *Sopranos* scene as they sit in a diner choosing pop songs from a jukebox. To be sure, this is just the most recent instance in a much longer history of mergers between politics and media entertainment; but it does demonstrate that the convergence between television and digital media is playing an increasingly significant role in 21st-century political culture. Whether this is a good or bad turn of events is a source of much anxious speculation, but it remains the case that in a society where less than half the eligible population votes, the electronic media are one of the keys means of creating public culture.

LABOUR, LEISURE AND DIGITAL CONVERGENCE

Underlying these transformations in media culture are fundamental shifts in daily life, and in particular changing relations of work and leisure. Orchestrated like trains to run on schedule, broadcasting was a hallmark medium of modernity, keeping the public attuned to the clocks of capitalist labour schedules and leisure time. The television schedule was historically organised in ways that meshed with the work hours and life cycles of its sponsors' target audience: the middle-class family consumer. From their breakfast news programmes to their late-night talk shows, broadcasters entrained their daily and weekly schedules to the timetables of work and recreation, the schedules of bourgeois domesticity, seasonal advertising cycles, and annual civic and religious calendars.[16] Assumptions about who was available to view at specific points in the day and week resulted in familiar programming forms such as the daytime soap opera, the dinnertime network newscast, and weekend coverage of live sporting events.

But all this is changing. In the new century, television networks are refashioning their schedules to reflect the 'social arrhythmia' of the new 24/7/365 post-industrial information economy.[17] In contrast to the eight-hour work shifts of the industrial economy of which broadcasting is a product, the information economy 'is characterized by the breaking down of the rhythms, either biological or social, associated with the notion of a lifecycle'.[18] Nowhere is this more evident than in the growing desynchronisation of traditional patterns of work and leisure. By the late 1990s, the portion of the American workforce working a traditional 40-hour week had dropped to just over 54 per cent. Meanwhile, contingent and part-time employment and flexible scheduling policies have grown more common, rendering the 9-to-5 workday a relic of America's industrial past.[19] And whereas the middle-class family of post-war America was predicated on the assumption of commuter suburbs where Dad worked downtown while Mom stayed at home, today only a minority of households are composed of nuclear families and most families contain either single or two parent workers who multitask across a spectrum of labour and leisure activities.[20] The compartmentalised bundles of free time that were the hallmarks of the 20th-century consumer society have now given way to 'neo-leisure', or snatches of time interspersed irregularly throughout the extended workday and workweek.[21] Just as David Harvey speaks of 'flexible labor' as a symptom of post-industrial capitalism, we can speak of 'flexible leisure' as a constitutive part of the 21st-century media environment.[22]

Television's changing scheduling patterns have both reflected and contributed to this shift in work and leisure time. Niche cable outlets like

SoapNet, CNN, and ESPN have built sizeable followings by re-running a limited menu of soap operas, news and sports coverage around the clock, allowing viewers to tune in to their favourite programmes on a catch-as-catch-can basis. Gradually, the traditional broadcast networks followed suit. Rather than *Thursday Night at the Movies*, or ABC's 'TGIF' ('Thank God It's Friday') line-up, the networks are now embracing strategies like 'multi-plexing' and Internet streaming that allow viewers to watch what they want, when they want, on the screens of their choice. The new digital time-shifting devices and services such as video on demand (VOD) and the digital video recorder (DVR) respond to and also help to change the rhythms of labour and leisure.[23] DVRs not only allow people to store and time-shift pro-grammes of their choice, they also allow viewers to pause or rewind programmes as they are transmitted into the home.[24] TV, in other words, is moving from being a *time-bound* medium based on simultaneous transmission from a local station (or its national network feed) to an *endless* activity based on 'storage' in and retrieval from decentralised data banks, ideally with global reach.

Although time-shifting technologies are still relatively rare among US television households, they nevertheless have important implications for media culture and the ways in which people perceive their own relation to it.[25] Rather than gathering audiences in shared viewing rituals, these devices and services operate on a new ideal of 'personal' media consumption that revolves around ideologies of individual choice. These choices are, of course, orchestrated in advance by large corporations like TiVo that provide people with a new form of 'feedback' in which viewers receive marketing reports on themselves ('If you liked *Survivor*, you'll like *Lost*'). In this respect, these new digital contraptions entirely invert the 20th-century broadcast ideal of public service. Rather than attempting to provide programmes that are in 'the public interest', these devices instead tell the public what they are 'interested in', and then market that knowledge as a consumer service. Moreover, at the turn of the 21st century, these devices seem poised to divide the audience into what one television industry insider terms a 'two-tier viewing popu-lation'. Indeed, DVR ownership has thus far largely broken down along socio-economic lines, with the majority of digital time-shifting devices being found in the households of wealthy and educated urbanites.[26] Digital time-shifters have emerged as the television audience's equivalent of the 'fast castes' described by Susan George, elites whose power and privilege 'is both reflected in and constituted by their control over greater speeds of motion and activity than enjoyed by most'.[27] For members of this self-segregating public, the decision of when – and on which digital platform – to view television is more than just a matter of convenience. It also becomes a lifestyle choice as important to the construction of a successful consumer identity as the car one drives.

In the well-worn tradition of planned obsolescence, the promotional discourses deployed by the consumer electronics industries increasingly suggest that 'real-time' viewing is as out of date as black and white receivers and bunny ears antennae. So too, advertisements for digital technologies conflate time shifting with a rebellious declaration of independence from the centralised forms of oversight embodied by the scheduling practices of the national television networks. They do so under the neoliberal banner of privatisation, inviting the self-reliant citizen-viewer to think of time shifting as akin to opting out of the industrial era's anachronistic collective leisure rituals. With slogans like 'TV Your Way', 'Program Your Own Network', and 'You Run The Show', companies like TiVo promote DVRs as machines that allow viewers to wrestle control of the schedule away from the moribund grip of network executives. Driving the point home, one advertisement for TiVo even depicts two gangsters throwing a network-programming executive out of the window of his corner office.[28]

In addition to these new dynamics of time shifting, the new technologies have also had a profound relation to the everyday experience of space and place. Whereas the mid-century TV receiver was a piece of living room furniture fixed in place and symptomatic of family viewing in the home, as television matured it became an increasingly mobile activity. First in the 1960s, the introduction of portable models (made possible by innovations with transistors) created new types of social fantasies around watching TV. During these years of the sexual revolution, advertisers promoted television as liberation from – rather than a retreat to – the private life of the family. Advertisements for portable sets showed young TV viewers on the beach, women carrying mini-portables in mod mini skirts while out on the town, and one humorous ad for Sony even showed viewers at a nudist colony gathered around a Sony portable receiver.[29] In the 21st century, mobility continues to be a key element of media experience. People receive TV over a host of mobile platforms including laptops, cell phones, iPods, and iPhones, and the Hollywood studios are creating 'mobisodes' designed distinctly for viewers on the go.[30] However, unlike the portable TV, which was promoted primarily as a leisure pursuit, today's mobile devices are aimed at the new lifestyle ideal of multi-tasking across a series of labour and leisure pursuits.

As testimony to this contemporary ideal of multi-tasking, television's new mobile screens are not just marketed as entertainment centres but also as productivity tools. Mobile technologies conflate activities of leisure and labour so that, for example, the cell phone watcher may at any moment receive a business call or the PC user can switch between watching a *Buffy* rerun and figuring out earnings on the latest stock reports. Whereas Thorstein Veblen famously coined the phrase 'conspicuous consumption' to characterise the bourgeois lifestyles circa 1899, today media industries promote a lifestyle of 'conspicuous production' where leisure and labour activities are wholly intertwined. Accordingly, a 1990s advert for ATT showed vacationers (or were they workers?) receiving a fax on the beach, while computer magazines routinely show a new generation of wired men and women lounging on sofas or patio decks while 'working' from home on their PCs.[31]

NATIONALISM, TRANSNATIONALISM AND GLOBAL FLOWS

The new mobile and time-shifting technologies are changing the prospects for broadcasting's national culture – or at least the fantasies of nationalism that network TV once offered viewers. For much of the 20th century, broadcasting provided American audiences with their most explicit reminders that they belonged to what Benedict Anderson calls the 'imagined community' of the modern nation state.[32] Media scholars have long remarked on television's capacity to forge and sustain a sense of national (or even global) unity, pointing to its live coverage of extraordinary events (including President Kennedy's assassination, the moon landing and Princess Diana's death) as illustrations of the medium's capacity to foster a sense of togetherness in the here and now.[33] But just as niche narrowcast channels fragment the audience into sharply defined taste publics, digital time shifting fragments the television audience *temporally*. Commenting on the trend, Michael Lewis of the *New York Times* observes that, after decades in which broadcasting formed the basis not only of the mass market but also of Americans' national identity, a 'technology [the DVR] appeared that can unravel the collective'.[34] More generally, critics and pundits have expressed alarm over these developments, cautioning that the desynchronisation of media consumption is tantamount to the 'breaking up of America'.[35] Only now, they suggest, the risk is no longer simply that of 'two Americas' divided by partisan lines, but rather of a multitude of Americas fragmented by niche tastes, time-shifting practices, and mobile forms of cultural consumption that no longer seem grounded in a particular place or shared sense of national identity.

However, even if these developments have weakened television's illusion of shared community (at least for those members of the audience that TV historically targeted as citizen-consumers), they simultaneously make it possible for viewers to participate in television publics that transcend national borders. In the context of media conglomerates' global marketing strategies and the diffusion of digital and networked technologies, television programming now circulates internationally at unprecedented speeds, through both authorised and unauthorised channels. While news programming has long crossed national borders (for example, via CNN and BBC newscasts, and more recently Al Jezeera), today viewers around the world can experience weekly episodes of their favourite entertainment series approximately in sync with US audiences, and people can participate with fellow fans in online discussions and web-based collaborative projects. Likewise, peer-to-peer file-sharing websites dedicated to the television, cinema, and music of specific nations enable US audiences to download programmes almost instantaneously after they have aired overseas. While the publics instantiated by these international media flows may be of little solace to critics alarmed by the dissolution of the national audience, their emergence in the aftermath of the 9/11 attacks suggests that the current media environment has now escaped its national borders, and that, despite momentary calls to patriotism, the media are no longer really 'American' – at least in the way that mid-century industry chiefs and government strategists hoped they would be.

In this respect, while television might have been the centrepiece technology of Luce's 'American Century', today TV is part of what Arjun Appadurai calls the image and economic flows of a transnational global culture.[36] In the Cold War era, radio and television programmes were incorporated into government sponsored campaigns to spread the American image abroad (for example, the Voice of America disseminated American jazz programmes overseas) and, by the 1960s, the television industry fully recognised the profits to be made in international syndication.[37] These circumstances led to wide-ranging disputes about American cultural imperialism through the media. In the 1980s, scholars and critics marvelled at the global embrace of the primetime serial *Dallas* (1978–91) and its reception worldwide. Yet studies of the global audiences for *Dallas* and other US media products suggest that worldwide audiences tend to interpret programmes according to their own cultural contexts and social backgrounds.[38]

Moreover, despite critics' fears of homogenisation, worldwide television programmes have not exactly imitated US productions; instead, international productions often express the values and beliefs systems of local cultures. Considering the transnational East Asian success of the '(post-) trendy' Japanese serial drama *Tokyo Love Story* (which aired in the early 1990s), Ien Ang argues that rather than thinking about globalisation as a worldwide phenomenon with uniform effects, it is more useful to think of the ways in which 'cultural proximity' (or shared influences, fashions and identities) among audience formations accounts for both programme popularity and the transnational flow of meanings across national boundaries.[39] Similarly, in their research on Chinese viewers of Japanese dramas in Singapore, Elizabeth MacLachlan and Geok-lian Chua show how different generations of Singaporean women interpret the shows differently and according to their own predilections for the perceived 'Western' values these programmes contain. Meanwhile, people are using the Internet to question US media stereotypes. For example, Pricilla Peña Ovalle shows how the website Pocho.com uses parody to critique the depiction of Mexican Americans on US television.[40] As these and other studies suggest, rather than thinking about American 'influence' on the rest of the world, it is more useful to think about 'disjunctures' in the way different nations and cultures experience media modernities.[41]

In this sense, the meaning of 'America' in the 21st century is itself subject to the transnational flows of a global 'image' market in which television and digital media play a central role. Not surprisingly, in the US the question of television's future is often bound up with larger trepidations about the future of America itself. When media pundits speculate on what TV and new technologies may do to 'us', they are also asking (whether consciously or unconsciously) what the media will do to 'America' as a whole way of life. As TV morphs into digital devices, as it splinters into narrowcast channels, and as it circulates in transnational flows, its future for the nation is uncertain. But, in the present century, as in the past, television's role – for good or bad – depends less on technological invention than it does on cultural inventiveness. Today, whether in Hollywood studios, the headquarters of multinational corporations, or on interactive websites like YouTube and grassroots chat rooms like moveon.org, the media are being re-imagined for a world no longer as 'American' as Luce and his contemporaries had once declared. In this respect, even though television still sends images of America around the world, at least when it comes to the media, the 'American Century' no longer prevails.

NOTES

1. See Lynn Spigel, *Make Room for TV: Television and the Family Ideal in Postwar America* (Chicago, IL: University of Chicago Press, 1992). For discussions of African Americans and early television see Melvin Patrick Ely, *The Adventures of Amos and Andy: A Social History of an American Phenomenon* (New York, NY: Free Press, 1991) and Donald Bogle, *Primetime Blues: African Americans on Network Television* (New York, NY: Farrar, Straus and Giroux, 2001).
2. See Spigel, *Make Room for TV*, p. 112; Newton N. Minow, 'The vast wasteland', in *Equal Time: the Private Broadcaster and the Public Interest* (New York, NY: Atheneum, 1964), pp. 45–69.
3. Marshall McLuhan and Quentin Fiore, *War and Peace in the Global Village* (New York, NY: Bantam Books, 1968).
4. For more on television and 9/11 see Lynn Spigel, 'Entertainment Wars: Television culture after 9/11', *American Quarterly*, 56(2), June 2004, 235–70.
5. Victoria Johnson, '"Welcome home?" CBS, PAX-TV, and "heartland" values in a neo-network era', in Robert Allen and Annette Hill (eds), *The Television Studies Reader* (London: Routledge, 2004), pp. 404–17.
6. This is not to say that the standards of 'objectivity' were without their own ideological underpinnings. The fact that in the US news anchors were historically virtually always white men already suggests the failings of objectivity in TV journalism.
7. John T. Caldwell, 'Convergence Television: aggregating form and repurposing content in the culture of convergence', in Lynn Spigel and Jan Olsson (eds), *Television After TV: Essays on a Medium in Transition* (Durham, NC: Duke University Press, 2004), pp. 41–74.

8. Robert McChesney, *Corporate Media and the Threat to Democracy* (New York, NY: Seven Stories Press, 1997), p. 6. See also Patricia Aufderheide, *Communications Policy and the Public Interest: The Telecommunications Act of 1996* (New York, NY: Guilford Press, 1999).

9. See Federal Communications Commission, Docket 06-93 (Washington, DC: Government Printing Office, 24 July 2006); 2006 Review of the Media Ownership Rules, http://www.fcc.gov/ownership/.

10. Herman Gray, *Watching Race: Television and the Struggle for 'Blackness'* (Minneapolis, MN: University of Minnesota Press, 1995); Beretta E. Smith-Shomade, *Shaded Lives: African American Women and Television* (New Brunswick, NJ: Rutgers University Press, 2002).

11. Smith-Shomade, *Shaded Lives*, p. 38.

12. 'Latinos hardly visible on prime time television, UCLA study finds', Press Release, UCLA Chicano Studies Research Center, 3 April 2003.

13. Charlotte Brunsdon, 'Lifestyling Britain: the 8–9 slot on British television', in Spigel and Olsson (eds), *Television After TV*, pp. 75–92; Lisa Parks, 'Flexible microcasting: gender, generation, and television-internet convergence', in Spigel and Olsson (eds), *Television After TV*, pp. 133–56.

14. For example, *Joe Millionaire* delivered Fox's highest ratings in its time slot in eight years among adults aged 18–49. Leslie Ryan, 'Are short-run reality series a long-term fix?', *Electronic Media*, 13 January 2003, 1A, 55.

15. Laurie Ouellette, '"Take responsibility for yourself": Judge Judy and the neoliberal citizen', in Susan Murray and Laurie Ouellette (eds), *Reality TV: Remaking Television Culture* (New York, NY: New York University Press, 2004), pp. 231–50; Henry Jenkins, *Convergence Culture: When Old and New Media Collide* (New York, NY: New York University Press, 2006).

16. Nick Browne, 'The political economy of the television (super)text', *Quarterly Review of Film Studies*, 9, 1984, 174–83; Paddy Scannell, *Radio, TV and Modern Life: A Phenomenology of Broadcasting* (London: Blackwell, 1996).

17. Manuel Castells, *The Rise of the Network Society* (Oxford: Blackwell, 1996), p. 475.

18. Scott M. Lash and John Urry, *Economies of Signs and Spaces* (London: Sage, 1994), p. 245; Castells, *The Rise of the Network Society*, p. 476.

19. Lonnie Golden, 'Flexible work schedules: what are we trading off to get them?', *Monthly Labor Review*, March 2001, 50.

20. According to the US Census Bureau, as of 2000, only 22.4 per cent of American households contained married couples living with their children. Frank Hobbs, *Examining American Household Composition: 1990 and 2000* (Washington, DC: US Census Bureau, 2005), p. 6.

21. 'A spy in the house of work', *Fast Company*, October 1993, http://www.fastcompany.com/magazine/00/spy0.html/.

22. David Harvey, *The Condition of Postmodernity: An Enquiry into the Origins of Cultural Change* (London: Blackwell, 1989).

23. Time shifting was possible with the videocassette recorder (VCR) in previous decades. But the new digital services and devices allow for a much more automated and regularised time-shift system.

24. In 2007, Nielsen reported that approximately half of all broadcast primetime programmes viewed by DVR households are time shifted. Mitch Burg, 'DVRs

and ads: a whole new dimension for time', *Television Week*, 26(3), 15 January 2007, 11.

25. As of March 2007, fewer than 15 per cent of US television households owned DVRs; approximately 25 million homes patronised VOD services in 2006. Jack Neff, 'New study finds DVR usage saps product sales', *Television Week* 26(10), 5 March 2007, 22; Daisy Whitney, 'VOD: getting bigger, but not better yet', 23 April 2007, http://www.tvweek.com/article.cms?articleId=31833/:.

26. Mike Bloxham, 'The DVR divide', 8 August 2007, http://blogs.mediapost. com/tv_board/?p=136/.

27. Susan George, *The Lugano Report: On Preserving Capitalism in the Twenty-first Century* (London: Pluto Press, 1999); Susan George, 'Beyond the WTO', 1999, http://www.tni.org/detail_page.phtml?page=archives_george_speed&print_format=YGeorge, S.; see also David Morley, *Home Territories: Media, Mobility, and Identity* (London: Routledge, 2000), pp. 198–200.

28. William Boddy describes this advertisement in *New Media and Popular Imagination: Launching Radio, Television, and Digital Media in the United States* (New York, NY: Oxford University Press, 2004), p. 128.

29. Lynn Spigel, *Welcome to the Dreamhouse: Popular Media and Postwar Suburbs* (Durham, NC: Duke University Press, 2001), pp. 60–103.

30. Max Dawson, 'Little players, big shows: format, narration and style on television's new small(er) screens', *Convergence*, 13(3), August 2007, 231–50.

31. Lynn Spigel, 'Designing the smart house: posthuman domesticity and conspicuous production', *European Journal of Cultural Studies*, 8(4), 2005, 403–26. For Thorstein Veblen's original thesis see *The Theory of the Leisure Class* (New York, NY: Dover, [1899] 1994).

32. Benedict Anderson uses the phrase 'imagined community' to discuss the way newspapers joined strangers together across geographical spaces and helped to create a shared sense of belonging to the modern nation state. See Anderson, *Imagined Communities: Reflections on the Origin and Spread of Nationalism* (New York, NY: Verso, 1999), p. 35.

33. Daniel Dayan and Elihu Katz, *Media Events: The Live Broadcasting of History* (Cambridge, MA: Harvard University Press, 1992).

34. Michael Lewis, 'Boom box', *New York Times Magazine*, 20 August 2001, 66.

35. Joseph Turow, *Breaking Up America: Advertisers and the New Media World* (Chicago, IL: University of Chicago Press, 1998); Cass Sunstein, *Republic.com* (Princeton, NJ: Princeton University Press, 2007).

36. Arjun Appadurai, 'Disjuncture and difference in the global cultural economy', in Bruce Robbins (ed.), *The Phantom Public Sphere* (Minneapolis, MN: University of Minnesota Press), pp. 269–95.

37. Michael Curtin and Lynn Spigel, 'Introduction', in Lynn Spigel and Michael Curtin (eds), *The Revolution Wasn't Televised: Sixties Television and Social Conflict* (New York, NY: Routledge, 1997).

38. For studies of the audiences for *Dallas* see, for example, Elihu Katz and Tamar Liebes, *The Export of Meaning: Cross-Cultural Readings of 'Dallas'* (New York, NY: Oxford University Press, 1990) and Ien Ang, *Watching Dallas: Soap Opera and the Melodramatic Imagination* (London: Methuen, 1985). For a classic theory of media interpretation and social context, see Stuart Hall, 'Encoding/decoding', in Hall

et al. (eds), *Culture, Media, Language* (London: Hutchinson, 1980), pp. 128–38.

39. Ien Ang, 'The cultural intimacy of TV drama', in Koichi Iwabuchi (ed.), *Feeling Asian Modernities: Transnational Consumption of Japanese TV Dramas* (Hong Kong: Hong Kong University Press, 2004), pp. 303–10; Joseph D. Straubhaar, 'Distinguishing the global, regional and national levels of world television', in Annabelle Sreberny-Mohammadi *et al.* (eds), *Media in Global Context: A Reader* (New York, NY: Edward Arnold, 1997), pp. 294–8.

40. Elizabeth MacLachlan and Geok-lian Chua, 'Defining Asian femininity: Chinese viewers of Japanese TV dramas in Singapore', in Iwabuchi (ed.), *Feeling Asian Modernities*, pp. 155–75; Priscilla Peña Ovalle, 'Pocho.com: reimagining television on the Internet', in Spigel and Olsson (eds), *Television after TV*, pp. 324–41.

41. We borrow this formulation from Appadurai, 'Disjuncture and Difference', in Robbins (ed.), *The Phantom Public Sphere*, pp. 269–95.

18. ANIMATION AND DIGITAL CULTURE

Paul Wells

The digital revolution happened without marches, placards and conflict; it was not about the overthrow of monarchs and governments; it was played out by corporate culture in cahoots with scientists, engineers and technologists. There was no conspiracy. For some, clinging to the term 'new media' meant that there was a modicum of resistance. There was still 'old media' – print, television, cinema – but with each passing day, these too were absorbed within the digital realm. Some suggested that it was the end of history, the end of cinema, the end: a quiet apocalypse that ironically found a key touchstone in the tragic spectacle of 9/11 and the War on Terror played out by the Bush administration. The revolution will not be televised, but nowadays it will inevitably be digitised.

As the YouTube, MySpace and Second Life generation enjoys its apparently democratic presence on the Internet, and the economies of domestic acquisition of digital equipment and software applications change to facilitate back-bedroom studios, issues in production, exhibition, distribution and, crucially, representation have inevitably changed. Shilo McClean has noted that 'this raises an extensive array of philosophical issues when what we view in images moves from recording to representational technologies, substituting idealised and stylised imagery for the indexical record'.[1] Kay Hoffman qualifies this, though, by noting that 'with digitisation we may have to adjust to a new magnitude of constructedness of the image, when it comes to how "reality" is presented to us in film and television, but the principle and the problem are as old as the cinema itself'.[2]

The early 21st century is a time of ubiquitous email, the omnipresence of mobile phones, the cinema of post-production, computer-gaming cultures, the vacuity of reality television, and of the multi-channel society. There is an implied sense of a global community though and, arguably, as most citizens move from being merely consumers to becoming producers, we live in a time of both famine and feast. The computer defines the data, the desk and destiny. Inevitably new identities form; ideological, ethical and spiritual principles become confused, challenged or re-defined to take on an often extreme clarity. Conspiracy culture proliferates, suggesting that all the things that in the past one dared to believe in are no longer certain. This, then, is the 21st-century version of the postmodern terrain.

It has always been the case, of course, that the arts and humanities have sought to engage with and address the major questions that arise from such conditions of existence, and that each disciplinary stance has used its sometimes highly specific tools to interrogate important agendas. For the purposes of this chapter, the nature of digital culture will be explored through the medium of animation. For so long associated with the achievements of the American animated cartoon, the Disney classical style, and the branding of Mickey Mouse, Bugs Bunny and Betty Boop, animation has now become, like new media, an almost redundant term in the way that it embraces every cross-disciplinary, multidisciplinary or interdisciplinary context or environment. There is the self-evident presence of the animated feature film, the television sitcom, the independent short or the web-toon (all essentially versions of animation cinema), but it is also an omnipresent language in other disciplines from architectural design to medical imaging. Animation has always embraced 'the other arts' – painting, sculpture, dance and theatre – but now, faced with the impact of digital technologies, it has been rent from its status as a pro-filmic creation in which phases of movement progress linearly and incrementally frame by frame. It is now a creative practice in which the mere manipulation of 'the frame' and ability to edit within the frame has changed the nature of how animation might be understood.

While a number of writers have suggested that if animation was once a subset of cinema, it is now the constituent language of cinema itself, this is still to render animation as a particular *langue*.[3] It is the language of metamorphosis, condensation, fabrication, penetration, symbol and metaphor and sound illusionism. It insists upon its filmic credentials in the material preparation for creating rather than recording a model of cinema. This has become a richly nuanced language, though, and its achievements have been recognised as a core modernist practice, as the redefining condition of the filmic apparatus, and a term by which the discourses of art might be played out.[4] This re-engagement with animation has inevitably recast the practice as a metaphysical principle rather than a specific application: for example, in the video artist Tom Sherman's case emphasising the form's mnemonic tendency:

Animation is the hard copy of memory, accessed while it is being rendered by hand, or by hands assisted by machine. In general, animation is memory that moves and evolves … I am saying that animation – memory in the act of forming – alludes to something essential, yet unattainable: the imagination itself.

Added to this:

Animation is a complex category of meta-media phenomena, a manner of creative behaviour quite capable of attracting and sustaining attention in all manner of media environments. Animation has marched through cinema, television, and now video, without missing a beat, because it is the concrete process of manufacturing records of psychological memory.[5]

Sherman's view is persuasive: that animation is a process which most directly accesses imagination through the act of memory and uses technology to manufacture concrete records of interior states. Canadian artist and animator, Pierre Hebert, however, insists that animation has also become a way of recording the experience in using and living through technology, noting that 'every work of art is an implicit statement about technology'.[6] In many senses, animation has always been concerned with the tension between the physical and the metaphysical; the material and the meaning; and, most importantly, the visualisation of psychosomatic experience to provoke cultural and philosophical questions.

THE NEW TRADITIONALISM

It would be easy then to look at the major animated features produced in the United States in recent years – what Shilo McClean calls 'the new traditionalist' work – as the core indicators of aesthetic, technological and philosophical preoccupation. This focus would report on the aesthetic shift from Disney's classical 2D styling to Pixar's 3D computer-generated plastic realism, or the technological interventions that have overcome the holy grails of simulated water or human hair, while never quite creating the plausibly human 'synthesbian'. Equally, it might record the philosophical preoccupation with looking backward to embrace a more populist and easily understood myth of America in the face of the digitised adventures of flawed heroes and dystopian ideas about progress. Brad Bird's *The Incredibles* (2004), for example, may finally vindicate the heroic versatility and moral outlook of the Parr family – superheroes attempting to live a normal suburban life in the face of the possibility that they might be sued by those who do not wish to be saved – but its enduring and resonant message lies in the anxiety *The Incredibles* plays out about conformism, the debilitating routines of daily existence, the failings of family life and social mentoring, and the over-whelming question of what remains to be saved in the midst of such moral relativity. It was little wonder that Disney narratives – for all their recent leftist critique – survived for so long as enduring examples of family-friendly mass entertainment, refusing nuance, ambivalence or ambiguity in the con-struction of easily understood notions of good and evil and the deployment of popular archetypes.[7] So embedded was this ideological imperative in Disney's classical 2D styling, however, that it has not survived into the 3D era. The new relativities of digital creativity have essentially moved the feature animation aesthetic into a less familiar terrain of relative values.

The Disney text has always been subject to critical interventions, but none have essentially transcended the 'brand' value of Disney narratives, or challenged the power of archetypal heroism and villainy so readily under-stood by a public eager for clarity and moral certainty. It is significant that the loss of Disney's classical styling, and its replacement by the new digital orthodoxies in 3D feature animation finally provoked a crisis in represen-tation some ten years after *Toy Story* (John Lasseter, 1995), the first fully computer-generated animated feature, and still a triumph of cinematic storytelling and cultural populism. It was not until the arrival of a critical mass in the production of computer-generated animation – a certain number of features produced annually rather than merely the long-awaited latest release from Pixar or DreamWorks – was there a critical shift in focus of the films.

For so long the 'wow' factor associated with computer-generated animated features overwhelmed the view that they might actually have something to say, or have meaning and affect. Only with the arrival of a glut of poorly received films was there an engagement with content. *Barnyard* (Steve Oederkerk, 2006) came under particular attack: 'this could be the film that snaps everyone's patience with Hollywood animations which have a Dell computer chip where their heart should be'.[8] Interestingly, seemingly poor films were associated with the 'cold heart' of the computer, and the implied longing for the intimacies of old style, hand-crafted storytelling. Never-theless, *Barnyard* still lent itself to an arguably bizarre allegorical interpretation: 'Ben is Bush senior fighting the first Gulf War, Otis is Bush Junior, revenging his father after 9/11, and the coyotes are the terrorists. Unlike the astringently pessimist *Animal Farm*, this feel good movie is Orwell that ends well'.[9]

Although this reading of *Barnyard* is a highly forced grounding of the film in a political discourse, it does at least suggest that animated films can carry seriousness of purpose, or a pertinent subtext. Championed, however, were films that seemed to privilege an overt leftist intervention: most notably, Blue Sky's *Ice Age* (Chris Wedge, 2002), *Ice Age 2: The Meltdown* (Carlos Saldanha, 2005) and Australian George Miller's *Happy Feet* (2006) with their ecological concerns. Exploring the normal liberal tensions between individualism and the mass, which is common to most American movies (animated or otherwise), *Happy Feet* tells a left-leaning tale of humankind's deliberate exploitation and abuse of the oceans, and the ways in which a fundamentalist rhetoric is employed to blame liberals and non-white groups for not being faithful Republicans committed to trusting the government and the political status quo. During a historical phase in which Hollywood movies have become predicated on what Phil Melling describes as an 'adversarial imagination', the reclamation of left-leaning or small 'c' conservative values has been important in reasserting the localness of traditional Republican and Democrat identity (arguably lost to a past mythology) in the face of broader ideological and spiritual struggles played out on a global stage in the War on Terror.[10] It is important to stress, though, that this reading relates to what might be termed as mainstream or institutional animation. The economies of the Hollywood animation (as well as the traditional filmmaking) industry have embraced the digital shift as a way of re-determining the modality of animation and the execution of visual effects, but this is still largely within the traditional paradigm of classical narrative. Crucially, though, the embrace of digital technologies has empowered filmmakers and animators in other ways, and the potential radicalisation of the animated image has resulted in a possible radicalisation of the means to narrative, in addition to refreshing ideological and political perspectives.

Richard Linklater's *Waking Life* (2001) employs digital rotoscoping, which works as an almost literal vindication of Lev Manovich's view that 'cinema can no longer be distinguished from animation. It is no longer an indexical media technology but, rather, a subgenre of painting'.[11] Embracing an old animation technique first used by the animators of the Disney and Fleischer Brothers' studios in the 1930s, this new model of rotoscoping digitally traces and paints over live-action footage, enhancing or revising the original material into a much more richly encoded text, more readily aligned to the dream state or an alternative mode of consciousness than the literal record can achieve.

The characters in *Waking Life* ruminate on a variety of personal, political and philosophical enquiries and anecdotes, thereby revising notions of classical Hollywood narrative by prioritising vocal performances. These performances act as a catalyst for interpretation by the animators, whose visualisations foreground, intensify and comment on the moods and emotions of the speakers. Thus, the abstract vocal performance of the actors might be said to support the contemplative abstractions of the characters. It also heightens a consideration of human endeavour and purpose as forms of 'narrative' or 'the quest for a new story' – a proposal ironically offered by a chimpanzee at a lecture in *Waking Life*.

These subjective histories once more delineate notions of the relativity of reality, whilst their representation dismisses the claims of photorealism to embrace that reality. More pointedly, a drive-by political campaigner broadcasting his vision, played by Alex Jones, who reddens and darkens with the intensity of his anger, dismisses the core political axes in American life, played out by the Republicans and Democrats, as 'two sides of the same coin; two management teams bidding for control of the CEO job of "Slavery Incorporated"'. The fundamental mistrust of American political life, or the notion of a coherent or common 'waking life', underpins the quasi-existential questioning process that serves as narrative in the film, positing the notion of the unconscious, the dream, the fantasy or solipsistic consciousness as an alternative engagement with lived experience. Recalling the mnemonic tendency in animation, cited earlier, and making figural the intrinsic ability of animation to visualise and capture interior states, *Waking Life* demonstrates the liberation of digital technologies. Animation is used as an interrogative language and the search for meaning in an era of relativity, challenging received knowledge of political dogma and ideological orthodoxies.

NOT-SO-SPECIAL EFFECTS

Linklater's *Waking Life* resists the heightened photorealism enabled by digital technologies, and which is often viewed as the norm. Indeed, while it is almost uniformly the case that digital interventions take place in all films, it is still clear that digital processes are most often understood as 'visual effects', or what were previously known as 'Special Effects' before their special status disappeared into code. When they are visible – most notably in the early excesses of 'the morph' or in the array of creatures, aliens and mythic beings – they essentially resemble *Waking Life* in the privileged use of animation as a signifying language.[12] This level of overtness in the texts normally signals the presence of the animator and suggests the intrinsically self-figurative and self-reflexive nature of animation, but it is also the case that animation in its new digital guise is taking place in less obviously exhibitionist contexts.

It is useful to delineate, therefore, what commonalities traditional definitions of animation and the typologies of visual effects share. It becomes clear that the diversity and application of visual effects is not dissimilar to the variances and breadth of purpose in traditional animation: what I have described elsewhere as the movement between *orthodox animation* (essentially classical Disney hyper-realism or 'the new traditionalist' model), *experimental animation* (non-linear, non-objective works) and *developmental animation* (playing out degrees of difference between them).[13] This is more pithily expressed by Maureen Furniss as the space between 'mimesis' and 'abstraction',[14] and directly echoes the typology discussed by Shilo McClean (see Table 18.1).

This effects model demonstrates the gradual but perceptual movement from photorealist representation to abstract expression. However, the model

Table 18.1. Typology of special effects adapted from McClean's analysis[15]

Type of effect	Definition	Example
Documentary	Visualisation of abstract and technical concepts and theories unimaginable unless graphically realised	*How the Twin Towers Collapsed* (Discovery, 2002) *Inside the Twin Towers* (Discovery, 2006)
Invisible	Deliberately concealed and undetectable interventions preserving the reality of the diegetic world; audience must not suspect or detect effects use	*Children of Men* (2006)
Seamless	Seemingly invisible effects *but* actually discernible and detectable if given consideration (most often in 'period' films)	*Titanic* (1997) *Gladiator* (2000)
Exaggerated	What would happen realistically in the unreal or excessive circumstances of narrative; 'perceptual realism but cognitive improbability'	*The Day After Tomorrow* (2004)
Fantastical	'Shows us things to be untrue, but with such conviction that we believe them to be real' (Albert La Valley); 'sublime or excessive imagery'; 'extending real world into the world of fantasy'	*The Lord of the Rings* Trilogy (2001–3)
Surrealist	Deliberately noticeable imaginative or spectacular effects that must be read as a concept or metaphor	*Amélie* (2001)
New Traditionalist	Narrative and cartoonal tradition of long form animation features	*Toy Story* (1995) *Toy Story II* (1999)
HyperRealist	Completely animated computer-generated figures and environments	*Final Fantasy* (2001) Gollum in *The Lord of the Rings* Trilogy (2001–3)

includes the recognition that a 'digital effect' in the 'HyperRealist' style may still be identified by the *completeness* of its application, and its commitment to a total level of constructedness in the computer environment, rather than the partial mix of elements described by Lev Manovich in his seminal definition of digital cinema as 'live action material + painting + image processing + compositing + 2D computer animation + 3D computer animation'.[16]

It is important, though, to interrogate the term 'computer animation' in this formulation a little more closely. There are three distinct categories, which might enable a fuller understanding of the breadth of material that could be viewed as computer animation:

(1) First, *computer-assisted animation* as the use of the computer in the determination of motion control; the deployment of specific kinds of software in the completion of process tasks normally undertaken by hand; replacing the camera as a recording device. Essentially this means the use of digital technologies *as a media aid*.

(2) Second, *computer-facilitated animation* in which the computer is deployed in the revision and re-determination of other already established, principally 2D, material approaches: drawing, painting, collage and scanned photo-montage; data used from motion capture or rotoscoping also informs this category as it operates as an index of performance motion. In this case, digital technologies function as *adaptive media*.

(3) Third, *computer-modelled animation*, which sees the computer as the core context in the construction of 'worlds' within a 3D environment, and might readily be called *digimation*. This model uses digital technologies as *origination media*.

It is important to note that these aspects may overlap and combine in some projects, particularly multimedia works.

Interestingly, at present it is clear that computer-assisted animation is, in effect, a relative orthodoxy, present in most forms of animation or film production to some degree. Computer-facilitated animation, though, appears the province of more experimental or progressive and largely independent work, whilst computer-modelled animation, represented here in McClean's work, predominantly as 'new traditionalist', has hyperrealist and documentary applications. Even with these distinctions and categories, there is acknowledgement of a significant movement towards the view that traditional filmmaking practices are not merely being overtaken by digital processes, but that the aesthetics of such films are moving closer to the visual codes, conventions and dynamics of animated film. Robert Skotak, a visual effects supervisor at 4-ward Productions notes: 'Overall I think that synthetic images are promoting a sense of illustration in visual effects. You come across a castle in the mist, and it is the ideal time of day, it is backlit, the mist is just so … It feels too much like an animated film, because it's all pretty, all controlled'.[17]

PROOF BY ANIMATION

David Clark has remarked that 'animation's trajectory into new media has radically altered the techniques of the medium, but perhaps more importantly it has fundamentally altered the metaphors by which we imagine time and change'.[18] Such metaphors have been increasingly bound up, however, with the dominant iconography of erotica and violence, which are brought together controversially in Edouard Salier's 2006 animated short *Flesh* (available on YouTube). Salier's vision is predicated on the idea that corporate America is preoccupied with its own obsessive indulgences, here played out as the mainstreaming of pornography, conflating titillating masturbatory images of Playboy-styled models with the phallic infrastructure of the New York architectural skyline. Pornography has become a multibillion dollar industry in the US and the everyday evidence of a consumer-led culture that sits uneasily with the old-style moralities of fundamentalists or even the neoliberal sensibilities of the political mainstream. When Salier, as a deliberate provocateur, uses the events of 9/11 in combination with pornographic content, the ethical implications of the images are extremely challenging.

In *Flesh* the terrorist planes plough into a World Trade Center now embellished with erotic images, releasing explosive, jagged edged spears, frozen in an angular configuration. But this is not the end of it. Further planes emerge, each crashing into more and more buildings, thereby reducing the attack on the city to the status of a computer game; its infrastructure 'virtually' destroyed, the 'flesh' of its citizens arbitrarily dismissed or abused. Although such imagery recalls the idea of the 'pleasures of war' and the cathartic arousal which may come with the heightened and abandoned energies of assault and brutality, Salier's film is less about the titillation of tyranny and terror and more concerned with the deep-rooted complacency of a nation caught up in the belief in its own mythic narratives and undermined by the excessive exploitation of liberty. Indeed, Salier's film concludes with the rebuilding of America from the debris set against the Statue of Liberty. Nevertheless, it is clear that normal service has been resumed: a 'pornographic' America survives, a slave to its own appetite for power and insistence upon control, epitomised in the erotica mapped on to the sky-scraping banks and businesses of New York.

Clearly this is not a Disney-take on animation or national identity, but one that in employing the expressive resources of computer-generated, neogaming, neo-realist digital animation challenges received understanding of 9/11 iconography and the competing mythologies now attached to it. Like Holocaust deniers before, some believe 9/11 to be an elaborate hoax; conspiracies abound and reality seems entirely relative. It is perhaps ironic, then, that increasingly animation is being viewed and used as a tool by which 'the truth' might be understood; some sort of legitimate proof in the equally ironic light of the deep betrayal of traditional media to sustain truth and appease our 'camera-never-lies' eyes. The mistrust of the indexical nature of reality assumed in photorealism – always illusory, of course – has led to the notion of accepting animation as an arbiter of insight because of its self-evidently authorial intention and the foregrounded nature of its artifice.

Animation is almost always intrinsically metaphorical and insists upon self-reflexively interpreting its own meaning. As he searches for an ambivalent stance that seeks to embrace both the Muslim perspective and American culture, Salier's work may be less ideologically coherent than this reading suggests, but it does highlight an important point about the use of pornographic imagery set against news footage.

For all the crassly staged and performance aspects of pornographic material, it might be argued that, perversely, such 'sex acts' have become a closer indexical record of the real in the contemporary imagination, and a fundamental reflection of a primal underbelly which is lost and repressed beneath legitimate corporate culture and populist social veneer. While there are clearly ethical difficulties in accepting this view, especially when it does not take into account the production of what might be regarded as 'non-mainstream' pornographic scenarios and practices, it is clear that one of the reasons why Salier uses the Playboy or Private-styled, girl-centred, soft-focus imagery is to illustrate and reveal its systematised embeddedness in a highly phallocentric stage of late industrial capitalism. *Flesh* becomes the outcome of a culture in which the business of sex become a bizarre index of 'the real' in the face of the collapse of ideological certainty, the mistrust of lens-based media and the escalation of simulated experience, best epitomised in the synthetic violence of computer games, played while the reality of brutal conflict escalates across the world. The animated film has rarely exhibited the illusionism or contradictions of contemporary existence so pertinently, but unsurprisingly *Flesh* is not alone in addressing 9/11 as a touchstone of an America in crisis.

Lazyboy Animations epitomise a low-rent approach to making animated films. Fan-generated, the work is made with Flash animation using the controversial observations of the *Nobody Likes Onions* comedy broadcasts as their soundtrack. Launched in 2005 *Nobody Likes Onions* – 'it's like taking a cold shower in sarcasm' – is actually Patrick Melton, Dagre and Johnny B., three comedians from the Tampa Bay area in Florida, producing a thrice-weekly podcast of topical satire. Representing a more radical critique of American culture in the style of *South Park* or Don Hertzfeldt, the trio are deliberately provocative in their views and opinions. The animation itself does little more than visualise some of the more contentious statements for easy comic effect, but nevertheless exploits both the ease in which digital applications enable the simple apprehension of the podcast, the minimal construction of the animation itself using basic software, and its wider exhibition and dissemination on the Internet. The '9/11 Tribute' (2006) looks at the tragedy five years on and imagines the World Trade Center as a toy called 'Towery', with attached spinning planes, charred bodies that fall out if the toy is shaken, and the warning: 'Careful Kids, It's Flammable'. Further along, the towers are imagined as 'Twin Tower Salt and Pepper shakers', and the original footage dismissed with the comment 'You see the plane crash into the towers, and you say, like, where's the popcorn?' *Nobody Likes Onions* conclude their gags by suggesting that the people running up and down the stairwells in the towers could be best remembered running to the British comedian Benny Hill's chase theme, 'Yakkity Sax', as the whole thing had become 'a farce': the last phrase uttered on the '9/11 Tribute'.

Tasteless or not, the simple animation of these statements supports the jokes and, in some ways, vindicates the underlying critique which suggests that 9/11 has become as much of a commercial vehicle as any other event and, for all concerned, has become about making money rather than recognising what has been lost and why. The rhetoric of corporate America has seemingly triumphed over the most powerfully affecting political act in the US in the last 50 years. Salier and Lazyboy clearly share this view, and both implicitly make the claim that the very things that are supposedly at the spiritual heart of American politics and identity are vehicles by which its hypocrisy and contradiction might be exposed. As Salier notes of the attacks by the multiple planes in his film:

> those attacks have finally no effect on the town; on the contrary, they only increase the spectacular decadence they are trying to knock down. The more the planes attack the town, the more debauchery, gigantism, images of violence and the 'hellish' town proliferate.[19]

The essential message of these films is that the nation has learnt little from its history, but, ironically, in the digital era it is this sense of history and notions of historiography that are most under threat.

This is illustrated by a final consideration of a 9/11 film predicated on using animation. Mike Wilson of Integrated Consultants' *Design to Reality* project creates a visualisation of Flight 77's flight trajectory as it crashes into the Pentagon. This authoritative vision is based on 'Forensic Engineering: Recreating events in the form of Newtonian physics-based visual communication that offers forensic dispute resolution', but which is nevertheless, as the voiceover at the beginning of the movie explains, 'a Solidworks generated animation showing the physics of a dynamic situation to help offer explanations when a particular incident has a counter-intuitive outcome'. While such rhetoric is reassuring for some in its implied sense of inevitable rightness, the piece still operates through the artifice of animated sequences, supposedly proving the official version of what occurred on the morning of 9/11 to more sceptical conspiracy theorists, here described coyly as those with a counter-intuitive view of the matter. The animation essentially shows the descent of the aircraft knocking over lamp-poles; the low flight trajectory recorded by a security camera video; the reason for the apparently unscathed lawn and untouched cable spools; the particularity of the plane's entry into the building, which resulted in major internal destruction but only minor external damage; and the place of external debris. The animation is supported by photographic evidence but its intended sense of record is determined by the way the animation creates a narrative for the available photographic evidence and not the reverse.

Design to Reality no more proves that this was an aircraft than it might effectively dispute the conspiracy theorists' view that this could have been a missile. Merely animating the idea that the aircraft flew into a building leaving an aircraft shape in the same way as Tom might leave a cat-like figure when running through a wall in a *Tom and Jerry* cartoon is hardly persuasive, but there is an intrinsic belief that the truth is clarified and proven by the controlling determinacy of computer animation. It is clear that the photographs prove that lamp-poles were knocked over, debris was found and that a generator and ground structure damage were recorded, but it is the animation that actually penetrates the unimaginable or unspeakable conditions which attended the crash and created its physical outcomes.[20] While it is often the case that animation is particularly adept at revealing technical, mechanical, organic or psychological interior states, the assumption here is that what amounts to any counter-intuitive interpretation of events is somehow effaced by quasi-scientific creative solutions offered by business consultants, surely commissioned to uphold the official version. Animation here, then, becomes 'dispute resolution'.

Intriguingly, such a principle – in many senses like those proposed in the critiques offered by Salier and Lazyboy – seemingly offers a notion of what Niall Ferguson has described as 'virtual history' based on hypothetical or counterfactual propositions. At a time when the facts seem increasingly relative, such virtual histories can take on increasing authority supported by the visual determinacy of digitally animated interventions. As Ferguson notes,

> the business of imagining such counterfactuals is a vital part of the way in which we learn. Because decisions about the future are – usually – based on weighing up the potential consequences of alternative courses of action, it makes sense to compare the actual outcomes of what we did in the past with the conceivable outcomes of what we might have done.[21]

VIRTUAL HISTORY

The three animations I have discussed here are but a step from saying that actual outcomes and conceivable outcomes might be one and the same thing. The literal and metaphoric deployment of animation suggests that virtual histories may be constructed out of the deeply subjective and relative contexts of the contemporary period, which define and underpin a new version of historiography. Ferguson notes that there have been two distinct kinds of counterfactual which have been used by historians: those which are essentially the products of imagination but (generally) lack an empirical basis; and those designed to test hypotheses by (supposedly) empirical means, which eschew imagination in favour of computation.[22]

Filmmakers are not historians, but it is not hard to place Salier and Lazyboy's work in the former category and Wilson's in the latter, and merely confirm their counterfactual equivalence. The relegation of causation as a determining model of understanding events (largely because causes often seem indeterminable or at least contestable) and the rise of an inclusive structural analysis (embracing a range of sociologically determined factors as the contextual provocateur or imperative of the historical moment) has in fact enabled contingency and indeterminacy to become significant aspects of the new historiography. Arguably, this model remains too complex and broad without an organising principle, but in some senses it is clear that the traditional historiographic certainties of the past have come to play second fiddle to the highly visible and seemingly transparent representations offered up by the unprecedented presence and intervention of media technologies. History, under these circumstances, is inevitably constructed more as commodity than concern, or more about commodity as a concern, or in line with Francis Fukuyama's instrumental view that 'history' is at an end.

Such postmodern playfulness and mock finality is belied, however, by the insistence of history and the deep-seated requirement to know that what has gone before *did* matter. The urge to preserve, conserve and know again, persists and every new tool of expression is thus applied to the excavation of the past – however, immediate or transient – as a 'lost world'. One need only take the image of the computer-generated dinosaur in such entertainments as *Jurassic Park* (Steven Spielberg, 1993) or quasi-documentaries like *Walking with Dinosaurs* (Tim Haynes, 1999) as a key symbol of such history. Prehistoric creatures are created in the computer, legitimised through the codes and conventions of the wildlife documentary, and made into history by speculative assertion. These are the new archives and new texts, a more subjective substitute for the object of history, validated both by the evidence that informs knowledge *and* the creative practice of imagined epistemologies embodied in persuasive visual signs. Simply, 'history' is not only that which is determined by historians and scholars, but by those who can creatively interrogate the past and produce a narrative which invites the maintenance of its significance, not at the level of social and cultural change but at the more individualised portal of local effect and emotional spectacle. It is not enough to know and critically embrace; history must be 'felt'. The rise of the 'psycho-historian' and the 'micro-history' is thus inevitable, but aided, abetted and enabled by hard copy of memory in the animus, the animation, and the animator of digital intervention.

Under such conditions, it is sometimes hard to deny that the past is another country. Ironically, animation techniques which foreground their own self-reflexive process in revealing change, reinventing the past, and reconstructing the old as new, seek to evoke not merely an alternative view, but the process by which it has been determined. It is perhaps perverse to accept that it is the potentially anarchic freedoms of animation as a mode of record which might best reveal this to us, but there is much in its artifice that remains much more appropriate to the recall of the psychology, physiology, emotion and the material culture of history than has been previously allowed. It might now be viewed as the most pertinent of temporal and archaeological excavators. By using the capacity of animation, and the digital shift to reveal the metamorphosis in everyday events throughout history, in the service of a better understanding and preservation of the past, it is perhaps the final irony that it is possible to challenge the belief in our own more problematic fictions.

NOTES

1. Shilo McClean, *Digital Storytelling: The Narrative Power of Visual Effects in Film* (Cambridge, MA: MIT Press, 2007), p. 60.
2. Thomas Elsaesser and Kay Hoffman (eds), *Cinema Futures: Cain, Abel or Cable? The Screen Arts in the Digital Age* (Amsterdam: Amsterdam University Press, 1998), p. 166.
3. See Alan Cholodenko (ed.), *The Illusion of Life: Essays on Animation* (Sydney: Power Publications, 1991); Paul Watson, 'True Lye's: (re)animating film studies', in Paul Wells (ed.), *Art & Animation* (London: John Wiley/Academy Group, 1997), pp. 46–9; and Lev Manovich, *The Language of New Media* (Cambridge, MA: MIT Press, 2002).
4. For modernist practices of animation, see Esther Leslie, *Hollywood Flatlands: Animation, Critical Theory and the Avant Garde* (London: Verso, 2002) and Paul Wells, *Animation and America* (Edinburgh: Edinburgh University Press, 2002); for discussion of redefined filmic apparatus, see Vivian Sobchack (ed.), *Meta-Morphing: Visual Transformation and the Culture of Quick-Change* (Minneapolis, MN: University of Minnesota Press, 2000) and Suzanne Buchan (ed.), *Animated 'Worlds'* (Eastleigh: John Libbey, 2006); and for animation and art, see Chris Gehman and Steve Reinke, *The Sharpest Point: Animation at the End of Cinema* (Ottawa: YYZ Books, 2005) and Benjamin Cook and Gary Thomas *The Animate! Book: Re-Thinking Animation* (London: Lux, 2006).
5. Gehmann and Reinke, *The Sharpest Point*, pp. 194–5.
6. Pierre Hebert in interview with Paul Wells, December 2005.
7. See, for example, Wells, *Animation and America*, pp. 102–25.
8. Philip Bradshaw, Film review: 'Barnyard', *The Guardian*, 20 November 2006.
9. Philip French 'Thoroughly modern Marie', *The Observer*, 22 October 2006.
10. See Philip John Davies and Paul Wells (eds), *American Film and Politics from Reagan to Bush Jnr* (Manchester: Manchester University Press, 2002), pp. 182–201.
11. Manovich, *The Language of New Media*, p. 195.

12. See Annette Kuhn (ed.), *Alien Zone II: The Spaces of Science Fiction Cinema* (London: Verso, 1999).
13. See Paul Wells, *Understanding Animation* (London: Routledge, 1998).
14. See Maureen Furniss, *Art in Motion: Animation Aesthetics* (Sydney: John Libbey, 1998).
15. McLean, *Digital Storytelling*, pp. 69–103.
16. Manovich, *The Language of New Media*, p. 301.
17. Jody Duncan (ed.), *Cinefex*, 100, January 2005, p. 65.
18. Gehmann and Reinke (eds), *The Sharpest Point*, p. 150.
19. Edouard Salier in interview with Paul Wells, April 2007.
20. The concept of 'penetration' in animation is fully defined and explored in Wells, *Understanding Animation*, pp. 122–6.
21. See Niall Ferguson, *Virtual History: Alternatives and Counterfactuals* (London: Pan, 2003), p. 2.
22. Ibid., p. 18.

BIBLIOGRAPHY

Abrahamian, Ervand, 'The US media, Samuel Huntington and September 11', *Middle East Report*, 223, Summer 2002, 62–3.

Adas, Michael, *Dominance by Design: Technological Imperatives and America's Civilizing Mission* (Cambridge, MA: Harvard University Press, 2006).

Anderson, Benedict, *Imagined Communities: Reflections on the Origin and Spread of Nationalism* (New York: Verso, 1999).

Appadurai, Arjun, 'Disjuncture and Difference in the global cultural economy', in Bruce Robbins (ed.), *The Phantom Public Sphere* (Minneapolis, MN: University of Minnesota Press, 1995), pp. 269–95.

Appadurai, Arjun, *Modernity at Large: Cultural Dimensions of Globalization* (Minneapolis, MN: University of Minnesota Press, 1996).

Bacevich, Andrew J., *The Imperial Tense: Prospects and Problems of American Empire* (Chicago, IL: Dee, 2003).

Bacevich, Andrew J., *The New American Militarism: How Americans are Seduced by War* (New York, NY: Oxford University Press, 2005).

Baer, Ulrich (ed.), *110 Stories: New York Writes After 9/11* (New York, NY: New York University Press, 2002).

Barber, Benjamin R., *Jihad vs. McWorld* (New York, NY: Times Books, 1995).

Battle, Juan, Michael Bennett and Anthony J. Lemelle (eds), *Free at Last? Black America in the Twenty-First Century* (New York, NY: Transaction, 2006).

Baudrillard, Jean, *The Spirit of Terrorism*, trans. Chris Turner (London: Verso, 2002).

Beckman, Ludvig, *The Liberal State and the Politics of Virtue* (London: Transaction, 2001).

Bellah, Robert N., 'Civil Religion in America', *Daedalus*, 96(1), Winter 1967, 1–21.

Bellah, Robert N., *Habits of the Heart: Individualism and Commitment in American Life* (New York, NY: Harper and Row, 1985).

Bellomo, Michael, *The Stem Cell Divide* (New York, NY: AMACOM, 2006).

Bender, Thomas, *A Nation among Nations: America's Place in World History* (New York, NY: Hill and Wang, 2006).

Berger, Dan *et al.*, *Letter from Young Activists: Today's Rebels Speak Out* (New York, NY: Nation Books, 2005).

Bhagwati, Jagdish, *In Defense of Globalization* (Oxford: Oxford University Press, 2004).

Biskind, Peter, *Down and Dirty Pictures: Miramax, Sundance and the Rise of Independent Film* (London: Bloomsbury, 2004).

Boal, Iain, T. J. Clark, Joseph Matthews and Michael Watts, *Afflicted Powers: Capital and Spectacle in a New Age of War* (London: Verso, 2005).

Boddy, William, *New Media and Popular Imagination: Launching Radio, Television, and Digital Media in the United States* (New York, NY: Oxford University Press, 2004).

Borgmann, Albert, *Crossing the Postmodern Divide* (Chicago, IL: University of Chicago Press, 1992).

Braudel, Fernand, *On History*, trans. Sarah Matthews (London: Weidenfeld and Nicolson, 1980).

Brauer, Ralph, *The Strange Death of Liberal America* (Wesport, CT: Praeger, 2006).

Brenner, Robert, *The Boom and the Bubble: The US in the World Economy* (London: Verso, 2002).

Brenner, Robert, *The Economics of Global Turbulence: The Advanced Capitalist Economies from Long Boom to Long Downturn, 1945–2005* (London: Verso, 2006).

Brigham, Robert K., *Is Iraq Another Vietnam?* (New York, NY: Public Affairs, 2006).

Brinkley, Alan, *Liberalism and it Discontents* (Cambridge, MA: Harvard University Press, 1998).

Buchan, Suzanne (ed.), *Animated 'Worlds'* (Eastleigh: John Libbey, 2006).

Burk, Kathleen, *Old World, New World: The Story of Britain and America* (New York, NY: Little, Brown, 2007).

Butler, Judith, *Precarious Life: The Powers of Mourning and Violence* (London: Verso, 2004).

Cannon, Lou, *Governor Reagan: His Rise to Power* (New York, NY: Public Affairs, 2003).

Carey, Alex, *Taking the Risk Out of Democracy* (Urbana, IL: University of Illinois Press, 1997).

Carson, Rachel, *Silent Spring* 30th Anniversary Edition (New York, NY: Houghton Mifflin, 1992).

Castells, Manuel, *The Rise of the Network Society* (Oxford: Blackwell, 1996).

Chambers, Whittaker, *Witness* (Washington, DC: Regnery, [1952] 2002).

Corn, Joseph J. (ed.) *Imagining Tomorrow: History, Technology, and the American Future* (Cambridge, MA: MIT Press, 1986).

Cotkin, George, 'The Democratization of Cultural Criticism', *The Chronicle of Higher Education*, 50(43), 2 July 2004, B8.

Cotton, Charlotte, *The Photograph as Contemporary Art* (London: Thames and Hudson, 2004).

Cox, Michael, 'American power before and after 11 September: dizzy with success?', *International Affairs*, 78(2), 2002, 261–76.

Crockatt, Richard, *After 9/11: Cultural Dimensions of American Global Power* (London: Routledge 2007).

Davies, Philip John and Paul Wells (eds), *American Film and Politics from Reagan to Bush Jnr* (Manchester: Manchester University Press, 2002).

Dawson, Max, 'Little players, big shows: format, narration and style on television's new small(er) screens', *Convergence*, 13(3), August 2007, 231–50.

de Crèvecoeur, J. Hector St John, *Letters from an American Farmer and Sketches of Eighteenth Century American Life* (New York, NY: Penguin, [1782] 1981).

DeLillo, Don, *Mao II* (London: Vintage, 1991).

DeLillo, Don, 'The Power of History', *New York Times Magazine*, 7 September 1997, 60–3.

DeLillo, Don, 'In the Ruins of the Future', *Harpers*, December 2001, 33–40.

DeLillo, Don, *Falling Man* (London: Vintage, 2007).

de Tocqueville, Alexis, *Democracy in America* (London: David Campbell, [1835–40] 1994).

Diggins, John Patrick (ed.), *The Liberal Persuasion: Arthur Schlesinger, Jr. and the Challenge of the American Past* (Princeton, NJ: Princeton University Press, 1997).

Dimock, Wai Chee and Lawrence Buell (eds), *Shades of the Planet: American Literature as World Literature* (Princeton, NJ: Princeton University Press, 2007).

Dixon, Wheeler Winston (ed.), *Film and Television after 9/11* (Carbondale, IL: Southern Illinois University Press, 2004).

Dorrien, Gary, *The Making of American Liberal Theology: Crisis, Irony and Postmodernity: 1950–2005* (Louisville, KY: Westminster/John Knox Press, 2006).

Draper, Robert, *Dead Certain: the Presidency of George W. Bush* (New York, NJ: Simon and Schuster, 2007).

D'Souza, Dinesh, *Letters to a Young Conservative* (New York, NY: Basic Books, 2002).

Dumbrell, John and David Ryan (eds), *Vietnam in Iraq* (London: Routledge, 2006).

Dworkin, Ronald, *Life's Dominion: An Argument about Abortion, Euthanasia and Individual Freedom* (New York, NY: Vintage Books, 1993).

Easterly, William, *The White Man's Burden: Why the West's Efforts to Aid the Rest of the World Have Done So Much Ill and So Little Good* (New York, NY: Penguin, 2006).

Eck, Diana, *A New Religious America: How a 'Christian Country' Has Become the World's Most Religiously Diverse Nation* (New York, NY: HarperCollins, 2001).

Eckes, Alfred E. and Thomas W. Zeiler, *Globalization and the American Century* (Cambridge: Cambridge University Press, 2003).

Edsall, Thomas Byrne, *Building Red America: The New Conservative Coalition and the Drive for Permanent Power* (New York, NY: Basic Books, 2006).

Edsall, Thomas Byrne and Mary Edsall, *Chain Reaction: The Impact of Race, Rights, and Taxes on American Politics* (New York, NY: Norton, 1991).

Edgerton, David, *The Shock of the Old: Technology and Global History since 1900* (New York, NY: Oxford University Press, 2007).

Edwards, George C. and Philip J. Davies (eds), *New Challenges for the American Century* (New York, NY: Pearson Longman, 2004).

Edwards, Mark Evan, 'Uncertainty and the rise of the work-family dilemma', *Journal of Marriage and Family*, 63(1), February 2001, 183–96.

Elshtain, Jean Bethke, *Who Are We? Critical Reflections and Hopeful Possibilities: Politics and Ethical Discourse* (Grand Rapids, MI: Eerdmans, 2000).

Ericson, David and Louisa Bertch Green (eds), *The Liberal Tradition in American*

Politics: Reassessing the Legacy of American Liberalism (New York, NY: Routledge, 1999).

Etzioni, Amitai, *The Common Good* (Cambridge: Polity, 2004).

Etzioni, Amitai, 'The Real Threat: An essay on Samuel Huntington', *Contemporary Sociology*, 34(5), 2005, 477–85.

Evans, Mark (ed.), *The Edinburgh Companion to Contemporary Liberalism* (London: Fitzroy Dearborn, 2001).

Faludi, Susan, *The Terror Dream: Fear and Fantasy in Post 9/11 America* (New York, NY: Metropolitan Books, 2007).

Ferguson, Niall, *Virtual History: Alternatives and Counterfactuals* (London: Pan, 2003).

Flett, Kathryn, 'Images that mocked all power of description', *The Observer*, 16 September 2001.

Florida, Richard, *The Flight of the Creative Class: The New Global Competition for Talent* (New York: HarperCollins, 2007).

Frank, Thomas, *What's the Matter with Kansas: How Conservatives Won the Heart of America* (New York, NY: Metropolitan Books, 2004).

Friedman, Thomas, *The Lexus and the Olive Tree*, rev. edn (New York, NY: Anchor Books, [1999] 2000).

Friedman, Thomas, *The World is Flat: A Brief History of the Globalized World in the Twenty-First Century*, rev. edn (New York, NY: Picador, [2005] 2007).

Fukuyama, Francis, 'The End of History?', *National Interest*, 16, Summer 1989, pp. 3–18.

Fukuyama, Francis, *The End of History and the Last Man* (New York, NY: Free Press, [1992] 1996).

Fukuyama, Francis, *After the Neocons: America at the Crossroads* (London: Profile, 2006).

Galston, William, *Liberal Pluralism: The Implications of Value Pluralism for Political Theory and Practice* (Cambridge: Cambridge University Press, 2002).

Gehman, Chris and Steve Reinke, *The Sharpest Point: Animation at the End of Cinema* (Ottawa: YYZ Books, 2005).

George, Susan, *The Lugano Report: On Preserving Capitalism in the Twenty-first Century* (London: Pluto Press, 1999).

Gerstle, Gary, 'The Protean Character of American Liberalism', *The American Historical Review*, 99, October 1994, 1043–73.

Gibbs, Nancy, 'America by the numbers: home truths', *Time Magazine*, 168(20), 6 November 2006, 24–33.

Giroux, Henry A., 'Reading Hurricane Katrina: Race, class, and the biopolitics of disposability', *College Literature*, 33(3), Summer 2006, 171–96.

Gitlin, Todd, *The Intellectuals and the Flag* (New York, NY: Columbia University Press, 2005).

Goldsmith, Jack L., *The Terror Presidency: Law and Judgement Inside the Bush Administration* (New York, NY: Norton, 2007).

Gore, Al, *The Assault on Reason* (New York, NY: Penguin, 2007).

Gottlieb, Robert, *Forcing the Spring: The Transformation of the American Environmental Movement* (Washington, DC: Island Press, 1993).

Griffin, Michael 'Picturing America's "War on Terrorism" in Afghanistan and Iraq', *Journalism*, 5(4), 2004, 381–402.

Griffin, David Ray and Peter Dale Scott (eds), *9/11 and American Empire: Intellectuals Speak Out* (Northampton, MA: Olive Branch Press, 2007).

Griffith, R. Marie and Melani McAlister (eds), 'Religion and Politics in the Contemporary United States', Special Issue of *American Quarterly*, 59(3), September 2007.

Guyatt, Nicholas, *Another American Century? The United States and the World after 2000* (Sydney: Pluto, 2000).

Habermas, Jürgen, *The Divided West* (Cambridge: Polity, 2006).

Halliwell, Martin, *American Culture in the 1950s* (Edinburgh: Edinburgh University Press, 2007).

Halstead, Ted and Michael Lind, *The Radical Center: The Future of American Politics* (New York, NY: Doubleday, 2001).

Haltunnen, Karen, 'Transnationalism and American Studies in Place', *The Japanese Journal of American Studies*, 18, 2007, 5–19.

Hamilton, Lee H., *The Iraq Study Group Report* (New York, NY: Vintage, 2006).

Hanson, Jim, *The Next Cold War? American Alternatives for the Twenty-First Century* (Westport, CT: Praeger, 1996).

Hardt, Michael and Antonio Negri, *Empire* (Cambridge, MA: Harvard University Press, 2000).

Hardt, Michael and Antonio Negri, *Multitude: War and Democracy in the Age of Empire* (New York, NY: Penguin, 2004).

Harrold, Eve, *Stem Cell Wars: Inside Stories from the Front Lines* (New York, NY: Palgrave Macmillan, 2006).

Hartz, Louis, *The Liberal Tradition in America* (New York, NY: Harcourt Brace Jovanovich, 1955).

Harvey, David, *The New Imperialism* (Oxford: Oxford University Press, 2005).

Haskins, Ron, *Work Over Welfare: The Inside Story of the 1996 Welfare Reform Law* (Washington, DC: Brookings Institution Press, 2006).

Hazen, Don *et al.* (ed.), *After 9/11: Solutions for a Saner World* (San Francisco: AlterNet, 2001).

Heclo, Hugh and Wilfred M. McClay (eds), *Religion Returns to the Public Square: Faith and Policy in America* (Washington DC: Woodrow Wilson Center Press, 2002).

Held, David and Anthony McGrew (eds), *Globalization Theory: Approaches and Controversies* (Cambridge: Polity, 2007).

Henkel, Kristin E., John F. Dovidio and Samuel L. Gaertner, 'Institutional discrimination, individual racism, and Hurricane Katrina', *Analyses of Social Issues and Public Policy*, 6(1), 2006, 99–124.

Hing, Bill Ong, *Making and Remaking Asian America Through Immigration Policy, 1850–1990* (Stanford, CA: Stanford University Press, 1994).

Hirsch, Marianne, 'The day time stopped', *The Chronicle of Higher Education*, 25 January 2002, B11, http://chronicle.com/free/v48/i20/20b01101.htm.

Holland, Suzanne, Karen Lebacqz and Laurie Zoloth (eds), *The Human Embryonic Stem Cell Debate: Science, Ethics and Public Policy* (Cambridge, MA: MIT Press, 2001).

Hollinger, David, *Postethnic America: Beyond Multiculturalism* (New York, NY: Basic Books, 1995).

Hollinger, David, 'Jesus matters in the USA', *Modern Intellectual History*, 1(1), 2004, 135–49.

Hollinger, David (ed.), *The Humanities and the Dynamics of Inclusion since World War II*

(Baltimore, MD: Johns Hopkins University Press, 2006).

Houen, Alex, *Terrorism and Modern Literature, from Joseph Conrad to Ciaran Carson* (Oxford: Oxford University Press, 2002).

Howard, John W. and Laura C. Prividera, 'Rescuing patriarchy or saving "Jessica Lynch": the rhetorical construction of the American woman soldier', *Woman and Language*, 27(2), 2004, 89–97.

Hunt, Michael H., *The American Ascendancy: How the US Gained and Wielded Global Dominance* (Chapel Hill, NC: University of North Carolina Press, 2007).

Hunter, James Davison, *Culture Wars: The Struggle to Define America* (New York, NY: Basic Books, 1992).

Huntington, Samuel P., 'The Clash of Civilizations', *Foreign Affairs*, 72(3), Summer 1993, 22–49.

Huntington, Samuel P., 'The Hispanic Challenge', *Foreign Policy*, March–April 2004, 30–45.

Huntington, Samuel P., *Who Are We? America's Great Debate* (London: Free Press, 2005).

Huston, Walter (ed.), *In Search of America* (Englewood Cliffs, NJ: Prentice-Hall, 1959).

Iwabuchi, Koichi (ed.), *Feeling Asian Modernities: Transnational Consumption of Japanese TV Dramas* (Hong Kong: Hong Kong University Press, 2004).

Jacoby, Russell, *The Last Intellectuals: American Culture in the Age of Academe* (New York, NY: Basic Books, 1987).

Jacoby, Russell, *The End of Utopia: Politics and Culture in an Age of Apathy* (New York, NY: Basic Books, 1999).

Jameson, Fredric, *Postmodernism, or, the Cultural Logic of Late Capitalism* (London: Verso, 1991).

Jenkins, Henry, *Convergence Culture: When Old and New Media Collide* (New York, NY: New York University Press, 2006).

Jenkins, Philip, *The Next Christendom: The Coming of Global Christianity* (New York, NY: Oxford University Press, 2002).

Johnson, Victoria, '"Welcome Home?" CBS, PAX-TV, and "Heartland" values in a neo-network era', in Robert Allen and Annette Hill (eds), *The Television Studies Reader* (London: Routledge, 2004), pp. 404–17.

Johnson-Cartee, Karen S. and Gary A. Copeland, *Strategic Political Communication* (Lanham, MD: Rowman and Littlefield, 2004).

Jumonville, Neil and Kevin Mattson, *Liberalism for a New Century* (Berkeley, CA: University of California Press, 2007).

Kaufman, Eric, 'Nativist Cosmopolitans: institutional reflexivity and the decline of "double-consciousness" in American nationalist thought', *Historical Sociology*, 14(1), 2001, 47–78.

Kazin, Michael and Joseph A. McCartin, *Americanism: New Perspectives on the History of an Ideal* (Chapel Hill, NC: University of North Carolina Press, 2006).

Kennan, George F. 'The Sources of Soviet Conduct', *Foreign Affairs*, 25 July 1947, 566–82.

Kercher, Stephen, *Revel With a Cause: Liberal Satire in Postwar America* (Chicago, IL: University of Chicago Press, 2006).

Kloppenberg, James T., *The Virtues of Liberalism* (Oxford: Oxford University Press, 1998).

Knight, Peter, 'Outrageous Conspiracy Theories: popular and official responses to 9/11 in Germany and the United States', *New German Critique*, 103(35), Spring 2008, 165–93.

Krauthammer, Charles, 'The Unipolar Moment', *Foreign Affairs*, 70, 1991, 23–33.

Kristeva, Julia, *Nations without Nationalism*, trans. Leon S. Roudiez (New York, NY: Columbia University Press, 1993).

LaFeber, Walter, 'The Bush Doctrine', *Diplomatic History*, 26(4), Fall 2002, 543–58.

Lewy, Guenther, *Why America Needs Religion: Secular Modernity and Its Discontents* (Grand Rapids, MI: Eerdmans, 1996).

Lieven, Anatol, *America Right or Wrong: The Anatomy of American Nationalism* (London: HarperCollins, 2004).

Linker, Damon, *The Theocons* (New York, NY: Doubleday, 2006).

Lott, Eric, *The Disappearing Liberal Intellectual* (New York, NY: Basic Books, 2006).

McClean, Shilo, *Digital Storytelling: The Narrative Power of Visual Effects in Film* (Cambridge, MA: MIT Press, 2007).

McKibben, Bill, *The End of Nature* (London: Penguin, 1990).

Magnum Photographers, *New York September 11* (New York, NY: PowerHouse Books 2001).

Maienschein, Janet, *Whose View of Life? Embryos, Cloning and Stem Cells* (Cambridge, MA: Harvard University Press, 2003).

Mann, Michael, *Incoherent Empire* (London: Verso, 2003).

Manovich, Lev, *The Language of New Media* (Cambridge, MA: MIT Press, 2002).

Marable, Manning, 'Race, Class, and the Katrina Crisis', *Working USA: the Journal of Labor and Society*, 9(2), 2006, 155–60.

Mattson, Kevin, *When America Was Great: The Fighting Faith of Postwar Liberalism* (New York, NY: Routledge, 2004).

Matusow, Alan, *The Unraveling of America: A History of Liberalism in the 1960s* (New York, NY: Harper and Row, 1984).

Mearsheimer, John, *The Tragedy of Great-Power Politics* (New York, NY: Norton, 2001).

Michaels, Walter Benn, *The Trouble With Diversity: How We Learned to Love Identity and Ignore Inequality* (New York, NY: Henry Holt, 2006).

Mir, Hamid, Interview with Osama Bin Laden, 'Muslims have the right to attack America', *The Observer*, 11 November 2001.

Mirzoeff, Nicholas, *Watching Babylon: The War in Iraq and Global Visual Culture* (London: Routledge, 2005).

Moeller, Susan, *Shooting War: Photography and the American Experience of Combat* (New York, NY: Basic Books, 1989).

Mooney, Chris, *The Republican War on Science* (New York, NY: Basic Books, 2006).

Moore, Curtis and Alan Miller, *Green Gold: Japan, Germany, the United States, and the Race for Environmental Technology* (Boston, MA: Beacon Press, 1994).

Morley, David, *Home Territories: Media, Mobility, and Identity* (London: Routledge, 2000).

Morrison, Philip and Kosta Tsipis, *Reason Enough to Hope: America and the World of the Twenty-First Century* (Cambridge, MA: MIT Press, 1999).

Murray, Susan and Laurie Ouellette (eds), *Reality TV: Remaking Television Culture* (New York, NY: New York University Press, 2004).

Nash, George, *The Conservative Intellectual Movement in America* (New York, NY: Basic Books, 1976).

Neuhaus, Richard John, *The Naked Public Square: Religion and Democracy in America* (Grand Rapids, MI: Eerdmans, 1984).

Nevins, Joseph, *Operation Gatekeeper: The Rise of the "Illegal Alien" and the Making of the US-Mexico Boundary* (New York, NY: Routledge, 2002).

Newman, Judie, *Fictions of America: Narratives of Global Empire* (London: Routledge, 2007).

Pallitto, Robert M. and William G. Weaver, *Presidential Secrecy and the Law* (Baltimore, MD: Johns Hopkins University Press, 2007).

Parson, Ann B., *The Proteus Effect: Stem Cells and their Promise for Medicine* (Washington, DC: Joseph Henry Press, 2004).

Pease, Donald E. and Robyn Weigman (eds), *The Futures of American Studies* (Durham, NC: Duke University Press, 2002).

Peck, Dale, *Hatchet Jobs* (New York, NY: The New Press, 2004).

Pfaff, William, *Barbarian Sentiments: How the American Century Ends* (New York, NY: Hill and Wang, 1989).

Pogge, Thomas, *World Poverty and Human Rights: Cosmopolitan Responsibilities and Reforms* (Cambridge: Polity, 2002).

Powell, Lawrence N. and Claence L. Mohr (eds), 'Through the Eye of Katrina: The Past as Prologue?', Special Issue of *Journal of American History*, 94(3), December 2007.

Rawls, John, *Political Liberalism* (New York, NY: Columbia University Press, [1993] 2005).

Reich, Robert B., *The Work of Nations: Preparing Ourselves for 21st Century Capitalism* (New York, NY: Vintage, 1991).

Reich, Robert B., *Reason: Why Liberals Will Win the Battle for America* (New York, NY: Knopf, 2004).

Reimer, David M., *Unwelcome Strangers: American Identity and the Turn Against Immigration* (New York, NY: Columbia University Press, 1999).

Renshon, Stanley and Peter Suedfeld (eds), *Understanding the Bush Doctrine: Psychology and Strategy in an Age of Terrorism* (New York, NY: Routledge, 2007).

Risen, James, *State of War: The Secret History of the CIA and the Bush Administration* (New York, NY: Free Press, 2006).

Ritter, Jonathan and J. Martin Daughtry (eds), *Music in the Post 9/11 World* (New York, NY: Routledge, 2007).

Rodin, Judith and Stephen P. Steinberg (eds), *Public Discourse in America: Conversation and Community in the Twenty-First Century* (Philadelphia, PA: University of Pennsylvania Press, 2003).

Rodrik, Dani, *Has Globalization Gone Too Far?* (Washington, DC: Institute for International Economics, 1997).

Rorty, Richard, *Achieving Our Country: Leftist Thought in the Twentieth Century* (Cambridge, MA: Harvard University Press, 1997).

Rothenberg, David and Wandee J. Pryor (eds), *Writing the World: On Globalization* (Cambridge, MA: MIT Press, 2005).

Rowe, John Carlos, *The New American Studies* (Minneapolis, MN: University of Minnesota Press, 2002).

Royal Academy, *USA Today: New American Art from the Saatchi Gallery* (London: Royal Academy of Arts, 2006).

Rubenstein, Richard E. and Jarle Crocker, 'Challenging Huntington', *Foreign Policy*, 96, 1994, 115–17.

Rushefsky, Mark E., *Public Policy in the United States: At the Dawn of the Twenty-First Century* (New York, NY: M. E. Sharpe, 2007).

Ryan, David, *US Foreign Policy in World History* (London: Routledge, 2000).

Said, Edward, *The Politics of Dispossession: The Struggle for Palestinian Self-Determination 1969–1994* (London: Chatto and Windus, 1994).

Said, Edward, 'The Clash of Ignorance', *The Nation*, 22 October 2001, http://www.thenation.com/doc/20011022/said.

Sandel, Michael, *Democracy's Discontent: America in Search of a Public Philosophy* (New York, NY: Belknap Press, 1996).

Sassen, Saskia, *Territory, Authority, Rights: From Medieval to Global Assemblages* (Princeton, NJ: Princeton University Press, 2006).

Saul, John Ralston, *The Collapse of Globalism* (London: Atlantic, 2005).

Saxenian, AnnaLee, *The New Argonauts: Regional Advantage in a Global Economy* (Cambridge, MA: Harvard University Press, 2006).

Scanlan, Margaret, *Plotting Terror: Novelists and Terrorists in Contemporary Fiction* (Charlottesville, VA: University of Virginia Press, 2001).

Schiller, H., 'Manipulating Hearts and Minds', in Hamid Mowlana, George Gerbner and Herbert Schiller (eds), *Triumph of the Image* (Boulder, CO: Westview Press, 1992), pp. 22–9.

Schivelbusch, Wolfgang, *The Culture of Defeat: On National Trauma, Mourning, and Recovery* (New York, NY: Henry Holt, 2003).

Schlesinger, Arthur M. Jr, *The Vital Center* (Boston, MA: Houghton Mifflin, 1949).

Schlesinger, Arthur M. Jr, *The Disuniting of America: Reflections on a Multicultural Society* (New York, NY: Norton, 1991).

Schrecker, Ellen (ed.), *Cold War Triumphalism* (New York, NY: The New Press, 2004).

Scott, Eugenie C., *Evolution vs. Creationism: An Introduction* (Berkeley, CA: University of California Press, 2004).

Scott, Christopher Thomas, *Stem Cell Now: An Introduction to the Coming Medical Revolution* (New York, NY: Plume, 2006).

Smith-Shomade, Beretta E., *Shaded Lives: African American Women and Television* (New Brunswick, NJ: Rutgers University Press, 2002).

Snow, Nancy, *Propaganda, Inc.: Selling America's Culture to the World* (New York, NY: Seven Stories Press, 2002).

Snyder, Alvin A., *Warriors of Disinformation: American Propaganda, Soviet Lies, and the Winning of the Cold War* (New York, NY: Arcade Publishing, 1995).

Sobel, Richard, *The Impact of Public Opinion on U.S. Foreign Policy Since Vietnam* (New York, NY: Oxford University Press, 2001).

Spigel, Lynn, 'Entertainment Wars: Television culture after 9/11', *American Quarterly*, 56(2), June 2004, 235–70.

Spigel, Lynn, 'Designing the smart house: posthuman domesticity and conspicuous production', *European Journal of Cultural Studies*, 8(4), 2005, 403–26.

Spigel, Lynn and Jan Olsson (eds), *Television After TV: Essays on a Medium in Transition* (Durham, NC: Duke University Press, 2004).

Starr, Paul, *Freedom's Power: The True Force of Modern Liberalism* (New York, NY: Basic Books, 2007).

Stephanopoulos, George, *All Too Human: A Political Education* (New York, NY: Little, Brown, 1999).

Stiglitz, Joseph E., *Globalization and its Discontents* (London: Penguin, 2002).

Sturken, Marita, 'The Aesthetics of Absence: Rebuilding Ground Zero', *American Ethnologist*, 31(3), August 2004, 311–25.

Sturken, Marita, *Tourists of History: Memory, Kitsch, and Consumerism from Oklahoma City to Ground Zero* (Durham, NC: Duke University Press, 2008).

Sullivan, Teresa *et al.*, *The Fragile Middle Class: Americans in Debt* (New Haven, CT: Yale University Press, 2000).

Sunstein, Cass, *Republic.com* (Princeton, NJ: Princeton University Press, 2007).

Talisse, Robert B., *Democracy After Liberalism: Pragmatism and Deliberative Ethics* (New York, NY: Routledge, 2005).

Takacs, Stacy, 'Jessica Lynch and the regeneration of American identity and power post-9/11', *Feminist Media Studies*, 5(3), 2005, 297–310.

Tichenor, Daniel J., *Dividing Lines: The Politics of Immigration Control in America* (Princeton, NJ: Princeton University Press, 2002).

Tsing, Anna Lowenhaupt, *Friction: An Ethnography of Global Connection* (Princeton, NJ: Princeton University Press, 2005).

Turow, Joseph, *Breaking Up America: Advertisers and the New Media World* (Chicago, IL: University of Chicago Press, 1998).

Updike, John, *Terrorist* (London: Penguin, 2006).

Veseth, Michael, *Globaloney: Unraveling the Myths of Globalization* (Lanham, MD: Rowman and Littlefield, 2005).

Vettel, Eric J., *Biotech: the Countercultural Origins of an Industry* (Philadelphia, PA: University of Pennsylvania Press, 2006).

Virilio, Paul, *Ground Zero*, trans. Chris Turner (London: Verso, 2002).

Waldinger, Roger and David Fitzgerald, 'Transnationalism in question', *American Journal of Sociology*, 109(5), March 2004, 1177–95.

Walt, Stephen, *Taming American Power: The Global Response to US Primacy* (New York, NY: Norton, 2005).

Walzer, Michael, *Politics and Passion: Toward a More Egalitarian Liberalism* (New Haven, CT: Yale University Press, 2004).

Weigel, George, *The Final Revolution: The Resistance Church and the Collapse of Communism* (New York, NY: Oxford University Press, 2003).

Wells, Paul, *Animation and America* (Edinburgh: Edinburgh University Press, 2002).

West, Cornel, *The American Evasion of Philosophy: A Genealogy of Pragmatism* (Madison, WI: University of Wisconsin Press, 1989).

West, Michael D., *The Immortal Cell: One Scientist's Quest to Solve the Mystery of Aging* (New York, NY: Doubleday, 2003).

Whitfield, Stephen J. (ed.), *A Companion to 20th-Century America* (Oxford: Blackwell, 2004).

Williams, Rosalind, *Retooling: a Historian Confronts Technological Change* (Cambridge, MA: MIT Press, 2002).

Wills, John, *Conservation Fallout: Nuclear Protest at Diablo Canyon* (Reno, NV: University of Nevada Press, 2006).

Wombell, Paul (ed.), *Photovideo: Photography in the Age of the Computer* (London: Rivers Oram Press, 1991).

Woodward, Bob, *The Agenda: Inside the Clinton White House* (New York, NY: Simon and Schuster, 1994).

Wuthnow, Robert, *The Restructuring of American Religion: Society and Faith Since World War II* (Princeton, NJ: Princeton University Press, 1988).

Žižek, Slavoj, *Iraq: The Borrowed Kettle* (London: Verso, 2004).

INDEX